The Art of Compassionate Business

Main Principles for the Human-Oriented Enterprise

By
Dr. Bruno R. Cignacco

A PRODUCTIVITY PRESS BOOK

First edition published in 2019
by Routledge/Productivity Press
52 Vanderbilt Avenue, 11th Floor New York, NY 10017
2 Park Square, Milton Park, Abingdon, Oxon OX14 4RN, UK

Printed on acid-free paper

International Standard Book Number-13: 978-0-367-13925-4 (Hardback)
International Standard Book Number-13: 978-0-429-02922-6 (eBook)

Visit the Taylor & Francis Web site at
http://www.taylorandfrancis.com

Contents

Acknowledgements

This book is dedicated to the memory of my mother, who was the person who first introduced me to the principles which have deeply influenced this book. This text is also dedicated to the memory of my uncle Hugo Francesconi, for his continuous support and faith in me.

I am also deeply grateful to:

- Fayola Saunders, a very sweet and special person in my life who showed great enthusiasm in reviewing the manuscript
- My father, my sister, my nieces, and my godson
- My friends
- My clients
- The educational institutions I have taught at over my career
- The people working for the publisher for their significant support during the publishing process

Author

Dr Bruno R. Cignacco, Ph.D., is an international business consultant, international speaker, and business coach. For over 20 years, he has advised and trained hundreds of companies on international trade activities and international marketing. He is also a Principal Lecturer in Marketing. He teaches marketing management, international marketing, product innovation, public relations, and research methods at GSM London (in partnership with Plymouth University). He taught business modules at other universities in the UK, such as Birkbeck University, Lancaster University, University of Wales, and University of Central Lancashire, among others. He also taught business modules at universities in other countries. He has been lecturing both at undergraduate level and postgraduate level for more than 17 years. He is a member of the Centre for Research and Executive Education at GSM London.

He is a Senior Fellow of the Higher Education Academy (HEA) UK. He is also a Master Life Coach and Master NLP practitioner. He has studied disciplines related to personal development for more than 20 years and delivered countless talks, seminars, and conferences in several countries.

He is the author of business books such as *Fundamentals of International Marketing for SMEs* (Atlantic Publishers, 2010) which has been published in several languages, such as English (Atlantic Publishers, 2010), Spanish (Macchi Publishers, 2004), and Portuguese (Saraiva Publisher, 2009). His other business book is *Techniques of International Negotiation* (Macchi Publishers, 2014). He is also the author of personal development books published in different languages. His websites are www.brunocignacco.com and www.humanorientedenterprise.com.

Prologue

A human being is a part of the whole called by us universe, a part limited in time and space. He experiences himself, his thoughts and feeling as something separated from the rest, a kind of optical delusion of his consciousness. This delusion is a kind of prison for us, restricting us to our personal desires and to affection for a few persons nearest to us. Our task must be to free ourselves from this prison by widening our circle of compassion to embrace all living creatures and the whole of nature in its beauty.

Albert Einstein

Origins of This Book

In hindsight, I realise the germ of an idea for this book has been dormant in my mind for several years. The topics it contains are the natural development of several books I have written about business and personal development over more than a decade. This book also includes golden insights from my lengthy career as an international business consultant. These topics have been integrated to create a unique text for the readers.

There are excellent business books, general texts or specialised ones (on marketing, human resources, business economics, strategy, accounting, management, entrepreneurship and other topics). Most texts indeed offer relevant advice to avid readers who set up, work for, or lead business organisations.

These business texts have a clear focus on specific organisational objectives (e.g., increasing profits, obtaining a bigger market share, improving quality levels, etc.). These books also assume that businesses are operating in an unpredictable and threatening environment, continually facing several challenges, which must be dealt with efficiently. Most traditional business authors make several assumptions regarding the dynamics of business activities, for example:

a) Zero-Sum Game

All businesses are inserted into a competitive environment, where all participants, with no exception, try to outpace one another. In this "game" each "player" seeks to win at the expense of the others. Mutually beneficial agreements for all parties involved and co-operative bonds between organisations tend to be uncommon, or the exception to this rule.

b) Competitors as Threats

Other companies are usually perceived as threatening adversaries, which must be outsmarted whenever possible. Companies tend to focus on the external (e.g., allocating resources to beat competitors), rather than on the internal (for example, developing their own distinct capabilities to stand out in the market). Other organisations can never be perceived as valuable sources of inspiration and feedback, but as threats.

c) Imperative Innovation

Organisations run an endless race to improve their products, services, and processes. Their constant innovation stems from market trends (social, economic, technological, etc.), customers' needs, and the companies' capabilities. Most companies perceive customers as overly demanding and fuelled by a continuous search for the latest novelties (better design, improved performance, etc.). In this frantic race, companies that dare to take a rest risk being tossed out of the market by more innovative competitors.

d) Limited Resources

Another relevant tenet in the business world asserts that all companies count on limited resources, which restrains what they do, as well as how and when. Consequently, companies tend to efficiently co-ordinate and utilise their scarce resources, through strategies and other tools. New resources are generally perceived as difficult to generate, because they take extensive time and effort.

e) Difficult Customers

There is a widespread assumption that finding new customers and retaining current ones is always difficult. Gaining customers' loyalty tends to be a troublesome issue, because they are perceived as fickle. Customer behaviour is deemed to be difficult to predict. Consequently, many companies perform manipulative activities to seduce customers and prospects by, for instance, using misleading information in adverts, making exaggerated promises regarding products and services, and carefully hiding products' weaknesses, among others.

f) Believing in the Might of Technology

In this fast-paced era, many companies consider that technological devices allow them to achieve their objectives more efficiently. Nonetheless, the excessive use of technology also decreases the direct interaction with people, thus damaging the human connection between businesses and their most relevant stakeholders (customers, employees, suppliers, etc.). In extreme cases, technology can even replace the human resources, such as in the case of automated machines or robots.

g) Unloving Work Environment

In many companies, their work environments are affected by internal politics, for instance, one-upmanship, backbiting, disloyalty, and gatekeeping, among others. These aspects do not contribute to strengthening relationships between workmates and instead prevent them from co-operating with one another. Many of these tactics are driven by an egotistic attitude, which creates a distrust among employees. These political factors often hold people back from adopting a loving attitude with one another.

h) Commoditised People

Figuratively speaking, some companies treat employees as cogs of the organisational machine which can be replaced easily by others. Employees are considered as a "means" to achieve organisational objectives, instead of human beings with needs, emotions, and dreams which must be acknowledged and valued. Employees tend to be entangled in a web of rules, regulations, and procedures which leave them no leeway for taking initiative or being creative. Oftentimes, employees are heartlessly pushed by companies to the limits in order to achieve the goals of the latter. This continuous pressure pushes employees towards stress or burnout.

i) Widespread Conflicts

All organisations are affected by internal and external conflicts. Often, conflicts tend to be solved in an adversarial manner where one party wins at the expense of the other. These win–lose solutions also affect the relationships between the participants in a negative manner. Many companies are more interested in obtaining all the gains from conflictive situations with others than in preserving the relationships with them.

My Background and Expectations for This Book

I have been teaching business modules at several universities at an undergraduate and postgraduate level across the world and acting as a consultant to countless organisations for more than twenty years. I recognised the aforementioned assumptions in all types of organisations both in my professional experience, as well as in most traditional business bibliographies. At several points, I asked myself "Is there a way to perform business activities more humanely?" After years of dwelling on this thought-provoking idea, the answer to this paramount question can finally be found in this book.

In the following chapters, I will elaborate on relevant aspects of business which have been dismissed in most relevant business bibliographies. As an inquisitive cartographer, I will map out the main principles which drive authentic success in businesses that at the same time generate benefits for all the parties involved.

How to Reap the Most Benefits from This Book

All principles included in this book are based on a deep awareness of our essence as human beings. Nonetheless, many organisations are oblivious to these principles, despite their enormous benefits.

It is not the purpose of this text to deliver law-like generalisations. Nonetheless the paradigms exposed in this book can certainly be applied to any type of organisational environment and cultural background, for example:

- Small, medium sized, and big organisations
- Local, national, regional, and global organisations
- Organisations related to different sectors, such as primary (extractive, such as agriculture), secondary (transformative or productive), and tertiary (provider of services)
- Non-profit and profit-making organisations, as well as governmental bodies

This book delivers a heart-warming and hopeful message to organisations. These down-to-earth ideas will help them become more valuable, genuine, and meaningful. The advice provided in this book is timeless.

This text does not provide intricate strategic perspectives, but people-centred principles. Even though some guidelines enclosed in this book are often based on common sense and others counterintuitive, all of them are backed by profuse scientific research and professional experiences. Some of the relevant points explored throughout the book are:

- How to define a business mission with a positive impact on the world
- How to be more passionate with business activities
- How to adopt a prosperity mindset in business
- How to have more loving relationships with stakeholders
- How to create more connected conversations
- How to create a warmer work environment
- How to serve customers in a loving manner
- How to develop more innovative and impactful ideas

It is suggested that readers gradually test and implement the guidelines conveyed in this book, both in the business environment and the workplace. When these principles are put into practice, positive ripple effects are bound to affect other stakeholders. The users of this knowledge and those affected by them will undergo a profound internal transformation, which will change the way they perceive business situations.

This book provides guidelines to contribute to more loving work and business environments. This text also shows the obstacles on the way to achieving that objective. There are organisations that will need to change their well-ingrained attitudes and practices to implement the beneficial perspectives suggested in this book.

Chapter 1

Purpose and Mission

Only when we truly love our work will we put in the time, and take the care, to do it to the best of our ability.

Mark McGuinness

1.1 The Importance of a Business Mission

I slept and dreamt that life was joy. I awoke and saw that life was service. I acted and behold, service was joy.

Rabindranath Tagore

It is one of the most beautiful compensations of this life that you cannot sincerely try to help another without helping yourself.

Ralph Waldo Emerson

The terms "mission" and "purpose" will be used interchangeably. A mission is an organisation's main reason for existence in the marketplace. A compelling purpose is one of the most relevant success factors for any organisation. Some organisations' websites have distinctive links to their mission statements.

Kotler et al. (2009) highlighted that a mission should include a very narrow set of objectives and other aspects (the company's industrial sector, its unique qualities, its products and services, specific groups of customers served and the benefits obtained by them). These authors also observed that a business mission is closely linked to its vision, which includes the company's objectives or intentions for the future. In other words, the vision is the image of what the organisation wants to be in the future.

According to Price and Price (2013), the mission is what the company aspires to do with their daily activities; instead, the vision is what the company intends to become in the future. A well-defined mission always assists a company in the achievement of its vision. The vision can be reformulated once attained, while the mission is more prone to remain relatively unchanged over time. Both vision and mission should be widely communicated to the organisation's main internal stakeholders (for example, employees) and external ones (for example, customers). When an organisation follows its purpose, it attempts to answer the following questions:

- Why are we here in the marketplace?
- Who do we want to serve?
- Why do stakeholders (including customers) prefer our company?
- What is the general direction of our company?
- What makes us unique and distinct?
- What valuable things do we want to create for our stakeholders?
- What positive changes can we introduce in the marketplace?
- What is the best way to improve people's lives?
- How can we add the highest value to others?
- How can we use our resources (skills, talents, information, etc.) to positively impact the world?

A well-defined business mission will also try to answer some less obvious questions, on an individual level, such as:

- What is our authentic path in life?
- Who do we want to be in this world?
- How can we create more love, joy and peace around us?
- What activities give us a sense of fulfilment?
- How can we use our time productively to help others?
- What is our future legacy or contribution for others to enjoy?
- What is our true place in the world?

All organisations can become valuable instruments or catalysts through which people can introduce positive change into the world. The organisation's mission can also be defined as:

- A project aligned with an organisation's distinct potential and strengths
- A significant quest which drives all business endeavours
- A wholehearted cause the organisation stays true to
- A wellspring of passion the company's contributors are committed to
- A generator of shared expectations regarding the business venture
- A valuable endeavour to make the world a better place
- A motivator which prompts the organisation to endure challenging circumstances

In the following points, some characteristics of a meaningful mission will be explained. Some tips to discover or rediscover a business mission will also be enumerated.

1.2 Impact of a Well-Defined Mission

1.2.1 A Mission is Intrinsically Loving

Everyone has been made for some particular work, and the desire for this work has been put in his heart.

Rumi

Many companies wrongly define their business mission by considering their products or services, or their specific business activities, instead of focusing on how they are of assistance to others. A company's contribution to others should always be at the centre of all business activities. To put it simply, a well-defined mission is focused on serving others in the best manner. Edelman (1993) observed that "Service is the rent each of us pays for living."

A mission-driven company serves others in a unique manner because each organisation has its own set of distinct talents and capabilities. A well-designed purpose is expansive; it brings more good to the world. An authentic mission is always based on lofty values, such as integrity, transparency, fairness, and honesty, among others. The company mission should be aligned with these moral "lighthouses" in order to be authentically meaningful and widely impactful.

An organisation which pursues its mission shows its best side. Figuratively speaking, a mission-centred organisation becomes a wellspring of love; its activities spread love within the company and outside it. A purpose-driven company is prone to recognise the interconnectedness and interdependence with all significant stakeholders in the business environment. This is congruent with both principles of quantum physics and ancient spiritual traditions, which state that everything in the universe is interconnected.

A mission resembles a solid platform from which fruitful relationships with the organisation's stakeholders can develop. The purpose is like a bridge which links a company's internal stakeholders (management, employees) and its external ones (customers, suppliers, community). A clear mission always has a positive intention, which is to help people feel better (more joy, peace, love, etc.) or to reduce their negative states (such as anger, sadness, despair, etc.).

A clearly defined purpose is selfless because it helps an organisation generate positive change both internally and externally. A mission is heart-driven because a company's actions to pursue it tend to be driven by its employees' hearts. When a company follows its mission, all its strategies (marketing, production, financial, etc.) tend to be aligned with this purpose, which in turn causes a company's activities to be congruent with these strategies.

1.2.2 A Mission Generates Engagement and Commitment

> All men dream; but not equally. Those who dream by night in the dusty recesses of their minds wake in the day to find that it was vanity: but the dreamers of the day are dangerous men, for they might act on their dreams with the eyes open, to make it possible.
>
> **T. E. Lawrence**

A company which pursues a well-defined mission makes all its people feel valuable. Employees are more prone to feel uncompromisingly engaged to a company's mission when:

- The organisation regularly demonstrates to employees the importance of pursuing its mission.
- The company explains to employees the relationship between their tasks and its mission and its impact on the world.
- The organisation prompts employees to feel that they worthily contribute to that mission.
- The organisation frequently acknowledges and thanks employees for their valuable contribution to this purpose.
- The organisation allows employees to take ownership and initiative regarding their specific work tasks.

- The company is open to employees' ideas to attain its mission more effectively.
- The company has an attitude of service, which prompts employees to behave in an obliging manner.
- The organisation enables employees to fully use their distinct talents to pursue its mission.
- The organisation makes employees feel that products and services supplied to customers are of real worth.
- The company sets quality standards related to its purpose, to which employees adhere.
- The company activities create a positive impact not only on customers, but also on its other stakeholders, such as suppliers, intermediaries, partners, and the community as a whole.
- The company allows employees to participate in the (re)definition of its purpose.

When employees' contributions are regularly acknowledged with thanks, they are more prone to go the extra mile to support the company's mission. Bridges (2017) observed that "people will follow you if they see you are not just about the money but also about meaning." In some organisations, not only are employees committed to the company's purpose, but they are also proud to work for that organisation.

When the company's mission is relevant to its employees, they tend to feel an unbounded amount of energy and passion to make it come true. When they perform their work tasks, they feel they are not wasting their time but contributing to change the world on a small or large scale. These employees are also more resilient when the company goes through challenging times.

Some employees can also feel honoured because their activities at work contribute to leaving a legacy in the world, something bigger than them. Sometimes, a company's mission is totally aligned with the personal objectives of its staff members, which makes their commitment seem effortless and spontaneous. In those cases, they feel compelled to take continuous action toward this purpose.

Besides employees, a meaningful company's mission also prompts other individuals and organisations to contribute to this purpose. When a company's mission is pursued wholeheartedly, people and companies around tend to be naturally drawn to this purpose, creating a strong emotional connection with them. Stakeholders that relate to a mission-oriented company feel comfortable and willing to support it. In those cases, the company should continually remind these stakeholders of the positive outcomes that stem from achieving its mission. An interesting question a company should regularly pose is "Does our purpose connect us with people more deeply?"

1.2.3 A Mission Makes People More Proactive and Creative

The only true happiness comes from squandering ourselves for a purpose.

William Cowper

Webb (2016) states that there are two types of goals: "approach objectives," which are goals where people focus on what they want, and "avoidance goals" which are when people seem to avoid what they do not want. Approach goals are set "for" specific things, avoidance goals are set "against" specific issues. From this perspective, when people pursue approach goals, they tend to act in a proactive fashion. When people focus on avoidance objectives instead, they are prone to act in a reactive manner. A well-defined mission is worded as an approach objective; it always states what the organisation is for, not against. The paramount question a company should ask itself is: "What are we for?"

Fritz (1984) stated that there are two types of perspectives a company can adopt: a problem-solving approach, when it tries to eliminate its difficulties, and a creative perspective, when it focuses on creating something new. This author observed that the creative approach is superior to the problem-solving approach.

As a consequence, when a company defines its mission, it should always use the creative approach, not the problem-solving one. When a company's mission is defined as something new to create, people are more prone to adopt a proactive attitude toward it. A relevant question an organisation should pose to define its mission is "What do we want to create?"

All activities performed by the company should be congruent with the achievement of its purpose. Companies should always prioritise those tasks and projects which contribute to its mission. The mission constitutes the guiding light against which all company activities are judged and assessed, either as relevant tasks or irrelevant ones. A company which performs activities contributing to its purpose nurtures it, in the same way as the mother who loves her child. An organisation can keep its mission alive by devoting its time and energy to it.

1.2.4 A Mission Balances Short-Term and Long-Term

> Success without contribution is hollow and unsatisfying.
>
> **Norman Drummond**

The majority of businesses commonly devote most of their time to activities which are necessary, for example, paying the bills, obtaining more sales, etc. These activities are primarily focused on the short-term. Nonetheless, a company with a well-defined mission tends to articulate the short-term and long-term in a harmonious manner.

A business mission has a long-term perspective, because the company's activities performed to pursue that mission tend to contribute to a valuable legacy for posterity. A well-defined purpose is also transformational and humanistic because it aims to add impactful value to all the company's relevant stakeholders. Conner (2010) observed that a purpose-driven organisation always generates "a wake of positive influence on all constituencies it touches."

The purpose is also holistic because it tends to produce a positive change in humankind as a whole, to a small or great extent. A company which pursues its mission wants to create a beneficial impact on the present community and also on future ones. Csikszentmihalyi (2003) observed that a good business pursues profits, but also contributes to human well-being and happiness, and makes the world a better place. In order to do so, a company utilises its own unique resources, such as relationships, information, technology, talents, etc.

When a company is aligned with its purpose, it is less likely that one stakeholder wins at the expense of others. A mission-driven company aims at the so-called "threefold bottom line," which includes looking for incremental profits, but also caring for people and supporting the planet. Companies with this long-term orientation tend to bring about other positive effects, for example:

- An increase in employees' engagement and morale
- A lower turnover of employees
- A higher customer satisfaction
- A friendlier work environment
- A higher reputation
- A reinforced brand image
- Loftier quality levels

- More innovative products and services
- Outstanding levels of productivity

On one side, companies without a clear mission cannot see themselves creating a positive change in the world. They have a narrow view of their activities, which is constrained by well-ingrained limiting assumptions such as "The most important thing is to survive, not to contribute to others," "It is not possible to follow our purpose and obtain profits," "We will never be able to create any significant impact on the world," and similar ones. On the other side, mission-oriented companies know it is worth pursuing a meaningful purpose to create a positive effect on the wider community. These companies are willing to play their relevant part in transforming the world.

A mission is also related to the short-term. When employees are fully engaged in activities which contribute to a company's mission, they are naturally rooted in the now and are fully present. These employees harness their unique capabilities fully, and their actions tend to be more effortless and flowing. They are less prone to be diverted by worries and fears (which are related to the future) or regrets and guilt (which are linked to the past). According to Csikszentmihalyi (2003), when employees pursue a company's mission, they tend to enter a state of flow – also called "the zone" – and are more prone to focus on the present, namely on the task at hand.

1.2.5 A Mission Produces Economic and Non-Economic Rewards

Put money first, and you'll probably stay poor. Put purpose first, and you're headed toward riches.

David Schwartz

Mission-oriented companies try to answer the question "Why are we in the marketplace?" in order to discover the real motivation behind their purpose. Some entrepreneurs will easily offer an answer to this question, like "to make more money." It is true that companies seek to thrive in the business environment to gain profits. However, these sought-after economic benefits, which are the result of pursuing the company's mission, only represent a small part of the benefits available.

Nowadays, more organisations understand that being in business is not only about making more money; a well-defined mission implies other reasons for being in the marketplace. By following its mission, a company also brings about other benefits, namely, creating a positive impact on the business environment and the community as a whole.

Collins and Porras (2005) recognise two main objectives in any company: "pragmatic pursuit of profits" and "purpose beyond profit." These authors observed that profits represent the oxygen for any company, without which it cannot live. They also stated that profits are never a company's main goal, but only a valuable means to achieve loftier objectives, such as creating a positive impact on society.

According to Maslow (1954), these higher objectives are related to the concept of self-actualisation, which implies finding meaning and fulfilment by accomplishing one's dreams and harnessing one's full potential. The mission can also be related (according to Maslow, 1954) to the need for self-transcendence, which implies helping others in a selfless manner and contributing to an objective bigger than oneself.

This prestigious scholar became well-known for his pyramid of needs, which includes basic needs on the bottom (physiological and safety needs); on an upper level, more advanced needs (socialisation and esteem needs); and on the top, the most advanced needs (self-realisation and self-transcendence).

A mission-driven company understands that its activities never occur in a vacuum because the organisation is inserted in a community affected directly or indirectly by the company's activities. A company which pursues its mission has a very tangible impact on its external environment, for example:

- Generation of economic benefits for all partners involved related to the company (suppliers, intermediaries, etc.)
- Development of discoveries through the company's research and product development process, which benefit the marketplace and humankind as a whole
- Protection of environmental resources (land, air, etc.) as a result of green activities (recycling, use of renewable energies, etc.) performed by the company
- Increase in taxes collected by government from the company, which can be used for social purposes (education, infrastructure, etc.)
- Generation of employment, which gives rise to a decent living for the members of a community
- Support to communities through the company's social initiatives (sponsoring, donations, etc.)
- Increase in customers' satisfaction through the company's offering of high-quality products and services

De Botton (2016a) observed that companies can also bring about a positive impact on customers by creating "good demand," which is "consumer's choice that is in line with fruitful needs" and contributes to improving their life from the long-term perspective. Some companies' purpose is focused on supplying products and services which positively contribute to their customers' development. Some examples are companies which sell products and services like healthcare services (which contribute to customers' better health conditions) and educational courses (which enhance customers' skills), among others.

Therefore, companies should avoid pursuing a mission related to goods and services which creates "bad demand" in customers, such as junk food and weapons, which have demonstrated their detrimental effects on a society. The mission pursued by a company should always aim to make people's lives better, from the short-term perspective (instant gratification), but also from the long-term viewpoint (better health, thriving careers, increased knowledge, outstanding relationships, etc.).

To sum up, a well-defined mission has a significant transformative power, because it challenges the status quo and produces a positive change in the world. When a company defines its own mission, it recognises that the relevant needs of customers and other stakeholders (employees, communities, etc.) can be satisfied more effectively. A company's mission is always bigger than the organisation itself and goes beyond the company's self-interest, in order to positively trickle down into wider society.

1.2.6 A Business Mission Represents a Company's Map of the World

The man without a purpose is like a ship without a rudder, a waif, a nothing, a no man.

Thomas Carlyle

Human perception is intrinsically limited; people can never perceive the millions of stimuli there are in the environment. Besides, people's perceptive systems are guided by their distinct beliefs and values. For example, if a person believes in the abundance of opportunities, he is more likely to find them regularly, as compared with those who do not believe so. This phenomenon, called "confirmation bias," implies that people tend to focus on specific stimuli from the environment consistent with their beliefs, dismissing the rest.

The world is intrinsically complex and dynamic. According to the discipline called neuro-linguistic programming (NLP), every person has a distinctive map of the world which helps them go through it in a unique manner. These maps are simplified representations of reality. From this perspective, a mission is a shared map which guides the company's people in the performance of their business activities on a continuous basis.

From the psychological perspective, people use personal stories which help them as guidelines for their lives. These manufactured personal tales can be related to the person itself, other people, and the world in general. These narratives are not necessarily truthful, but credible and meaningful to the creator. People make sense of circumstances in a narrative manner, through their stories. In a similar vein, Zander and Zander (2002) observed the stories that people hold in their minds help them represent and interpret the world around them. Moreover, these stories *limit* the way they "see" reality.

A company's mission has shared stories embedded in it, especially the ones related to the questions "Why are we in the marketplace?" and "What is our relevant contribution to others?" These stories are continuous reminders which help a company pursue its mission in a more effective manner. These stories gather the company's people around the purpose and make them feel more optimistic about achieving this purpose.

A well-designed mission is always story-based, which is emotionally compelling. When a mission has an enticing narrative, it lulls people into pursuing it. Some story-telling aspects are implicit in the verbal definition of the mission. Other aspects are fully expressed when the mission is conveyed to others. Very significant narrative aspects related to the mission unfold when the company takes specific actions to pursue it. A mission tends to be pursued more effectively if its narrative is congruent with the personal stories of the people (for example, employees, etc.) contributing to it.

1.2.7 A Business Mission Is an Overarching Goal

The mission is the company's major guideline which is duly considered in any action performed by the organisation. A company's objectives must always be aligned with this general purpose. In the human brain, there is something called the "reticular articular system" (RAS). When people set specific goals, their own RAS helps them encounter people, things and circumstances related to these very objectives. The RAS acts like a filter which sifts through all the stimuli in the environment to concentrate on those significant to the person's objectives.

When people in a company share a mission, which in practice is an overarching goal, their RAS helps them pursue this purpose, in the same way as for minor objectives. Committed employees continually have the organisation's mission on their minds, and their RAS guides them toward situations, circumstances and people closely related to this very purpose. The company's purpose "moulds" their employees' perceptions, leading them to situations related to this mission. There is a well-known quotation which goes "What you focus on, grows; what you dismiss, dwindles." When a company follows its mission in a continuous manner, its employees concentrate their attention on this purpose in a single-minded manner.

According to Fritz (1984, 1999), primary purpose is the general aim or direction which all other purposes (called secondary ones) are subordinate to. This author stated that the primary purpose is the "organization's most meaningful organizing principle" (Fritz, 1999). From this perspective, the business mission can be considered the company's primary purpose to which all secondary goals (such as corporate objectives, marketing goals, production objectives, etc.) need to be aligned. In other words, the company's purpose is an overall guideline with which all strategies and tactics must be congruent.

A company's mission also dictates which business opportunities will be harnessed and which ones discarded. From this perspective, a company's mission eliminates the uncertainty regarding how to act before different courses of action, avoiding situations of paralysis from excessive analysis. Consequently, a company will choose only those courses of actions aligned with their mission.

A mission pervades each and every of the company's activities. Therefore, when employees pursue the company's mission, they tend to prioritise activities closely related to it. They avoid dissipating their energy on unrelated chores. Seemingly big challenges do not seem so overwhelming to the company, because it goes toward what it cares about the most.

1.2.8 A Mission Is Inspirational and Meaningful

> People are physically moved to a person who is vulnerable enough to make visible the deep essence of what their heart is giving.
>
> **Mark Silver**

A well-defined mission is meaningful because it clarifies why the company wants to achieve this purpose. The answer to the question "Why is our company in the marketplace?" is reflected in the business mission. A true mission is related to the concept of togetherness because it is truly inspirational to others. Most people realise when a company wants to make a difference to the world, and tend to be more willing to assist the organisation in that process. Mission-driven companies are also perceived as models to emulate.

People tend to feel enthusiasm when they do things they love. A well-designed mission elicits positive emotional states in people, which prompts them to pursue it. These people feel emboldened to take action. Therefore, inspired employees tend to contribute to the mission in a continuous and loving manner, even during challenging times. These employees experience good feelings by using their unique talents to add value to other people. These employees also know their actions are leaving a positive mark on the world, which represents a good reason to go to work and do their best.

Many people feel their lives are without meaning. Contrary to this, employees engaged with the company's mission find their lives motivating and meaningful because they are pursuing a purpose related to lofty values such as fairness, benevolence, care, and others. By contributing to that well-meaning purpose, these employees feel useful because their contribution is of real value to others. Frankl (2006) observed that what drives people is their meaning and purpose in life, which implies following their mission and carrying out the tasks necessary for its fulfilment.

A company which follows its mission radiates positive energy which not only animates employees but also its external environment. Mackey and Sisodia (2014) called the purpose a "magnet" which attracts the right human resources to the company. People can intuitively sense when a company focuses on worthwhile causes and tend to support it. According to Goleman (1996, 1998), emotional contagion implies that intense emotions tend to be naturally contagious. Therefore, employees who pursue the company's purpose in a wholehearted manner positively "infect" others around them, who are more prone to provide support.

Lastly, it has been stated that when people follow their calling, a decent livelihood tends to follow. Likewise, when a company follows its purpose and serves others in a genuine and valuable manner, their success is more prone to occur.

1.2.9 A Mission Is Socially Caring

Does this path have a heart? If it does, the path is good; if it doesn't, it's of no use.

Carlos Castaneda

A true mission is defined in a conscientious manner. A well-defined purpose considers the positive impact on all relevant stakeholders and avoids trade-offs among them. Companies which are not mission-oriented are instead more prone to benefit some stakeholders (for example, customers) at the expense of others (for instance, employees). An authentic mission is holistic, because it takes into consideration all the company's relevant stakeholders, even those with little power in relation to the organisation.

As seen previously, a company which pursues a clearly defined mission goes beyond profit-oriented goals. An authentic business mission is related to the concept of corporate social responsibility (CSR). This perspective implies caring for the external environment the company acts within. From this standpoint, the company's activities tend to have a deliberate beneficial impact on the members of its community. Right from its onset, this type of company intends to make a better world.

Some examples of CSR activities are: leading foundations, organising charitable events and donating resources to social causes, among others. This CSR perspective implies the adoption of a generous attitude. In a traditional (and non-generous) approach, a company mostly aims to *obtain* (more customers, more profits, more sales, etc.). The generous perspective, instead, means the company is willing to *give* valuable things to the wider community. A company that adopts this selfless perspective becomes more closely connected and integrated to the environment where it is doing business.

For ages, many maladies, such as wars, global warming, sexual exploitation, child labour, and others, have been affecting the world. A true business mission connected to CSR perspectives is aimed at producing a positive shift on the planet, and also brings some support, hope and solace to people suffering from these global predicaments.

1.3 Tips to Discover (and Rediscover) the Business Mission

People without a purpose go nowhere, accomplish little, and enjoy less.

David Schwartz

A company's mission is connected to its meaningful contribution to others, not related to fashions, fads or trends. Some companies mistakenly believe that they have to play small in the business environment. These companies must stretch themselves and set ambitious purposes. Companies should also avoid being short-sighted due to short-term urgencies and set lofty purposes with a positive long-term impact on others. Each company has a unique mission, which will help the organisation utilise its own distinct resources, talents and capabilities. Therefore, there is no "competition" among the missions pursued by different companies.

Some business people have serious difficulties discovering their purpose. They have hectic daily activities which prevent them from reflecting on their mission. It is important that these entrepreneurs set time aside and listen to their inner voice more attentively to discover their true purpose. They should think beyond self-interest and survival needs (which entails the development of a profitable company) and include a long-term perspective (which implies generating a positive impact on all the company's stakeholders).

Hillman (2006) developed the "acorn theory," which states that a person's mission is inborn. From this perspective, people's unique potential and possibilities are already inside themselves, prompting these individuals to fulfil them. Using a relevant analogy, an acorn always has the blueprint of the mighty oak contained within it.

The aforementioned author also observed that people came to this world to fulfil their mission, which includes a particular way of harnessing their distinctive potential through their work and also a unique way of being themselves in the world. From this perspective, a very important question to pose related to one's own mission is "How can I be of value to other people?" It is interesting to note that the acorn theory can be applied both to individuals and organisations. Business people can pose other questions to (re)discover and define their mission:

- Who do I admire for their passion and purpose?
- What is my main reason for being in business?
- What are my essential qualities and how I can share them?
- What activities give me joy, fulfilment or peace and why?
- What activities make me lose track of the time when I am engrossed in them?
- How can I use my unique talents to serve others and solve their problems?
- How can I create an authentic and loving connection with people around me?
- What endeavours connect me to my essence and allow me to give my best to the world?
- What do I want to be remembered for?

Business people should dwell on these questions on a regular basis to obtain insights and define their mission in a more accurate manner. A business mission is never written in stone; a company can always reformulate, update and rediscover it over time. Nonetheless, according to Duckworth (2017), entrepreneurs cannot discover their mission only by insights; they have to interact with the world to streamline their purpose.

Questions for Self-Reflection

- How can our business mission improve the lives of other people?
- How can I communicate our business mission in a more meaningful way?
- How can I co-operate with others to fulfil the company's purpose?
- How can our company's mission inspire others?

Chapter 2

Relentless Passion

Even the best business plan will not produce any result if it is not backed with passion.

Howard Schultz

2.1 Passion and Business

You cannot push a business you do not love. You cannot push a business in which you put no heart … Love for a business brings continually new thoughts, plans, ideas, and devices for so improving it. Love for a business brings new force ever to push that business.

Prentice Mulford

In different business meetings and entrepreneurial conferences, when business people were asked the question "What drives your authentic passion to run your business?", the most frequent answers were:

- I want total financial independence.
- I want to increase the level of profits.
- I want to deliver the best products or services in the market.
- I want to deliver innovative products and services.
- I want to enter new markets.
- I want to solve people's problems in an effective manner.
- I want to satisfy customer needs.
- I want to have more loyal customers.
- I want to beat my competitors.
- I want to improve quality and productivity levels.

However, in all these answers underlie some hidden reasons for making a company thrive. Some usual unmentioned reasons motivating many business people's activities are:

- To do what they are passionate about
- To utilise their talents and skills openly

- To make people's lives more fulfilling
- To create better relationships with others
- To successfully surmount challenges
- To learn new capabilities
- To become a better person
- To feel recognised by others
- To make the world a better place

In this chapter and the following ones, these valuable reasons will be explored in a more thorough manner.

2.2 Main Aspects of Passion

Visionary companies focus primarily on beating themselves.

James Collins and Jerry Porras

Many business people lack passion; they view their activities as a chore. In an almost predictable manner, entrepreneurs with no passion have the following characteristics:

- They dabble with their business activities, not making them a major priority.
- They are prone to give up when they face relevant challenges in their business endeavours.
- They do not remain true to themselves; they perform activities opposite to their values.
- They tend not to harness their distinct skills, and to underperform.
- They are worried about business problems instead of focusing on their solutions.
- They experience a large amount of resistance to taking unusual actions or considering new ideas.
- They get easily distracted by trivial activities.
- They are not fully committed to what they do.
- They do not feel vigorous and energetic when performing their daily tasks.
- They feel uncomfortable with uncertain and uncontrollable business scenarios.

Passion is the fuel which helps companies pursue their mission. Without passion, business objectives are less likely to be attained. There is no general agreement on an academic definition of the word "passion." Passion is an expression of love; passionate people lovingly give the best of their time, effort, and talents to pursue their mission. They truly love their purpose and pursue it with enthusiasm and single-mindedness. Passionate people's loving attitude toward their mission helps them endure tough situations during their business journey.

Therefore, passion represents a continuous heightened emotional state which drives people to follow their mission with tenacity. However, the emotional aspects are only a part of the passion equation. It also includes rational and pragmatic components. All these aspects are interrelated and will be explained in the following points.

2.2.1 Rational Aspect

If you sit and calculate all the risks before you do something you feel inspired to do, you will throw your highest dream away.

Jason Chan and Jane Robert

He who has a why to live for can bear almost any how.

Friedrich Nietzsche

The rational aspect is linked to a meaningful purpose a company wants to achieve. When a company's people are passionate about the organisation's purpose, they always have this purpose on their minds. All their business strategies and tactics are developed to achieve this mission. In relation to this, Blackburn and Epel (2017) observed that people who pursue their purpose are more resilient regarding stress and have better psychological health. Besides, when these individuals have a strong conviction their purpose can be attained, they are often open to innovative perspectives in order to pursue their mission.

Passionate business people are also more prone to organise and utilise company resources (funds, technology, information, personnel, etc.) in the most effective way to achieve the organisation's purpose. These people adopt an attitude of self-control and discipline, in order to avoid being distracted or diverted with any activity not conducive to the mission. Assagioli (1974) observed that discipline does not mean suppression or repression of one's expression, but its regulation so that one's biological and psychological energies are used in a productive manner. In other words, passionate people will regulate their expression so that they only perform activities related to their purpose, and avoid superfluous actions.

From the rational perspective, passionate people learn from their mistakes and setbacks to take necessary corrective actions on their way to the mission. According to Dweck (2012), these people have a growth mentality, which implies willingness to obtain useful feedback for their continuous improvement and development. When appropriate, these people can vary their approaches in order to choose activities more congruent with their mission. Passionate people are more prone to frame any circumstance, including seemingly challenging ones, in a positive manner. From this perspective, failures are interpreted as springboards to do things better next time.

These people also understand that a great number of the circumstances they will encounter during their business journey are beyond their control. They understand that they are always dealing with a myriad of uncertain, unpredictable, and uncontrollable factors; therefore, adopting a flexible attitude is key to their success. They therefore avoid resisting these situations or becoming negative about them.

Passionate people realise that they can truly control the way they perceive each circumstance in order to do their best. For example, these individuals tend to perceive troublesome situations as "challenges," instead of "problems." Moreover, in uncertain situations, these people use research to make more informed decisions, but they also adopt an exploratory attitude as they take action. These individuals realise that many aspects of the business process will be discovered by acting toward their purpose.

Some passionate individuals have an unshakeable conviction that circumstances affecting their business projects always unfold in the best way possible. They perceive these situations as part of a bigger picture which cannot be fully known in advance. Some entrepreneurs, like Steve Jobs (2008), observed that people can make sense in hindsight of how different situations are linked to one another.

Passionate people tend to avoid overanalysing each action to be taken. Instead, they are empowered to take continuous action and understand that there are no perfect ways to act and no ideal circumstances. Passionate people are willing to fine-tune their activities as they act. These individuals perceive their business endeavours as a learning process; their skills, talents, and actions are continually perfected as they pursue their purpose. In this process, feedback always provides invaluable lessons which help them evolve.

2.2.2 Emotional Aspect

> Necessity is always the first stimulus to industry; and those who conduct it with prudence, perseverance, and energy, will rarely fail … Attention, application, accuracy, method, punctuality, and dispatch, are the principal qualities required for the efficient conduct of business of any sort.

Samuel Smiles

> Desire is behind all purpose. Civilization rests upon it.

Orison Marden

Passionate people are tirelessly and obstinately committed to taking continuous actions to fulfil their purpose. Their sustained interest and unsated appetite for their purpose prompt these people to bring about positive change in the world, benefitting their company and others (e.g., customers, community, suppliers, etc.). Their sparkling emotional energy is fully focused on their purpose. Their clout and tenacity assist them on a continuous basis to do their best and use every fibre of their beings. In relation to this, Wiest (2013) observed that "passion is the spark that lights the fire; purpose is the kindling that keeps the flame burning all night."

Passionate individuals are truly convinced their purpose is worth achieving, which leads to them performing their tasks in a zealous and unwavering manner. Their steady resolve and temperance prevent them from giving up in challenging circumstances. They continually move forward, and do not feel disappointed when failure strikes them.

Passionate people understand that oftentimes valuable opportunities lie within difficult circumstances. Every time these people are pushed down, they tend to come back even stronger and with the benefit of insights. Figuratively speaking, setbacks have the same effect on them as the wind on a thistle plant, temporarily bending, but never breaking it.

Their focus is always narrowed down to what is contributory to their purpose. Passionate people have inexhaustible energy, and love learning from the challenges related to their endeavours. These people enthusiastically share their purpose with others (customers, business partners, etc.), inspiring them and gathering their support.

Passionate people are more prone to respond to difficulties in a proactive and fruitful manner, instead of reacting negatively to them. These individuals also avoid blaming, criticising, or complaining, because these actions are energy drainers which prevent them from going toward their purpose. Their positive attitude helps them discover the positive side of each circumstance they face, even negative ones. Their unremitting focus on their purpose helps them to perceive predicaments as learning experiences.

Passionate people are aware of their fears and realise these fearful states have an instinctive and protective function. However, they always face these fears, feel them, and boldly do what must be done to achieve their purpose anyway. These people also face the ambiguous and the unknown, and are sometimes even comfortable with it, prompted by the momentum of their continuous actions. These individuals are capable of stretching themselves beyond their comfort zone to take actions they have not taken before.

People who pursue their mission are prone to do what they truly love; therefore, they tend to be naturally positive and adopt a loving attitude toward others. Their enthusiasm and joy infect others, as people tend to replicate the emotional states of others around them. This phenomenon is called "emotional contagion."

Hawkins (2012, 2013) stated that individuals can access different states of consciousness: high ones (gratitude, peacefulness, love, etc.) and lower ones (shame, grief, fear, etc.) This scientist observed that when people experience high states of consciousness, they counteract the lower states of consciousness of a massive group of people around them. Therefore, with their enthusiastic attitude, passionate people tend to experience a higher state of consciousness which tends to positively transform individuals around them.

Sometimes, despite countless efforts, business people don't see any tangible outcomes from their actions. Leonard (1992) called this phase "plateau," and it is a critical time where most people become disheartened and are prone to give up. Nonetheless, passionate people never become disappointed; they know that the plateau is a necessary stage to fulfil their mission and they are willing to continually work toward it wholeheartedly. Moreover, passionate people tend to show appreciation during the plateau.

From the emotional perspective, passionate people enjoy pursuing their purpose, which is not considered "work," but something fun and rewarding. They do not feel obligated to pursue their mission, but they feel compelled to do so because they love it. Sometimes, these people are so obsessed with their mission that they end up creating an imbalance in other areas of their lives (family, health, etc.).

Lastly, Fritz (2003) observed that passion does not necessarily have to be an emotional experience of excitement, which he considers a temporary state. Instead, this author observed that passion can be considered as "the desire to bring a work into completion," which tends to be a more permanent state. In other words, passionate business people have the continuous desire to achieve the organisation's purpose.

2.2.3 Pragmatic Aspect

> It's OK to be discouraged. It's not OK to quit. To know you want to quit but to plant your feet and keep inching closer until you take the impenetrable fortress you've decided to lay siege to in your own life – that's persistence.
>
> **Ryan Holiday**

> The best time to move ahead is just before you are ready to move ahead.
>
> **Robert Fritz**

Passionate people doggedly wrap their minds around their purpose and take continuous deliberate action toward it. According to Fritz (1991, 2003), people should always focus outwardly, more specifically on their main purpose, and take actions accordingly, instead of centring inwardly (on their emotions, thoughts, and self-image).

Oftentimes, passionate people regularly visualise the main aspects related to their mission; this envisioning process helps them not to lose sight of their purpose. According to research, visualised actions activate the same brain cells as when the real actions are performed. Research also showed that, with every visualisation, the respective neural pathways are strengthened. Continuous visualisation of the purpose represents a simple way to gain motivation toward it.

Passionate people avoid making excuses regarding why things might not work out. A passionate company's people are determined but also flexible; their actions change over time when circumstances require it. They understand there is no such a thing as the perfect strategy to be applied to any situation. When taking action, these people tend to harness their innermost skills and capabilities.

These people are willing to perform unpleasant tasks which contribute to the purpose. All their actions are performed in a wholehearted manner. Tasks that would seem unachievable for people with no passion look doable to passionate individuals. Passionate business people are prone to perform tasks related to their purpose with gust and zest.

Passionate people know the value of small steps; each step sets the foundation for the following ones. Their frequent resolute actions get them nearer to their very purpose. These people realise that taking action generates more motivation and develops a virtuous cycle. They know that the greatest ideas have no value, if not properly implemented. Oftentimes, passionate people are disciplined and form positive habits supportive to the achievement of their purpose. Their disciplined attitude helps these people avoid short-term gratification in order to achieve their mission.

When passionate people are hit by setbacks, they avoid feeling disheartened and quickly stand up to keep on moving forward; setbacks are always perceived as temporary. These people know the journey to their purpose is a series of small sprints. They realise that persistent action always pays off; every single action counts. They understand that, oftentimes, companies improve in a progressive manner, not by quantum leaps. Consequently, these individuals are willing to take actions with all their heart, even when the circumstances are not the ideal ones. They know their actions can be improved on the way, as they get some feedback on the actions taken. They also know that to succeed in the achievement of their mission, their actions, thoughts, and emotions must be aligned with it.

Fox (2010) distinguished two types of actions: true ones and false ones. On one side, true action shifts things significantly and always comes from inside out. Genuine actions tend to be lively, graceful, and self-energising; they provide the performers with unbounded vitality. Passionate people tend to perform this type of action on a regular basis. In relation to this, Goleman et al. (1995) called passion "intrinsic motivation," and observed that passionate people feel internally driven to follow their purpose, without relying on any external incentive.

On the other side, false actions start outside in; these actions are externally driven and often disconnected from one's own interests and desires. In false actions, external factors (other people's opinions, ingrained social assumptions, etc.) have more relevance than one's innermost desires. This type of action is more connected to what must or should be done, instead of being related to one's genuine desires. These actions tend to be more mechanical and less inspired. Passionate people are less prone to perform this type of action.

Besides, passionate people tend to concentrate on the relevant business tasks at hand and avoid ruminating on past experiences (for example, through regret, guilt) or future ones (for instance, through fear, trepidation). These people pursue their purpose in a determined manner and avoid being sidetracked by trivial tasks which do not contribute to their mission, because they are fully centred on relevant business activities related to their purpose. Such people are prone to enter a state of flow (also called "the zone") which allows them to achieve higher performance levels.

Csikszentmihalyi (2002, 2003) observed that in the flow state, people are less self-conscious, more immersed in the present task and open to immediate feedback on their performance. As a consequence, their activities seem almost effortless, which allows them to work for extended periods of time without getting tired or distracted. The aforementioned author also mentioned other characteristics of the flow state, like clarity of objectives, control of the situation at hand, achievability of tasks in relation to one's capabilities, and challenges with some degree of complexity and richness.

Lastly, passionate people are resolute with their actions, but not stubborn. It is important to differentiate "determination" from "stubbornness." Passionate people are determined; they are mindful of their mistakes and make adjustments to their future actions and keep on pursuing their purpose. Stubborn people are unwilling to learn from their mistakes and continue acting in the same way again and again.

Questions for Self-Reflection

- Which activities make me feel more passionate?
- How does my passion contribute to the achievement of the company's business purpose?
- How does my passionate attitude help me face dire business circumstances?
- How does my passion help me distinguish relevant tasks from trivial ones?

Chapter 3

Prosperity Mindset

When you are oriented to abundance, you care less about being in control, and you take more risks.

Rosamund Stone Zander and Benjamin Zander

3.1 Business Mindset

3.1.1 General Aspects of Mindset

You can get everything in life if you will just help others to get what they want.

Zig Ziglar

Some define mentality or mindset as "mental perspective," "thought processes," "way to view the world," "personal paradigm," or "mental attitude." A mindset prompts a person to act in a specific way. Most psychologists observe that a person's mindset is affected by three important elements: beliefs, values, and emotional states. A mindset is related to an "inside-out" approach; one's internal resources bring about one's circumstances.

As seen previously, a mindset is related to beliefs. People's beliefs are subconscious rules governing what is true for them, even when not supported by evidence from reality. A person's beliefs stem from different sources: upbringing, relevant personal experiences, training received, communication with other people, and media messages, among others.

Beliefs dictate how people act, think, feel, and perceive reality, as well as how they see themselves (self-image). Beliefs always generate expectations consistent with them. These beliefs can be positive or negative; they are selective and self-confirming because they only allow a person to perceive things congruent with them and dismiss anything that contradicts this individual's beliefs.

Dilts (1994) stated that, on a lower level, beliefs are related to capabilities (which are specific strategies on how to act), behaviour (the actions that people take), and the environment (the external context the individual acts in). This author also observed that, on a higher level, beliefs are related to people's identity, which is in turn connected to their purpose or mission. The main aspects of mission have been analysed in Chapter 1.

Some examples of these levels can be observed in the following sentences: "We are one of the main companies worldwide helping people communicate better online" (identity), "Communication is necessary to develop a better world" (belief), "We have excellent technological skills" (capabilities), "We develop highly advanced online platforms" (behaviour), and "We will launch a new interactive multimedia platform for the Chinese market" (environment). Dilts (1994) also observed that identity relates to the question "Who?", beliefs and values answer the question "Why?", capabilities answer the question "How?", behaviour answers the question "What?", and the environment answers the questions "Where?" and "When?"

A mindset is also related to values. Values are specific beliefs about what is important for a person (for example, fun, stability, happiness, love, generosity, etc.). Values can act as personal moral guidelines, and help people assess what is right and wrong for them. In other words, value is what a person actually stands for, and what this individual rejects. Values are ordered in a hierarchical manner; in other words, some values are more important than others.

People tend to make decisions consistent with their highest values. In the case of a company, its most relevant values will affect its activities. The ideal situation for a company is that its employees' values are congruent or aligned with the company's values. According to Robbins (2001), there are "moving-toward values" which prompt people to take action toward pleasurable outcomes (e.g., success, comfort, wealth, etc.), and "moving-away-from values," which are those values which people tend to avoid (e.g., scarcity, failure, etc.), as they are painful.

A mindset is also related to emotions, which are states which people experience, like fear, anger, sadness, happiness, and others. These states bring about physiological changes (e.g., quick breathing, pupils' dilation, etc.) as well as interpretations and actions related to them. Emotional states are also reflected in body language (gestures, facial expressions, etc.). Dalmasio (2012) observed that emotions are "complex, largely automated programs of actions" performed by one's body which are complemented by "some ideas and modes of cognition." Besides, emotions continually interact with thoughts and "colour" how a person interprets circumstances.

According to Ellis and Harper (1997), emotions follow this sequence: a person goes through a specific experience, which in turn activates specific beliefs and thoughts, which bring about certain emotions and behaviours. These authors noticed that emotions are the result of a biased assessment of specific thoughts. Likewise, the Stoic philosophical school of thought observed that people are not upset by circumstances, but by their interpretation of them.

It is important to pinpoint that thoughts prompt specific emotions closely related to them (a person with negative thoughts is prone to experience negative emotional states). This aspect also works the other way around; certain emotional states are more conducive to specific thoughts: for example, happiness is more likely to trigger positive thinking. On a different note, Wiseman (2013) observed that emotions are mental interpretations of one's physiological sensations (like tension, accelerated heartbeats, etc.).

Lastly, mindset is a concept which can be related both to individuals and companies. In the case of a company, its actions, strategies, and business activities will be driven by the prevalent mindset of its people. These aspects will be explained more thoroughly in the following points.

3.1.2 Mindset and Business Activities

> We cannot choose the things that will happen to us. But we can choose the attitude we will take toward anything that happens.
>
> **Alfred Montapert**

In business, a positive mindset is the most important resource a company can count on. Every single activity performed by a company is dictated by the predominant mindset in this organisation. From this perspective, the prevailing mindset in a company will help it decide on certain aspects, such as:

- How to discover and harness business opportunities
- How to allocate the company's unique resources
- What goals to set for the business activities
- How to utilise the company strengths and talents
- How to add more value to others
- How to define the business the company is in
- How to present a unique offering to the market
- How to invest, save, and spend money
- What type of business strategy to develop
- How to develop new products and services
- How to be motivated by specific objectives
- How to handle customer service
- What type of technology to use in business
- How to recruit and empower employees
- What business model to follow
- What productivity and quality levels to set
- How to grow business activities
- How to leverage others' capabilities
- How to relate to other organisations
- What information to consider for decision-making
- How to interact with internal and external stakeholders
- How to tackle obstacles during the business journey
- How to learn and recover from business setbacks
- How to deal with uncertain or dire business scenarios
- How to solve problems in a creative manner

As previously seen, a mindset is related to beliefs, values, and emotions which in turn bring about a distinctive interpretation of reality and prompt actions related to it. In other words, every single action a company takes stems from ideas coming from the prevailing mindset of people working for this company. In a similar vein, Covey (1992) observed that things are always created twice; firstly, in the mind, and secondly in real practice, in the physical environment. For example, a company's strategy is first thought out thoroughly (mental creation) and then implemented by taking concrete actions to achieve its objectives (physical creation). This obvious idea is frequently forgotten by some entrepreneurs.

On one side, a company where there is a prevalent abundance mindset is more likely to generate ideas which bring about positive activities and outcomes. On the other side, a company with a prevailing scarcity mindset is more prone to generate ideas which lead to detrimental actions and results. It is important to pinpoint that mindsets are never carved in stone; they can be changed. Companies should be aware of the main characteristics of their predominant mindsets, in order to reflect on them and change them when necessary.

Yeager (quoted in Dilts et al., 2012) stated that a change in a mindset tends to occur when there is enough motivation, adequate knowledge about a strategy to produce change, and a clear opportunity to bring about this change. In this chapter, some recommendations on how to change the prevailing mindset in an organisation will be given.

3.2 Scarcity Mindset

> The greatest discovery of my generation is that a human being can change his life by altering his attitude.
>
> **William James**

3.2.1 *The Looming Threat of Scarcity and Competition*

> Life is not about having good cards, but of playing a poor hand well.
>
> **Robert Louis Stevenson**

In the business environment, a scarcity mindset supports the existence of scarce resources. Business people with a scarcity mindset believe in the threatening power of other companies offering similar products or services, known as "competitors." These two aspects will be analysed in the following points. Traditional economic theory observes that in the business environment, all resources (capital, technology, land, etc.) are intrinsically limited. From a wider perspective, some economists assert that the main world maladies (poverty, crime, wars, deforestation, etc.) stem from a natural lack of resources worldwide.

Most organisations believe that resources are scarce. Some companies, for instance, claim that there are not enough funds to perform business activities. Other companies complain about the lack of ideas, talent, technology, and time. Some entrepreneurs state that there are insufficient opportunities in the markets and that customers are scarce.

When resources are perceived as limited, organisations tend to continually seek these prized resources, driven by egotism and greed. The concept of "competitors" is closely related to the idea of scarcity of resources. A company "competes" with others because there is not enough (customers, funds, etc.) for all of them. In fact, most companies' strategies take into consideration their competitors as one of their main factors.

The word "competition" is commonly used in the professional sports environment. In any sport, one team (or player, in individual sports) aims to win at the expense of others. In these cases, the winner gets the sought-after prize and the loser gets nothing (or just a consolation reward). Winners also receive praise and recognition because of their skills, talents, or strategies. In sports, winning is associated with a state of superiority and high achievement.

From the social perspective, individuals are faced with the idea of "competition" in their early years. Several social institutions, starting firstly with the family, support the concept of "competition," encouraging their children to do better than others. Many families compare themselves with the neighbours next door and try to outpace them.

Schools are other social institutions which foster competition. At most of these institutions, children are encouraged to compete with one another. In most educational systems, students' academic performance is measured with grades; students with "better performance" are rewarded with higher marks than others, which implies competition between them. This grading system continues even when students enter high school and university.

Besides, media news is constantly feeding society with ideas of scarcity of resources and competition. For example, news about unemployment is widely promoted, suggesting that there are not enough jobs for everybody willing to work. Similarly, popular television contests prompt participants to compete with others for a prize. Most people are impressionable to these media messages, which contribute to the development of a scarcity mindset in them.

In all the aforementioned examples, there is a common framework known as a "zero-sum game," or "win–lose." This is an adversarial model where two or more participants compete for specific scarce resources, and one *always* wins at the expense of others and obtains all resources at stake. Some conflict-resolution methods – for example, lawsuits – are also based on zero-sum game.

3.2.2 Competition and Scarcity of Resources in the Business World

A mind when stretched by a new idea, never regains its original dimensions.

Oliver Wendell Holmes

As seen previously, most companies continually relate their activities to the concepts of scarcity and competition. Consequently, these companies are prone to use countless tools to deal with their perceived scarcity of resources, for example, business plans, budgets, cost projections, and others. These tools have two main objectives: firstly, to reduce uncertainty levels regarding future business scenarios, and secondly to use companies' limited resources (funds, technology, human resources, etc.) more efficiently.

In relation to the concept of "competitors," the majority of companies tend to act in a reactive way. In other words, these companies' activities are driven by their competitors. In these cases, a relevant objective of these companies' business strategies is to outsmart rival organisations. Only a small part of these companies' actions is proactive, which means acting without considering other organisations.

The concepts of "scarcity of resources" and "competition" are fundamental parts of the mindset predominant in most companies. These concepts prime companies' perception of the business environment and prompt them to act accordingly. In other words, companies with a prevalent scarcity mindset tend to perceive a lack of opportunities and resources in the marketplace, which prompts these organisations to "fight" over them.

These companies adopt a "warmongering attitude" because they perceive other organisations as "adversaries" to be defeated. These companies participate in carefully planned "market battles" with rival organisations. In this "battlefield," they use different "weapons" (e.g., strategies, tactics, etc.) to beat their "enemies." Most of the well-used business tools have obvious belligerent connotations.

3.2.3 Fear, Competition, and Scarcity of Resources

The concepts of "competition" and "scarcity of resources" are fundamentally based on fear. As mentioned previously (in Chapter 2), the scientist Dr Hawkins (2012, 2013) observed that there is a scale of states of consciousness, where fear is one of its lowest states, and love is the highest of this spectrum. From this perspective, business people who are fearful of other companies and of scarcity of resources have a very limited view of the business environment. These organisations cannot tune into a higher state of consciousness, such as love. In the business environment, fear is commonly observed in different ways, for example:

- Fear of being beaten by other companies
- Fear of not achieving the company's objectives

- Fear of taking certain business actions
- Fear of not surviving in the marketplace
- Fear of navigating uncertain business scenarios

A company's people can show their fear in various ways, oftentimes very subtle ones, such as doubts, worries, procrastination, complacency, stagnation, distrust, and aggressiveness, among others. Any state of fear is constrictive and limiting for business activities. A company driven by fear-based concepts like "competition" and "scarcity" tends to be reactive. This type of company tends to have a very narrow view of their business environment, which affects their relevant activities (mentioned in Section 2.2.) Companies which make their decisions based on fear are less prone to harness their full potential and embrace their uniqueness.

A company with a predominant scarcity mindset tends to take actions which are driven by fear. This type of organisation tends to act against perceived threats (e.g., competitors and scarcity of resources). From the psychological perspective, this reactive behaviour is related to the so-called fight-freeze-flight response. Therefore, an organisation with a prevalent scarcity mindset is prone to act in three possible ways:

- *Fight:* for example, a company takes specific actions in order to outwit its competitors.
- *Freeze:* for instance, a company remains passive before its competitors' actions.
- *Flight:* for example, a company abandons the marketplace where other companies act, to avoid confronting them.

In the above cases, companies' actions are prompted by an external threatening factor (i.e., competitors). In none of these cases is the company intrinsically motivated, which means acting in a spontaneous and proactive manner. When a company's employees act in fight-freeze-flight mode, their highest mental skills (analysis, synthesis, creativity, etc.) are temporarily impaired; these individuals cannot access their innermost resources fully. The topic of fear in business activities will be explored thoroughly in Chapter 5.

As mentioned in the previous chapter, Fox (2010) distinguished two types of actions: unauthentic actions (generated by external factors) and real actions (motivated intrinsically). When a company is driven by competitors or scarcity of resources, it tends to take actions which are reactive and inauthentic. From this standpoint, this type of organisation performs inauthentic activities.

These fear-driven companies cannot fully tap into their valuable resources (talents, technology, information, etc.). This type of company cannot provide its stakeholders (customers, employees, suppliers, community, etc.) with its distinctive value either. Employees working for these companies are also less prone to enter a flow state (explained in Chapter 2) where peak performance can be achieved. These companies bring about other negative effects, as follows:

- **Avoidance of potential beneficial partnerships:** A company continually focused on its competitors cannot fathom the possibility of developing partnerships with them. This type of company has an adversarial attitude toward other organisations, because it perceives them as opponents, instead of potential collaborators. Potential opportunities stemming from alliances with these companies are missed: for example, sharing or complementing resources (technology, business information, etc.), reducing costs, and assuming joint risks, among others.
- **Focus on negative factors:** The scarcity mindset is intrinsically limited and prompts companies to focus on obstacles, instead of helping these organisations to pursue their mission.

These companies are more concerned about threatening factors (other companies in the markets, negative economic situations, more challenging legislation affecting the sector, etc.) than on seizing and creating business opportunities. This type of company is also more worried about fixing their own weaknesses, rather than harnessing their strengths. These companies are more afraid of potential losses than interested in looking for probable gains stemming from their business activities. In short, in any given situation, these companies are centred more on the limitations affecting them than on the possible choices available. This limiting way of thinking does not allow companies to focus on what is really important, which is continuously pursuing their business purpose.

- **Insufficient development of internal resources:** A company mostly centred on external factors (e.g., competitors) is less likely to develop its own internal aspects properly. For example, this type of company might not train their human resources adequately or develop unique products, services, and technology. These companies tend to develop a very small amount of creative ideas because they act defensively, which stifles their employees' creative skills.
- **Impossibility of obtaining valuable feedback:** A company which only perceives other companies as threats cannot consider them as valuable sources of information or feedback. The products, services, business models, processes, and strategies related to these organisations cannot be taken as references to emulate, adapt, or improve, either.
- **Reduction of spontaneity:** A company which mostly acts in response to other companies is less likely to act according to its innermost goals and show its uniqueness and originality in the marketplace. As mentioned, this type of company is prone to act reactively, for instance, counteracting or neutralising competitors' moves. Consequently, this organisation is less likely to act proactively, for example, by developing new products or services. Oftentimes, this type of company acts against its distinct essence and spirit to respond to its rivals. Competition-driven companies are not totally free to be themselves, because they are slavish to others.

3.2.4 Other Characteristics of a Scarcity Mindset

The scarcity mindset is based on fear. As seen previously, a mindset is not only affected by emotions, but also by beliefs and values. A scarcity mindset has specific beliefs, which are generally very limited and rigid, for example:

- It cannot be done because we do not have enough resources.
- Other companies have more experience than us regarding this issue.
- If only we had the right information, we could make the right decision.
- We cannot offer customers anything different from other companies.
- We do not have the minimum capabilities to develop this project.
- We will be defeated by competitors if we go ahead with this.
- It is not the right time to undertake this project.
- This new idea is unlikely to succeed, better not to take the risk.
- Let's do things as usual; it is not time to rock the boat.
- We must take actions to counteract competitors' moves.

As observed, the scarcity mindset does not only include beliefs about limited resources and competition. The previous examples of constraining beliefs are also related to an inability to perform certain actions, incapability of offering something different from other companies, opposition to taking risks, and resistance to change, among other aspects.

Some limiting beliefs are based on the assumption that the company cannot offer distinct value to the marketplace. This type of company is usually convinced that it does not have any unique talents and capabilities as compared with other companies, so it cannot stand out in the eyes of customers.

All these limiting beliefs act as real obstacles to developing new ideas, products, services, or taking alternative courses of action in the business arena. These negative beliefs represent "mental cages" which restrain a company's performance within the limits of these very beliefs. In relation to this, Dilts et al. (2012) observed there are three main types of beliefs:

- **Beliefs related to objectives:** This type of belief is related to the attainability of one's objectives. Companies with a prevalent scarcity mindset have negative expectations regarding the achievement of their objectives. An example of this type of belief for a company with a prevailing scarcity mindset can be: "An increase in sales of 10% annually cannot be achieved."
- **Beliefs related to self-efficacy:** This belief is related to one's *capability* of achieving a certain objective. A company with a predominant scarcity mindset is not confident it is equipped with the right resources to attain its objectives. An example of a belief which limits a company's self-efficacy can be: "Our company lacks a trained customer service team, therefore we will struggle to attain a 10% annual increase in sales." Some authors like Cash (2013) observed that positive self-efficacy beliefs, alongside optimism, a sense of control, and support from close people make individuals and organisations more resilient. Consequently, there is a direct relationship between one's self-efficacy and the perception of one's resourcefulness.
- **Beliefs related to outcomes:** This type of belief is based on the link between a *cause* (for instance, an action) and an *effect* (a specific result). A company with a scarcity mindset believes its actions will not produce specific results. An example of a negative belief could be "The actions of our customer service will not produce an increase of 10% annual sales."

All the previous examples of negative beliefs are related to the concept of "scarcity." With these limiting beliefs, the company is convinced that it lacks specific resources (experience, time, distinctive products, valuable information, qualified personnel, etc.) to thrive in its projects.

A mindset is also affected by one's values. Companies with a predominant scarcity mindset tend to have values such as stability, safety, survival, risk-aversion, tradition, and control, which make them less willing to take significant risks or explore new ideas. These companies prefer to stick to what is known and avoid highly uncertain scenarios. Oftentimes, these companies have "away-from values" (scarcity, failure) instead of "moving-toward values" (recognition, wealth, etc.).

The scarcity mindset is also related to the concept of "fixed mindset," originally developed by Dweck (2012). From this perspective, companies with fixed mindset consider they have a given set of capabilities which cannot be changed or improved over time. Therefore, for these companies, it is not worth committing resources or making any effort to develop new capabilities. These organisations tend to avoid activities bringing about potential failures (and learning), and instead, they play it safe.

The aforementioned author observed that these companies are generally uncomfortable with criticism from internal and external stakeholders, and are closed to feedback. These organisations cannot enhance their self-efficacy and improve their capabilities. Besides, these companies are less likely to learn from their own mistakes, which prevents them from taking corrective actions to improve their future performance. People working for these companies tend to be envious of other companies' achievements.

As seen previously, companies with a prevailing scarcity mindset tend to focus mostly on their difficulties, incapacities, and constraints. These companies use most of their energy to solve problems, dwelling on them on a continuous basis; for example, worrying, catastrophising, or becoming paralysed by these challenges. These organisations are prone to magnify the negative aspects of each situation and sometimes jump to negative conclusions without a thorough analysis of the relevant issues.

These companies have a "no" mentality which is intrinsically narrow-focused and negative. They have multiple excuses and explanations of why things will not work out. This way of thinking tends to bring about a self-fulfilling prophecy; the results obtained by these organisations generally match their negative expectations. Companies with a prevalent scarcity mindset tend to have a restricted perception of the business environment, which prevents them from discovering opportunities around them. These organisations are mostly centred on threatening aspects of the business environment, such as competitors and scarcity of resources, which makes them less willing to play big in their endeavours.

By focusing on negative issues, these companies are less inclined to take full responsibility for their actions. These organisations are less likely to challenge their perceived internal or external limitations with questions like "What really impedes …?" or "What would happen if …?"

Research has shown that people have a natural tendency to adopt a mindset more biased toward the negative. Some researchers like Baumeister et al. (2001) observed a greater impact, duration, and pervasiveness of negative experiences (e.g., detrimental circumstances, undesirable people, harsh criticism, adverse impressions, unpleasant sensations, negative places, unloving attitudes from other people, harmful emotions, etc.) on people's lives, as compared with positive experiences. In other words, people's response to negative situations tends to be more intense than to that of positive ones.

These researchers also concluded that people are more inclined to avoid negative experiences than to seek positive ones. From the scientific perspective, this phenomenon is named positive-negative asymmetry effect. Research has also found this phenomenon has an evolutionary function, which means that primarily focusing on negative situations increases the likelihood of survival. Likewise, Kahneman and Tversky (1984) observed that negative emotions that people experience when they lose a certain amount of money are far more significant than the happy feelings they experience when they gain the same amount.

3.3 A Prosperity Mindset

What lies behind us and what lies before us are tiny matters compared with what lies within us.

William James

3.3.1 Importance of a Prosperity Mindset

People are always blaming their circumstances for what they are. I don't believe in circumstances. The people who get on in this world are the people who get up and look for the circumstances they want, and, if they can't find them, make them.

George Bernard Shaw

In this book, the terms "abundance mindset" and "prosperity mindset" will be used interchangeably with the same meaning. As mentioned previously, people working for a company with a prevailing scarcity mindset are prone to be afraid of competitors which can take customers from them. By contrast, a company with a predominant prosperity mindset realises there are always countless opportunities in the marketplace for every organisation. This type of organisation is not worried about other companies, and can even wish them well.

These companies never compare themselves with other organisations because they trust their own distinctive talents and capabilities, and embrace them to attain their business purpose. This type of company understands that every organisation can thrive by offering its distinct products and services, and harnessing its unique talents and skills.

Companies with a prevalent abundance mindset know that everything in the business environment is intrinsically dynamic; they are inclined to explore new possibilities ("What it could be") instead of focusing on how things are ("What it is"). These organisations continually ask themselves questions like "What if …?", "What else …", or "What other ways …?"

These companies assume that there is a solution for each business challenge and know that it is a matter of time and dedication to find the best solution to any problem. These organisations know that creative ideas generate countless resources (information, technology, funds, etc.), which can be valuable for their business mission. Besides, these companies understand that creative thinking is the most important resource an organisation counts on.

Companies with a prosperity mindset know that there are always opportunities for growth and development, even in the most challenging business scenarios. Wickham (2004) observed that an opportunity is "the gap left in a market by those who serve it" and "a landscape representing possibilities open to us" which is teeming with potential. This author also observed that opportunities give companies the chance to do things in a different and better manner (for instance, developing new products, innovative services, new practices, superior ways of managing information and relationships, etc.).

Companies with a predominant prosperity mindset have an entrepreneurial approach in relation to business activities. Drucker (2007) observed that "the entrepreneur always searches for change, responds to it, and exploits it as an opportunity." Consequently, companies with a prevalent abundance mindset are able to identify assess and capitalise valuable opportunities. They avoid complaining about factors affecting their businesses (e.g., inflation, taxes, etc.), but they are centred on increasing the value offered to their customers.

People working for these organisations do not waste time dwelling on external uncontrollable factors, but they take full responsibility regarding what they can actually manage (their thoughts, emotions, and actions). In this way, they free themselves from reacting to these external factors and also free themselves to make meaningful choices regarding what they think and do. These companies take full responsibility for what they can actually control, which makes them experience a sense of empowerment regarding their business activities.

People working for these companies have a positive mental attitude; they are not "delusionary dreamers." They know that their only limits in their business activities are their minds. In other words, they realise that oftentimes the hindrances they encounter are self-imposed. They also understand that the development of creative ideas and fresh perspectives can help them work around these constraints.

Companies with a prevalent abundance mindset never set goals which are "too realistic," but instead set big objectives, which can motivate these organisations to work on them with passion and determination. In practice, goals which are "too sensible" tend to limit a company's development and growth. Instead, big objectives help the company push its limitations away, and widen its perception of the business environment.

Besides, companies with a prevailing abundance mindset are continually centred on their mission, and are not overwhelmed by obstacles, which they perceive as temporary and surmountable. These organisations never ignore problems affecting them; they just deal with them as soon as these difficulties come up. Their mission is the steady guideline or horizon these companies always aim at.

As a priority, these companies focus on their unique capabilities, strengths, and talents. Nonetheless, these companies do not deny or neglect their weaknesses. Sometimes, these organisations try to convert their weakness into strengths. However, this usually takes time and implies a medium- to long-term approach. For example, if a company does not have a good customer service call centre, the organisation can train its employees to serve customers in a better manner.

Other times, these companies outsource activities related to their weaknesses. On these occasions, they can use external companies specialised in the areas they are not good at. Following the previous example, the company can contract the service of an external "call centre" to serve customers on the phone. This is a quicker approach and allows companies to focus on what they are really good at, what many authors call "core competencies."

Companies mostly centred on their strong traits are more prone to offer distinct products and services, and implement unique processes and systems. These companies also tend to add differentiated and significant value to their main stakeholders and are more prone to stand out in the marketplace. Besides, these companies are genuinely concerned about the strengthening of the relationships with their main stakeholders. These organisations are also keen on expanding their business activities, for example, by entering new markets and innovating their products and services. To that effect, Mulford (2015) observed:

> You cannot succeed in a business unless in mind you are ever increasing and expanding that business. All great enterprises are thought over and lived over and over again in thought by their projectors, long before the material results are seen. The thought or plan in advance is the real construction of unseen element… The man or woman who succeeds in any business is always in mind living ahead of their business of today.

According to Dr Maltz (2015), a company's people should frequently and empathically delve into the positives, while peripherally glancing at the negatives. From this perspective, people should look at negative circumstances and situations only when it is necessary to make adjustments and corrections.

Companies with a prevalent abundance mindset tend to avoid binary alternatives, which uses words such as "or" or "but." An example of binary thinking is when a company provides customers with high-quality products, but its manufacturing process pollutes the environment. In this example, customers benefit, but at the expense of the community. Instead, companies with a predominant prosperity mindset use inclusive approaches, which relate to words such as "and" and "besides." Following the previous example, this type of company can think of offering a high-quality product (which benefits customers) and which is produced with a clean manufacturing process (which supports the community).

Companies with a prevailing prosperity mindset adopt a broad outlook on their business activities, which helps them assess traditional and innovative options to handle their challenges. This open attitude also allows them to learn from their setbacks. These business people are prone to count on other relevant characteristics:

- Discerning skills to make the best decisions on any occasion
- Emotional stability and resilience to endure challenges

- Increased awareness to discover new opportunities
- Confidence in themselves and others
- Respect and care when relating to others
- Clarity to perceive circumstances in the best way
- Faith in things always working out well
- Continuous focus on what is meaningful or adds value
- Courage to take daring actions beyond their comfort zone
- Persistence to follow their mission despite setbacks
- Flexibility to change their course of action when required

The aforementioned skills are not the privilege of a few organisations; any company can develop them over time when they intend to do so. To that effect, companies with a prevalent prosperity mindset are more prone to develop these capabilities. These organisations have other distinct characteristics, such as positive thinking patterns, ongoing learning attitude, tolerance to ambiguity and uncertainty, and orientation toward action. Each of these characteristics will be explained in a thorough manner in this chapter and the following one.

3.3.2 Positive Thinking Patterns

All that we are is the result of what we have thought. The mind is everything. What we think we become.

Buddha

Watch your thoughts, because they become your words; watch your words, because they become your habits; watch your habits, because they become your character; watch your character, because it becomes your destiny.

Plato

3.3.2.1 Awareness of Regular Thinking Patterns

In the province of the mind, what one believes to be true either is true or becomes true.

John Lilly

Some business people consider "positivity" as a topic related to New Age literature. However, this is not true at all. Moreover, from the scientific perspective, there is a relatively recent discipline named "positive psychology," which has formally studied the impact of positivity on relationships, business, career, health, and other areas. According to this standpoint, entrepreneurs are not only successful due to the actions they take and the knowledge they possess and apply, but also because of the conditions of their minds.

Many people realise that their thoughts are the most significant resources they count on. Thoughts generate ideas which help people create what they want. In relation to this, Siebold (2010) observed that prosperous people "understand that money flows from ideas, it is an inside job, and since ideas are limitless, money is limitless." The aforementioned author also stated that the use of strategic thinking to outstandingly solve problems for other people is one of the main characteristics of people with a prosperity mindset.

Likewise, Neill (2013) observed that "we create our individual experience of reality via the vehicle of thought." This author also highlighted that "without thought, there would not be delineation in our world – no perception, no distinction, no variety of experience." Besides, this specialist stated that all people's experiences in life are created from their thoughts; reality is indeed an inside-out series of experiences.

It interesting to pinpoint that people have thousands of thoughts a day, but most individuals have the tendency to ruminate negative thoughts. Negative thinking also includes criticising, blaming, insulting, catastrophising, complaining, moaning, etc. Research has demonstrated that the human brain has a negativity bias; it is prone to easily recollect bad experiences, but forget positive ones.

Authors like Lieberman (1997) observed that many people dwell on negative thinking to avoid potential disappointments in case that negative news does arise, or to punish themselves because they feel undeserving. This author also observed that people tend to have negative thoughts when they lack a purpose and their minds wander aimlessly.

Therefore, people must be aware of their thoughts on a regular basis. Oftentimes, people cannot prevent negative thoughts from entering their minds, but they are free either to linger on them or to let them go. Every time their thoughts wander aimlessly into negative topics, they can redirect them toward positive ones. Thinking negatively is a habit and, like all habits, it can be changed with patience and determination.

When people continually focus on positive thoughts, they create a positive loop which prompts them to keep on thinking positively. Positive thoughts feed the subconscious mind, which is the warehouse of a person's knowledge, skills, and automatic behaviour. Some specialists estimate that around 90 per cent of all actions a person performs during a day are driven by the subconscious mind.

Some psychologists suggest that people should say to themselves the words "stop" or "cancel" when a negative thought pops up and quickly replace it with a more positive one. People cannot dwell on negative and positive things at the same time; when they dwell on the positive, the negative automatically dissipates. Another way people can replace negative thoughts is to evoke positive past circumstances or to be mindful of things they are grateful for.

When people have negative thoughts, they are more prone to experience negative emotional states. These people tend to become more demotivated, unproductive, and less creative. Their emotional states make them act more reactively, and oftentimes respond in a fight-freeze-flight mode. People who experience negative emotions are less inclined to learn new information or skills in a deep manner.

Positive thinking has several benefits for business activities. Liu and Noppe-Brandon (2009) observed that people who think positively are more open to analysing different circumstances affecting them. These authors highlight when people think positively, they tend to infect others, who in turn start thinking alike, creating a virtuous circle. A person who is positive also tends to be more agreeable with others, which prompts them to act more co-operatively.

People with positive thoughts tend to be more inquisitive and naturally perceive the positive side of any circumstances, including challenging ones. Research has also shown that when people think positively, they can handle stressful situations more effectively. History has shown countless examples of people facing the most unfavourable conditions and triumphing against all odds because of their positive mindsets. Therefore, it is important that a company's people are mindful of their detrimental thoughts; for example:

■ Our company is going through a dire financial situation.
■ It is difficult to obtain new customers.
■ We are continually beaten by competitors' offerings.

- These suppliers are trying to rip us off.
- We are incapable of increasing our sales.

Oftentimes, people say that the previous expressions just "describe" the circumstances their companies face. Nonetheless, situations never have a meaning *per se*; the person experiencing them assigns specific meaning to them, which can be positive or negative. In the previous statements, the focus is placed on the negative aspects of each situation. The same sentences can be reframed in a more positive manner; for instance:

- Our company is capable of improving the current financial situation.
- We aim to satisfy customers' needs more effectively.
- We can deliver a unique offering which stands out in the marketplace.
- It is important to obtain win–win agreements with these suppliers.
- We can develop new products which can boost our sales.

Seligman (2006) called the way specific events are explained by people "explanatory style." In the previous examples, the same events are framed in two different ways: firstly, negatively, and secondly, in a positive manner. This specialist observed that when events are explained in a negative fashion, the person is prone to feel helpless. Instead, when an event is explained in a positive manner, the person tends to feel more energised, confident, motivated, and can have a higher level of performance. These positive statements are more empowering and prompt people to feel more hopeful and in control, in order to take specific actions to improve their situation. Achor (2011) observed that "brains are literally hardwired to perform at their best not when they are negative or even neutral but when they are positive."

Research has also shown that when people frame events more positively, they are less prone to become stressed about them. People with an abundance mindset know that constructive thoughts and emotions make it easier to obtain the necessary resources (people, funds, technology, etc.) to pursue their business mission. Consequently, these individuals tend to be less fearful and hesitant; they also brood less over their setbacks but learn from them instead.

According to Covey (1992), every time people are affected by an external factor (or stimulus), they are able to choose how to respond to it; there is always a gap between stimulus and response. Every time people are aware of this gap and respond with positive thoughts and actions, these individuals become more empowered. Therefore, the small gap connecting stimulus and response is one's real point of power. However, as seen previously, people have the tendency to react negatively to threatening stimuli, which can be very challenging to them.

3.3.2.2 Other Relevant Aspects Regarding Thinking Patterns

People with frequent positive thoughts have a "for" mindset, instead of an "against" one. These individuals tend to focus more on what they want to create, instead of centring on what they want to eliminate. These people focus on solutions and things they want to create, instead of dwelling on troublesome situations. Besides, these people also have faith and a sterling conviction that things will work out well in their business activities, which propels them to take continuous actions forward toward their purpose.

These people do not have naïve or passive faith in their goals; these individuals know they are more likely to achieve their objectives when they perform the necessary activities to do so. Their unwavering confidence and positive expectations help them cast away fear or hesitation, and provide them with enthusiasm and grit to face challenging situations on their way to their mission. When new opportunities or innovative ideas arise, these individuals tend to ask themselves "What if this can be done?", instead of endlessly doubting themselves.

Besides, positive business people believe in their skills, capabilities, and talents, and in all the actions they take. These people are strongly convinced they can offer something unique and valuable to the work and business environments. These individuals always think of giving their best to others, instead of being continually focused on "getting" from them.

Negative thinking is usually based on a negative belief system. As mentioned previously, beliefs are one of the cornerstones of a person's attitude, which helps them navigate any situation they encounter. According to Bailes (2004), people's distinct beliefs constitute their main thought atmosphere. It is interesting to pinpoint that many people carry the same beliefs they formed a long time ago, without questioning them. Therefore, people should analyse their beliefs in a detached and continuous manner. Oftentimes, these internal "guidelines" are outdated or not supported by any real facts.

A company's people with negative thoughts can ask themselves questions like "What is the detrimental belief underpinning this thought?", "Is there any relevant evidence that backs this belief?", "What are the consequences of holding this belief?", "Is there any evidence which contradicts this belief", and "What positive belief can replace this unproductive one?", among others. These individuals can also jot down the insights into these questions. The objective of this introspective exercise is to challenge any useless beliefs and replace them with more positive ones.

There is a well-known principle called the Pareto Law (also named the 80/20 principle), which observes that a very minimal set of factors have a paramount importance in any situation; this principle also states the majority of factors has the minimum relevance. From this perspective, a company's people tend to have a few disempowering beliefs which create the majority of havoc in their business activities. These few detrimental beliefs should be discovered and replaced with more positive ones. It is important for people to discover the few detrimental beliefs limiting them in order to replace them with more positive ones.

Besides, a company's people can gradually change their limiting beliefs by acknowledging their achievements in the business arena, small or big ones, on a regular basis. They can also reflect on the lessons they obtained from their business setbacks. The frequent reflection on their achievements and learning experiences helps people enhance their self-efficacy skills to face future challenges more confidently. In this exercise, besides reflecting on external achievements (e.g., more sales, increased productivity, etc.), individuals can also reflect on more internal attainments (calm, patience, joy, kindness, etc.) experienced during their business journey. In relation to this, Wiest (2013) observed that individuals can change their beliefs system when they seek and navigate new real experiences.

Some business people take the time to openly celebrate their successful outcomes, for example, with the organisation of social events. These positive habits prevent people from minimising or taking their achievements for granted. In this way, these people's belief systems gradually become more positive.

As previously mentioned, beliefs are formed with information from various sources, for example, other people's opinions, media news, personal experiences, etc. Therefore, business people should be very watchful of information coming from their environment. For example, naysayers are intrinsically discouraging and infectious and can affect one's beliefs systems negatively. These negative individuals should therefore be avoided, whenever possible, or time with them should be kept to a minimum.

As a consequence, a company's people should interact with positive people, when possible. They should also talk to people with different perspectives, from whom they can learn new things. Individuals with a prevalent abundance mindset like motivated, thriving, and positive people to discuss relevant topics, but tend to avoid people keen on gossiping, moaning, and complaining.

A company's people should also be careful with media because their messages are mostly negative and sometimes catastrophic. This does not mean that a company should be uninformed; instead, it should avoid dwelling excessively on media negativity. Many websites, newspapers, magazines, and TV programmes convey only negative business news (e.g., bankruptcies, shut-downs, frauds, economic crises, stocks crashes, etc.).

This type of media shows negative news in an exaggerated and sensationalistic way, as part of their core strategy to grab the attention of a bigger audience. The media's insidious outlook on reality prompts most people to worry, which negatively affects their beliefs systems. As a consequence, people with an abundance mindset tend to analyse different sources of information in order to stay in the know; these individuals use their own discernment and experience and avoid continually delving into negative news.

3.3.2.3 Thoughts and Emotions

As seen previously, thoughts are always linked to emotions. Negative thoughts tend to bring about negative emotional states, and positive thinking is prone to generate positive emotions. According to disciplines like rational emotional behaviour theory and cognitive psychology, when people face an event, they think about it in a specific way, which brings about related feelings, which in turn prompt certain behaviour.

For example, when entrepreneurs face an event (they read negative economic news), this prompts specific beliefs and thoughts (e.g., "My company cannot survive in the current negative circumstances"), which generates an emotional state (these individuals start feeling overwhelmed). In turn, this emotional state prompts these business people to take action (for instance, they decide to shut down their companies). From this perspective, people can question or dispute the belief or thought which trigger their negative emotions. In this example, entrepreneurs can ask themselves "Is it true that this negative situation will affect my business?" to find more balanced thoughts.

By reappraising these thoughts, emotional states can be modified accordingly. Therefore, when people have negative emotions, they should focus on the disturbing thoughts which bring about these emotions, and positively reassess these thoughts, instead of trying to directly act on their emotions. In other words, people should reflect on their own thoughts. The skill of thinking about one's thinking is called metacognition. Some metacognitive questions about thoughts are "How does this thought make me feel?", "What is the evidence for this?", or "Are there alternative ways to think about this?"

Body language (gestures, posture, etc.) is also linked to emotions (and related thoughts). There is a continuous body–mind connection. Specific emotional states bring about their distinct aspects of body language. This also works the other way around; research has shown that specific body language can bring about related emotional states. For example, if people purposefully have a positive body language (e.g., they walk with aplomb, stand up confidently, move in a relaxed and assertive manner, and use open gestures), consequently they will tend to have positive emotions and thoughts. Scientists like Wiseman (2013) and Cuddy (2016) both observed that enthusiastic and energetic postures affect emotions and thoughts positively. In a similar vein, Lobel (2014) stated that when people use power postures, their testosterone levels significantly rise, which is a sign of increased dominance.

Besides, a company's people with a prosperity mindset tend to naturally dwell on positive emotional states, such as gratitude, peacefulness, and others. These individuals realise that concentrating on positive emotions brings about more positive thoughts, which helps them make more meaningful and discerning decisions. Likewise, Forgas et al. (1984) have observed that people in a positive mood are prone to make more positive assessments of situations affecting them.

When people experience positive emotions, their thoughts tend to be sharper, as compared with negative emotions like fear, which trigger a defensive response (fight-freeze-flight mode) that narrows their discerning capabilities. Likewise, Goleman (1996, 1998) observed that positivity widens a person's attention; this scholar also observed that positive people tend to be more persistent, motivated, and flexible, which contributes to improving their performance. Miller (2009) observed that positive people tend to become more resilient, overcome challenging circumstances more effectively, develop more fruitful relationships, enjoy their activities more, and experience an overall sense of wellbeing.

Achor (2011) also observed that when people experience positive emotional states, their brains are inundated with chemicals which foster a good mood (serotonin and dopamine), which in turn prompt the learning areas of their brains to perform in a heightened way. According to the aforementioned author, this helps these individuals organise, incorporate, and retrieve information more effectively, prompting them to develop more neural connections. As a consequence, these individuals tend to have creative thoughts, make better decisions, and develop a more thorough analysis.

Some schools of thought suggest that negative emotions can be replaced by positive ones in a very simple way. For instance, if people experience fear, they can focus their attention on experiences, people, or things they are appreciative for. In this example, these two emotional states, fear (negative) and gratitude (positive), are incompatible, which means they cannot be experienced simultaneously. Other schools of thought recommend that when people experience negative emotions, they should observe them, as an external witness, and let them go. This is a simple but effective way to avoid repressing, suppressing, or dwelling on negative emotional states.

The HeartMath Institute, a very prestigious scientific organisation based in the United States, observed that from the energetic viewpoint, negative thoughts and emotional states (so-called "energy deficits") reduce the body's energy. This renowned institution also stated that positive thoughts and emotions (so-called "energy assets") increase body energy, which improves the person's overall performance. This organisation also advises people to keep a journal with their daily energy deficits and gains in order to purposefully reduce the former and increase the latter (Childre et al., 2000).

Lastly, Seligman (2006) also observed the best perspective any person can adopt is the so-called "realistic optimism." This perspective implies the use of positive explanatory style of events, but oftentimes, a pessimistic view is also admitted so that people can connect to a sense of reality. In other words, realistic optimism implies positive thinking, but it also includes critical analysis of circumstances, which brings about a more balanced perspective.

In relation to this, Goleman (1996) observed that positive thoughts accompanied by a realistic view of reality protects people from experiencing states of hopelessness, apathy, and depression. This approach proves very valuable, especially when people face tough circumstances or when they navigate turbulent situations.

3.3.3 Frequent Use of Positive Words

3.3.3.1 Importance of Using Positive Language

> Sharp words make more wounds than a surgeon can heal.

Vern McLellan

Letterman (1962) observed that words can be considered the fuel of the mind. Many business people tend to use negative language. It is important to pinpoint that words are the external expression of thoughts; therefore, when people use negative words, their thoughts are not positive. People tend to use negative words when they are overwhelmed, stressed, frustrated, or angry. For example, a company's people might use negative vocabulary when they complain about a lost business deal or when their customers switch to other organisations. It is important that a company's people use positive language on a continuous basis.

As mentioned before, thoughts are connected to emotions on a continuous basis. As a consequence, when people use positive vocabulary, they are prone to experience positive emotional states, which in turn generate even more positive thoughts, creating a virtuous cycle. People with positive thoughts and emotions are more prone to effectively use their ability to discern.

Covey (1992) suggested that entrepreneurs should always use "proactive language" in their business activities. Examples of proactive language include sentences like "I choose …", "I prefer …", and "I will." This type of language makes people feel more in control of their responses, especially when they face threatening factors. Likewise, Wiseman (2013) highlighted that when people talk in a positive manner, their words are prone to influence their mood positively.

According to Covey (1992), proactive language is different from reactive language; the latter includes sentences such as "I can't …", "I must …", and "I have to." When a company's people use reactive language, they tend to feel they have little or no control over their responses. The use of these reactive words also prompts a company's people to have rigid and absolute patterns of thinking, which prevents them from exploring alternative approaches in relation to relevant business topics. Oftentimes, the use of reactive words is based on an underlying state of fear.

Consequently, business people should avoid, when possible, the use of self-defeating vocabulary, such as "difficult," "struggle," "cannot," "limitation," "impossible," or similar words. These negative words prompt people to experience negative emotions and bring about more negative thoughts, which prevents people from analysing important topics clearly and taking effective actions.

According to Robbins (2001), business people should always magnify the positive words they use and minimise negative ones, in order to increase their positive emotions and reduce the intensity of their negative ones, respectively. For example, if a business person wants to say, "I obtained a good business deal," this individual should exaggerate this statement by saying "I obtained an amazing business deal." This last sentence not only enlivens the previous expression but also prompts this person to feel better.

On the contrary, when a person wants to say, for instance, "I feel very angry about losing this customer," this individual should minimise this with a sentence like "I feel slightly frustrated about losing this customer." The use of this sentence prompts this person to feel less negative. In relation to this, Letterman (1962) wisely observed that words are the fuses of emotional states. This author observed that the words people used to frame their experiences actually become their experiences.

As mentioned previously, people can find different ways to explain events affecting them. Lieberman (2001) observed that negative situations could be explained more positively when they are shown as temporary, one-off, and unimportant, instead of them being perceived as permanent, continuous, and relevant. When people word negative circumstances in a more positive manner, their negative emotional reactions toward these circumstances are also decreased or even eliminated, which helps them adopt a more discerning perspective to tackle these situations effectively.

In relation to this, Seligman (2006) added that a negative event can be explained in a personalised manner, which means that the person affected is a "failure," or the cause of this very event. This is an unproductive way to explain negative events. On the contrary, a negative event can be explained in an impersonal manner, which means the person affected by the event did not cause it, this event was brought about by external factors. This second perspective implies a more positive explanation of events. Seligman (2006) also observed that negative events can be perceived and explained as general or universal, which means that they always happen. Besides, negative events can also be interpreted as specific ones (not universal), which is always a more productive interpretation of these situations.

3.3.3.2 Other Aspects of Positive Language

The words a person frequently uses with others are very powerful; these words can strengthen or weaken a relationship. For example, when a company uses words of recognition, gratitude, encouragement, and support with its stakeholders (employees, customers, etc.), these words strengthen relationships with these very stakeholders. The opposite happens when the company uses words which imply manipulation, harsh criticism, and resentment.

Schwartz (1979) suggested that a company's people should talk to other people in a positive manner and encourage them to take action. Moreover, when a person communicates with others positively, they are more prone to co-operate. This author also observed that positive vocabulary is useful when a person (e.g., a manager) sets a plan for another (e.g., an employee) to implement. In this example, the manager can present the plan as an "opportunity for expansion," not only for the company but for the employee on a professional level.

Oftentimes, a company's people do not say negative words overtly, but as part of their unproductive self-talk. These people should adopt a wary attitude toward their internal dialogue, and regularly ask themselves "Is this internal dialogue constructive or destructive?" If they discover ongoing negative self-talk, they should apply the tips previously explained to improve their thinking patterns.

It is important that people have a positive mental dialogue with themselves and become their best friends. This means frequently talking to themselves in a kind and loving manner. People with positive self-talk become their best coaches, continually encouraging themselves to harness their innermost skills and talents. When people improve their inner conversation, they are more prone to explore non-traditional approaches and possibilities, which were previously stifled by their negative inner dialogue.

People with a prosperity mindset also tend to use positive metaphors. Authors like Haidt (2006) observed that "human thinking depends on metaphor" A metaphor is a suggested but implicit comparison, in which one thing is used to designate a second one. Metaphors are always meaningful and easily understandable.

From the psychological perspective, metaphors are very powerful because they synthesise a large amount of information in a terse sentence; besides, metaphors act directly on a subconscious level. It is important that entrepreneurs use more positive metaphors. Many people believe metaphors are only used in prose and poetry; nonetheless, metaphors are regularly used by people in all areas, including business activities.

A negative metaphor commonly used in business is "The marketplace is a battlefield," which uses a war concept to refer to the marketplace. This metaphor is negative, because it presupposes that companies act like enemy bands, which try to outpace one another. In this example, more a positive metaphor to be used is "The marketplace is a playground." In this case, a company can adopt a more experimental and explorative attitude toward its external environment, which can help this organisation develop more innovative approaches regarding its business activities.

In relation to this, Morgan (1997) observed that metaphors are like lenses which help organisations perceive themselves and their business issues in different ways. This specialist also stated that metaphors are different ways to relate to reality which can help companies gain new insights about specific situations and develop new strategies to implement.

Lobel (2014) observed that people tend to embody the metaphors they frequently use, and act them out. For example, if a person says, "This problem is weighing me down," this individual will tend to *feel* physically and emotionally drained and tired. In other words, the metaphors people use have a concrete impact on their thoughts, emotions, and actions.

Therefore, a company's people should always choose positive metaphors; they should regularly ask themselves questions like "What positive metaphors can we use to define our company and business activities?", "What constructive metaphors can be used to define the marketplace?", and "What other metaphors can we utilise to define other companies in the marketplace?", among others.

3.3.4 Positive Perception

> Life affords no higher pleasure than that of surmounting difficulties, passing from one step of success to another, forming new wishes and seeing them gratified.

Samuel Johnson

As seen previously, each business situation can be perceived in different ways. When people adopt a grateful attitude, they tend to focus on the positive aspects of circumstances affecting them. Appreciative people tend not to adopt a defensive attitude (or fight-freeze-flight mode), and consequently, they can access their discerning and creative capabilities more easily. For example, companies can be grateful to employees (for their co-operation in business projects) or to customers (for their loyalty). Companies can even be appreciative for the lessons obtained from their setbacks. The topic of gratitude is analysed thoroughly in Chapter 7.

Business people can also participate in playful activities in order to have a more positive perception of reality. These events put people in a good mood and help them release stress and tension. When people have frequent enjoyable time off, they are less prone to burnout. Research has demonstrated that playful activities also contribute to the enhancement of individuals' cognitive capabilities. Playful events prompt people to experience positive emotions and contribute to their overall wellbeing. This topic will be dissected later, in Chapter 7.

A third way to have a more positive perception is by being more generous with others. Generous people do not focus on lack or scarcity, they give because there is more than enough to share with others. When people give to others, they tend to become more positive. For example, a company can give their employees material things (e.g., a salary increase) or non-material ones (e.g., recognition for their contribution to the company).

A company's people can also be generous with other stakeholders (suppliers, customers, etc.). Companies with a prevailing scarcity mindset are unable to be generous because they are continually focused on *getting* from others (more profits, more revenue, more market share, more customers, etc.). Their greed-driven mentality prevents them from *giving*. This topic will be explored in Chapter 7.

Companies with a predominant prosperity mindset avoid perceiving factors of the business environment (e.g., changes in the economic conditions, other organisations with similar products, new regulations, etc.) as threatening. In other words, these organisations avoid adopting a defensive attitude toward these factors. Instead, these external factors are perceived as opportunities to grow and evolve.

These companies frequently pose questions like "How can we perceive this factor in a more positive manner?", "What are the opportunities hidden behind these factors?", or "How can this factor affect our company more constructively?" With this positive perspective, companies are more equipped to explore these factors more constructively and find beneficial aspects related to them.

Companies with a prosperity mindset also perceive their setbacks in a positive manner. From this perspective, "failures" become opportunities to do things differently in the future. These organisations can ask themselves questions such as "What can we learn from this?" and "How can we act differently next time?" In other words, these setbacks are considered as learning experiences which can help these organisations avoid similar mistakes in the future.

In a similar vein, Hill (1928) observed that "every failure brings with it the seed of an equivalent advantage." From this standpoint, each time these companies fail, they are confident in their own capabilities to work things around for the better in future situations. These organisations do not expect their past failures to be repeated in the future or allow these failures to condition them in any way.

Besides, companies with a prevalent abundance mindset tend to focus on the positive qualities of every person they interact with. When they meet a person for the first time, they are prone to have positive assumptions about this individual. These organisations also value their relationships with different stakeholders, acknowledging and respecting their distinct views. Furthermore, these companies tend to express their gratitude to their stakeholders for their contribution to the business activities.

These companies continually connect with people in an honest, supportive, and friendly manner. These organisations also tend to solve all conflicts with them in an amicable manner, without attacking or threatening them. Besides, these companies are prone to develop win–win agreements with all relevant stakeholders, which fairly consider the interests of all parts involved. These organisations always believe it is possible to develop co-operation bonds with any relevant stakeholder. They understand that their business activities are built on a network of meaningful relationships, which must be preserved and strengthened over time.

Companies with a prevailing prosperity mindset try to avoid win–lose situations, where a party wins at the expense of others, which are more related to a scarcity mindset. To that effect, these organisations perceive every business situation involving their stakeholders (suppliers, customers, employees, etc.) as a valuable opportunity to develop win–win agreements, in which all participants have their needs duly satisfied. These organisations know that win–win agreements also strengthen their relationships over time.

Lastly, a company's people with a prosperous mindset are always aware of their own distinct positive values (for example, kindness, honesty, respect, wisdom, etc.). Their noble values act like a compass for their activities. Besides, these people tend to review their list of values on a frequent basis, and change them in order of importance, when necessary. These people regularly remind themselves of their most important values and prioritise those business projects aligned with these relevant principles. As a consequence, they do not waste time with activities which do not honour their main values.

Questions for Self-Reflection

- What are the main fears hindering our company's activities?
- How can I develop a more positive business mindset?
- What are my positive and negative beliefs regarding our company's activities?
- How can I frame a negative business circumstance more positively?

Chapter 4

Additional Aspects of a Prosperity Mindset

4.1 Ongoing Learning Attitude

There are few human beings who receive the truth, complete and staggering, by instant illumination. Most of them acquire it fragment by fragment, on a small scale, by successive developments, cellularly, like a laborious mosaic.

Anaïs Nin

4.1.1 Knowledge and Learning

Tapscott (1996) observed that the current economy is knowledge- and innovation-based, which implies that the most significant value will be added by brain, not brawn. In other words, the creative skills which add value to others in a non-traditional way are appreciated in this economy. The know-how regarding research, development, production, and marketing of products and services is one of the most important assets companies can count on.

Covey (1992) observed that learning and training represent non-urgent but significant activities which all companies should prioritise. Most business people tend to give a lot of importance to learning and self-learning; these people are pragmatic, which means they know that knowledge put into action is power. Likewise, Hill (1928) stated that power is "organized knowledge, expressed through intelligent efforts."

There are different types of knowledge. Polanyi (1967) differentiated tacit knowledge from codified knowledge. The former is developed through specific experiences and practices that a company's people go through, and it is context-specific and difficult to transfer to other environments. The latter is systematised (for example, video courses, books, etc.) which makes it more general and transferable.

Fromm (1976) differentiated "having knowledge" (possessing available knowledge) from "knowing" (which is related to thinking productively). He also observed that "knowing" always implies going beyond the surface of things, to arrive at its core roots, so as "to 'see' reality in its nakedness," and "to strive critically and actively in order to approach truth more closely."

Therefore, knowing implies a higher level of awareness; when people are more knowledgeable about a topic, their beliefs and values tend to be affected by it.

Lundvall and Johnson (1994) suggested that there are different types of knowledge: know-how (procedures on how to do things, for example, managerial, manufacturing, and design procedures, etc.), know-who (knowledge on who has a specific expertise), know-why (general principles which explain why things are done a certain way, for example, why products must be tested before being launched), and know-what (explicit codified content which includes concepts, facts, frameworks, techniques, tools, etc.).

It is possible to add to this typology "know-when" (knowledge about when to perform specific actions, for instance, when to hire new personnel, or develop new products) and know-where (specific knowledge about places, for instance, which markets to enter, which countries to obtain supplies from, etc.). Collison and Parcell (2004) use another classification of knowledge, which include the knowledge obtained before, during, and after performing an activity.

4.1.2 Prosperity Mindset and Knowledge

People with a prosperity mindset do not believe they know everything. They have a humble attitude toward learning. Oftentimes, these people are less reliant on formal training and more confident in self-education. They tend to be self-educated and teachable; therefore, their capabilities can be developed.

These people are interested in a variety of topics, even those seemingly unrelated to their company and sector. For them, learning is pleasurable; they are intrinsically driven to become more knowledgeable. In order to do so, they are willing to tread the path of self-discovery and self-knowledge. These people look for any type of knowledge which could potentially improve their company activities and enhance their capabilities and talents.

These individuals are more keen on practical and specialised knowledge, rather than theoretical and general knowledge. However, they are willing to learn not only conceptual knowledge (facts, models, terms, etc.), but also soft skills: for example, creativity techniques, tools for rapport in business relationships, effective uses of body language, and team-playing capabilities, etc. They realise these skills help them make better choices in the business arena. Every potentially valuable piece of knowledge is researched deeply and intently. Oftentimes, these people do not apply the knowledge they acquire in a literal way, but instead adapt it to the distinctive reality of their company activities.

People with an abundance mindset adopt an open and curious attitude toward knowledge; they are keen to be continually updated. A frequent question these people ask themselves is "What do I need to learn to achieve the business mission?" and reflect on insights thoroughly. They really understand that knowledge is a meta-resource, a resource of higher order which generates many other resources (capital, technology, etc.). They also understand that the business environment is complex and dynamic, and it can only be clearly understood through continuous learning. They also know that knowledge is power, providing it is applied in a specific way.

People with an abundance mindset know they must first become more knowledgeable in order to become more successful. Therefore, continuous learning is always a priority goal for these individuals, and is as important as other business objectives (for example, productivity, increasing sales, improving quality, etc.). Moreover, practical knowledge will facilitate the achievement of these other objectives.

Individuals with an abundance mindset also have what some oriental traditions call "beginner's mind": they are always willing to learn. Autry and Mitchell (1998) observed that the beginner's mind is not hindered by fixed ideas, but instead open to countless possibilities. These people are hungry for useful knowledge and act like relentless scavengers. The usefulness and impact of the knowledge they obtain is valued from the short- and long-term perspectives. Oftentimes, the validity of this knowledge for specific financial, productive, administrative, and marketing purposes is also considered.

The consideration of different perspectives makes these people more adaptive to changes in the business environment. These individuals are willing to let go of conservative or previously defended ideas, in order to explore others. Their intrepid, passionate, and inquisitive spirit prompts them to look for valuable insights in a myriad of sources, even seemingly trivial ones, for example:

- Past mistakes and setbacks
- Business reports and comments from opinion leaders
- Insightful questions posed by themselves or others
- Activities performed by other companies
- Traditional media (books, magazines, newspapers, etc.) and non-traditional media (websites, blogs, social networks, etc.) with diverse viewpoints
- Any type of training (workshops, conferences, seminars, etc.)
- Other external references (successful entrepreneurs, great men and women, artists, humanitarians, philosophers, scientists, etc.) to model or emulate their outstanding aspects
- Non-traditional sources (contact with nature, family or friends' meetings, etc.)

People with an abundance mindset also gather insights from formal or informal feedback from interactions with different company stakeholders (customers, employees, suppliers, intermediaries, etc.). Individuals with a prosperity mentality are even open to obtaining insights from people who do not think like them, whose beliefs systems and preferences are different. The variety and diversity of viewpoints always enriches their own knowledge mental databank. Their circle of influence and mutually beneficial relationships are greatly valued as sources of knowledge, insight, and support.

People with an abundance mindset are also dedicated observers of the current and potential trends in the marketplace. Their analysis of the business environment is multidimensional and includes its economic, socio-cultural, legal and technological aspects and their complex interrelationships. These individuals are even willing to look out for valuable ideas in different or unrelated contexts. For instance, if their company belongs to the food sector, they might seek valuable ideas from other sectors (e.g., car manufacturing sector, education sector, etc.). Sometimes they are even open to explore other fields (arts, sport, politics, etc.) to look for new ideas to be applied to their organisation.

According to Hendricks and Ludeman (1996), prosperous business people usually learn from three main sources: the messages conveyed by their own emotions, the reflection on their past experiences, and the analysis of feedback provided by others. In a similar vein, Rogers (1961) observed that an individual's own experience has the highest validity of all sources of learning, even over opinions, guidance, and guidelines delivered by others. This scholar also stated that "Experience, for me, is the highest authority ... no other person's ideas, and none of my own ideas, are as authoritative as my experience."

As mentioned, people with a prosperity mentality also look for role models, contemporary or past ones, to emulate. These models can include business luminaries, artists, politicians, spiritual masters, and others. Information about these models can be found in articles, books, biographies, etc. People with an abundance mindset tend to dissect the main positive traits of these models and try to replicate and apply them to their own activities.

Lastly, these people are also willing to participate in mastermind groups, which are composed of individuals who want to support each other. These inspirational groups hold regular meetings where each participant expresses their challenges and receives feedback from the rest.

4.1.3 Relevant Aspects of the Learning Process

From the neuro-linguistic programming perspective, the learning process generally goes through four stages: unconscious incompetence (people do not know that they do not know a skill), conscious incompetence (people start practising a skill, but they are not good at it yet), conscious competence (people have the skill, but they have to concentrate to use it), and unconscious competence (the skill is used automatically, freeing people's energy for additional activities.) A company's people who are very good at certain business activities are prone to perform these tasks at the level of unconscious competence, while when people carry out specific business activities for the first time, they are more prone to be at the stage of conscious incompetence.

Kolb (1973) observed that the learning process is comprised of four stages: reflective observation (which includes research and collection of data), developing hypothesis (which implies conceptualisation, conjecturing, speculation, etc.), testing (which includes active experimentation and trial), and audit (which encloses activities such as verification, scrutiny, etc.). This series of stages is circular and allows continuous improvement of the learning experience based on the result obtained from practical application of the knowledge.

Dixon (2000) observed that there is a learning cycle that any organisation goes through, composed of several stages. Firstly, the organisation produces relevant information from internal sources (R+D, past achievements, unsuccessful results, etc.) and external ones (e.g., suppliers, customers, etc.). Secondly, this data is disseminated and integrated within the organisation. Thirdly, people in the organisation collectively interpret that information, through inclusive conversations and respectful debates. Oftentimes, these interactions aim to challenge ingrained assumptions in the organisation.

Lastly, people working for the company are ready to take action based on the agreed meaning of the data analysed in the previous stage. Most organisations go through these stages, but oftentimes the stages overlap with one another. In relation to this, Chaston (2004) observed that this organisational knowledge represents a valuable asset and a core competence for a company, which can be disseminated through systems, platforms, and networks created for that purpose.

O'Connor and McDermott (1997) observed that there are two types of learning processes: simple learning and generative learning. In simple learning, a person considers feedback stemming from the learning process and make adequate adjustments. These authors mention some examples of simple learning, such as trial and error approach, and learning of new capabilities, among others. Simple learning does not produce any change in the learner's mental attitude.

According to these specialists, in generative learning, people receive feedback that transforms their mental attitudes and challenges their beliefs and assumptions, which helps them expand their future experiences and courses of action. These authors give some examples of generative learning, like learning to learn, analysing situations from different perspectives, or questioning one's own beliefs.

People with a prosperity mindset are prone to go though both simple and generative learning. From this perspective, some questions generative learners are prone to ask themselves are: "What are other contexts or areas where this knowledge is useful or meaningful?", "What are other viewpoints on this knowledge?", "What are other possible connotations of this knowledge?", "How does this piece of knowledge relate to others?", and "What are the assumptions to be challenged by this knowledge?", among others. These people are also open to considering feedback delivered by others (e.g., employees, suppliers, business partners, etc.). The topic of constructive feedback is analysed in Chapter 9.

People with an abundance mindset never accept new knowledge at face value; instead, they critically assess it. When they get in contact with new knowledge, they analyse it with an open and receptive mind, temporarily leaving their individual and collective assumptions aside. They often sift the knowledge learnt with their critical discernment skills. Sometimes, they contrast and compare information from different sources to test its feasibility, meaningfulness, validity, and truthfulness.

Every time these individuals obtain relevant pieces of knowledge, they are prone to dissect and break them down into their main parts to analyse their main interrelationships. These people can also consider a specific piece of knowledge in a wider context. For example, the analysis of specific customers' behaviours can be analysed within the cultural context that customers are in. People with prosperous mindsets also tend to relate each piece of knowledge with others, even with those not overtly interrelated. They are also willing to share this knowledge with other people in the company, in order to discuss it or apply it, when necessary.

People with an abundance mindset are also willing to unlearn, which means reflecting on past knowledge in order to discard those pieces which are not relevant or valuable any longer. Not only do these individuals reflect on knowledge obtained from different sources (books, events, etc.) to obtain insight into it, but they also reflect on their own past actions and experiences. Therefore, these people are prone to ask themselves questions like "What were the main obstacles I faced?" and "How could I have done things differently?" In other words, people with a prosperity mindset see everything that occurs to them as a learning experience.

During their learning process, people with an abundance mindset are open to going beyond their comfort zone and trying new approaches and challenges, which oftentimes enhances their self-efficacy skills and contributes to their business mission. With a deliberate attitude toward learning, they realise they can only grow in proportion to their mental expansion. Csikszentmihalyi (2003) observed that entrepreneurs who learn new skills tend to become more confident and empowered to go through more complex business challenges.

4.1.4 Other Aspects of the Learning Process

People with a prosperity mindset know that all circumstances, negative and positive, are stepping stones on their learning journey; therefore, they are willing to reflect on their own mistakes, in order to avoid them in the future. However, they never feel stuck, ashamed, or frustrated because of their failures, but receive them with a collected attitude. People with a prosperity mindset consider their setbacks as valuable feedback in the overall process, dissecting their setbacks to obtain insights into them. Every time they make mistakes, they frame them in a constructive manner and ask themselves questions, such as "What can I learn from this setback?"

In relation to this, Baumeister et al. (2001) observed that people are prone to learn much more quickly from negative events (which implies a certain degree of punishment) than from positive experiences (which entails reward). Sometimes people with a prosperity mindset can even learn from mistakes made by others (customers, suppliers, etc.). They are keen on "borrowing" lessons learnt by other individuals or organisations in order to apply them to their own business activities.

People with an abundance mindset realise that oftentimes, in order to learn more effectively, they have to do the very things they want to learn. Race (1995) called this type of process "learning by doing." From this perspective, mistakes can never be avoided, and they are an important part of the business journey. According to Rogers (1961, 1969), the main characteristics of this empirical way of learning are: proactive and direct involvement and self-evaluation.

People with an abundance mindset do not make excuses (such as insufficient time, other priorities, etc.) to avoid learning regularly. Instead, these individuals take their time to invest in increasing their own knowledge on a regular basis because they value a lifelong education. Their ongoing learning process makes them more resourceful in order to achieve their mission. These people are also keen on simplification: they like to summarise complex ideas in simple terms, which requires thorough and deep comprehension of various data. These business people act, as it is known in sociology, as symbolic analysts, the ones who manage knowledge and creative ideas as relevant strategic assets.

People with an abundance mindset realise that their business ventures are not destinations themselves, but instead valuable development processes. These people choose a learning process which is self-directed and their learning is intrinsically motivated (e.g., to enhance their mental skills, to generate new ideas and perspectives, etc.), but also extrinsically driven (for instance, to achieve specific business objectives). They also consider the learning process to be a relevant catalyst to loosen their own self-restricting beliefs and widen their awareness.

Business people with a prosperity mindset follow their own learning and development path. Sometimes, their learning path is structured, systematic, and methodical, which implies setting clear learning objectives and positive learning habits. Oftentimes, their learning process is intuitive and they are open to unplanned learning, for example, valuable lessons stemming from adverse situations affecting their company. These unexpected learning sources are welcome and fully embraced.

These individuals have a patient attitude toward their learning process. Research has shown that proficiency always takes time; there is no such thing as instant mastery. These people also have an explorative attitude, which makes them resemble curious toddlers eager to discover the wonders of their environment. These people are willing to ask various questions, even the most obvious ones, about any relevant topic, in order to open paths to new perspectives. Asking frequent questions helps them never take things for granted, even when everything seems to be working well.

These people enjoy the learning process because it contributes to their personal and professional development. Their continuous learning path creates new neural pathways in their brains, which broadens their perspective of their activities and the business environment. These individuals consider the process of learning as expansive because it provides them with a more enhanced and refined perception. New knowledge always helps them "read" reality in a clearer and more through manner. These learning people are more prone to "see" new aspects of the business environment they could not have perceived otherwise. In other words, the learning process helps them make meaningful and valuable, and often subtle, distinctions of different aspects of the business context.

Lastly, people with a prosperity mindset know they don't have to learn everything to run their business efficiently. They generally look for expert advice and professional support when necessary. These people also understand that the knowledge needed for their company's success is multidisciplinary, involving many areas of expertise (legal, marketing, finances, computing, etc.) which are required to support thriving business activities.

4.1.5 Other Relevant Aspects of a Learning Attitude

People with a prosperity mentality have a "growth mindset," a term coined by Dweck (2012). According to this author, these people can improve their skills over time with effort and commitment. Their perseverant attitude prompts them to engage in challenging activities, instead of avoiding them. Whenever these individuals face setbacks, they keep on acting resiliently and use the feedback stemming from failure to improve their future performance. Consequently, these people are more prone to have higher achievements over time.

Many of these people become even more enduring and resilient after having overcome their failures. Cyrulnik (2009) observed that resilience is one's ability to cope with one's adverse circumstances, while realising that negative events don't inevitably determine one's destiny. According to this author, resilient people are prone to ask themselves "What am I going to do with the adverse situation?" in order to get valuable insights to help them to bounce back and move forward. Reivich and Shatté (2002) observed that "resilient people are able to derive meaning from failure, and they use this knowledge to climb higher than otherwise they would." These authors also observed that resilient people tend to transform setbacks into success. In other words, their setbacks prompt them to develop wiser comebacks. This approach is consistent with cognitive behavioural therapy which states that people's feelings and related behaviour are not generated by events affecting them, but by their personal interpretation (beliefs and related thoughts) of these very events.

There is another important topic to pinpoint. Business people generally learn and apply different business models or frameworks to improve their performance. These instruments help companies analyse business circumstances more simply. These instruments integrate different pieces of information and assist companies in their business decisions. For instance, SWOT is a tool most companies use to assess their own strengths and weaknesses, and opportunities and threats in their environment.

However, companies must bear in mind that all these models are like simplified maps. None of these models consider every single factor of a business situation; valuable aspects are always left aside. Companies should also understand that a model is always a means to aid business decisions, but is never an end in itself. Even when some companies are keen on the use of certain models, these organisations should avoid forcing business circumstances to fit into models, but instead keep in contact with real business circumstances.

Cohen and Prusak (2001) observed that "ground truth" is "the complex reality of authentic experiences" which is different from theoretical models and generalities. It is important that companies realise that there is always a gap between these frameworks and the real circumstances. Companies can only bridge this gap through practice, which means navigating real-life business circumstances.

4.2 Tolerance to Ambiguity and Uncertainty

4.2.1 General Aspects of Uncertainty

> Only those who will risk going too far can possibly find out how far one can go.
>
> **T.S. Eliot**

The business environment becomes increasingly complex, which always entails dynamism and unpredictability. This environment is affected by several actors (e.g., customers, other organisations, communities, etc.) and macro factors (economic aspects, technological discoveries, cultural factors, environmental issues, and political and legal aspects). These actors and factors are interrelated in a very intricate and dynamic manner.

Oftentimes, a company is uncertain about potential changes in external factors (for example, advances in technology, or modification of the regulation in force). It is impossible for any company to fully "predict" what is about to occur in future scenarios. Some organisations even profit from the intrinsic uncertainty of the business environment, for instance, insurance companies, economic researchers, financial advisors and others. Some companies are often uncertain about the occurrence of internal circumstances (for instance, changes in employees' behaviour).

Lorenz (1993) observed that tiny changes in an environment can potentially create unpredictable massive outcomes, which is known as the "butterfly effect." A very well-known metaphor stated that a butterfly flapping its wings could affect the conditions of a tornado that later develops far away. Therefore, business people should view all their actions as important, even those that seem to be insignificant. It is difficult to estimate the long-term effect of a company's actions, both small and large ones.

Many business people feel anxious and doubtful when dealing with uncertain scenarios; these people are prone to devise plausible explanations for uncertain factors. Other people tend to over-analyse uncertain situations by gathering as much information as possible. Most companies try their best to eliminate, or at least mitigate uncertainty levels affecting their activities. De Mello (1990) wisely quipped that people are not fearful of the uncertain, but afraid of losing what is certain, their current circumstances.

Weick (1995) observed that there are three types of uncertainty: a) state uncertainty, which means that companies do not know how specific factors are changing; b) effect uncertainty, which includes the ignorance of the impact of specific factors on the company; and c) response uncertainty, which implies not knowing the possible ways to respond to change. Similarly, Simon (2016) observed that, when making decisions, people might have uncertainty about the number of options available, the consequences and usefulness of their choices. This author also stated that in uncertain situations, people tend to decide based on several factors: handy information, things they are acquainted with, or opinions from specialists.

Klein (2003) observed that "the five types of uncertainty are missing information, unreliable information, conflicting information, noisy information and confusing information." From this perspective, noisy information is when relevant data is mixed up with irrelevant data. In all these cases, it is difficult for companies to make effective business decisions.

4.2.2 Companies' Attitude before Uncertainty

Most companies perform a series of activities to handle their "fear of the unknown." According to Meares and Freeston (2008), companies deal with uncertainty in different ways, for example, being over-vigilant regarding future scenarios, becoming endlessly indecisive, avoiding commitments, procrastinating, looking for reassurance from experts, and shunning tasks via delegation, among others. These authors observed that some business people are inclined to worry about uncertain scenarios because this behaviour motivates them and helps them prevent problems, or protects them against them.

Klein (2003) observed that people tend to face uncertainty in different ways, for instance, by deferring their decisions, looking for additional information, increasing their attention on the available information, making assumptions on information gaps, making up possible interpretations of the available information, and taking actions despite uncertainty. The aforementioned author observed that people also deal with uncertainty by projecting future scenarios, making simpler and more flexible plans, planning for the worst-case scenarios, taking incremental steps, taking preventive actions, and embracing uncertain scenarios.

Cialdini (2009) commented that oftentimes, in uncertain circumstances, people see how others act and tend to take them as external valid references and imitate them, which is called the "social proof principle." Oftentimes, other people are incorrect, therefore when taking others as references as to how to act, some relevant questions like "Is there any evidence that these people are acting in the best way?" and "Are there better ways of acting in this situation?" should be asked to avoid being misguided by social proof.

Some people tend to become immobilised before uncertain situations, thus they avoid taking any action. They feel comfortable with the known and fret over new experiences or unfamiliar projects. In order to reduce the uncertainty levels associated with future scenarios, some companies use different tools, such as:

- Setting of the business mission and vision
- Developing various strategies and tactics
- Setting clear policies, procedures, and systems
- Preparation of budgets and business projects
- Conducting or contracting research studies
- Analysing, comparing, and extrapolating information about trends
- Writing meticulous contracts
- Using well-proven techniques and tools
- Assessing and managing potential risks
- Pre-testing feasibility of potential processes, products, and services
- Depicting hypothetical scenarios about future events
- Contracting insurance policies

These well-used tools are valid instruments to deal with uncertainty related to business activities. These tools help companies handle their "fear of the unknown." Nevertheless, none of these strategies completely eliminates the uncertainty of future scenarios. These tools have a common factor: they are used to attempt to control what will happen. In other words, their users are fearful of losing control in uncertain scenarios. From the perspective of social psychology, most people experience the so-called "illusion of control," because they believe they have more control over their own world than they actually have.

In business activities, risk is often related to the outcomes stemming from future scenarios. Valtonen (2016) observed that companies facing risky scenarios can adopt four courses of action: tolerating potential risky scenarios, taking specific actions to reduce their risk, transferring this risk to other companies, and terminating business projects to avoid risk. Most companies will assess the potential impact of future circumstances and try to take appropriate preventive measures. To that effect, there is profuse literature, as well as professional qualifications, concerning risk management techniques which help people analyse this topic more thoroughly.

Some entrepreneurs believe they are capable of predicting future scenarios. There is no such thing as "foreseeing" future scenarios because companies are affected by so many interrelated variables which cannot be fathomed in an accurate manner. Therefore, business predictions should be put into perspective; these formalised forms of guesswork are always subject to errors.

Even though no entrepreneur has the gift of predicting the future, some business people do use their intuitive insights and reflections on past circumstances to expand their vision of uncertain scenarios. This type of person is prone to imagine the future continuation of some current trends, and even intuit the emergence of new patterns in the marketplace.

Some business people can see the bigger picture, which includes unobvious linkages between current circumstances, and past and future ones. These individuals tend to become leaders, because they do not wait for the future to come, but create, shape, and mould it in their minds and with their actions. This foresightedness also includes the "prediction" of the potential consequences of present business activities.

4.2.3 Mental Biases, Uncertainty, and Complexity

When analysing information about future scenarios, business people are prone to misinterpret available data. Their interpretation of facts tends to be clouded by numerous cognitive distortions, called cognitive errors or mental biases. These mental distortions are prone to modify the information from the environment, eliminate it, generalise it, or even avoid it.

Dobelli (2014) observed that these biases represent deviations from logic and prevent people from thinking optimally about a given situation. These defective patterns of thinking are generally subconscious. These mental biases help business people interpret circumstances more simply and quickly. Nonetheless, these cognitive distortions commonly prompt people to come to incorrect or unfounded conclusions regarding uncertain scenarios.

Copious research has demonstrated numerous examples of cognitive distortions which affect the analysis of uncertain scenarios, for instance, minimising or exaggerating the importance of certain factors, selecting specific pieces of information and discarding others, seeking confirmation of one's beliefs, using stereotypes, confusing typical factors for likely ones and over- or underestimating the likelihood of the occurrence of events. Other distortions are: blindly trusting a group's opinion or an expert, linking unrelated factors, confusing cause for correlation, personalising impersonal events, relying exclusively on recent or available information, misevaluating current resources, believing in the repetition of past events, and generalising unique or random factors, among others.

As previously explained, the business environment is so complex that no company can take into account all its factors. Therefore, companies tend to perceive situations in a partial manner, ignoring some factors, oftentimes relevant ones. Any organisation counts on incomplete information, they can never gather all the possible data surrounding the business environment because of its complexity and dynamism. In other words, all "educated" decisions a company makes about their future are based on incomplete information. Many of the missing pieces of information are prone to pop out as the company takes action.

Consequently, no company should avoid acting in uncertain scenarios because they do not have all the information needed. Moreover, companies can never be fully ready for the uncertain. When in doubt, a company should take the most positive course of action for all involved. Oftentimes, an organisation realises how to deal with specific situations as they unfold, not in advance.

In order to avoid complacency and continually thrive, a company should be willing to navigate uncertain scenarios. Companies with a predominant prosperity mindset tend to fully embrace uncertainty and imagine future scenarios in a flexible and open-minded manner. These companies use a multidimensional analysis which includes as many relevant factors as possible. Some of these organisations are even keen on uncertain scenarios because these environments are considered fertile ground to develop creative ideas and projects.

4.2.4 Abundance Mindset and Uncertainty

A company with a prevalent abundance mindset tends to analyse uncertain scenarios in a provisional or tentative manner. This type of company prefers general plausibility over precision. Therefore, for these companies, plans or projects related to uncertain scenarios are never carved in stone, but subject to continuous changes and fine-tuning as actions are taken.

Oftentimes, people with a prosperity mindset tend to make tentative decisions, moved by approximation. These individuals adjust their actions along the way, based on feedback which prompts them to confirm or correct their course of action. These people realise that each business circumstance is affected by a myriad of mostly unknown factors.

Moreover, these individuals understand that many factors affecting their future business activities are beyond their control. Therefore, when business circumstances do not play out well, these people avoid interpreting them negatively. Their plans tend to be flexible because many future events affecting them cannot be predicted. Consequently, these companies never set goals in a rigid manner, but as references or guidelines which can be changed over time.

People with an abundance mindset tend to adopt a more explorative and curious attitude regarding future business scenarios. Instead of looking for security and certainty; they develop a sense of wonder and discovery as circumstances unfold, casting away rigid approaches and adapting to changing circumstances. Instead of resisting the "wave" of change, they are prone to "surf" it.

Besides, people with a prosperous mindset perceive their business endeavours as adventures into the unknown and recognise their main point of power is the present moment. By knowing that no future scenarios can be accurately predicted, they are empowered to take full responsibility and act in the best way possible each moment according to the available information and resources. These people tend to feel less anxious and worried about the uncontrollable future, because they focus on what is actually under their control: the now. Because future circumstances cannot be fully foreseen, they also avoid having negative expectations about these situations.

Covey (1992) observed that there are situations when a company does not have any influence called "circle of concern." From this perspective, in any situation involving others (organisations, government, etc.) a company has limited influence, and never total control over the circumstances. This author also highlighted that there are areas where a company can respond effectively, called its "circle of influence," such as its own actions at each moment. Likewise, the ancient Stoic philosophical school of thought also observed that people can only fully control their thoughts, emotions, and actions; all the rest is beyond their control.

As seen previously, no company has all the information to make the perfect decision about future business scenarios. Therefore, the information gathered by the company should be reasonable, avoiding excessive information gathering. It is better to obtain a sensible amount of information and update and adjust it on a regular basis. In the same way, companies should avoid over-analysis of data in an attempt to predict future possibilities.

Business people with a prosperous mindset never give up or get stopped by uncertain scenarios. These people act in a determined and daring manner, focusing on their purpose in a continuous and wholehearted manner. These individuals are less likely to be concerned about uncertainty affecting their activities. They know that the next steps to take are often discovered as they walk their talk. Small actions contribute to their mission and generate positive momentum which drives these people forward.

When people are at ease with uncertainty, they continually stretch their comfort zone. The zone of comfort is safe, known, and certain, while exploring new business activities, developing new products and services, and entering new markets implies a certain degree of uncertainty and risk. Business people with a prosperity mindset are prone to tread unconventional paths and undertake non-traditional endeavours. These people know not taking any risks represents a very risky business perspective.

These people take action in a faithful manner. They make the mental choice to believe that if they are doing their best, then things are likely to work out. Even though they do not have the complete picture of how things will unfold, they are willing to take one step at a time toward the achievement of their purpose.

4.3 Orientation to Action

> Knowing is not enough, we must apply. Willing is not enough, we must do.
>
> **Goethe**

4.3.1 Importance of an Action-Oriented Attitude

In a previous point, the importance of continuous learning was explained. Nonetheless, even the most relevant knowledge is useless without taking any action on it. People with a prosperity mindset consider their actions as fundamental parts of their business journey. They know that even though their actions cannot guarantee success, their inaction tends to bring about failure. Some business people have great ideas that never come to fruition, as they are reluctant to take effective action. Ideas tend to be forgotten if they are not nailed down by putting them into practice. Individuals with an abundance mindset know that being inactive is prone to make them restless, anxious, hesitant, fearful, or insecure. They realise that their actions can add value to their organisations and also society as a whole.

Most business books profusely highlight the importance of any organisation having a big vision and clear goals to achieve, but only a few authors analyse the significance of taking continuous actions. In that sense, Fritz (1984, 2003) observed that actions are paramount to create anything in the business environment, because they close the gap between a company's current reality (the status quo) and its vision (where the company wants to go). From this perspective, no creation can be brought to life without any action. This author also suggested that oftentimes, actions should be taken before one feels completely ready to take them.

Action-oriented people are more vital because they are always taking charge; they go beyond survival and security mode to focus on their growth and development. They know the best action has not been taken yet, because there is always room for improvement. Not only do they take action, they also follow through on actions taken previously.

People oriented to action avoid being perfectionist. They always choose the most plausible action. Perfectionists are instead prone to get stuck in negative behaviour, such as:

- Comparing their performance with others
- Finding negative traits in their actions
- Becoming anxious about their performance
- Fretting over setbacks
- Over-controlling their tasks
- Planning excessively
- Procrastinating or making excuses
- Waiting for the ideal circumstances
- Setting unachievable standards
- Harshly criticising themselves

Paradoxically, the aforementioned behaviours prevent perfectionistic people from taking due action. It is important to pinpoint that taking action always creates momentum and motivation, which defeats people's complacency and inertia. Ellis and Harper (1997) observed that "inertia has a tendency to feed on itself." When people take action, their energy is in motion, which prompts them to take even more action. Instead, when people are not used to taking continuous action, it seems harder for them.

Successful business people have a ruthless can-do attitude. They do not stop at the level of intention; they actually take action. They know they will be judged by others for their actions, not their promises or resolutions. They take continuous action, which expands their beliefs about what is possible. They realise that each day is a brand-new opportunity to take action and they are willing to roll their sleeves up to make it happen; they also understand that small commitments create a virtuous cycle, which bring about bigger commitments. As their actions build up gradually, their persistence and discipline eventually pay off.

Bandura (cited in Egan, 1994) states that people are more prone to take action when they expect that their behaviour will lead them to the desired outcomes (also called outcome expectations) and when they feel their capabilities are adequate for that action (also called self-efficacy). When people take continuous action, their expectations tend to improve and they feel more self-efficacious.

Continuous action helps people overcome any feelings of incompetence and inadequacy. From the psychological perspective, people improve their self-efficacy through the feedback they obtain from their previous actions. Figuratively speaking, people continually adjust their trajectory, like a rocket heading to outer space.

4.3.2 Traits of Action-Focused Business People

Action-prone people are more enduring and tolerant to frustration. They are willing to go the extra mile without giving up, even during challenging circumstances. Their actions give these people an edge and staying power to navigate dire situations more effectively. They delay instant gratification stemming from the natural comfort and ease of not acting, in order to take valuable actions to pursue their purpose.

People with an abundance mindset are continually coaching themselves into action because they do not settle for mediocrity; they know that their present actions contribute to their business future outcomes. These individuals are willing to harness their innermost greatness, which makes them unstoppable. People with an abundance mindset are also willing to step into the unknown and act differently. Sometimes these people are perceived as slightly naïve or childlike because of their experimental ways of doing things.

Siebold (2010) observed that people with an abundance mindset are *"comfortable being uncomfortable."* Successful business people are always willing to take action, even when they feel demotivated or moody. Their feelings never prevent them from taking action. They know that as soon as the first step is taken, the following actions get easier and more manageable.

Whenever possible, these people take actions while remaining positive and calm. They avoid having negative expectations, which never contribute to their success. Their emotional stability and continuous focus on their purpose sharpen their discerning and creative skills and improve their performance.

According to Miller (2009), there are four main types of mood people can experience: action mood, calm mood, anxiety mood, and depression mood. This author observed that people in the action mood become positive, experience high energy, and tend to adopt a can-do attitude. This author stated that, in this mood, people tend to be more confident, communicate more openly, and are more likely to analyse new alternatives.

From this perspective, people should strive for balance between the action mood and the calm mood. The calm mood helps people replenish their energy, reflect on their actions, learn from their mistakes, and plan to act differently in the future.

People do not have to wait to be in an action mood in order to act. To that effect, when people start taking action, these activities prompt them to experience the action mood. In other words, when people take action, their mood is boosted accordingly.

According to Robbins (2017), people should force themselves into action, because they are never going to feel like acting. This author presents a case for people continually parenting themselves and taking action. Likewise, Schwartz (1979) observed that people should crank up their mental engine in a mechanical manner and take action at the moment, avoiding waiting for their spirit to move them. Some people trick themselves into action, for example, by setting tight deadlines.

People with an abundance mindset take full responsibility. According to Rosenberg (2005), some people tend to avoid responsibility in different ways, such as abiding by the opinions of others, reacting to external forces (for example, economic factors), blaming others for their faulty character (e.g., lazy, indecisive, etc.), complying with external rules, being driven by their own impulses, etc.

People who take full responsibility do not pay attention to harsh criticism from others, nor do they retreat before these comments. These people take action without looking for approval from others. After they have taken action, they never feel regret, shame, or guilt. When their actions produce negative outcomes, they are open to learning from them.

Some business people mistakenly wait for the ideal circumstances in order to take action. They use sentences like "I will take action when …" or "I will take action if there is …," and similar ones. These individuals take a long time getting themselves ready to take action. It is important to pinpoint that there is no "perfect" situation or time to take action. A company's people with an abundance mindset harness the present circumstances and take the best action possible at that moment. They take action, even when they do not feel completely ready, and make adjustments on their way.

Action-oriented people search for new opportunities and challenges they can act on. These individuals never refrain from taking risks if these actions might lead them closer to their mission. Their courage and grit prompt them to act whenever it is necessary. Oftentimes, their actions challenge the status quo and what is considered possible in the business environment.

Business people with a prosperity mindset take action to harness their unique strengths and capabilities (and the ones from their company) to add distinct value to the company's stakeholders. These individuals avoid copying other companies' offerings by highlighting their own perspective through every action they take.

4.3.3 Continuous Action, Fear, and Growth

Cuddy (2016) observed that taking action always reinforces future action, because each time people take action, they tend to recall their previous experiences of acting, which makes it easier for them to take action again. These people also realise that they are the most important obstacle holding them back from acting. Action-oriented people progressively expand their comfort zone because they abhor becoming stagnant. These people often seem to move beyond what is considered reasonable by the average person. These individuals dare to perform activities most people do not even dare ponder.

By taking continuous actions, people with abundance mindset are empowered to set higher goals over time. These people believe that big objectives can be achieved with determination and flexibility. These individuals know that their true potential is limitless; they realise that extraordinary results can be brought about if they adopt an attitude of commitment. Wattles (2013) observed that business people should take action with the impression of increase, which means having the intention to advance themselves and the people around them. This author also stated that this intention has very tangible effects. Likewise, Schwartz (1979) expressed that actions should always add value to oneself and others.

Some business people are fearful of taking some actions. Ferriss (2017) opines that these people should ask themselves about the worst possible outcomes if actions are taken, the different ways to prevent these potential negative outcomes, and their solutions in case they occur. This author also suggests estimating the benefits of taking action, as well as the cost of not taking these very actions.

Wiest (2013) observed that when a person feels fear of doing something, this task tends to be both frightening, but also worthwhile to this individual; in other words, fear often indicates what is worth doing. This author wisely stated that "Fear means you're trying toward something you love, but your old beliefs, or unhealed experiences are getting in the way."

In order to keep fear of action at bay, Robbins (2017) suggests a simple technique called the "five-second rule." From this perspective, when people feel the need to act, in that moment they should mentally count down from five to zero and immediately take action without second-guessing. This technique proves to be efficient to overcome negative states people experience when they are about to take action, such as hesitation, lack of confidence, indecisiveness, immobility, and over-analysis.

Thompson (1992) observed that when people act despite their fears, their bodies release adrenalin which provides their actions with more vigour. When people are dominated by fear, their bodies instead release *excessive* adrenalin which renders them inactive and overwhelmed.

There is a technique some psychologists use with some patients (with phobias, compulsive behaviour, and anxiety problems) called progressive exposure. The technique requires gradually exposing oneself to the factors which prompt one to feel fearful, without reacting in any way. This increasing exposure makes one more habituated to the seemingly threatening factors. As a consequence, all negative reactive responses toward the perceived threats eventually get extinguished.

For example, if salespeople feel fearful of making phone calls to customers, they can progressively expose themselves to this situation, by making a few calls, despite their original discomfort and uneasiness. Then they can progressively increase the amount of calls over time, because they will feel more at ease and less threatened by that situation.

Action-oriented people are proactive and less prone to react to external circumstances (for instance, changes in the economic conditions, new legislation, etc.). These individuals preferably use sentences in active voice ("I do …," I choose …," etc.) rather than phrases in passive voice ("I am affected by …," "I am defeated by …," etc.). Their proactive orientation prompts them to explore different alternatives around the circumstances they face. They are also willing to harness valuable opportunities which appear in the marketplace. These people reveal how they truly are through their action; their true essence is shown through the steps they take.

When people take action, they tend to feel more empowered, not more helpless, because they focus on what they can control (their behaviour) instead of being centred on the uncontrollable (external circumstances). Action-oriented people are in the driver's seat; they are not victims of circumstances. Psychologically speaking, their locus of control is internal, not external. Walter (2005) observed that all behaviour can be placed on a spectrum, which has a "reactive attitude" on one extreme, and "active attitude" on the other. This author stated that people can gradually move from being reactive to becoming more active, by taking little but consistent steps.

When people with an abundance attitude take action and achieve their objectives, they give sufficient credit to people who supported them during that path. They know the achievement of goals is always the result of co-operative teamwork. Therefore, these people encourage assistance from others, and they are explicitly grateful for their co-operation.

Action-oriented people are keen on flexible planning. As seen previously, most companies commonly use plans as tools to co-ordinate their resources and deal with uncertainty. Even though plans have a future-orientation, they can never predict forthcoming situations precisely. Besides, plans are always based on imperfect information which is gradually completed, amended, or updated when actions regarding these plans are taken. Consequently, their plans are flexible and can be changed over time as these individuals take action.

Sometimes, action-oriented people visualise themselves taking a specific action before actually performing a certain activity. In other words, these individuals form vivid mental images of them performing an activity in an effective manner and also experiencing positive emotions while doing so. Many athletes and other sports people use visualisation techniques to improve their performance levels in their competitive field. Besides, some research studies corroborate that when people visualise themselves taking action, the same areas of their brains are activated as if they were taking real action. The main aspects of visualisation are explored in Appendix G.

4.3.4 Tips to Become More Action-Oriented

Some companies spend excessive time developing their plans, because they tend to over-analyse information, which brings about "paralysis by analysis." Therefore, planning should be done in a reasonable time in order to take timely action. No plan will ever be perfect; a company can always make adjustments as it takes action. Besides, the factors of the business environment (legislation, technology, economy, etc.) are dynamic, so oftentimes a company takes unplanned actions. Organisations with a prosperity mindset also take into account these aspects:

- When these organisations face setbacks, they never remain passive; these companies see failures in perspective and gain insights in order to come back and act more intelligently. Failures only imply these organisations have not attained their aims yet. Every action taken, even failed ones, gets these companies closer to their business purpose. Each business project can be considered as a work in progress, and obstacles are perceived as opportunities for improvement.

- These businesses also learn from their achievements. When this type of company attains its goals, it thoroughly analyses what worked well, in order to repeat and improve it in future projects. These companies build up momentum on their past successes so as to foster their future successes.

- These organisations give their best each time they take action. In other words, they never make tentative moves or halfway effort. Their actions are wholehearted and passionate. When these companies face failure, their people remain calm because they have given their best.

- These companies know when to discontinue overtly inviable projects, even when they have invested sufficient time and effort. Psychologically speaking, most people are affected by a phenomenon called self-justification, which implies justifying their previous assessments of ongoing projects to continue them, even when these projects have not produced tangible results for a significant time.

- People working for these organisations take their time to recharge their batteries after having taken action. Therefore, these individuals take time to do some fun things, such as hobbies, travelling, parties, etc. These activities revitalise them, and help them think in a more insightful manner when they resume taking action.

- These organisations set clear, but reasonable, deadlines for actions to be completed over time. Deadlines represent valuable constraints which prompt the companies' people to do their best in order to meet these signposts, and prevent them from procrastinating indefinitely. These companies are prone to extend these deadlines, if more time is needed.

- People working for action-oriented companies prefer to work smart rather than hard. Therefore, these individuals avoid taking mindless actions. These people tend to analyse situations before acting on them. They assess the risks and implications of their actions, without overanalysing these aspects. However, these people also take some actions on the spur of the moment. These seemingly erratic actions are based on gut instinct, hunches, or intuition. The topic of intuitive insights will be thoroughly analysed in Chapter 15.

- When taking action, these organisations are focused on their mission and objectives. Therefore, these companies avoid being distracted by other organisations, nor do they compare themselves with them. Action-prone businesses know that the best way to succeed in the business environment is to continually compete with themselves, and become better every day. Before taking any action, individuals working for these organisations often ask themselves "Is this action aligned with our business mission?" If the answer is affirmative, the action is taken; if negative, the action is fully discarded.

- Action-prone organisations divide complex business projects, including various actions, into smaller and more actionable "chunks." By doing so, these projects become more manageable and less overwhelming. Individuals working for these companies become more capable when dealing with smaller steps contributing to an overall project. They also believe in the power of small wins which create valuable momentum for future wins.

- These organisations know that not all actions are equal. Therefore, these companies take their time to prioritise actions. Actions which contribute to the achievement of business mission and those which strengthen business relationships with stakeholders are given priority over the rest, when possible.

- These companies encourage their employees to take one action at a time and focus their energy on the action at hand, but also take consistent steps over time. In that sense, multitasking is strongly discouraged due to its intrinsic ineffectiveness; this is backed by profuse scientific research. These organisations also empower their employees to balance their work tasks with other relevant areas of their lives. These individuals do not exclusively devote their time to business activities, but they try to look for equilibrium with other areas, such as health, family, etc.

- Action-oriented organisations always take the most suitable actions at each moment. If these actions proved them wrong, these companies are always willing to try alternatives courses of action. To that effect, these companies are flexible and feel comfortable with change; they are open to adapting their actions according to dynamic scenarios. These organisations also know there is not one way to approach every business situation. These companies, according to Kay (2011), tend to achieve their objectives indirectly. From this standpoint, companies are prone to go through a lot of exploration, iteration, and continuous adjustments of their actions on their way to achieving their goals.

- These organisations take action from a perspective of service to all their relevant stakeholders. Their actions represent effective ways to connect to these stakeholders and strengthen the relationship with them. For example, by improving customer service activities, a company is more capable of satisfying customers' innermost needs effectively and thus adding more value to them.

■ These organisations continually assess the outcomes of their actions. They regularly ask themselves this question: "Are our actions taking our company toward where we want to be?" and take corrective actions when necessary.

■ These companies allow people to delegate activities to others, when possible. Employees do not have to be directly responsible for every single relevant action. Each employee takes certain actions, preferably those they are actually outstanding at, and delegate the rest. The remaining actions will be performed by other employees or external advisors.

■ These organisations frequently celebrate their achievements, small and large; they never take these accomplishments for granted. These companies show gratitude to those people whose actions contributed to those successful outcomes.

Action-oriented individuals know that, with continuous repetition and reinforcement, most actions become automatic over time. Therefore, these people thoroughly evaluate their current habits in order to keep the ones which contribute, directly or indirectly, to the company's mission, and discard the rest. Oftentimes, these individuals tend to discard certain detrimental habits, such as overanalysing information before taking any action.

Action-prone individuals are prone to form new positive habits. Wiest (2013) observed that, when people develop a positive habit, this is constructive, because it gives these individuals a sense of purpose and provides them with emotional stability and predictability. This author also stated that the new positive habit formed by people is beneficial because it affirms their previous decisions, validates their capabilities to take specific actions and encourages self-regulation of their actions.

Lastly, according to Wattles (2013), companies with an abundance mindset take actions which are always focused on creating value for others; their actions are never based on fear of other organisations. This creative attitude will help the company harness business opportunities, which are always abundant in the marketplace. The topic of creativity will be explored in Chapters 14 and 15.

Questions for Self-Reflection

■ How can I harness uncertainty in a more productive manner?
■ What type of knowledge is necessary for my organisation to succeed in the marketplace?
■ What type of actions are necessary to pursue the company's mission?
■ What is preventing me from taking the following obvious next step?

Chapter 5

Love and Business Activities

There is something peculiar about human beings. We are loving animals. I know that we kill each other and do all these horrible things, but if you look at any story of corporate transformation where everything begins to go well, innovation appears, and people are happy to be there, you will see it is a story of love.

Humberto Maturana Romesin and Gerda Verden-Zoller

5.1 Main Meanings of Love

Listen, my friend. He who loves, understands.

Kabir

In the world, the lack of love is observed through countless examples: terrorism, racism, human trafficking, wars, corruption, pollution, and other excruciating problems. In the business environment, companies with an unloving attitude display countless examples of misbehaviour: exploiting employees, ripping customers off, acting without integrity with intermediaries and suppliers, using misleading advertising, polluting the environment, using non-renewable resources, and bribing governments, among others. Within most companies, some employees also adopt an unloving attitude toward others, for instance: backbiting, one-upmanship, power struggles, stealing other people's credit, and bullying, among others.

Hamilton (2010) observed that people are naturally hardwired to behave in a loving manner with others. Likewise, Griffith (2016) stated that human beings have an instinctive orientation to behave "in an unconditionally selfless, all-loving, co-operative moral way." Nonetheless, many people tend to frequently act with others in a selfish and uncaring manner. Some negative values (egocentrism, carelessness, manipulation, defensiveness, etc.) present in most social contexts commonly reinforce people's selfish attitude.

Montagu (1957) observed that love is intrinsically social and it is a basic emotional need, as relevant as food. This author also stated that love for others implies active interest, caring support and involvement regarding their well-being and their development as human beings. A person with a loving attitude toward others is keen to support them in their innermost needs and interests.

Loving people care for others, even when the latter do not request the support from the former. This type of person acknowledges, accepts, and appreciates others as unique human beings. Loving people never judge others, but treat them tenderly. These people develop a profound sense of connectedness with others.

Maturana and Verden-Zoller (1996, 2008) observed that, from the biological perspective, each emotion is a bodily disposition of what a person can or cannot do in relation to others, and "love is the domain of those behaviours or bodily dispositions in which another arises as a legitimate other in coexistence with ourselves." Moreover, these authors stated that love is "a biological phenomenon ... through which social life arises and is conserved." They concluded that "love is our natural condition, and *it is the denial of love that requires effort*" (emphasis added) (Maturana and Verden-Zoller, 1996).

Research has corroborated that a loving attitude toward others brings about countless positive effects. Hamilton (2010) observed that the brains of people with a loving attitude release opiates, serotonin and dopamine, which lift their mood and make them feel more optimistic. This specialist also stated that adopting a loving attitude toward others generates oxytocin, which is a substance that prods people to behave kindly and selflessly, co-operate, share, and trust others. This author also stated that when a loving person is near another, the latter gets "infected" by the kindness of the former and is prone to act alike.

Sunderland (2007) observed that loving people are less willing to behave aggressively and more inclined to experience lofty values, like kindness, compassion, and altruism. This author stated that "Loving in peace means that your moment-to-moment stream of consciousness, your thoughts and feelings take you to a warm world inside your head."

Maturana and Bunnel (1998) observed that, when people adopt a loving attitude, their discerning and creative skills are enhanced. The HeartMath Institute concluded that when people experience loving feelings in the area of their hearts, they enter a state of coherence, where all their body systems act in sync (Childre et al., 2000). As seen previously, Hawkins (2012) concludes that love is one of the highest states of consciousness that exists.

The word "love" cannot easily be defined; there are different possible "definitions" of this term. The list below is not exhaustive, but only exemplificative.

- Love is the link which connects everything that exists.
- Love is the straightener of negative thoughts and emotions.
- Love is continuous care for oneself and others.
- Love is a gentle opener of all possibilities.
- Love is a torch providing clarity in confusing situations.
- Love is the most valuable capital of a human being.
- Love is the main engine of progress and positive change.
- Love is an alchemic shortcut to contentment and peacefulness.
- Love is an internal motivator in challenging situations.
- Love is an enabler of inclusiveness and diversity.
- Love is the silent positive observer of everybody and everything.
- Love is the bridge which shortens any distance between people.
- Love is the overt demonstration of support and affection.
- Love is the facilitator of a more meaningful communication.
- Love is a natural pacifier for any conflictive situation.
- Love is service to others, not servitude nor slavery.
- Love is the true connector of each individual with others.
- Love is the origin of every creative endeavour.
- Love is pure authentic essence, beyond distracting appearances.

- Love is the core element of all fruitful relationships.
- Love is the most powerful antidote to fear.
- Love is the smoothest way to overcome others' defensive behaviour.
- Love is an enlivening principle pervading everything in the universe.
- Love is the truth beyond any type of speculation.
- Love is an open standpoint which welcomes diverse perspectives.
- Love is pure kindness and respect for others.
- Love is the beautiful side in everything that exists.
- Love is the most comforting respite in dire times.
- Love is the state which melts any resistance away.
- Love is the most precious energy needed for triumph.
- Love is the preventer of control and manipulation.
- Love is the balm which enlivens organisational environments.
- Love is the most significant fuel for passion and action.
- Love is a sense of togetherness and integration.
- Love is the uniting substance of all relationships.
- Love is the main driver to attain an authentic mission.

On one side, love is the natural heightener of people's human qualities. In other words, when people adopt a loving attitude, their positive human side is gracefully enhanced. On the other side, when people adopt an unloving attitude, even their greatest human qualities are degraded. According to Scheffer (1990), without love, some relevant human virtues become negative qualities. From this author's perspective:

- When people are righteous but lack love, they become intolerant.
- When faithful people have no love, they become fanatical.
- When powerful people are unloving, they become brutal.
- When committed people act without love, they become peevish.
- When orderly people experience no love, they become centred on petty things.

A similar perspective was observed by some ancient Greek philosophers. From their perspective, love naturally lights up all natural human attributes and humanises their rough edges. Besides, with love, all human interactions are smoother, deeper, and more meaningful. It is also possible to define love by its opposite, which means that love is never:

- Being indifferent or nonchalant with others
- Neglecting other people's valuable needs
- Dismissing the unique attributes of other people
- Condemning people overtly or covertly
- Not recognising people's contribution to a project
- Threatening people or guilt-tripping them
- Being dishonest or untruthful to others
- Controlling or manipulating people
- Willingly hurting others

Bevelin (2017) observed that people are more prone to act based on their self-interest. This author also stated that when people act in a loving or kind manner with others, their behaviour can be explained from a perspective of self-benefit. To that effect, this author stated that "social recognition, prestige, fear of social disapproval, relief from distress, avoidance of guilt, a better after-life or social expectation are some reasons behind 'altruistic' behaviour" (Bevelin, 2017). In a similar vein, De Mello (1990) observed that loving and supportive individuals give themselves the pleasure of helping others, which is based on selfishness.

5.2 The Absence of Love in Business Activities

One who loves is always right.

Peter Deunov

Many terms commonly used in the business world come from the military disciplines. Words such as "strategy," "defeating a position," "tactics," and others are related to a defensive and non-loving attitude. As seen previously in this book, the widespread use of these terms implies that there are external threatening forces, which a company should guard itself from. This terminology prompts companies to adopt actions primarily based on fear, not love.

Another great wealth of words commonly used in the business world come directly from the industrial field, such as rationalisation, quality levels, and Key Performance Indicators, among others. The majority of these relevant terms are quantitative by nature, related to figures to be precisely monitored and measured. Most companies are keen on measurement tools, such as budgets, estimated costs, plans, etc. Nonetheless, love cannot be measured; it is qualitative by nature. Even though love cannot be quantified, its impact on relationships with stakeholders, productivity levels, customer service, sales amount, and the bottom line is very tangible.

Some oriental philosophical schools of thought imbue love with feminine traits, such as compassion, care, integration, and nourishment, among others. In the business environment, most organisations are prone to focus more on masculine characteristics, such as productivity, effectiveness, efficiency, and others. Here the terms "feminine" and "masculine" do not refer to genders; these terms are related to complementary forces or principles which, for example, are shown in the concept of yin and yang.

Manby (2012) observed that most organisations tend to set "do goals," instead of "be goals." From this perspective, "do goals" are about what the company wants to achieve, and "be goals" are how objectives will be achieved. For instance, a company sets the following "do goal": "to obtain an X level of profit in a specific period of time." In this example, the respective "be goal" could be "by being caring with the community." In this example, the "do goal" is as important as the "be goal." In this example, the company wants to attain an X level of profit (do goal), not by any means but by creating a positive impact on the community (be goal).

Most organisations tend only to measure and reward the achievement of "do objectives," but they dismiss or do not even consider "be goals" for their business activities. A company should always set "be goals" which imply loving traits (e.g., compassion, kindness, generosity, gratefulness, benevolence, etc.) toward its stakeholders.

5.3 Love Is the Opposite to Fear

There is no difficulty that enough love will not conquer … No door enough love will not open … No gulf that enough love will not bridge … No wall that enough love will not throw down …

Emmet Fox

Some spiritual schools of thought consider love as the opposite to fear, not to hatred, as many people tend to think. As seen previously, fear is a powerful negative emotional state expressed in different ways in the business environment. McBride-Walker (n.d.) observed that fear is the "lived experience of a defensive state constructed with the purpose of self-preservation," which includes a cognitive and emotional response toward a perceived threat. Fear can be considered a natural response human beings inherited from their ancestors, whose survival was threatened by predators, shortages of food, and other dangerous factors.

Every time people are fearful, they do not feel able to effectively respond to a perceived threat. It is interesting to pinpoint that what is considered threatening tends to vary from person to person, depending on their past experiences, personal assumptions, and even genetic aspects, among other factors. Fredrickson (2013) observed that, when people are scared, they cannot behave lovingly because their survival defences override any possible loving attitude.

The bodies of fearful people release two powerful hormones called cortisol and adrenaline, which in turn prompts their focus to narrow down to the menacing factor. Goleman (1996, 1998) observed that fear has physiological aspects (e.g., blood rushes to the legs, the face becomes blanched, heart rate speeds up, etc.) which are opposite to the traits observed in a person who demonstrates love to another.

When fear is widespread in a company, people working for it tend to adopt a defensive attitude toward real or perceived threats (for instance, rival companies). These threatening factors are often perceived in a magnified or exaggerated manner. As a consequence, when a company's environment is teeming with fear, people are less inclined to adopt a loving attitude toward others. To put it simply, fear is utterly intimidating and immobilising for most people; it does not bring about any positive change within a company.

Fear is intrinsically protective and restrictive. According to Jeffers (1991), when people feel fear, they feel less capable of handling situations they face at present or in the future. Fearful people's typical behaviour includes, for instance, procrastination, avoiding problematic situations, reluctance to team-play with others, maintenance of a negative status quo, and drawing catastrophic conclusions about future scenarios, among others.

5.4 Business People's Default Response

Take away love and our Earth is a tomb.

Robert Browning

Most business people tend to experience fearful states which prompt them to perceive the business environment as dangerous. As explained before, fear is the opposite of love and prevents business people from adopting a loving attitude toward others. This defensive mode makes business people focus on potential threats and prevents them from adopting a more proactive and creative attitude. This fear-based perspective prompts organisations to act in specific ways to navigate the business environment. Some common fears most companies face regarding their endeavours are, for example:

- **Fear of not achieving the company's objectives:** This is related to the so-called fear of failure. These objectives can include goals related to increased productivity, increment of sales and profits, cutting costs, development of new products and services, increase of market share, entry to new markets, improvement of quality levels, training of staff, betterment of customer relationships, widespread public recognition, and internal restructuring of the organisation, among others. These organisations only set "realistic" objectives according their own capabilities and resources. For example, a company's objectives can be related to their current products and markets, avoiding the exploration of new ones. These companies avoid setting objectives that stretch them too much, because they are fearful of not attaining them.

■ **Fear of being out of business:** This is an extreme expression of the fear mentioned in the previous point. This is the fear of not surviving, for example, by not obtaining enough profits, shutting down, or filing for bankruptcy. Many entrepreneurs have continuous gnawing ruminations preventing them from taking "excessive" risks which could take them out of business. These business people tend to adopt an overly conservative attitude and take the well-trodden business path. These companies' defensive attitude prompts them to focus mostly on how not to be wiped out of the market.

■ **Fear of innovating:** This fear is also related to the penultimate point. Some companies tend to avoid any change by all means; change implies developing new products or markets, introducing innovative administrative systems, trying out new suppliers, and contracting new employees, among others. This type of company is prone to adopt a cautious attitude toward activities with uncertain results. These conservative companies tend to avoid those courses of action that do not offer them guarantees of success. These organisations prefer to play safe by focusing on well-known scenarios; they fear uncertain situations they cannot fully control. They avoid rocking the boat, even when new ideas might potentially be more beneficial than traditional ones. For example, a company keeps on focusing on the national market, instead of going international, because the internationalisation process, albeit potentially more profitable, is perceived as a riskier endeavour. When facing uncertain scenarios, these organisations become over-reliant on various data to "predict" scenarios, such as updated reports, expert advice, economic news, etc.

■ **Fear of inadequacy:** This fear is related to the perceived lack of the necessary resources to undertake business endeavours. This fear can be related to a lack of tangible resources (capital, technology, human resources, etc.) or intangible ones (specific capabilities, knowledge, time, experience, etc.). Some companies feel continually threatened by business challenges (financial shortages, technological changes, manufacturing hold-ups, etc.) because they do not know how to handle them effectively.

■ **Fear of being deceived:** This fear relates to potential swindling stratagems undertaken by internal or external company's stakeholders. In other words, an organisation fears possible deceptive behaviour from others, such as disloyal employees, unreliable suppliers, and delusory retailers, among others. This can also include the fear of the company's innovative ideas being stolen by other organisations. These companies thoroughly analyse trustworthiness of people (e.g., employees, suppliers, etc.) related to them. For these organisations, trust tends to be gained gradually; individuals are untrusting by default. These companies take special care to have their own interests fully covered, for instance, through the widespread use of thorough contracts and forms, and utilisation of various passwords, among others. Their distrusting attitude also prompts them to set varying policies and procedures to regulate different company activities (e.g., cash management, working time, purchases and sales, etc.). Companies should be cautious with people related to them, but oftentimes, organisations become excessively zealous and protective, which prevents them from harnessing their valuable resources effectively.

■ **Fear of being outpaced by competitors:** This common fear shows up as a reactive response to other organisations perceived as rivals. A fearful organisation does not want its products and services to be outsmarted by other companies' offerings. This type of company implements strategies that are mostly focused on what other companies do, reacting to their moves instead of adopting a proactive attitude.

■ **Fear of using their resources ineffectively:** Most companies have the assumption that all their resources are limited. These organisations spend significant time coordinating these scarce resources in the most effective manner, to avoid their wastage. These companies utilise an arsenal of tools, like budgets, strategies, planning spreadsheets, schedules, control of resources, etc. Nevertheless, these organisations do not take into account that some resources, for instance, staff's creative skills, cannot be depleted; these resources can always generate more resources.

■ **Fear of not satisfying customers:** All companies know their customers are their most significant source of income; customers are the organisations' paramount "assets." Some companies adopt an attitude of customer "retention," which is based on fear of losing them. These organisations have an all-pervading fear of losing their customers because of not satisfying their customers properly. Oftentimes, these organisations are afraid of receiving complaints or objections from customers. These companies also dread negative word of mouth (for example, negative online reviews).

■ **Fear of being rejected by other stakeholders:** Some organisations fear customers will reject their product or services. Their fear of not meeting prospects' expectations is related to their perceived lack of originality and distinctiveness of products and services offered. Companies that launch new products have an underlying fear that innovative items will not be accepted by the market, especially when they have not been duly tested beforehand. These organisations also fear being rejected by other stakeholders, for example, other organisations for potential business partnerships, financial institutions for possible loans, media companies for publicity, and the wider community for acceptance and support, among others.

■ **Fear of developing relationships with stakeholders:** Many companies tend to interact with their stakeholders in a goal-oriented and utilitarian manner, which oftentimes fails to consider the human side of the latter. Relationships with stakeholders are often so formal that they are devoid of real substance; countless conventions and rules override any potential meaningful connection with these stakeholders. These meaningless relationships are called "empty forms" by Fritz (2007). Consequently, some companies recognise the need for more meaningful human contact in order to deepen relationships with their main stakeholders.

■ **Fear of conflicts with stakeholders:** Most companies consider conflicts to be a natural part of business dynamics. However, some organisations, when interacting with their stakeholders (for example, government, employees, customers, suppliers, etc.) try to avoid conflicts with them at all cost, or alternatively try to solve them in the best way possible. As a consequence, these companies are prone to use a wealth of tools, such as conflict prevention, negotiation, conciliation, etc.

■ **Fear of success:** As they become bigger, some companies become more concerned about the increasing complexity and investment required to go ahead with their business activities. As a company grows, more suppliers, customers, and employees are needed. Some big companies are also prone to offer a wider range of products. Successful companies tend to have more resources at stake. If business goes well, rewards are significant; if not, losses become overwhelming. Bigger companies also tend to be perceived as more difficult to manage. For this reason, most companies are inclined to adopt a cautious and conservative attitude, as their activities grow over time. These organisations often limit their growth rate by taking only reasonable risks.

Even though all businesspeople aim to be successful in their endeavours, in the depth of their hearts some tend to experience a straining feeling of not deserving the best outcomes. This is observed in some unintentional self-sabotaging actions, such as promoting their products and services inadequately, misinforming customers, firing talented people, etc. These incongruent actions are prone to become more common when a company is doing well in the market.

5.5 Love Can Improve Business Activities

> Genuine love is volitional rather than emotional. The person who truly loves does so because of a decision to love. This person has made a commitment to be loving whether or not the loving feeling is present.
>
> **M. Scott Peck**

> Love is not primarily a relationship with a specific person; it is an attitude, an orientation of character which determines the relatedness of a person to the world as a whole, not toward an 'object' of love.
>
> **Erich Fromm**

I have delivered countless talks and seminars worldwide and oftentimes my audience is composed of business people; some of them lead the destiny of hundreds of employees. When I engage with entrepreneurs, I regularly say to them "It is necessary to introduce more love into your business activities." Some of them are confused and astonished by this statement.

Many entrepreneurs have told me that love has nothing to do with their business activities. These business individuals clearly believe that the most relevant objective for their companies is to offer goods products and services and increase their revenues and profits over time. Love does not appear among their priority business objectives.

In relation to this, Sanders (mentioned in Holden, 2008) observed "The most powerful source in business isn't greed, fear or even the raw energy of unbridled competition. The most powerful force in business is love." Kevin Roberts, CEO of the biggest advertising agency in the world, Saatchi & Saatchi, stated that this organisation is in the pursuit of love and what that means for its business activities. This global company agrees that people cannot live without love (Roberts, 2004).

As seen previously, love is wishing others the best, supporting and recognising them as human beings. Most business people tend to link love with non-business environments, for example, close relationships with partners, relatives, friends, and acquaintances. Nonetheless, this sentimental view of love is very limited.

Love is related to qualities such as connection, closeness, affinity, sympathy, care, support, gratitude, support, generosity, compassion, and others which can be applied to any type of relationships, even business ones. Relationships are a key component of any business; without them no company can thrive, regardless of the unique traits of its products and services and the deftness of its marketing strategy.

A loving attitude is the foundation of fruitful relationships, both business and non-business ones. According to Lowell and Joyce (2007), relationships are one of the most important intangibles in any company, because they contribute to add value to the company's products and services through the development of valuable networks.

Rogers (1961) concluded that some people are fearful of having a warm, loving, and caring attitude toward others, and tend to act in an impersonal, distant, or "professional" manner.

Oftentimes, this type of attitude is detrimental to the development of thriving relationship with others. In relation to this, Fromm (1956) observed that people who adopt a loving attitude toward others want to bridge the state of separateness between them, while also keeping their own individuality.

Manby (2012) stated that "treating someone with love regardless of how you feel is a very powerful principle," and also observed that "this type of love is the basis for all healthy relationships, bringing out the best in ourselves and others." The Greeks called this type of love "agape," and it can be defined as an affectionate and caring treatment toward others. According to Abrams (2017), this love is "of a higher order," because it requires an act of will and a continuous commitment.

When a person adopts a loving attitude toward others, there is no reservation toward them. This attitude is non-judgmental, and stems from one's deliberate choice. A loving person is naturally kind with others and does not expect reciprocal treatment from them. A person with this attitude treats others in a loving manner, just because they are unique and valuable human beings.

According to Von Hildebrand (2009), a loving person tends to be warm-hearted and generous with others and also assumes the best of people, even when they have not shown any benevolent qualities. To put it simply, people with a loving attitude toward others tend to have positive assumptions regarding them. Schein (2009) observed that assumptions about others are a relevant factor of any organisation's corporate culture. Moreover, corporate culture includes shared and implicit assumptions which set specific ways of thinking, feeling, and perceiving in relation to the company's adaptation to the external environment and the integration within the organisation.

Therefore, when people working for a company have positive assumptions about others inside (personnel) and outside (suppliers, customers, etc.) the company, the company's culture and the organisation's overall performance are affected in a beneficial way. Besides, people with a loving attitude toward others naturally generate more rapport with them and their relationships with them are strengthened.

Drucker (1999) observed that "Manners are the lubricating oil of an organization." This scholar concluded that saying "thank you" and "please" to others, calling them by their name, and asking about their families helps people relate to one another in a better way. These are just a few examples related to a loving attitude toward others. Loving people are always easier to deal with, because they tend to shorten the distance with others, and seek mutually beneficial agreements with them. When there is a widespread loving attitude toward others in an organisation, this company is prone to act as follows:

- The organisation does not attempt to deceive customers or manipulate them. Instead, this company continually cares for its customers and guides them to make their best buying decisions.
- The company does not consider other organisations as enemies to defeat. Instead, these companies are considered as valuable sources of information, and oftentimes potential partners.
- The organisation does not de-skill its employees with monotonous and repetitive work. Instead, the company allocates diversified tasks to its employees and encourages them to learn new valuable skills continuously. The organisation tends to assign its employees tasks aligned with their talents and capabilities.
- This company does not have high profits as its sole objective, but also sets relevant social goals, such as supporting communities, caring for the environment, and contributing to a better world, among others. These companies are less calculating and more generous than others. Kay (2011) observed these purpose-driven organisations tend to be more successful than other organisations.

- The company avoids exploiting employees or just paying them enough to get by. Instead companies are proud of paying their employees fairly, which in turn increases their employees' satisfaction and productivity. This type of company makes sure that all their personnel's significant needs are covered, so they can live with dignity.
- This organisation does not treat employees as a means to an end to achieve company objectives. In other words, employees are never considered replaceable cogs in the company's machinery, but instead as valuable resources to be appreciated for their individual distinctiveness.
- This company looks for more natural, hearty, and personal ways to communicate with its main stakeholders. Therefore, this organisation avoids the exclusive use of technology (emailing, phone, etc.) to get in contact with its stakeholders. Formal ways of communication (meetings, protocols, appointments, etc.) are used alongside informal channels (for instance, casual chats, social events) in order to develop deeper bonds with stakeholders.

A company with a loving attitude tends to use quality data (research, focus groups, etc.) to make decisions, but is also open to act on intuitive insights, instinct, or inspiration. This company sets in force rules and procedures to act in specific ways, but is also open to acting in an adaptive and innovative manner, especially in changing circumstances.

A company's people should not wait for others to start adopting a loving attitude. They should start themselves with this change and observe the ripple effects pervading the rest of the organisation and its external stakeholders. A company's people should frequently ask themselves a very relevant question: "Is love present in the business environment?"

Questions for Self-Reflection

- How does love relate to our organisation's activities?
- How can we be more loving toward our stakeholders?
- Which fears are hindering our organisation's performance?
- How can love improve our business activities?

Chapter 6

Stakeholders and Love

The essence of love is not what we think or do or provide for others, but how much we give of ourselves.

Rick Warren

6.1 How to Treat Different Stakeholders with Love

Darkness cannot drive out darkness; only light can do that. Hate cannot drive out hate; only love can do that.

Martin Luther King Jr.

In the business environment, love is commonly seen as a feeling totally alien to the cultures of most organisations. Some renowned authors have even observed that love could undermine important business variables or Key Performance Indicators (e.g., productivity, quality levels, competitiveness, efficiency, etc.). Most companies focus on improving these indicators, instead of centring on love. It is important to pinpoint that these indicators are always the result of the interactions of an organisation and its internal and external stakeholders. Therefore, when a company adopts a loving attitude toward its stakeholders, these indicators tend to improve naturally.

An organisation with a loving attitude develops continuous goodwill and mutually beneficial relationships with all its relevant stakeholders; this company is more likely to succeed in the business arena. Stakeholders are individuals and organisations with an interest in the company; they can be external (e.g., suppliers, intermediaries, competitors, communities, media, government, etc.) or internal (management and the rest of the employees). All stakeholders have their distinctive objectives and agendas.

A company which develops beneficial relationships with its stakeholders is more likely to be supported by them when needed. When a company acts in a considerate manner with stakeholders, they tend to respond in a reciprocal fashion. In order to strengthen its bonds with its stakeholders, an organisation should identify their distinct needs and expectations in order to cater for them in the most effective way.

Some specific tools (e.g., meetings, open telephone lines, emails, surveys, focus groups, etc.) can be used to discover stakeholders' specific interests. A company should always take into account stakeholders' unique needs when it develops its strategies and makes relevant business decisions. When a company continually cares for its stakeholders, its public image tends to improve significantly.

Sometimes the company discovers that its employees must be trained in order to meet its stakeholders' expectations properly. Oftentimes, the participation of employees from different departments (marketing, finance, etc.) is necessary to meet stakeholders' expectations.

With some stakeholders, a company has formal bonds (for example, suppliers); with other stakeholders, the organisation could have more informal ties (for instance, the community). In some cases, the company can engage stakeholders, by consulting them or deciding with them, before taking specific actions, especially in situations with potential significant impact on these stakeholders. In other cases, the company makes decisions and then informs or educates stakeholders about the actions taken. In all cases, actions performed by the company should take into consideration the plurality of interests of its stakeholders.

When a company adopts a loving attitude, all its activities (e.g., buying, selling, developing, and launching new products, etc.) are based on the development of mutually beneficial relationships with internal and external stakeholders. Strong relationships with stakeholders are always a relevant source of power, which gives an organisation an edge in the marketplace.

A company with a loving attitude performs business activities which do not benefit some stakeholders at the expense of others. This type of organisation, for instance, offers quality products to customers, pays good salaries to employees, develops fair agreements with suppliers and also adopts a caring attitude for the environment. In this case the company cares for the well-being of all its stakeholders (customers, employees, suppliers, and community); no stakeholder is considered more valuable than the others.

Kofman (2013) observed that there are three dimensions to be considered by any organisation regarding its endeavours: the "I" dimension, whose focus is on a personal or individual level; the "We" dimension, which is focused on relationships between a person (or organisation) and others; and the "It" dimension, which takes into account the organisation as a whole. Therefore, when a company nurtures its relationships with its stakeholders, it is adopting the "We" dimension. This author also stated that companies which develop the "We" dimension tend to adopt an attitude of solidarity and connectedness with their most relevant stakeholders.

6.2 Towards a Wider Definition of Love

As seen previously, outside the business environment, people naturally feel love toward others (friends, relatives, partners, etc.). Many people also effortlessly experience love toward animals, plants, things, places, objects, ideas, and experiences. This type of love does not *exist a priori*; people are prompted to feel love *in response* to a specific target (person, thing, place, etc.).

In this book, the definition of love is wider; it includes the general attitude of connection and genuine care for others. In a company, it implies that people adopt a deliberate and *a priori* loving attitude toward *all* individuals in the business environment. This standpoint is based on the assumption that all people deserve to be loved; they are intrinsically loveable. A person who adopts a purposeful loving attitude toward everyone relates to them in a more meaningful and deeper manner.

This proactive and non-judgemental type of love is called "unconditional love," or "love for no reason." People with this loving attitude toward others do not expect anything in return from them. This is love toward anyone, without any motive, regardless of who they are and what they do.

Fromm (1956) observed that "To love one's flesh and blood is no achievement … only in the love of those who do not serve a purpose, love begins to unfold." Metaphorically speaking, this type of love is like a rose which spreads its fragrance to be enjoyed by everyone around it, regardless of their condition or attitude.

A person with this loving attitude focuses mostly on the good qualities of others. This love is kind, forgiving, inclusive, grateful, generous, compassionate, caring, and supportive. This love is also trusting, non-judgemental and undemanding. People with a loving attitude toward others can connect to the human side of each person inside and outside an organisation. When people working for a company adopt this loving attitude toward all stakeholders, the latter are more prone to feel acknowledged, recognised, and appreciated. Consequently, a loving attitude creates an atmosphere of deeper communion among people, which in turn improves business activities in a more effortless fashion.

A very important aspect of a loving attitude is affection. When people are truly affectionate with others, they relate to them in a respectful and caring manner. A loving person avoids any negative form when addressing others (e.g., slandering, gossiping, criticising, guilt-tripping, etc.), but makes continuous and supportive comments to them, especially when they go through challenging times. A loving person makes others feel at peace with themselves and in their own skins, which also makes them more co-operative and easier to deal with. On the contrary, when people are not treated lovingly, they are very prone to behave in an anxious, restless, scared, and even aggressive manner.

In relation to this, Baumeister et al. (2001) observed that a person's positive (loving) behaviour toward others (e.g., smiling, listening to them, etc.) will not affect the relationships with them as much as when this individual decreases negative (unloving) behaviour toward others (e.g., stopping frowning at them or avoiding insulting them). Gottman (1994) also concluded that a relationship can only succeed when the participants' positive interactions outnumber the negative ones by at least five to one.

When a company adopts a loving attitude toward others, its conflicts with them are handled in a more peaceful and conciliatory fashion. A loving attitude helps people consider the interests of everyone involved in a conflicting situation. Loving people are more open to consider diverse perspectives on a topic, as these views enrich its discussion and understanding.

A loving attitude is the great pacifier and harmoniser of a company's relationships with its stakeholders. Moreover, when a company's people adopt a continuous loving attitude, they will try to prevent any potential disagreements with other stakeholders. According to their research study, Barsade and O'Neill (2014) have observed that the adoption of a loving attitude in the workplace brings about very tangible positive results such as increased customer satisfaction, higher employee satisfaction, lower absenteeism and turnover, and decreased stress levels, among others.

Another relevant characteristic of this loving attitude is authenticity. In a company, when people adopt a loving attitude, they become more credible and trustworthy in the eyes of others. A true loving attitude always comes from the heart, and it makes interactions with others smoother and more truthful.

In an organisation, people with a loving attitude communicate with others more deeply, going beyond rigid social masks, business personas, or work roles. A person with a loving attitude encourages others to show themselves as they truly are, with their strengths and talents and their insecurities and vulnerabilities. In a loving environment, people can communicate their needs and viewpoints more openly without the fear of being criticised. Loving people understand that relationships can only prosper when all parts have their needs fulfilled.

The development of loving relationships is never a one-off attempt, but a continuous process. In other words, all of a company's relationships should be continually nurtured and strengthened; they are like plants that must be regularly watered to grow stronger. In a company, people with a loving attitude continually ask themselves "Does our attitude toward others contribute to a more loving relationship with them?" and "Are we infusing more love to people related to us?", among others.

A company's people with a loving attitude are more emotionally intelligent. According to Goleman (1996, 1998), emotional intelligence not only includes the awareness and regulation of one's own emotions, but also management of relationships and social awareness or empathy. According to Gardner (2006), the capability to relate to others in a loving manner can be included as a relevant skill related to interpersonal intelligence, which implies the capabilities to relate to others effectively. This author observed that this type of intelligence "builds on a core capacity to notice distinctions among others – in particular, contrasts in their moods, temperament and motivations" which allows people to "read the intentions and desires of others, even when they have been hidden."

Lastly, in the business world, there is a well-known classification of skills: hard skills and soft skills. From this perspective, on the one side, hard skills are the specific knowledge (tools, techniques, concepts, frameworks, skills) necessary to be effective in a certain discipline (marketing, logistics, management, etc.). On the other side, soft skills are the set of personal qualities and capabilities necessary to relate to other people in a better manner.

These soft skills include, among others, flexibility, integrity, commitment, communication, leadership, teamwork, and work ethic. From this standpoint, the capability of adopting a loving attitude toward others can be included in the group of soft skills. Both type of skills (soft and hard skills) are necessary to be successful in the work and business environments.

6.3 Main Reasons to Be More Loving with Stakeholders

To love one person with a private love is poor and miserable; to love all is glorious.

Thomas Traherne

People might find it challenging to adopt a loving attitude toward others, especially when others behave in a deceptive or manipulative manner. The default response toward these behaviours is prone to be a defensive one, instead of a loving one. Some psychological schools of thought opine that adopting a loving attitude toward others can always be learnt. It can be mastered like any other life skill, with continuous practice and commitment in order to become a positive habit.

In relation to this, Assagioli (1974) observed that people can master a loving attitude toward others in the same way as in any artistic expression: love needs patience, persistence, and discipline. According to this author, when people adopt a loving attitude, they are intervening actively and committing themselves to treat others lovingly.

Bodian (2006) observed that people might find it more difficult adopting a loving attitude toward others, especially when the former regularly behave in a reactive manner toward the latter. Some examples of this reactive behaviour are: being resentful, jealous, suspicious, fearful, or angry with other people. All these reactive responses tend to preclude all possible love being given to others.

According to Salzberg (2014), some individuals have difficulties to adopt a loving attitude toward others because they tend to be continually self-centred and preoccupied, which prompts them to interact with others only using a "veneer of civility." Instead, when people behave in a generous, understanding, co-operative, and thankful way with others, the former tends to find it easier to adopt a loving attitude toward the latter (Salzberg, 1995).

Some spiritual perspectives also state that all people, beyond their outer appearances, are living expressions of love. All people are full of love to give to themselves and others; moreover, people have the need to express their love to others. The expression of love is applicable to any context, including the business environment. In a company, there are several reasons for adopting a loving attitude toward its stakeholders:

- **Reciprocal response:** In social psychology, the principle of reciprocity affects all social interactions. According to this principle, if a person adopts a loving attitude to others, the latter tend to feel compelled to respond to the former in a loving manner. The opposite also applies; if a person relates to others in a harsh and uncaring manner, they are prone to adopt an unloving attitude toward this individual.

- **Positive colouring:** When people experience positive emotions toward others, such as the ones stemming from a loving attitude, the thoughts and actions of the former tend be affected positively. People with a loving attitude tend to have a wider, more lively and vibrant perception of the circumstances affecting them. These individuals are more inclined to connect to others, because any defensive behaviour of the former tends to be cast aside.

- **Like attracts like:** Another well-known principle states that "what you focus on, becomes augmented." In practical terms, when a person adopts a loving attitude toward others, this individual tends to attract loving circumstances, people, and situations. The opposite happens when a person has an unloving attitude toward other people. Dr Hawkins (2012) observed that feelings are in fact energy which send out a vibration – "we are sending and receiving stations" – therefore, "the more we love, the more we find ourselves surrounded by love."

- **Heightening of consciousness:** The aforementioned scientist stated that love represents one of the highest states of consciousness, above fear, greed, anger, or any other lower states. This scholar also observed that when people express their love to others, this lofty state can effortlessly transform lower consciousness states (for example, fear) in a myriad of people around them.

- **Interconnectedness:** Some spiritual standpoints have observed that all people are interconnected; seeming separation from one another is an egoic illusion. From a systemic perspective, people are naturally interdependent, like components or parts of the same system. A system is set of components which relate to one another. From this perspective, every time people adopt a loving attitude toward others, they end up experiencing this very love themselves. The systemic perspective of relationships will be explored more thoroughly later on in this chapter.

- **Acknowledgement of others:** A loving attitude toward others is a fundamental way of recognising them as valuable human beings, with special and unique qualities. Likewise, Maturana and Bunnel (1998) observed that "love is the domain of those relational behaviours through which another (a person, being, or thing) arises as a legitimate other in coexistence with oneself." Instead, when a person is unloving with others, this individual is negating them as valid individuals.

- **Enhanced mental capabilities:** Research backs the fact that love constitutes a generative and expansive energy, which helps people harness their innermost mental capabilities (analysis, synthesis, combining, comparing, and contrasting, etc.). The aforementioned scholars also concluded that the majority of problems experienced by companies can be sorted out through love, because when people experience this enabling state, their intelligence and creativity are naturally expanded.

- **Increased trust and co-operation:** Many people are naturally cautious with others, especially when they do not know each other well, or the actions of one can affect the former on a personal level. A person with an unloving attitude tends to behave in a deceptive, disrespectful, unfair, or manipulative manner with others, which makes this individual untrustworthy in their eyes. In those cases, these people might even perceive that the unloving person aims to harm them, which makes them behave in a less co-operative manner with this individual. The opposite happens when a person adopts a loving attitude; in this case, others are more willing to co-operate with this individual.
- **Contagious effect:** Goleman (1996, 1998) stated that all emotions a person feels when interacting with others are likely to be mimicked by them. This transference of emotional states is due to the existence of the so-called "mirror neurons" in the human brain (Goleman, 2006). The main function of these neural cells is to replicate the emotions experienced by others in social interactions. As a consequence, when a person adopts a loving attitude toward others, they tend to naturally experience the same emotional state (love) as this individual because of their mirror neurons. In other words, a loving attitude is contagious and contributes to improve the work and business environments.

Likewise, Fredrickson (2013) observed that, people who adopt a loving attitude toward others brings positive resonance, which means not only that the former share their positive emotions with the latter, but also that the behaviour and biochemistry of the former become in sync with the behaviour and biochemistry of the latter. From the physiological perspective, people with a loving attitude toward others are also prone to experience a state of warmth, calm, ease, and openness in the area of their chests.

6.4 Main Aspects of a Loving Attitude to Stakeholders

> Love is not a problem, not an answer to a question. Love knows no question. It is the ground of all, and questions arise only insofar as we are divided, absent, estranged, alienated from that ground.
>
> **Thomas Merton**

6.4.1 Mutual Satisfaction of Needs

Thriving relationships are always based on the mutual and continual satisfaction of each party's needs. Unilateral gain, unfair agreements, opportunism, and manipulation prevent relationships from prospering and oftentimes lead to a relationship breakup. In any relationship, including business and work ones, members must be continually aware of each other's needs to satisfy them properly. Consequently, each party should be encouraged to communicate their needs to the other.

An organisation should attempt to find a balance between its own needs (for example, achieving a certain level of revenues and profits, reducing costs, improving quality levels, eliciting employees' engagement, etc.) and the needs of its main stakeholders, both external (suppliers, intermediaries, community, etc.) and internal (employees, management). Oftentimes, the alignment of these two types of needs (company's needs and stakeholders') can be challenging.

For example, as an employer, an organisation can satisfy the needs of its employees in different ways, such as paying them a fair salary and providing them with decent work conditions.

When workers' needs are duly satisfied, these employees are more prone to satisfy the needs of the employer, for instance, by co-operating at the workplace and giving their best performance. Instead, when employees' needs are not properly satisfied (e.g., employees are not compensated fairly, or they are not being cared for by the employer), they tend to avoid satisfying the needs of the organisation (for example, they become purposely unproductive or uncollaborative).

In most circumstances, things are not as simple as the previous example. Individuals are multidimensional beings, with a multitude of needs to be satisfied. Maslow (1954) observed that all individuals have different types of needs: basic physiological needs (such as hunger, thirst, and sleep), and more advanced needs related to safety (which includes physical protection, financial security, and health and wellbeing). From this author's perspective, individuals also have social or belonging needs (e.g., relating to others) and esteem needs (which imply self-respect and validation from others).

From this standpoint, there are also self-actualisation needs (which include accomplishing personal dreams and harnessing one's full potential). This author also related this last category of needs to self-transcendence, which implies assisting others altruistically and contributing to a goal bigger than oneself. From this perspective, people cannot satisfy their higher-level needs (for instance, self-actualisation needs) if their lower level needs are unmet (for instance, safety and security needs). Maslow (1968) observed that when an individual adopts an unloving attitude toward others, it is generally because some of this person's relevant needs have not been met.

In a company, employees tend to satisfy several of the needs in Maslow's model. For example, the paying of economic compensation (salary, etc.) is prone to satisfy employees' physiological needs (such as, hunger, thirst, etc.). When employees work in a safe and secure workplace, their safety needs are likely to be met. The existence of a friendly, warm, and co-operative work environment tends to satisfy employees' social and belonging needs.

In this example, when employees are praised and thanked for their contribution to the company, their self-esteem can be met. When employees are offered opportunities to thrive in the company, for example, through job promotions, their need for self-actualisation may be catered for. When people feel they are contributing to the company's mission in a meaningful manner, their needs for self-transcendence are met. These are just examples relating to employees, but a company must apply the same perspective for all the rest of its main stakeholders (suppliers, customers, suppliers, community, etc.).

Alderfer (1972) developed a model called ERG to classify Maslow needs into three categories, and it includes needs, such as existence, relatedness, and growth. From this perspective, the existence needs include safety and physiological needs; the relatedness needs include social needs and certain esteem needs, especially the need to develop relationships with others; and growth needs include self-esteem and self-actualisation needs (McKenna, 2012a). This author observed that none of these types of needs takes precedence over the other, and that an activity (for example, working for a company) can satisfy many needs at the same time (Alderfer, 1972).

Some authors like Sirgy and Lee (2018) observed that, in general, people always look for a balanced satisfaction of all their needs. These authors also observed that individuals are more prone to achieve life balance and an overall state of well-being when they obtain satisfaction from different life domains (e.g., work tasks, family life, community activities, etc.) in an equilibrated manner.

Herzberg (mentioned in De Board, 1978) observed that all individuals have two main needs, which are avoiding discomfort and pain, and developing and growing from the psychological perspective. For example, a company should prevent its employees from experiencing pain and discomfort by setting up a safe and secure workplace.

In this example, organisations can go further and allocate tasks to employees which harness their innermost skills to foster workers' growth and development. Employees can also be acknowledged and praised for their performance for the same purpose. These factors which support employees' development and growth tend to be more motivating than those preventing workers from pain and discomfort.

6.4.2 Other Aspects Regarding Needs' Satisfaction

Some authors like Schwartz et al. (2010) state that all individuals have a wide range of needs related to different aspects: material (related to survival), physical (for example, health and fitness), emotional (e.g., feeling valued and cared of, etc.), mental (for instance, expression of capabilities), and spiritual (for instance, search for meaning). It is possible to include two more types of needs: social (which implies the development of relationships with others) and environmental (which implies relating and caring for the environment).

Employees can have their physical needs satisfied, for instance, through working reasonable hours. Employees' mental needs can be met, for instance, through the performance of stimulating and challenging tasks prompting them to use their mental skills. Employees' spiritual needs can be met by making them feel that they are making a meaningful contribution to a relevant social cause with their work. Employees' emotional needs can be met when they are appreciated by the company.

Following this example, employees can meet their social needs with a warm and friendly work environment where they can relate to others, such as colleagues and management. In relation to employees' environmental needs, employees can perform tasks contributing to a more sustainable world, for instance, when they perform environmentally friendly activities (e.g., recycling, use of "green" packaging, etc.) for the company they work for.

Some authors like Robbins (2014) argue that all individuals have six specific types of needs which are: search for certainty (or stability), quest for change (or uncertainty), search for one's growth, quest for one's uniqueness and specialness, the need for connection with others, and the quest for making a relevant contribution.

From this perspective, employees might find their needs for stability are met with their monthly pay cheque, and their need for change can be met when they are continually assigned varying and novel tasks, not repetitive ones. Employees can meet their needs for growth when they are offered the chance to be promoted, or work on more advanced tasks. Employees' need for uniqueness can be met when they are being rewarded for their distinctive attributes and contribution to the company they work for.

Employees' need for connection can be satisfied when they develop more meaningful relationships with their colleagues in their company. Lastly, employees can satisfy their need for contribution when they feel their work activities meaningfully create a significant change for society in a direct or indirect manner. Management, when possible, should explain to employees about the relevant value the latter add to society.

Other schools of thought include other needs, for example, the need for expression, the need for autonomy, and the need for physical possession of material goods. Some research has observed that individuals have a need for power, which means influencing or persuading others, which can be used in a benevolent or manipulative manner; this need is closely related to the need for respect and recognition from others. This need is also closely related to the concept of organisational politics, which will be discussed in Chapter 10.

In most cases, these additional needs can be subsumed in the previous categories. In the previous example, employees' need for expression can be met when they have a voice in some of the company's relevant work projects. Employees' need for autonomy can be satisfied when they are empowered to make significant decisions at work without any superior's authorisation. Employees' need for possession of material goods might be met when they have their own desks in the workplace where they can work at ease. Employees' need for power and recognition can be satisfied when an employee is promoted to a higher position.

Lastly, some scholars observed there are only two types of needs: the need for material things (for example, in the case of employees, their need for economic compensation, their need for a safe and secure workplace) and the need for immaterial things (in the example of employees, their need for frequent recognition, their need for improving their skills, their need for contribution to a bigger cause, their need for social bonding, etc.). Nonetheless, it is argued that all needs for material things also have an underlying intangible aspect. For example, in the example of the material need for economic compensation, there is an intangible need to feel financially secure and economically confident, which is evidently intangible.

6.4.3 The Overarching Need for Love

> Love is an incurable disease. No one who catches it wants to recover and all its victims refuse a cure.
>
> **Ibn Hazim**

6.4.3.1 Love Underpins All Other Needs

Stakeholders have a myriad of needs, which must be met in order to develop long-term and mutually beneficial relationships with them. All their main needs (not just some of them) must be satisfied in order for relationships with these stakeholders to prosper. For example, if employees are only offered economic compensation for their work (salary, bonus, etc.), but their other needs (such as feeling understood, heard and respected, etc.) are not properly met, the relationships with these stakeholders are unlikely to thrive. A company should use the same approach with other stakeholders; each stakeholder's needs must be met adequately, while pursuing the organisation's objectives.

There is an overarching need that most needs directly or indirectly relate to: the need for love. This need includes the need to love others and the need to be loved by them. Montagu (1957) observed that all "needs must be satisfied in a particular manner, in a manner which is emotionally and physical satisfying" and that "the basis of all social life has its roots in this integral of all basic needs which is the need for security, and the only way it can be satisfied is by love." The term "love" is used here from a wider perspective, which includes appreciation, recognition, keenness, preference, collaboration, care, support, and other similar connotations.

Sometimes this need is overtly expressed as such, but it is often subtler. For example, when employees look for recognition and appreciation from their superiors, the former look for expressions of love from the latter. In that sense, recognition and appreciation are qualities directly derived from love.

A company which offers products and services to its customers in the marketplace always looks for the acceptance of these offerings by these customers. In other words, this company desires that customers love its products and services. At the same time, every time customers buy any product or service from an organisation over others, they do so because they love this very product or service. To put it differently, their custom is the way that customers express their love for certain goods and services, and in turn, for the organisation offering them.

Each time an organisation searches for a mutually profitable agreement (win–win) with others (customers, suppliers, intermediaries, etc.), this company aims to fairly consider the other party's needs, not only its own ones. The recognition and discussion of the other party's needs implies adopting a loving attitude toward this very party.

Another example of this is when a company donates funds for a relevant social cause; this generous and supportive attitude is a way for this organisation to express its love to the community. Lastly, when sales people provide customers with the best advice according to the needs of the latter, the supportive and sympathetic attitude of these sales people toward customers is a way to express love to these customers.

Consequently, the need for love is extremely relevant not only inside a company, but also outside it. In a similar vein, Wiest (2013) observed that through most of their actions, people aim to earn love from others. Several scientific studies corroborated that babies without love are prone to die or suffer from serious illnesses. This need to be loved is not exclusive to babies, but applies to everyone. To sum up, all people, without exception, have the basic need to be loved by others and to love them, which is covertly or overtly related to other needs.

Some specialists observed that love is also closely related to the enhancement of mental skills. To that effect, Buzan (2000) concluded that the human brain's needs are: biological nutrition, oxygen, and information, but also love. Consequently, when people have loving relationships with others, this will impact on their mental capabilities in a positive manner.

6.4.3.2 Love Is Developing Affinity Bonds with Others

People are naturally gregarious, which means that they are intrinsically social. Affinity is the drive to develop connections with others. Nardi (2005) observed that "affinity is achieved through activities of social bonding in which people come to feel connected with one another, readying them for further communication." Ornish (1999) observed that lonely people have a chance of disease and premature death up to 500 per cent higher as compared with people who regularly relate to others. The need to relate to others is directly related to love.

Montagu (1957) stated that love "is the principal developer of qualities for being human, it is the chief stimulus to the development of social competence." This author also observed that love is "the only quality of the world capable of producing a sense of belonging and relatedness to the world of humanity that every human being desires and develops."

People satisfy their affinity need by joining groups and collective projects. Social psychologists observed that when people belong to a group, they feel acknowledged, understood, validated, and supported by this group. Their personal identities are connected to the group they belong to. A group can also give meaning to its members' lives, especially when the group undertakes activities that have a positive social impact.

In a similar tone, Baumeister and Leary (1995) suggested that people have a need of belongingness that implies looking for regular, positive, and stable relationships with others, in which they show mutual affective concern, support, and care for the welfare of one another. These authors also stated that the development of these relationships tends to be related to positive emotional states (e.g., peacefulness, happiness, etc.), whereas the deprivation of these relationships or threats against them could bring about stress and anxiety, as well as other physical and mental problems.

Hamilton (2010) concluded that this need to belong is purely biological; there is a hormone called oxytocin which prompts human beings to gather together and develop relationships with others. This author further observed that this hormone is also responsible for people's tendency to behave in a compassionate and caring manner with others.

Fredrickson (2013) stated that oxytocin also creates a "calm-and connect response." Zak (2013) called oxytocin the "moral molecule"; its release makes people experience positive emotional states and reinforces their prosocial behaviour (such as caring for others, collaborating with them, etc.). This scientist also said that when a person is being trusted by others, this individual has a rush of oxytocin, which makes this individual feel good. This prompts this person to respond to others in a reciprocal manner.

In a company, employees can satisfy their need for affinity, for example, by participating in collective team projects. Employees who perform these collective activities tend to develop stronger bonds with the other participants. Another way of meeting the affinity need is by inviting employees to company meetings so that they can give their opinions on relevant projects regarding the company's destiny.

A company can satisfy the affinity need of its suppliers and intermediaries (wholesalers, retailers, etc.), when this organisation is in continuous contact with them and makes them feel they are valuable contributors to the process of adding significant value to customers. For example, a company can satisfy its suppliers' affinity need when it praises them for the quality of the raw material they provide. Sometimes these suppliers' needs can also be satisfied when a company gives them kind advice on how to improve their quality levels.

In the case of retailers, a company can satisfy their affinity needs by being thankful with them for their contribution to the promotion of its products. Oftentimes, the affinity need of these retail outlets can be met when the company offers them recommendations on how to show its products to customers in a more attractive manner.

A company also satisfies customers' belonging needs when they are offered products with the highest value possible and also when they are given valuable suggestions regarding products and services meeting their specific preferences. Customers who bought a product from a company that met their expectations form part of the group of satisfied buyers; these customers tend to be proud of being connected to the company and its products. These customers are more inclined to support the company, and in turn promote its products to potential customers, prompting them to try these very products.

Satisfied customers are in love with the company's offerings and they want to share this love with others: friends, colleagues, acquaintances, etc. These customers, for example, might even write positive reviews online about a company's products; their unsolicited endorsement is called "word of mouth," and it is more credible than other forms of promotion, such as advertising, or promotional discounts. Solomon et al. (2006) observed that nowadays word of mouth becomes more relevant due to "the decline in people's faith in institutions."

6.4.3.3 Love Is Harmonising Relationships with Others

> Love has a warming effect even on the coldest of hearts.
>
> **Bernie Siegel**

Love is a natural harmoniser of relationships, even business ones. A person with a loving attitude toward others prompts them to put any defensive response aside. This makes the person's interactions with others smoother and more graceful, and the relationships with them tend to become stronger. Research concluded that when people have a more harmonious and loving relationship with others, their creative skills are enhanced, and their productivity and co-operation increased. However, an unloving person tends to make others feel unappreciated, undervalued, and even disrespected, which weakens the relationships with them over time.

Sometimes a company adopts an unloving attitude toward its stakeholders by being careless, ungrateful, or manipulative. In these cases, the company's relationships with these stakeholders deteriorate, even when their economic needs (for instance, fair compensation) are fairly satisfied by the company. If stakeholders' non-economic needs (for example, feeling acknowledged and appreciated by the company) are not met, these stakeholders tend to experience negative emotions (fear, resentment, etc.), which negatively affects their relationships with this organisation.

Oftentimes, a company's non-loving attitude toward its main stakeholders is a negative habit, which can be changed. Most companies tend to focus excessively on solving short-term problems (for example, paying the bills, dealing with suppliers, obtaining more customers, etc.) and do not take the time to develop long-term loving relationships with their stakeholders. These companies tend to be so overwhelmed with the urgent matters that it prevents them from adopting a loving attitude toward others.

Therefore, people working for a company should frequently ask themselves "How can I be more loving in this relationship?" and "How can I make this relationship closer for both parties?" This type of question raises people's awareness and provides them with insights into how to develop more loving relationships with other stakeholders. The insights garnered from these questions can also help people to connect to the human side of others more deeply. Most business and work relationships only scratch the surface of their potential purposefulness and meaningfulness.

When people adopt a loving attitude toward others, their relationships are harmonised because these people can feel comfortable and at ease. A person working for a company who adopts a loving attitude toward others tends to avoid, when possible, confrontations or disputes with them. If any conflict with these stakeholders arises, the issue tends to be resolved in the most amicable manner; any adversarial ways to tackle this conflict (lawsuits, etc.) are avoided. The use of aggressive approaches, such as threats and ultimatums, to handle the conflicting situations is also put aside.

A conflict between people always implies that their needs are not fully satisfied. From this perspective, the most effective way to solve any conflictive situation for the parties involved is to work out an agreement which duly contemplates their needs. These agreements – called win–win, where no party wins at the expense of the other – are only possible when the parties adopt a loving attitude to one another. This type of agreement makes both parties feel at ease and more connected with each other, which strengthens their relationship over time.

In order to develop win–win solutions to conflicts with others, people working for a company should ask themselves questions like "What are my needs in relation to this stakeholder?", "What are this stakeholder's needs in relation to me?", and "How can the needs of both parties be duly satisfied?" Sometimes, a person really does not know the needs of a stakeholder. In those cases, one can ask this stakeholder questions such as "What are your relevant needs that are not being met in this situation?" and "What solutions do you suggest in order to have your needs satisfied?", among others.

6.4.3.4 Love Is Recognising and Validating Others

> When you are socially intelligent, you understand and appreciate the very different personalities you meet, as well as what motivates them, what their personal needs are, and how you as an individual can make them comfortable and pleased with you.
>
> **Tony Buzan**

A person with a loving attitude shows interest in others. When a person displays interest in others, this individual is not self-centred, but focused on them. Honest interest in other people implies wishing the best for them and trying to meet their unique innermost needs in the best way possible.

In other words, when people adopt a loving attitude toward others, they are more naturally selfless and also more generous to them. Genuine concern and care for others impacts positively on their sense of self-worth. This loving attitude also contributes to making relationships with others stronger over time. A significant question that people should regularly ask themselves is "How can I be more interested in this person?"

For example, an employer can become more interested in their employees by holding frequent meetings with them in order to know their unique value, interests, dreams, and aspirations. In these interactions, employees can also be asked to express their fears and challenges, as well as their recommendations regarding aspects of the company that need improvement. These encounters also help an employer connect to the human side of its employees, which makes them feel more valued by the company. When duly acknowledged, these employees are more inclined to engage with a company's undertakings and projects in a more co-operative manner.

All people need to feel they are relevant to others, that their unique traits and capabilities really count. Employers can satisfy this relevant need by regularly telling their employees that their contribution to the company's success is fundamental. An employer can even explain the specific reasons as to why an employee's activities are valuable for the company. This is a significant way to express love to the company's employees and validate them as worthy human beings. This loving perspective can be applied to any of the company's stakeholders (suppliers, intermediaries, etc.).

In order to validate stakeholders on a frequent basis, a company's people should ask themselves "What do I appreciate in relation to this stakeholder?" This type of question prompts people to focus on the positive aspects of others around them, instead of being self-centred. This question is useful to gather insights into how to relate to others in a kinder, more appreciative, and more humane manner. These insights usually prompt people to overtly express their appreciation to others, which in turn contributes to the development of more meaningful and purposeful relationships with them.

6.4.3.5 Love Is Exploring Commonalities with Others

> The human side is the interesting thing ... People aren't interested in "cold" facts.
> They want to know you are human.
>
> **David Schwartz**

Research shows that when two individuals discover they have some aspects in common (for example, country of origin, preferences, hobbies, values, etc.) these commonalities naturally create a stronger bond between them. Therefore, a very effective way to develop stronger relationships with others is to explore and look for shared aspects with them.

Most people, by default, tend to focus on distinct aspects regarding others (for instance, different opinions, diverse preferences, etc.), instead of looking for similar aspects with them. When a person focuses on dissimilarities regarding others, these differences tend to separate this individual from these very people instead of creating stronger bonds with them. This perspective of separation (and its close neighbours, discrimination and segregation) are always detrimental to the development of fruitful relationships.

When an individual finds common aspects (experiences, beliefs, values, preferences, etc.), even seemingly trivial ones, with another, a sense of communion and belongingness is spontaneously developed. It is important to pinpoint that a person who looks for commonalities with other people when interacting with them does not have to forsake his unique views and qualities.

The search for commonalities with other people has the objective of setting a basis which improves the sense of togetherness and rapport between these individuals. These shared aspects help people shorten the distance with others, especially when they have different social façades (roles, economic position, etc.). Social psychology research has corroborated the theory that similarity of attitudes and values develops more affinity between people.

When people find common ground, they are also more likely to drop any defensive mental responses toward one another; their conversations also tend to flow more gracefully and flowingly. Consequently, every time people interact with others, they should mentally ask themselves questions like "What do I have in common with this individual?", "How can these commonalities bring about a closer and deeper relationship between us?", and similar ones.

From a wider perspective, all human beings share their human side or humanness with others. For example, all individuals, with no exceptions, are affected by both positive and negative thoughts and emotions. Likewise, all people have dreams and expectations, but also fears and moments of tribulation. With no exceptions, all people feel confident about certain tasks, and doubtful about others.

As part of their humanness, all individuals have weaknesses and strengths; people are "a work in progress" on their way to improve and develop their potential. Psychologically speaking, all individuals try to do their best, according to the knowledge available to them at each moment, the specific circumstances affecting them, and their past experiences.

All people are continually learning, knowingly or unwittingly, how to become better human beings, and they do so *by living*, through their varying attainments and failings. When people bear in mind the aforementioned aspects when relating with others, they will find it easier to find common ground with them and also be more loving to them.

6.4.3.6 Love Is Praising Others

Many companies reward their stakeholders in tangible or material ways, for example, offering discounts to retailers, or bonuses to employees. However, there is a more meaningful way to recognise and validate others: giving them compliments. Compliments can be defined as the positive evaluation a person explicitly makes of other people, but praising can also be considered an expression of love for others. Oftentimes, these psychological rewards bring more satisfaction to the receiver than tangible rewards.

According to Leech (1983), an important maxim for conversations states that people should increase comments which imply the approval of others (praises) and also decrease comments implying their disapproval (dispraise). Likewise, Schwartz (1979) observed that *"people do more for you when you make them feel important."* In a similar vein, Lieberman (2001) observed that when a person compliments others, the receivers of the compliments tend to like and respect this individual more and their connection becomes stronger.

People love to receive honest praise from others because these compliments make them feel good about themselves and boost their self-esteem. Moreover, research has concluded that praises to others can improve their performance. Figuratively speaking, compliments are keys opening the doors to any relationship, even those that have been slammed shut.

When a person does not praise others, this individual is generally taking them for granted. The easiest way to take up the positive habit of praising others is to notice anything interesting in them, even minimal. Compliments to others should always be authentic; people should avoid complimenting others out of duty or political correctness. Consequently, formal compliments to ingratiate oneself with others should be avoided.

Whenever possible, praising should be specific. Some ways to deliver kudos to people are: "Thank you for … (explaining the reasons this person is thanked for)," "I am very delighted because you …," "Our company is pleased that you …." A person should say these sentences in a warm and friendly tone. In some cases, the compliments can be implied or more indirect, for example, "You seem to be doing a very good job because …."

Some psychologists suggest that the person delivering the compliment should not be included in it. For example, the compliment "You contributed to …" is preferable to the compliment "I love that you contributed to …" to place the focus on the person receiving the kudos. Nonetheless, other specialists observed that when the person delivering the compliment is included in it, the kudos is valid and it has a more appreciative tone. From the perspective of this book, the last option is more advisable, because it indirectly highlights the current relationship between the sender and receiver of the compliment.

Some specialists have observed that kudos to others, when expressed publicly, is more impactful than when it is delivered privately. Novak and Bourg (2016) observed that a company should frequently acknowledge and praise their people for their good ideas, which encourages them to generate more of them. These authors also observed that praising people for their achievements represents an important catalyst for better company's results.

Murray (1964) observed that people have the need for achievement, which implies accomplishing challenging tasks and overcoming problems. Consequently, when a person praises the achievement of others, this individual satisfies this important need. This author also stated that people have the need of succourance, which means being supported, guided, sustained, and loved by others. Therefore, compliments given to others are ways of supporting them, which caters to their succourance need.

A person can deliver a compliment to another, even when the former wants to raise the issue of a mistake made by the latter. In this case, the person should start the contact with the person who made the mistake with some compliments, and later comment on the blunder. When praise is harmoniously dovetailed with constructive criticism, people tend to be more receptive to it.

For example, if an employee made a mistake, the manager can tell this person "You are always … (highlighting positive aspects of the recipient's past performance) and I would like for you to be more attentive to … (kindly explaining the mistake made by the recipient) and try to … (suggestions on how to avoid similar mistakes in the future)."

Dweck (2012) observed that a person should avoid complimenting personal qualities of others (punctuality, tidiness, etc.), but instead praise the process they go through (which includes effort, time, and commitment) to achieve their goals. This approach is related to the so-called "growth mindset." People with a growth mindset believe they can always better themselves; they know their attributes and capacities are not fixed.

From the perspective of a growth mindset, all activities performed by a person are valuable regardless of their results, because committed and continual action contributes to the development of their capabilities. Likewise, Dyer (1976) observed that with sufficient effort and time, people can develop any skill, but to do so, they must make the choice to develop that capability.

For example, sometimes managers want to compliment their employees for their valuable participation in a successful work project. In this case, the manager should never say to the subordinate "You are very capable …" or "You are very co-operative." This type of praise is inappropriate because it highlights the personal qualities of this employee.

Instead, a more appropriate compliment for this situation will be, for example, "You did your best, fully committing your time and giving your best efforts to achieve the results for this project." This praise is not centred on the employee's personal qualities, but on the process of growth and development that this individual went through to contribute to this work project. This type of compliment tends to pinpoint relevant aspects of that process, such as zest, passion, commitment, effort, discipline, etc.

Lastly, Dweck (2012) observed that a person who delivers praise to another should also pinpoint the specific positive impact of the actions of the latter during the process. In the previous example, the manager can say to the employee things like "Your continuous effort produced a complete change in the company's system of sales."

Companies should make a habit of acknowledging the precious value of others and their relevant contribution to business activities. Consequently, the frequent use of sentences like "Our company is very pleased we have you because ..." helps organisations relate to their stakeholders in a more humanised way.

6.4.3.7 Love Is Acknowledging the Emotional Side of Others

All people have positive and negative feelings which are relevant parts of themselves. Consequently, people need to be acknowledged as sensitive human beings by others. Nonetheless, many companies tend to focus primarily on the rational aspects of their stakeholders, dismissing their emotional traits.

Most business people are naturally goal-oriented, which implies the active and continuous use of their analytical skills. Therefore, emotional aspects tend to be considered as hindrances which disrupt levels of performance, productivity, and growth. Consequently, the free expression of emotions is discouraged by most companies.

Companies must realise that human beings are multidimensional, which includes physical, mental, spiritual, and emotional aspects. For instance, many companies tend to exclusively focus on the talents and capabilities brought to work by employees, but only few organisations consider and care for other valuable aspects, such as the various emotional states of these individuals.

In the business environment, most people are reluctant to openly express their feelings to others. When people have unexpressed negative emotions, their perception of reality tends to be detrimentally coloured by these very emotional stakes, which affects their thoughts and actions in a non-constructive manner. Oftentimes, people do not notice the effect of their undisclosed emotions on their perception and interpretation of circumstances and reactions to them. In other words, every time people are not fully aware of their emotional states, these emotions are more prone to control these people's lives.

When a person adopts a loving attitude toward others, this individual encourages them to express their emotional aspects. By acknowledging and understanding these very emotional aspects, people can develop a deeper connection and more meaningful communication with others.

When interacting with others, a person can ask them, for example, "Would you like to tell me how you feel about ...?", or more directly "How do you feel about ...?" These questions welcome emotional aspects of experiences by other people, making them feel more whole as human beings.

The regular use of this type of question also cleans up any "emotional debris" and makes the interactions between both parties more authentic and livelier. These questions empower people to express their feelings in a safe and non-judgemental environment, which makes them feel duly acknowledged as valuable beings who deserve to be understood and cared for.

6.4.3.8 Love Is Respecting Others

All individuals want to be respected when they interact with others. Murray (1964) observed that people have a relevant social need called "infavoidance": they tend to avoid any embarrassing, disrespectful or humiliating circumstances. Consequently, people should always intend to relate to others in a kind, warm, and friendly manner. Maturana and Bunnel (1998) observed that an individual who has a loving attitude toward another accepts and recognise the latter as a legitimate human being.

Any type of condemnatory comments to others like harsh criticism, offensive comments, and snide remarks should be left aside. These negative comments always affect a relationship in a detrimental manner because they negate others as valuable individuals. According to Murray (1964), "defendance" is the need of people to defend themselves from negative comments from other people. These comments tend to be perceived as threats by the receiver, which prompts this person to respond to them defensively. This response is related to the so-called fight-freeze-flight mode analysed in Chapter 3.

According to De Board (1978), when individuals adopt a defensive attitude, their mental energy is mostly used to protect themselves from the threatening factors, which prevents this energy from being used in more productive activities (for instance, analysis, creation, comprehension, etc.). To put it more simply, in defensive mode, a person's analytical and reflective skills tend to shut down or be severely impaired. Therefore, when people feel attacked by comments from others, the performance levels of the former tend to naturally dwindle.

According to Webb (2016), the mental state opposite to the defensive mode is called discovery mode. A person who adopts a discovery mode does not feel endangered and is open to engage in communicational interactions with others. In this mode, this person also becomes naturally curious and thoroughly analytical. The discovery mode makes people become more resourceful, which allows them to approach challenging situations more creatively. The aforementioned author also observed that in this mode, people tend to feel naturally competent, smart, and autonomous.

A person who adopts a respectful attitude toward others welcomes each person's uniqueness and distinctiveness. This type of individual is interested in discovering and exploring people's different perspectives, values, opinions, and preferences. Respectful people always welcome comments from others, even when the comments of the latter differ from the views of the former. An individual with a respectful attitude toward others encourages them to express their uniqueness with phrases such as "Please tell me more about your viewpoint."

When a respectful person has views on a topic which are different from the ones of other people, they say phrases like "I understand your view and I respect it, and I have a different perspective on this topic." This type of individual kindly welcomes and acknowledges different points of view, which does not mean agreeing with them. When a company frequently uses this inclusive approach with its main stakeholders (employees, suppliers, etc.), the relationships with them become stronger over time.

The need for respect is related to a well-known "golden rule," which states: "Treat others as you want to be treated." This widespread rule is sensible and very practical and it has been accepted by the most important religions in the world. A person who applies the golden rule is inclined to adopt an attitude of benevolence and avoid any attitude of malfeasance.

For example, if employees do not feel they are fully cared for, respected, and understood by the company they work for, they tend to behave in a reciprocal manner. In this case, the company is acting in an unloving manner toward its personnel; therefore, these employees will also tend to adopt an unloving attitude toward this company, which implies for example, behaving in an uncooperative manner, and "doing just their job."

In this example, the company's lack of love to its employees has a very tangible effect, which is the decrease in employees' co-operation at work. Their uncooperative attitude, in turn, is likely to affect the company's productivity and quality levels, which can eventually drive profits down. It is important to highlight that the golden rule can be applied not only to a company's employees, but also to other relevant stakeholders (such as suppliers, retailers, customers, community, etc.).

According to Alessandra and O'Connor (1998), the "platinum rule" states that you should always treat others in the way *they* want to be treated. From this perspective, a company should discover the most important and unique needs of each stakeholder in order to cater to these very needs. Companies that use a marketing approach, which implies being customer-oriented, try to thoroughly research their customers' needs in order to meet them in an effective manner, which includes treating them in the way they want to be treated.

Respectful people naturally treat others in a kind and loving manner. Hamilton (2010) observed that people are genetically wired for kindness, which means that kindness is in their genes. This author observed that when people are kind to others, not only will this better their relationships with them, but it will also improve their health condition and mood, slowing down their ageing process.

Not only do people feel respected when they are treated in a kind way, but also when they participate in agreements with others which are fair and reasonable, commonly known as win–win. In these agreements, the needs of both parties are duly acknowledged and considered. People are also more likely to feel respected when they perceive that others are not acting arbitrarily with them, but in a well-justified manner.

In the work and business environments, the concept of respect is closely connected to the term "face." In this context, "face" means a person's self-image in public (or public image). Goffman (1967) observed that face is a person's image of themselves, which is "delineated in terms of approved social attributes." According to this author, people are prone to react emotionally, positively or negatively, regarding their face whenever they interact with other individuals.

A person tends to experience positive emotions in those situations perceived as enhancing the face of this individual. Nonetheless, in circumstances that are perceived to put this individual's face at risk, this person is more prone to experience negative emotional states. The aforementioned author wisely concluded that "as sacred objects, men are subject to slight and profanation" from others (Goffman, 1967).

According to Brown and Levinson (1987), there are two main aspects of a public face: a positive aspect (the desire to be positively perceived, liked, approved, and accepted by others) and a negative aspect (the desire that one's actions are not prevented by others). When any of these two aspects are not duly considered by other people, a person's face is at risk, and the individual might feel disrespected.

These authors also observed some actions of others which can affect people's positive face: ignoring these individuals, overtly disapproving or not valuing their comments, embarrassing and harsh criticism of them, and not allowing them to express their ideas, among others. According to these authors, there are some actions performed by others which can affect a person's negative face, for example, manipulative commands, threats, and ultimatums, refusing to provide help when requested, etc. A person who adopts a loving attitude toward others naturally avoids actions which can potentially threaten the positive or negative face of others.

According to these authors, some valid strategies to protect the negative face of others are, for example: delivering requests in a tactful manner ("Could you please move the chair?") instead of formulating direct requests ("Move the chair now!") and using apologetic words when making requests to others ("Sorry, could you please move a bit ahead?"), among others. These specialists also pinpoint actions to preserve people's positive face, such as considering the person' interests and needs adequately, avoiding disagreements with the individual whenever possible, and allowing the person to partake in important decisions, among others. In relation to this, Goffman (1969) calls the techniques used by people to protect the impression conveyed by others "protective actions" or "tact."

Other examples of actions which can potentially enhance the positive self-image of others are: delivering compliments to them and being publicly appreciative of their contribution. Lastly, a person with a loving attitude toward others naturally respects them and tends to regularly use the aforementioned strategies to save their face.

6.4.3.9 Love Is Having Positive Assumptions about Others

Assumptions are the termites of relationships.

Henry Winkler

Every time a person working for a company meets others for the first time (for instance, new employees, new suppliers, new customers, etc.), this individual should have positive assumptions about them. Whenever a person has positive assumptions regarding others (for instance, this individual assumes they are benevolent, honest, credible, etc.), these assumptions affect the way this person perceives others.

It is interesting to note that people never relate directly with others, but through their own mental representations of these very people. These representations about other people are very subjective, but never precise nor complete. Steiner (1986) stated that our knowledge about others begins with, but cannot go beyond, our representation of them. These mental representations can have different names, for instance, assumptions or mental images, among others.

These assumptions (positive or negative ones) toward other people are mental projections, which act like glasses colouring the way others are perceived. For instance, when a person has positive assumptions about others, their words and actions are filtered through these assumptions and tinted positively in the eyes of this individual. A person who holds positive assumptions about others is also more inclined to treat them kindly, which contributes to the development of deeper and more meaningful relationships with them.

In other words, when a person intentionally has positive assumptions about others, this individual's overall attitude toward them becomes more constructive. This person is more inclined to have positive thoughts, emotions, words, and actions toward these people, which in turn prompts them to behave accordingly, that is, in the same positive way they are treated. According to the psychological principle of consistency, a person tends to naturally behave in accordance with how they are treated by others.

For instance, a person who assumes others are co-operative treats these people as if they were really co-operative. In this example, these people will tend to behave collaboratively with this individual. Likewise, research demonstrates that when a person has high expectations of another individual, the latter is prone to show improved levels of performance. Psychologically speaking, this is also called the "Pygmalion effect."

There is a very simple technique people can use to have more positive assumptions about another person. Before interacting with this individual, people should say to themselves "My positive assumptions about this person are …". This sentence should be completed with some positive attributes and qualities regarding the other person.

When people use this technique, their perception regarding others is affected positively, as a result of the constructive assumptions of the former about the latter. Even though this technique is very simple to use, its powerful effects should never be dismissed. As a consequence, a company's people should give this tool a try in order to improve their relationships with the organisation's main stakeholders.

This technique of purposely adopting positive assumptions about others can be applied to people one meets for the first time. An individual can also apply this tool to known people, especially those whom were involved in past feuds or disagreements with this person. When a person has positive assumptions about others, this person's perception of them is shifted almost instantaneously, making the communication with them more constructive and pleasurable.

To sum up, having positive assumptions about others always helps a person see them in the best light and prompts these people to adopt a congruent attitude, which in turn makes interactions more flowing and graceful. The opposite is also true; when a person has negative assumptions about others, they tend to behave according to these very unproductive assumptions, which makes communication less spontaneous and more defensive.

6.4.3.10 Love Is Showing Compassion for Others

Human compassion, or what I sometimes call 'human affection' is the key factor for all human business.

His Holiness the Dalai Lama

Compassion implies listening to others in a non-judgemental manner, and oftentimes offering them care and support. When a person is compassionate with others, interactions with them become more flowing and relationships with them become stronger. Compassion always begets a stronger connection with others. People who face challenging circumstances are in need of a helping hand from others.

- **Non-judgemental:** According to Rosenberg (2005) a compassionate person does not make moralistic judgements or condemnatory comments about others. Compassionate people try to understand the challenges experienced by others in a non-judgemental way, taking into consideration the unique perspective of the latter.
- **Understanding:** A compassionate person is not self-centred, but instead is focussed on others. This person is authentically concerned for others and identifies with their experiences as if they were their own. This person tries to be in the shoes of others to understand them in the best way possible, from the emotional, rational, and behavioural perspectives. The compassionate person tends to offer solutions which are suitable for the other person, when appropriate. A compassionate person is open to understanding the human side of the person affected by challenging life experiences.
- **Depth:** A compassionate individual tends to understand what really affects others, without grasping their issues in a superficial or intellectualised manner. Rosenberg (2005) stated that when a person is compassionate with others, these people tend to feel more empowered to dwell on deeper aspects of themselves. This exploration prompts people to experience a sense of relief regarding the issues affecting them.
- **Sensitivity:** A compassionate person who interacts with people facing difficult times and experiencing pain or grief tends to feel authentically connected to their feelings. It was mentioned in this book that people have mirror neurons which allow them to experience the same emotions of the people they interact with. Moreover, a compassionate individual validates the feelings and experiences of others and listens to these individuals in a loving and active manner. A compassionate person is fully present before others and willing to offer them full support, when appropriate.

Gray (2015) observed that compassion implies a person's skills to recognise pain in others, identify with their suffering, and emotionally connect with them because of this individual's own painful experiences. From this perspective, the compassionate person tends to use sentences such as "I can truly recognise your pain because of my own painful experiences." Compassionate individuals realise that painful experiences are commonalities affecting all human beings, which helps them authentically connect to others when they suffer. These circumstances are valuable opportunities to adopt a more nurturing, collaborative, and connecting attitude toward others.

For instance, a person working for a company can adopt a compassionate attitude toward one of the organisation's suppliers. Let us imagine a supplier that was not able to deliver an order placed by the organisation on time because of unforeseen circumstances. In this case, the compassionate employee will kindly ask this supplier about the reasons for the delay of the delivery.

In this example, not only will this employee acknowledge the justifications given by the supplier, but this employee will give, when possible, additional time for that delivery without penalising this supplier. This compassionate employee is also likely to give valuable suggestions so that this supplier could avoid similar delays in the future. The compassionate attitude adopted by the employee toward this supplier is bound to have a positive impact on their relationship, increasing the trust levels between them.

It is important that a company's employees adopt this kind and assisting attitude toward a company's stakeholders, especially if they showed goodwill and commitment toward the company in the past. Compassionate employees understand the difficulties experienced by others in a caring and non-judgemental manner, providing them with assistance when possible.

Oftentimes, a compassionate person helps others abreact, which means prompting them to release their emotional tension in a cathartic manner, through their meaningful articulation of thoughts and emotions. Troubled people tend to feel more relieved when they can vent their feelings and ideas with a person who is not judgemental, but relaxed, supportive, and caring. In a similar vein, Gilbert (2009) observed that when a person is compassionate with others, they tend to feel more safe, nurtured, soothed and cared for, and less stressed, which can help them navigate their challenges in a more confident manner.

Kukk (2017) observed that the evolutionary process in humankind is more based on the "survival of the kindest" instead of "the survival or the fittest." According to this specialist, research has shown that people are hardwired for compassion and that compassionate behaviour toward others is a fundamental human instinct; when people adopt a compassionate attitude toward others, the hormone oxytocin is released in their brains, which makes them experience positive emotions.

In work and business environments, many people do not adopt a compassionate attitude toward others for different reasons, such as goal-orientation, busyness, lack of personal communication, over-reliance on formal procedures, self-centredness, and negative aspects of organisational politics (one-upmanship, gatekeeping, turf wars, etc.), among others. Lastly, research concludes that people with a powerful position in an organisation are less likely to behave in a compassionate manner with others. Instead, when people have low power in a company, they are more inclined to treat others in a compassionate manner.

6.4.3.11 Love Is Acting with Integrity with Others

People want to be treated fairly by others. From this perspective, people believe that their good actions must be duly acknowledged, appreciated, and, if possible, rewarded. When people feel that their accomplishments are not properly recognised, they are prone to feel resentment towards those who should have acknowledged them.

For instance, an employee who works overtime every day for a company that does not acknowledge this person's additional contribution is likely to consider this situation unfair. In this example, the employee devoted additional valuable time performing the company's tasks, without receiving any recognition from the company. As a consequence, this employee is prone to become more demotivated and this person's support to the company will dwindle over time.

The company could have acted more fairly and recognised this employee's additional effort in different ways, for example, a salary rise, bonus, or additional annual leave, among others. This company could also have openly expressed its gratitude to this employee. If the company had acknowledged this employee's valuable contribution, this individual might have been more inclined to keep on co-operating with this company in the future.

There is another relevant point to highlight. Even though deceitful behaviour is socially condemned, deceptive actions tend to be widespread in the business environment. However, most people do not tolerate dishonest individuals and companies. In other words, there is an urgent need to deal with transparent and authentic people and organisations.

In the business environment, many organisations act without integrity. These businesses regularly implement a wide range of manipulative stratagems which affect their internal and external stakeholders in a negative fashion. Some examples of these deceptive behaviour are: threatening others, making others feel guilty, lying to them, providing others with unfelt praise, using double discourse, and hiding relevant information, among others.

Organisations that use the aforementioned ruses intend to control others in order to take advantage of them. When these ploys are discovered, the individuals and companies affected tend to adopt a distrusting and uncooperative attitude toward these organisations, which affects the relationships with them in a negative manner.

It is interesting to pinpoint that most individuals and organisations have the need to avoid being controlled by others. Murray (1964) calls "autonomy" the social need "to resist coercion and restriction" and "avoid or quit activities prescribed by domineering authorities." People who are controlled by others are prone to feel that their natural freedom of choice is reduced, which makes them experience negative emotional states.

In Section 4.3.8, the main aspects of saving people's face or maintaining their public image were thoroughly explained. One of these aspects is people's desire to avoid their actions being prevented by others. When people's autonomy is reduced by other people, the former are likely to perceive that their public image or face is threatened, which makes them feel disrespected by the other people.

Research concluded that some common causes of stress in the work and business environments are situations in which individuals perceive they have no control. When a person feels the unfolding or outcome of a specific circumstance is in the hands of other people, this individual tends to feel fretful and restless.

There is another point to highlight regarding the topic of control and autonomy. When people feel that they are being controlled by others, the former tend to adopt a defensive attitude toward the latter. This protective response is related to the fight-freeze-flight mode which was previously explained in this book. As a consequence, these person's relationships with those attempting to control them tends to be impacted in a negative manner.

Exerting control over other people can be overt and blatant, or oftentimes, subtle. For example, in most companies, employees are overtly controlled, when their superior gives them specific orders or commands regarding how these subordinates must act. Most companies also have an intricate myriad of procedures and policies in order to control employees' behaviour. These rules are set with the purpose of bringing more order and predictability to the work environment, but they often become utterly constraining and even stifling regarding employees' natural need for autonomy.

In other cases, employees are covertly controlled, especially when their roles offer little or no discretion to act spontaneously. In other words, these employees' freedom of action in the workplace is very limited, as they need their superiors' permission to make most relevant decisions. Employees' freedom of action can also be restricted when they are not encouraged to express their voice regarding company activities.

It is important to pinpoint that exerting control over others is never good, more especially when it is excessive. Control generally creates friction in relationships, and it brings about different degrees of resistance from the person being controlled. In the business and work environments, the best way to relate to others is allowing them to have an important degree of autonomy. For example, instead of the superior commanding a subordinate on the actions to take, the former can invite the latter to make joint decisions on the steps to be taken. In other cases, the manager can give general guidelines on a project undertaken by the subordinate, so that the latter works out the details on how to proceed considering those guidelines.

These recommendations should not be applied only to a company's employees. The perspective of increased autonomy should also be applied, when possible, to other company's stakeholders, such as suppliers, customers, intermediaries, etc. Consequently, a company's people should frequently ask themselves questions like "How can I give this stakeholder more autonomy?" and "How does this stakeholder's increased freedom of action contribute to more efficiency regarding our business activities?"

6.4.3.12 Love Is Expressing Creativity

All people have the relevant need to show others their uniqueness, which implies harnessing their distinct talents and capabilities, and standing out from others in a differentiated manner. To put it more simply, people have the need to express themselves, in various ways, openly and creatively.

When people connect to their creative essence, they become less bound to widespread rigid structures (e.g., social conditioning, well-ingrained assumptions, self-judgement, assessment from others, etc.). When these individuals aim to satisfy their creative needs, they feel empowered to develop things that did not exist previously (for example, new projects, products, services, ideas, etc.). The need to be creative also includes going through novel experiences (e.g., visiting new places, learning new topics, etc.). People who dare to be creative can be more "themselves," because they harness their unique talents in a more complete manner.

Rogers (1961) observed that people who satisfy their natural creative needs tend to harness their potentialities more fully and actualise themselves. Fritz (1984) stated that the creative process is an act of love itself. The topic of creativity will be explored in Chapters 14 and 15 in a more thorough manner. Several recommendations on how people working for companies can become more creative will also be examined in detail.

6.5 Some Interesting Perspectives about Relationships with Stakeholders

6.5.1 Bank Account Approach

This perspective was suggested by the legendary management guru Covey (1992). This well-known perspective is called the "bank account approach." Metaphorically speaking, every relationship a company has can be likened to a bank account. In the same way as a bank account, the relationship has "deposits" and "withdrawals." The "deposits" are positive actions or gestures from one person to the other in the relationship. These "deposits" make the relationship stronger, and increase the rapport and affinity between the relationship members. Some examples of these positive actions or gestures are:

- Being grateful, loving, and kind with the other person
- Being generous to the other party, freely and unconditionally, offering them affection, time, advice, support, information, etc.
- Acknowledging the other person's opinions, interests, dreams, difficulties, and concerns
- Respecting the word given to the other person and always acting with integrity
- Recognising the other person's uniqueness, talents, and capabilities
- Spending quality time with the person and listening to this individual actively
- Recognising when the other person was hurt by one's actions
- Admitting one's mistakes affecting the other person promptly and compensating this individual when possible
- Being compassionate and forgiving for the other person's mistakes
- Using positive vocabulary with the other person and avoiding delivering any snide remarks or abrasive criticism to this individual

Negative actions and gestures or "withdrawals" are the opposite to the aforementioned examples. An example of "withdrawals" is adopting an unloving attitude with others, which implies being ungrateful, self-centred, uncompassionate, etc. From this perspective, a relationship can only thrive when there are more "deposits" than "withdrawals" on both sides of the relationship.

When a member of the relationship has made continuous "deposits" over time and occasionally and unintentionally makes a mistake ("withdrawal") affecting the other, their relationship is unlikely to suffer in a relevant manner. The precedent of these "deposits" acts as a "cushion," which makes the relationship solid and strong enough for this type of contingencies. When, instead, at least one of the relationship members has "overdrawn" with the other, their relationship tends to wither. Consequently, some paramount questions people working for a company should ask themselves on a frequent basis are:

- How can I make more "deposits" in the "bank accounts" in each of my relationships?
- What "withdrawals" regarding these relationships must I avoid?
- What relationships are "overdrawn" and how can I reverse this?

6.5.2 Substance over Form

This approach was suggested by the insightful author Robert Fritz (2007). This perspective can be applied to any company stakeholders (employees, suppliers, intermediaries, etc.). From this standpoint, the different relationships with stakeholders must be regularly and thoroughly analysed to discover how they can become more vital, true, precious, and real. In order to do this, Fritz (2007) advises dwelling on the essence or substance of each person involved in these relationships.

Most companies tend to focus, not on the essence of people, but instead on their external aspects (role, function, position, etc.). When people only focus on the external aspects of others, their relationships tend to become cold or formal, and oftentimes lifeless. Therefore, each member of a relationship should aim to discover the "substance" of the other. Their essence is what makes them precious and unique as human beings, and it should be regularly analysed and acknowledged.

Not only is it important to examine the human side of the other person, but also the relationship as a whole. In this sense, Duncan (2002) stated that people tend not to focus properly on the essence of relationships, but instead on their formal aspects. When participants focus on the essence of their relationships, these relationships tend to become more meaningful and thrive. Some important questions people working for a company should frequently ask themselves are:

- What are the main human aspects of these relationships? Are these human aspects duly taken into account by our company?
- How can each person in these relationships uniquely contribute from the human perspective?
- How can I be more loving in these relationships?

6.5.3 *Vulnerable Beings*

This is an alternative perspective on relationships, suggested by certain psychological schools of thought, which can be used with any of the company's main stakeholders. People can use this approach especially when they engage in one-to-one interactions with others, in person, on the phone, or in any other way. The regular use of this perspective significantly increases the connection and rapport with others.

From this perspective, every time a person interacts with others, this individual should perceive them as vulnerable human beings. Most people see others and themselves as vulnerable only when they have had an accident, a serious illness, or a life-changing event. Nonetheless, all people are intrinsically vulnerable and sensitive; this is a common trait of all human beings. Consequently, all stakeholders should be perceived beyond their social masks, and treated with care, compassion, understanding, patience, and affection. All stakeholders are intrinsically valuable and special, with their skills and capabilities, and their contradictions and shortcomings.

In order to apply this perspective, it is advisable to see others as if they were newborns. Most people perceive babies as sources of utter innocence, purity, and brilliance. Babies only prompt most people to feel positive emotions, such as peacefulness or joy. When people interact with babies, they tend to adopt a tender, kind, and playful attitude. Therefore, by perceiving others as if they were vulnerable beings like babies, a person can connect to them in a more sensitive, smooth, and loving manner (De Botton, 2016b).

6.5.4 *Interdependence and Interconnectedness*

You are at once a beating heart and a single heartbeat in the body called humanity.

Wayne Dyer

It really boils down to this: that all life is interconnected. We are all caught in an inescapable network of mutuality, tied into a single garment of destiny. Whatever affects one destiny, affects all indirectly.

Martin Luther King Jr.

All people are connected to others around, even if they are not aware of this. Covey (1992) observed that there is a constant state of interdependence which links all people. From the business perspective, no company can achieve its business objectives (increasing profits, decreasing costs, launching new products, etc.) without the participation of others (suppliers, employees, intermediaries, customers, community, etc.). From a wider perspective, Castells (1996) observed that our society is a complex grid composed of countless networks whose purpose is to develop activities related to production, consumption, power reproduction, and experience, through meaningful interactions.

The business environment is an intricate and dynamic network of relationships, in which each participant has its share of contribution to the whole. Cohen and Prusak (2001) observed that the participants of these networks are "brought together by common interests, experiences, goals or tasks" and "imply regular communication and bonds characterised by some degree of trust and altruism." These authors also observed that "networks form because people need one another to reach common material, psychic and social goals."

From a systemic perspective, each person is a relevant component of a system and interacts with others in various ways. Consequently, for this system to work flowingly and efficiently, the continuous contribution of all its components is needed. From this standpoint, there are systems, which belong to bigger ones. Each system also contains subsystems.

For instance, a company can be considered a system which is composed of subsystems (such as divisions, departments, employees, etc.). In this example, the company also belongs to bigger systems (for example, a group of companies serving similar customers, industrial sectors, etc.). From a wider perspective, a company also belongs to even bigger systems, such as communities, regions, countries, and the world itself, with all the implications this represents. Organisations which are oriented to social causes and those that are environmentally friendly consider this holistic perspective and contribute to the well-being of the community and the planet as a whole, respectively.

In other words, people and organisations that realise their interconnectedness with others relish belonging to the systems they form part of. They purposefully contribute with their best to these very systems. These individuals and organisations know that every positive action they take, even the smallest one, will make a significant beneficial impact on the whole. They are also aware of the subsystems they enclose.

People working for a company should frequently ask these questions: "How can I add more value to the systems I belong to and also to my subsystems?" and "What are the potential consequences of my actions on these systems and subsystems?" This systemic approach is analysed more thoroughly in Appendix D.

Questions for Self-Reflection

- How can I satisfy the unique needs of each our company's stakeholders more effectively?
- How can I acknowledge and respect our stakeholders in a clearer manner?
- How can I adopt a more compassionate attitude toward our company's stakeholders?
- How can I create a stronger connection with our stakeholders?

Chapter 7

Loving Ways to Relate to Stakeholders

7.1 Generosity

7.1.1 Generosity, Abundance, and Stakeholders

> Kindness in words creates confidence. Kindness in thinking creates profoundness. Kindness in giving creates love.
>
> **Lao Tzu**

Generosity is a very important way to improve relationships with a company's external and internal stakeholders. Some examples used in this chapter relate to specific stakeholders, but nonetheless, this powerful tool can be applicable to any stakeholder. The word "generosity" comes from the term "genere," which has its origins in an old Latin term that means "beget," "bring about," or "produce." Generosity is a valuable by-product of adopting a loving attitude toward others.

Most people only act generously only on specific occasions, such as birthdays, weddings, graduations, etc. It is important to pinpoint that this chapter suggests the adoption of a continuous generous attitude toward internal and external company stakeholders, not an occasional act of generosity.

People who are generous with others are focussed on them, rather than on themselves. Fromm (1956) stated that "love is primarily giving, not receiving." This author also observed that the act of giving is an expression of real power and strength, but also a display of joy and aliveness. As in the case of respiration where inspiring is always linked to expiring, giving can never be separated from receiving.

When a person is generous with others, this makes them feel especially acknowledged and cared for, which in turn has a positive impact on this individual's relationship with them. In other words, the act of giving recognises others as valuable human beings, who always deserve to be supported. Schwartz (1979) observed that likeability is the natural consequence of generosity. In other words, a person who is generous with others is more prone to be liked by them. On a similar note, Hyde (2012) observed that a generous person erases the boundaries separating this individual from the receiver which makes their emotional connection stronger and closer.

In a company, a person who adopts a generous attitude toward other stakeholders gives with no strings attached. Authentic generosity means giving unconditionally, without expecting anything in return. A person who gives with the expectation of receiving back is not actually generous, but calculating. This type of manipulative attitude is easily detected by others and it often results in a negative impact on the relationship with them. An honest generous person is focused on others, this individual does not have any hidden agenda and gives selflessly.

Most companies tend to adopt the opposite attitude; they try to receive. Most forces in the business environment push organisations to "get," instead of being generous. Oftentimes, these organisations focus on "getting" in a very disguised way. For their projects, objectives, and actions, these companies use more subtle words such as "achieving," "developing," "attaining," "attracting," "obtaining," "cashing in," and similar terms. All these terms are synonymous with "getting" or "receiving." Some examples of organisations centred on receiving, instead of giving, are for example:

- Companies that try to attract more new customers
- Companies that try to retain current customers
- Companies that try to obtain more profits and revenues
- Companies that try to get more efficiency from employees
- Companies that try to have a better brand image and reputation
- Companies that try to obtain positive word of mouth in the marketplace
- Companies that try to have lower costs regarding their business activities
- Companies that try to achieve higher levels of quality and productivity
- Companies that try to attain more overtime from their employees
- Companies that try to obtain better deals from suppliers and intermediaries (wholesalers, retailers, etc.)
- Companies that try to achieve higher objectives over time

It is important to pinpoint that there is nothing inherently wrong with the aforementioned activities. However, most organisations tend to be excessively focused on "getting" activities, while paying little or no attention to their "giving" ones. From the perspective explained in this book, companies should aim to keep their "getting" and "giving" activities more in balance.

The key to knowing if a company is giving or receiving can be deduced by a simple question: "Who is benefiting directly with this company's action?" If the company is the only party benefitting from its own action, then this organisation is not adopting a giving attitude, but a receiving attitude. If instead others (for instance, customers, employees, community, suppliers, etc.) are the primary beneficiaries of a company's actions, this company is adopting a generous attitude.

The adoption of a generous attitude is related to the abundance mindset, which was thoroughly explained in Chapters 3 and 4. People with a prosperity mindset give because they feel they have enough abundance to share with others. These individuals give wholeheartedly, they do not experience any sense of loss, and their focus is on others, not on themselves; their giving is based on love, not fear.

By contrast, when a company's people focus on what they do not have and try to get it from others, they adopt a scarcity mindset. These people adopt a "receiving" mode, instead of a generous attitude. As seen in Chapter 3, this scarcity mentality is based on fear (of not having enough), which is never beneficial for the company's growth and development. These people do not dare to give, because of their underlying fear of losing what they have. Oftentimes, a company's people who are primarily (or solely) focused on receiving from different stakeholders, instead of giving, tend to be perceived as manipulative, selfish, careless, forceful, and cajoling.

7.1.2 Generosity and Business Activities

> Put giving first and getting takes care of itself. The generous prosper. The selfish don't …
> Prosperity varies in relation to generosity.

David Schwartz

Some will argue that if the company only gives, instead of focussing on receiving, this company will find it hard to perform any of its relevant business activities. But this is only a half-truth; all companies are actually giving, in many cases unwillingly, to perform their daily activities. For instance, when a company pays salaries, advisors' fees, taxes, supplies, or utility services, this organisation is giving.

An organisation is also giving when, for example, it allocates its resources (time, personnel, technology, etc.) to perform specific activities (e.g., showing its products to customers, arranging good deals with suppliers, recruiting and training employees, designing a customer-oriented strategy, developing new products, designing an attractive company website, setting up new branches, opening new markets, etc.). All these activities represent a company's expenses which are related to giving. In general, every item that appears as an expense (for example, advertising, salaries, etc.) in the company's financial report known as an "income statement" is related to giving.

The generosity perspective explained in this chapter does not imply that companies should only be giving. As mentioned previously, it is important that a company achieves a balance between giving and receiving. A company should aim to progressively increase its "degree of giving," which implies being more generous over time. In relation to this, a company's people should frequently ask themselves this relevant question: "How can we be more generous with this stakeholder?" Most company's people ask the opposite question "How can get more from this stakeholder?"

Companies with a generous attitude focus primarily on others. In other words, these organisations put others (customers, employees, community, suppliers, etc.) first, and by doing so, these organisations become naturally more prosperous and successful over time. For instance, a generous company will always try to offer customers the best quality possible, the most outstanding performance and impeccable customer service, among other aspects of high value. This type of company acts in the same generous manner, not only with its customers but also with its other stakeholders (suppliers, employees, community, etc.).

Not only do these companies aim to offer the best value possible to every stakeholder they relate to, they also try to improve the value offered to them over time. As a consequence, customers tend to become more loyal and recommend the company's products and services to friends and acquaintances. Employees become more committed, suppliers become more obliging, and the community is more prone to offer its support to these organisations.

As explained previously, when a company is generous with others, they are the main beneficiary of the company's actions. Nonetheless, there are some specific benefits a company's people usually obtain from being authentically generous with others, as follows:

- A generous person tends to develop stronger trust bonds with others. When a company's employee is genuinely generous with stakeholders, they tend to be more receptive and open to interact with this individual. A generous person is more prone to bypass the default defensive attitude some stakeholders tend to adopt toward others, especially at the beginning of a relationship.
- A company's people who adopt a generous attitude become a good example, or role model to be emulated by other stakeholders. These generous people are also less self-absorbed

and more people-oriented. Employees who are generous with others also create a positive impact on the business environment, which makes their actions more meaningful. Research backs the fact that a generous attitude toward others has a triple-positive effect: it makes the receiver feel appreciated, it generates good feelings for the giver, and it prompts people witnessing the giving act to experience positive emotions.

■ Some research studies have concluded that people who perform altruistic actions become less stressed, which improves their overall state of wellbeing. Wiseman (2009) observed that "people become much happier after providing for others rather than themselves."

■ A generous person does not try to get anything from the receivers, but to benefit them instead, which brings about more rapport between them. A person with a generous attitude toward others prompts them to behave in a more attentive and co-operative manner.

■ A generous attitude is related to a principle known as reciprocity thoroughly analysed by Cialdini (2009). For example, when a company's employee adopts a generous attitude to other stakeholders, they naturally feel compelled to reciprocate and give back to this individual. In other words, receivers feel "indebted" to the giver, which prompts them to act in a reciprocal manner, which implies "paying their debt back."

■ According to Dr Hawkins (2012), a company's people who are in "getting mode" (which is opposite to a generous attitude) have a lower state of consciousness, commonly related to greed, fear, or any other negative emotion. Instead, in a company that adopts a generous attitude, the company's people have a higher state of consciousness, related to love and thankfulness. This specialist observed that an individual who has a high state of consciousness (e.g., a generous attitude toward others) positively affects thousands of individuals with lower consciousness states (such as fear, shame, greed, etc.) (Hawkins, 2013).

■ According to Salzberg (1995), generous people tend to experience a state of freedom, glee, brightness, and expansion and become more welcome and popular in groups. This scholar also observed that giving is a powerful way to express equanimity, joy, and compassion for others, and also helps individuals let go of any state of withdrawal, aversion, and disconnection with others.

■ When a company's people act in a generous way toward other stakeholders, this company's image is improved exponentially. A generous company is likely to become more attractive in the eyes of talented employees, who work or might want to work for this organisation. Companies never want to be seen by stakeholders as exploitative, greedy, corrupted, or heartless. When a company is exclusively focused on getting (for example, obtaining more profits, increasing market share, getting more customers, etc.), this company is prone to be seen in a negative light by its stakeholders.

Abrams (2017) observed that when a person is generous with others, his oxytocin levels are increased, which produces a flood of feel-good hormones (such as endorphins and the neurotransmitter called dopamine, which is highly addictive), prompting this individual to be generous again and again, to have this positive feedback loop repeatedly. This author interestingly stated that the aforementioned positive side effects are also experienced by a person who follows a meaningful purpose which contributes to the improvement of other people's lives.

7.1.3 Generosity and Corporate Social Responsibility

The whole concept of corporate social responsibility (CSR) is based on the concept of giving something back to the community. This CSR includes activities such as helping communities and specific groups, through charitable endeavours, donations, philanthropy, and other meaningful social causes. Oftentimes, companies have their CSR projects clearly separated from the rest of their other activities.

Many companies tend to misuse the CSR perspective because they support a community only with a purpose of "cleaning up" or improving their image. In these cases, the company is not adopting an authentically generous attitude, because it only supports the community in order to get something back (for instance, an improvement of the company's image). This type of company does not behave generously in an unconditional manner and this tends to be perceived by stakeholders.

The generosity approach explained in this book is radically different. Firstly, companies that adopt this generous attitude give fully and wholeheartedly. Their attitude is unconditional and loving, because they give with no expectation of receiving anything in return. These companies behave generously with only the aim of benefitting their stakeholders. Their generous attitude is not speculative, transactional, or manipulative. This type of company adopts a proactive and continuous generous attitude toward others. In other words, these companies act in a generous manner as a fundamental and natural way of doing business, which is fully integrated with all their activities.

A company which adopts this giving attitude acknowledges their interconnection with other stakeholders in the business environment. This company realises that all business activities are performed within a network of stakeholders, who are always interdependent. Therefore, for a company to thrive, its activities should always be flowing, which implies both giving to and receiving from stakeholders, instead of only receiving from them. When a generous company brings about benefits for its stakeholders, this very organisation also vicariously benefits, as a part of this intricate network.

7.1.4 Different Types of Gifts

Many companies argue that they cannot give because they lack resources. Nonetheless, any company can give two type of things: tangible and intangible ones, whose examples can be found below:

1. **Tangible things**: For example, the company can give free gifts to customers (e.g., samples, merchandising items like pens or calendars, etc.). Customers can also be given, for instance, bonuses and discounts. In relation to its employees, a company can pay them, for instance, a salary higher than the minimum legal wage, or additional holiday time. In the case of suppliers, the company can offer better conditions to them (for instance, a more lenient timeframe to deliver their supplies). In relation to retailers, the company can give them free goods with their orders. In the case of the community, a company can donate goods to social groups in need in that community.

2. **Intangible things**: A company can give, for example, thanks to its employees for continuous commitment and contribution to company objectives. In relation to customers, for instance, an organisation can give them outstanding and comprehensive information so they can make the best decisions according to their needs. A company can also provide customers with free services (free delivery, free training, etc.); services are intrinsically intangible, but with very tangible effects on customers. In relation to suppliers, a company can give them compliments for providing goods ordered on time. In relation to retailers, for example, the company can give them ongoing support and advice on how to exhibit goods in their outlets and market these products more efficiently. In the case of a community, for instance, a company can give their time to train its members free of charge.

People working for a company can also give other intangible valuable things to others. For example, a person can give a smile, a warm handshake, a supportive pat on the back, and valuable assistance. People can also give others their appreciation, encouragement, and vision. Oftentimes, an individual can also give others valuable references, an expert opinion, relevant contacts, kind endorsements and the time to listen to them, among other things.

The attitude of giving also implies giving up or letting go of one's own negative thinking and unproductive qualities. To that effect, people working for a company should give up deception, manipulation, untruthfulness, malevolence, and any other negative trait or detrimental behaviour. In other words, any unloving attitude should be given up in order to create space to adopt a loving perspective toward others.

7.1.5 Generosity and Employees

As seen previously, a company should be generous with all its stakeholders, for instance, customers, employees, suppliers, business partners, community, etc. In the following, some specific examples of the adoption of a generous attitude related to a company's employees will be explained.

Many employees feel that they participate in an unfair exchange with the company they work for. In this exchange, these employees feel their work activities are not dully valued economically (for example, a fair wage) and non-economically (e.g., respectful treatment of employees, acknowledgement of their achievements, gratitude for their contribution to company's projects) by this organisation. Oftentimes, these employees feel that the company takes all the gains at the expense of them; they feel short-changed or deceived by this organisation.

Many employees regularly complain, in an overt or silent manner, against the organisation they work for. Oftentimes, these employees say that they give the best of their time, energy, and skills to undertake projects in the workplace, but their efforts are not fairly recognised by the company they work for. These working individuals perceive that the company does not adopt a generous attitude with them.

Many companies pay the minimum salary established by the legislation in force. In those cases, companies do not take into account the unique contribution of each employee in order to compensate them accordingly. Consequently, these employees do not feel motivated to contribute with their valuable and distinctive skills and talents to forward the company's endeavours. Novak and Bourg (2016) wisely observed that "people won't care about you if you don't care about them."

These unmotivated employees are prone to act in an unproductive and uncooperative way in the workplace and do only the minimum work possible for their specific roles. These employees are unwilling to fully harness their analytical and creative skills; this uninterested attitude in turn tends to be negatively reflected in the company's economic indicators.

In these common situations, it is paramount that the company adopts a generous attitude toward employees, which in turn gracefully resolves issues with them. Generous companies always make sure that their employees are prodigally compensated. When a company is bountiful to employees, they will be grateful. A thankful employee is prone to work in a happier and more productive manner, and this in turn will have a positive impact on the company's economic development.

According to the principle of reciprocity analysed in this chapter, when a company acts generously with its employees (for example, paying them higher salaries for their work), these individuals are more inclined to reciprocate (e.g., they willingly work harder and work overtime, when necessary). Besides, when a company adopts a generous attitude toward employees, its relationships with them are strengthened over time. Therefore, a company can be more generous with its employees in different ways, for example:

- The company offers higher salaries to their employees, as compared to the minimum set legally. The company pays employees bonuses and additional benefits not required by law.
- The company allows employees to take longer breaks at work and allows more generous holidays. This extended non-working time will help employees resume their work tasks having been refreshed and revitalised.
- The company offers several benefits to employees (e.g., free coffee and tea or meals, discount vouchers, free transport passes, free relevant training, free use of technological equipment like laptops and mobile phones, free medical insurance, etc.).

All companies, including the ones that adopt a generous attitude toward their employees should frequently ask themselves this question: "How can we be more generous with our employees?" All companies can become more generous over time; there is no limit to generosity. These organisations should always remind themselves that satisfied employees tend to be more productive, co-operative, and creative in the workplace.

A company can also be generous with its employees via intangible things, such as congratulating employees on their contribution to the company's projects, for example, with a personalised letter signed by the company's management. As seen before, when a company is generous with its employees, these individuals tend to adopt a more generous attitude toward the company's customers. For example, a generous employee will be more willing to provide customers with the best advice according to their needs.

Motivated employees are also prone to adopt a generous attitude with other employees. For example, a generous employee is more prone to provide colleagues with advice, technical information, and warm support, and co-operate with other workmates, even when they are not formally required to do so. Moreover, generous employees also tend to adopt a generous attitude toward other relevant company stakeholders, such as the community, suppliers, etc. In other words, when a company is generous with its employees, they act generously, which creates a virtuous cycle, spreading gradually over the work environment and also toward external stakeholders.

7.2 Gratefulness

Don't forget your thank-you notes! ... Appreciation, applause, approval, respect – we all love it!

Tom Peters

7.2.1 Importance of Gratitude for Stakeholders

Feeling gratitude and not expressing it is like wrapping a present and not giving it.

William Arthur Ward

The term "*appreciation*" has two main distinct meanings. The first meaning of this word is to recognise the value or quality of something (a person, a thing, a place, idea, or an experience). From this perspective, when people are appreciated, they tend to focus on the positive sides of things around them; a person who is grateful cannot adopt a negative attitude.

Appreciation, also called gratitude or thankfulness, has a second meaning that is "increasing the value of things." For example, when a national currency has appreciated in relation to others, the former has a higher value than the latter. Likewise, when people appreciate things around them, these things become of higher value in their eyes; they are not taken for granted. According to Hyde (2012), gratitude implies a person's sense of indebtedness toward someone or something, which prompts this individual to value them.

Hellinger et al. (1998) observed that in all relationships, there is a natural need for members to keep equilibrium between what they give and receive. These authors stated that "expressing genuine gratitude is another way to balance giving and taking." For instance, employees who regularly work overtime to meet a company's deadlines might feel the time and effort they devote is imbalanced compared to the salary they are paid by this organisation.

In this example, the organisation could show its thanks to the employees, and pay them a more attractive salary recognising their effort and dedication to company's endeavours. In this way, the organisation re-establishes the balance between what was given by these employees and what they receive. Oftentimes, the organisation can be more grateful with its employees in a simpler manner, for example, by giving them a personalised gratitude note.

Gratitude should never be occasional, but a continuous attitude. A company's people should make a habit of being thankful to other stakeholders, which will strengthen the relationships with them over time. All companies are interdependent with their internal and external stakeholders; no business is self-sufficient. Consequently, when an organisation is grateful, not only does it recognise these stakeholders' contribution to the company's activities, but it also values the interdependence with them.

In the following points, some positive effects of adopting a grateful attitude in the work and business environments will be analysed. It is important to pinpoint that this enumeration is only illustrative. To that effect, some positive effects of being thankful to stakeholders are:

◼ A person who is appreciative to others tends to behave in a more loving and thoughtful manner when interacting with them. A thankful person tends to see the positive in others, instead of their faults, which lifts their self-esteem and self-confidence. Schwartz (1986) observed that that all individuals want to feel needed and useful, and showing gratitude toward them is a good way to achieve this. In the business environment, adopting a grateful attitude creates a better connection with internal and external stakeholders.

◼ When people are thanked for their contribution, their mood tends to become more positive. Gratefulness gladdens the heart of the receiver and also the heart of the giver. Ashkanasy and Ashton-James (2007) observed that employees tend to experience positive moods in the workplace as a consequence of a series of cumulative small uplifts, such as being regularly appreciated for their work, which in turn motivates them to keep on contributing to the company's projects.

◼ When a company's people are appreciative with stakeholders, the level of conflict is diminished and oftentimes eliminated. Appreciative people tend to focus on the positive aspects of their relationships with others, instead of concentrating on their conflicting traits. In other words, when people are grateful to others, their relationships become more harmonious and peaceful. Research concluded that when people are frequently grateful to others, these positive effects built up.

◼ Thankful people tend to be more caring and compassionate to others. Gratitude also shows humility and kindness toward others. When a person is thankful to others, they tend to be more co-operative with this individual.

- Grateful people tend to be in a good mood. When people are grateful, their perception of circumstances is shifted toward the positive and their stream of thoughts tags along. A person who adopts a thankful attitude also tends to be more calm and peaceful. No person can be appreciative, and experience negative emotional states (anger, sadness, fear, etc.) at the same time. When a thankful person interacts with others, their emotions are positively shifted because of this person's emotional state. People tend to experience the emotional states of others around them because of mirror neurons. The topic of mirror neurons was explained in Chapter 6 of this book.

- Grateful people are less prone to criticise, moan, or complain, as they become more aware of the positives surrounding them. In the business environment, grateful people naturally perceive the positive aspects of each situation they face, especially challenging circumstances. Moreover, thankful people are more prone to perceive business opportunities, even in situations which are seemingly dire. When people are grateful on a continuous basis, they build up positive habits and a virtuous cycle regarding gratitude which feeds itself over time.

Childre et al. (2000) call gratefulness an "energy asset" or "heart feeling" because it contributes to the general state of well-being of an individual. As an "asset," thankfulness also helps people release any tension stemming from stress. Thankful people tend to feel more alive and happier, which has a positive impact on their overall performance.

7.2.2 Practical Aspects of a Thankful Attitude toward Others

Reflect upon your present blessings of which every man has plenty; not on your past misfortunes of which all men have some.

Charles Dickens

Show the people in your life that you appreciate what they do, whether they are in your main cast or your background crew.

Jaime Thurston

Companies are urged to show their gratitude to their main external and internal stakeholders in an overt and authentic manner. As seen previously, a grateful attitude toward others can never be excessive; in other words, gratitude cannot be overdone. Rosenberg (2005) observed that a complete expression of gratitude should be specific and include the reasons why the person is grateful as well as the feelings related to that experience. Some examples of ways of expressing gratitude to stakeholders can be found below:

- I really appreciate your contribution regarding …. This is very important to me because … and I feel … because of this.
- Your co-operation regarding … is greatly appreciated because … and I feel … because of your kind assistance.
- You are very kind because …. Thank you very much for …. I feel … because of your support.

A thankful person can always add their personal touch to express their gratitude to others. For example, a person can give thanks to others by sending them a personal, handwritten, and signed letter. Companies should not only recognise their stakeholders for their performance, but also for their distinctive traits.

Figuratively speaking, every time a company's people express their gratitude to stakeholders, they act like gardeners tending to and watering their plants. Moreover, people who show their gratitude to others prompt them to act in a reciprocal manner, which contributes to the development of more fruitful relationships. A person can express gratitude regarding other people's significant achievements or contributions, but also be grateful for their small gestures.

In the case of a company's personnel, there are several reasons for being grateful with them. An example could be an employee offering creative insights to improve a company's systems and processes, or an employee treating customers in a warm and kind manner, among others. In some cases, a company can be appreciative to its employees in a more indirect manner, by involving them in relevant company decisions. In this case, the company can say "We appreciate your commitment and hard work and we would like to hear your opinion on …".

A company can express gratitude to its customers for several reasons, for instance, these customers have trusted the organisation, the customers have recommended its products to others, etc. A company can also be thankful to its suppliers for a myriad of motives, for example, the suppliers have delivered their supplies on time, the goods provided are of the highest quality, and the packing used in their deliveries is safe, among others.

A company's employees can use gratitude in advance to make polite requests to others. For example, an employee can say to one of the company's suppliers "I appreciate you sending the shipment by the end of the week" or "Your co-operation on this topic is greatly appreciated." In this case, the appreciation "in advance" also subtly prompts the supplier to deliver the goods on time.

This type of request is friendly and is prone to dissolve any type of resistance from the receiver. Besides, in this example, the grateful person has positive assumptions about the attitude of the other individual, which prompts the latter to behave congruently with these assumptions. This topic was explained more thoroughly in Chapter 6.

It is advisable not to use plain sentences like "Thank you" but to include the specific reasons for gratitude "Thank you for …" in order to make thankfulness more complete and meaningful for the receiver. When gratitude is accompanied by generosity, they are a powerful combination, which enhances the relationships with others. For example, when a person is grateful with others, and also gives them a valuable present for their contribution, the positive effects of gratitude are significantly magnified.

7.2.3 Ungratefulness and Its Negative Effects

> A hundred of times every day I remind myself that my inner and outer life depends on the labour of other men, living and dead, and that I must exert myself in order to give in the same measure as I received and am still receiving.
>
> **Albert Einstein**

Many people are not accustomed to being grateful. These individuals are more keen on criticising, moaning, or focussing on the negative. Oftentimes, these people take valuable things around them for granted, which prevents them from being appreciative. Some people behave ungratefully out of entitlement; they do not feel they need to be appreciative for their belongings or experiences, because they believe they just deserve them.

Some individuals cannot be appreciative because their thoughts are focussed on what is missing, instead on what can be cherished. Other people say they do not have time to be appreciative, because they have more urgent things to do, or because they do not believe they have attained enough to be grateful for. Oftentimes, individuals negatively focus on their past (for instance, regrets) or their future (for example, worries), instead of being centred on what there is to be grateful for at present.

In the business environment, many companies act in an ungrateful manner. This type of company demands a lot from their stakeholders but does not show its appreciation to them. An ungrateful company, for instance, demands its employees work long hours every day, but it does not recognise their additional contribution. In another example, a company receives goods from its supplier before the time agreed, but this organisation does not express its gratitude to this very supplier. A company can also be ungrateful with customers, for instance, when it does not send them an email to them thanking for their purchase.

In these previous examples, the company takes these stakeholders for granted; they are not acknowledged as valuable human beings. When stakeholders are not appreciated by a company, they are more likely to behave in a non-cooperative and unmotivated manner. Oftentimes, these stakeholders become resentful and might criticise the company because they feel they are not being recognised and cared for. It is possible that the communication between the company and these stakeholders is negatively affected. An unappreciated employee, for example, might comply only with the minimum work requirements, or might even sabotage the company's activities.

Goldsmith and Reiter (2008) observed that gratitude always represents a form of recognition of others; it is like the beautiful ribbon that wraps around the jewel boxes that other people are. These authors also stated that when a person is not grateful with others, they are deprecating them.

Lastly, a company that frequently celebrates its business achievements (for example, increase in sales, growth in market share, launching of new products, etc.) tends to adopt a generous attitude toward its stakeholders. These accomplishments can be celebrated in several ways, for instance, providing gifts to employees and organising social events (dinners, balls, retreats, etc.). A company which celebrates its past successful outcomes does not take them for granted, but it also gives credit to people who contributed to these accomplishments. Some companies focus so much on achieving their goals and pursuing their purpose that they do not take the time to acknowledge and celebrate their past achievements.

7.2.4 Appreciative Inquiry

> The supreme happiness of life is the conviction that we are loved; loved for ourselves, or rather, loved in spite of ourselves.
>
> **Victor Hugo**

Appreciative inquiry is another topic related to thankfulness. Appreciative inquiry is a tool that many organisations use on a regular basis. The concept of appreciative inquiry is indeed simple. Bushe (2013) stated that this tool "advocates collective inquiry into the best of what is, in order to imagine what could be" and it is "followed by collective design of a desired future state that is compelling." This author also observed that, when this tool is used, there is no need to incentivise people in order to introduce change in an organisation.

Companies are prone to use problem-solving techniques that tend to focus excessively on the negative aspects of issues affecting them. Organisations that use these tools tend to dwell on the causes of the problems in order to devise possible solutions to efficiently "fix" these issues. Oftentimes, this way of solving problems proves ineffective because its primary focus is on the negative aspects of a challenging situation which needs a solution.

People who use appreciative inquiry recognise and value the positive aspects of a troublesome situation, which means they adopt a grateful attitude. These people also aim to envision possible ways in which this situation can work better for the company. When people focus on positive aspects of a challenging situation, and are appreciative of them; they are more capable of devising creative and compelling alternatives to deal with this very issue.

The main stages of appreciative inquiry are: discovery (the company highlights what is working positively, such as strengths, processes, capabilities, functions, etc.), dreaming (the company creatively visualises what is prone to work positively in the future), design (developing a suitable plan with emphasis on what could work in a positive manner), and destiny (which implies the commitment to implement specific actions to fulfil the goals previously set, as well as learning from this implementation). This tool can be applied to a specific issue affecting the organisation, or to the company as a whole (Bushe, 2013; McKenna, 2012a).

The approach of appreciative inquiry is closely related to the creative approach explained by Fritz (1999). This specialist observed that most companies use a "problem-solving approach," which implies analysing a problem to eliminate it. This author also suggested that a company should instead use a "creative approach," which implies acknowledging and recognising its current situation (and its problematic aspects) and generating the future desired state this organisation wants to create. This second approach is primarily focused on what a company wants to generate, as compared with the traditional problem-solving approach which is centred on what the company wants to eradicate.

7.3 Collaboration

7.3.1 Competition and Collaboration

> Competition is an acquired, not an inborn drive ... Competition is, however, not a basic need of any kind.

M. F. Ashley Montagu

As previously seen, society supports competition. In the business environment, for instance, many companies continually aim to outwit other organisations, known as rivals or competitors. In the work environment, employees compete for a promotion and candidates compete for a job. Different suppliers compete with others to provide a specific company with their goods and services.

However, a company that adopts a competitive approach with its stakeholders can never develop a mutually beneficial relationship with them. This competitive approach implies a scarcity mindset, which is based on fear and implies that there are scarce resources available to fight for. Consequently, a company that acts competitively with its stakeholders always tries to outpace or defeat them.

The competitive approach implies a zero-sum game in which a company attempts to get all the gains at the expense of others. This approach (also called win–lose) implies that there is a winner that takes all the gains at the expense of others. Sometimes, a company can even use this approach with its customers, when it tries to get as much as possible from them, without giving enough value in return.

When a company adopts a competitive attitude toward its stakeholders, no fruitful relationships with them can be developed. The use of a competitive perspective generates negative emotional states, such as fear of losing, resentment, and mistrust. An organisation adopting a competitive attitude tends to act in a defensive manner, instead of being proactive, because it aims to care and defend its access to available resources, which are perceived as scarce.

From this perspective, the competitive approach is the opposite to the co-operative perspective. While the former is based on fear because resources are perceived as scarce, the latter is based on love and trust toward others and the view that resources are abundant. On one side, in the competitive approach, a company believes it can only access resources when battling for them with others. On the other side, from the co-operative perspective, a company aims to develop synergetic alliances with stakeholders because it believes that resources can be shared and even generated collectively. Some examples of the use of the co-operative approach can be found below:

- A company adopts a co-operative approach with customers when it provides them with good value for their money. In other words, the company does not try to take advantage of customers, by misleading, manipulating, or ripping them off. Instead, this company offers customers the best products and services in a fair exchange for these customers' money. This company also provides them with the most complete and truthful information about its products and services so that they can make the most appropriate decisions according to their unique needs. A company adopts a co-operative attitude with customers when it offers them relevant incentives, such as samples, bonuses, free services, discounts, etc.
- A company adopts a co-operative attitude with its employees when it fairly recognises the effort and time they devote to the company. This company offers employees a fair compensation (economic and non-economic one) for their services and aims to enhance employees' capabilities through training, mentoring, coaching, or other relevant upskilling activities. A company that adopts a co-operative attitude toward its employees allows them to overtly express their opinions regarding the company's important decisions.
- A company adopts a co-operative approach with other companies (such as suppliers, wholesalers, retailers, etc.) when it only looks for fair agreements (win–win) with them. In these agreements, the needs of both parties are duly satisfied. A company that adopts a co-operative approach toward other companies is understanding, supportive, and patient with these organisations when they face challenges.
- A company is co-operative with other companies offering similar products and services (commonly called rivals) when it tries to develop partnerships with them. Some objectives of these partnerships could be sharing resources, such as technology, contacts, technical information, customers, human resources, facilities, and distribution channels, among others. These partnerships can have other goals, for example, researching, manufacturing, and promoting in a joint manner, spreading business risks more effectively, and reducing costs by sharing resources, among others.
- A company that adopts a co-operative attitude toward the community tries to support social causes, through donation, free training of community members, and other activities. The co-operative company performs these philanthropic activities without expecting anything in return. This company only aims to benefit its community without any hidden agenda or ulterior motives. As a consequence, the company's ties with the members of this very community tend to strengthen over time.

When companies adopt a co-operative attitude with one another, some transaction costs linking these organisations are lowered significantly. Transaction costs are the expenses of buying or selling products or services in relation to other independent organisations. Some examples of these costs are: preparation of contracts to be signed by the parties, the enforcement of these contractual aspects, and the supervision of the obligations assumed by the parts, among others.

For example, when a company and its supplier adopt a co-operative attitude, the costs of enforcing and monitoring contractual aspects tends to be significantly lower. In this case, the parties trust one another and are committed to complying with the terms of the contract linking them, which helps them lower the aforementioned transaction costs.

7.3.2 Other Aspects of Co-Operation

Some experts observed that people are naturally inclined to co-operate with others. Schrage (1990) noted that when people adopt a co-operative attitude toward others, their relationships can become purposeful. These relationships can have different aims, such as working together to solve intricate problems or creating something new, etc.

When people support one another and consider each other's needs, they tend to act in a more cohesive manner. Co-operative people avoid social loafing, which is not to be fully supportive and proactive when working in a collective project. A co-operative person tends to pose questions like "Is there anything I can be of assistance with?" and "How can I help you with this?" This type of person also frequently uses statements like "Let's do this together," or "Let me help you."

A person who adopts a co-operative attitude toward others tends to purposely use more positive words (such as "right," "good," etc.) instead of negative criticism or complaints (such as "impossible," "not feasible," etc.). A co-operative individual is also inclined to use a more inclusive vocabulary (for example, words such as "and," "we," "our," "ours," "us," etc.), instead of words which imply an individualistic approach (such as "I," "my," "mine," etc.). These inclusive terms connote a sense of togetherness with others, implying everyone is on the same side and trying to achieve shared objectives.

Co-operative people tend to be grateful for the contribution of others ("Thanks for your kind support regarding ..."). In a co-operative environment, every person feels that their support is of great value, and their unique contribution can improve collective projects in a significant manner. The adoption of a co-operative attitude toward others is related to a systemic approach to business activities. In this approach, a company and its stakeholders are perceived as relevant parts of the same system; all components are interdependent and their harmonious interaction is crucial to bring about valuable collective results.

A co-operative attitude helped our primitive ancestors co-ordinate resources to perform relevant survival activities, such as defending themselves from dangerous predators or obtaining food for the group, among others. Montagu (1957) observed that "man is born with strong co-operative impulses, and all that they require is strong support and cultivation."

This author also stated that co-operation has a biological basis which "has its roots in the same sources as social behaviour, namely, in the process of reproduction" and that "social co-operative behaviour is the continuation and development of the maternal-offspring relationship." This specialist concluded that "social behaviour which is not co-operative is diseased behaviour," because "the basis that informs that all behaviour ... is biologically healthy is love." From this author's perspective, love and co-operation are closely related.

Most people's early upbringing unfolds within a network of co-operative relationships, which includes close relatives and friends. From a wider perspective, Montagu (1957) observed that a society is a complex set of co-operative interactions between its members for a common life, where co-operation has a relevant value for each individual's survival.

Human beings have a gregarious nature, which means they are prone to socialise and relate to others in a co-operative fashion. Many social psychologists recognise "affiliation" as a relevant human need, which implies people's desire to belong to groups. People want to form part of a group because they want to feel identified with its values and activities, and also be acknowledged and valued by other group members.

In the same view, Murray (1964) observed that co-operation is closely related to affiliation which means "to draw near and co-operate or reciprocate with an allied other." The concept of co-operation can also be related to what is known as "brotherly love." Fromm (1956) observed that this type of love implies loving others, regardless of their differences and distinct attributes. An individual who adopts this loving attitude toward others is willing to assist them, whenever needed.

7.3.3 Co-Operation within the Company

If you don't believe in co-operation, look what happens to a wagon that loses a wheel.

Napoleon Hill

Within an organisation, co-operation is a key factor to develop strong relationships between employees. Employees have specific roles and activities related to these roles, which makes the interdependence of employees a relevant factor in the workplace.

Besides, most companies meticulously divide their work projects into specific tasks, which are assigned to different employees. Therefore, an employee never undertakes an entire project, but only a part of it. Sometimes employees interact and work together for each of the stages of projects. Nowadays, many employees are connected in a virtual way, for example, by email. Employees need to support one another for the company to thrive in the marketplace. Collaborative employees realise that successful outcomes often stem from everyone working on the same side.

According to Cornelissen (2017), co-operation contributes to the development of "communities of practice" within a company. These communities are self-managed networks composed of employees from the same or different departments, who have common interests and are linked by shared tasks or projects. In these communities, people adopt an attitude of mutual support and understanding toward each other, which aligns their actions. Some employees only behave co-operatively for specific collective projects; other employees adopt a co-operative attitude on a continuous basis. In most cases, co-operation among colleagues represents an expansive experience for them.

According to Fritz (1991), in the work environment, there are two possible types of co-operation: consensual and hierarchical. The consensual way is used when there is no chain of command and employees work at the same level. Hierarchical co-operation is used instead when superiors and subordinates work in a joint manner. Some advantages of adopting a co-operative attitude with other employees are:

■ When employees adopt a co-operative attitude, a more amicable and loving work environment is developed.
■ Co-operative employees have team spirit and a sharing attitude; they aim to frequently support one another because they realise that nobody is self-sufficient.
■ When employees co-operate with one another, the tasks related to a collective project can be allocated among them in a more efficient manner.
■ When employees work on a joint project, each participant's skills complement one another; no employee has an overarching set of skills to solve every single problem.
■ In collective projects, employees are compelled to relate to others, which helps them know each other better and learn from one another.

- Co-operative employees develop a stronger bond with their colleagues; trust and rapport among them is naturally increased.
- In co-operative projects, participants are more prone to support one another whenever difficulties or challenges arise.
- In a co-operative work environment, each employee is recognised for their unique skills and capabilities and their contribution to collective results, which makes these employees feel more comfortable and engaged.
- Co-operative employees do not adopt a defensive attitude toward others; they can be more at ease because they form part of a group which contains and supports them.
- In complex projects, co-operative employees can jointly develop a deeper analysis of the different alternatives and generate more creative courses of action, as the result of profuse interaction between all participants.
- In joint projects, co-operative employees are naturally open to contributions from others; they willingly welcome different opinions from others.
- Co-operative projects create synergy because the collective results are not the simple sum of employees' individual achievements, but an enriched combination of all of them.

Besides, the existence of a widespread co-operative attitude in the workplace often discourages some common detrimental practices in relation to an organisation's politics, such as backbiting, favouritism, one-upmanship, and gatekeeping, among others. These unproductive behaviours are related to a competitive approach, which is based on fear.

In a co-operative work environment, employees are not on their own; they know they will be assisted by others. By being supported by others, these staff members feel more confident and empowered to face and overcome work challenges. To put it more simply, co-operative employees develop mutually supportive relationships with others.

This co-operative attitude also implies providing others with insights into relevant topics, giving others useful advice, creating value jointly, and clarifying unclear topics. Co-operative people also tend to solve disagreements with others in a fair and amicable manner. In co-operative environments, collective decisions are encouraged whenever possible.

Co-operation is closely related to love; employees who interact with others adopt a loving attitude toward them. In the workplace, co-operative employees avoid outpacing one another, but work side-to-side with colleagues. Co-operation also generates an atmosphere of camaraderie, where people are more inclined to support one another. Besides this, co-operative environments are very suitable spaces to use a creative technique like brainstorming, which will be analysed in Chapter 14.

However, social psychology research has concluded that co-operative projects are also likely to have some disadvantages, for example, groupthink (which means that the group members conform to a unique view, without challenging it), less individual effort made by each participant, problems of co-ordination, taking a longer time to make decisions and perform activities, and interference of members in each other's actions, among others. Oftentimes, co-operative projects can have other negative effects, such as ineffective communication between the participants, formation of conflictive subgroups, and lack of consensus. When participants adopt a loving attitude toward one another, this mitigates these negative effects.

7.4 Forgiving Attitude

When you plant lettuce, if it does not grow well, you don't blame the lettuce. You look for reasons it is not doing well. It may need fertiliser, or more water, or less sun. You never blame the lettuce. Yet if we have problems with our friends or family, we blame the other person. But if we know how to take care of them, they will grow well, like the lettuce. Blaming has no positive effect at all, nor does trying to persuade using reason and argument. That is my experience. No blame, no reasoning, no argument, just understanding. If you understand, and you show that you understand, you can love, and the situation will change.

Thic Nhat Hanh

7.4.1 Effects of a Lack of Forgiveness

The quality of mercy is not strained; it droppeth as the gentle rain from heaven upon the place beneath. It is twice blessed – it blesses him that gives and him that takes.

William Shakespeare, *The Merchant of Venice*

Forgiveness is not only applicable to non-business relationships (such as relatives, friends, lovers, etc.), but also to business relationships. In the business environment, some individuals discriminate against others, make aggressive comments to them, behave in an intolerant manner, or use manipulative stratagems to deceive other people, which might prompt the recipients of this behaviour to feel resentful with these negative individuals. When people are affected by harsh criticism, unfair treatment, and lack of recognition from others, they are also prone to hold grudges.

In all these situations, the individuals offended by others have not had their personal needs duly met by them. Moreover, these people tend to become resentful, because they believe that their personal limits have been trespassed on by others. Consequently, these resentful people are more prone to become bitter, unmotivated, aggressive, uncooperative, less productive, and critical, especially with the people who disrespected them. These resentful individuals tend to cling to continuous negative ruminations about people who have mistreated them. These negative thoughts cloud their perception and affect their actions in a detrimental manner.

Resentment implies a lack of forgiveness because it keeps negative past issues in an unproductive loop. When a person is feeling resentful toward another individual, their relationship is not likely to thrive. Resentful individuals always adopt an unforgiving attitude toward their offenders, which prompts the former to continually grieve over the past wrongdoing of the latter. A person who is continually resentful tends to be avoided by others.

Resentful people carry very heavy emotional baggage; their intense emotions related to past offenses prevents them from experiencing current circumstances fully. Their discerning skills tend to be clouded by these powerful negative emotions, which also make them act in a defensive manner. Resentful people find it difficult to be kind to those who have mistreated them; they also cannot acknowledge and appreciate the distinct qualities of others. In the business environment, when people cannot forgive others, simple disagreements become more relevant and intense, leading to conflicts escalating and becoming more personal. Resentful people are also less prone to co-operate with others who they feel offended by.

Oftentimes, people do not forgive themselves because of negative words they have said to others, unintentional negative actions affecting other people, or mistakes made. These individuals hold on tightly to their own past errors, which keeps them stuck in a negative unforgiving attitude toward themselves.

7.4.2 *Meaning of Forgiveness*

People who adopt a forgiving attitude are more capable of releasing grief and pain related to past issues that could have affected them negatively; these individuals are also more open to experiencing positive emotional states. When people forgive others, the attitude of the former has an impactful and restorative effect on their relationships with others. These people release any negative judgement or condemnation of those who offended them, as they realise that blaming others is useless, because it does not make them feel better, nor does it improve their interaction with others.

Therefore, when people decide to give up any negative emotional wounds caused by other people, they allow themselves to relate to others in a more meaningful manner. Forgiving individuals realise that all suffering and frustration stemming from offences caused by other people prevents the former from harnessing their own innermost potential.

Forgiveness transmutes negative emotions toward others; it also transforms separation from others into connection with them. A person with a forgiving attitude toward others tends to treat them in a more compassionate manner. Dr Hawkins (2013) observed that many people wrongly believe that forgiving others is debilitating, when in fact it is very empowering. Research has shown that forgiveness makes people less stressed and more positive.

Some people have an unforgiving attitude toward themselves; these individuals should learn the lessons stemming from their own past mistakes in order to release them for good. People who cannot forgive themselves tend to feel guilty and fretful, which clouds their discerning skills and unique resources. In order to forgive themselves, people should realise that in the past, they have always done the best they could, according to the available knowledge and experience at that moment.

When people think that they (or others) could have done better in relation to certain issues, they analyse this in hindsight. These people examine the past mistakes from the present vantage point, considering the learning obtained, and counting on a different set of circumstances and personal resources.

7.4.3 *Resolving Misunderstandings Promptly*

> Life forgives you when you cut your finger ... Newer cells build bridges to cover the cut.
>
> **Joseph Murphy**

As seen previously, when a person offends or disrespects others without apologising for this, these people tend to become resentful with this individual. As a consequence, when a person realises that others are resented because of actions performed or words said by this individual, this person should tackle this issue in a prompt, friendly, and straightforward manner, leaving formalities aside, if possible. Shapiro and Shapiro (1994) observed that asking for forgiveness puts the person in a position of vulnerability, in which this individual recognises the pain caused to others, as well as the participation in it, but also shows care and respect for them.

The best way to handle this type of issue is to humbly apologise to the person who feels offended. People who offer authentic and overt apologies to others should take full responsibility for their own mistakes, without minimising, denying, or hiding them. Whenever possible, apologies should be made in person in a private meeting; therefore, emails or letters should be avoided.

People willing to apologise for their past mistakes understand that relationships are the most precious resource in the work and business environments. They understand that their wrongdoing might have affected the relationship with others in a negative way; consequently, they are willing to offer their apologies to those affected in order to care for their relationships with them.

People should never be ashamed or hesitant to ask for forgiveness, but instead offer their apologies in a humble manner. People who truly recognise their mistakes adopt an attitude of humility and integrity toward others. Oftentimes, these individuals are prone to ask others to forgive them, even when they are not completely sure they have offended them.

People who offer their apologies to others can also promise to avoid similar mistakes in the future. Sometimes, apologies are not sufficient and a compensatory action must be offered to people offended; this compensation aims to assuage the pain or trouble caused. These actions are beneficial to preserve and strengthen the relationships between the company and stakeholders. Dr Maltz (2015) wisely observed that people who have been hurt by others should always be willing to forgive them, even when there is no sensible reason to do so, because through forgiveness, their emotional wounds can be healed.

As seen previously, a person who forgives others forsakes judgement, grudges, or blame toward them, and negative emotions related to the incident. The forgiving person understands that all human beings make mistakes, which deserve to be forgiven. Some psychological schools of thought observe that people always try their best, according to their specific circumstances and personal resources. People with a forgiving attitude are aware of this and adopt a more compassionate attitude toward others.

7.5 Fun, Playfulness and Humour

Play is the highest form of research.

Albert Einstein

7.5.1 What Is Not Playfulness

Seriousness is the only refuge of the shallow.

Oscar Wilde

We are most nearly ourselves when we achieve the seriousness of a child at play.

Heraclitus

Playfulness is not a topic traditionally related to business activities. On the contrary, most people tend to relate business activities with terms which are the complete opposite of playfulness, such as sacrifice, hard work, huge effort, Spartan discipline, and other similar phrases. Many people believe that business activities should be performed in a serious, hard, and monotonous manner.

Dodgson and Gann (2018) observed that most organisations set a myriad of rules, policies, and procedures, which oftentimes prevent people from being playful. Besides, many companies share a widespread but detrimental assumption that their employees must be on duty 24/7 (and more, if this were possible) to progress in a challenging and complex business environment. Most business people associate business success with abnegation. The term "abnegation" implies an attitude of self-denial, responsibility, dutifulness, and sacrificing one's desire to favour others' desires.

Consequently, abnegation does not seem to be related to the concepts of "fun" and "playfulness." In a company, abnegated staff are prone to renounce their own interests to achieve the company's goals. The business approach based on abnegation is borne out in different ways:

■ Working hard, fatiguingly, and drudgingly in a continuous manner
■ Setting business activities as a priority over everything else
■ Taking massive action in the shortest time possible
■ Being worried about any problem, even small ones
■ Overanalysing situations in order to solve them
■ Forcing things to happen in a specific way
■ Performing activities on automatic pilot
■ Being over-committed to the goals previously set
■ Following successful formulas that worked for others
■ Doing things in the same way as usual
■ Focusing exclusively on "serious" and traditional activities
■ Being exclusively focused on economic aims

The behaviours shown in these examples tend to generate negative feelings, unproductive thoughts, and tension in most people. When people act in any of these ways, they are prone to feel stressed and fretful. These people are also inclined to adopt a defensive attitude (fight-freeze-flight mode) which prevents them from harnessing their high mental capabilities (such as creativity, synthesis, analysis, etc.). Likewise, Marden (1917) observed that "over-seriousness depresses the mental faculties and tends to lower efficiency."

In other words, being too "serious" or abnegated regarding work and business activities can bring about negative effects. For example, people who continually work hard are more likely to burn out. When people perform massive action in a short time, in order to be efficient, they are more prone to make innumerable mistakes. Besides, people who perform activities on automatic pilot lack the minimum discernment regarding their performance. Individuals who consider work and business activities as their only priority tend to become imbalanced in other relevant areas of life (such as health, family, etc.) which end up affecting their productivity negatively.

People who are continually worried about business problems tend to be more stressed and less creative in tackling these issues. These people are prone to over-analyse possible solutions to their problems, which prompts them to feel tired and scatty. When people push hard for things to happen, they are prone to affect their relationships in a negative manner.

People who are over-committed to their goals do not take enough time to reflect and change these objectives when necessary. These people tend to adopt a rigid attitude toward these aims, which is unproductive when relevant changes in the business environment make these goals meaningless.

When people follow the "successful formula" used by others, they are unwilling to tread their unique path, considering their own distinctive resources (skills, capabilities, information, etc.) and set of circumstances. In the same way, when people do things the way they have always done before, their conservative attitude prevents them from going beyond their comfort zone and exploring alternative approaches.

Lastly, when people exclusively focus on the economic rewards of their business activities (e.g., obtaining more profits, increasing revenues, etc.), they tend to dismiss other relevant aspects, for example, building fruitful relationships with stakeholders, offering a better service to customers, or creating a better work environment, among others. These other positive outcomes of business activities tend to be as important as a company's economic returns.

7.5.2 *Importance of Playfulness*

> Every now and then go away, have a little relaxation, for when you come back to your work, your judgement will be surer; since to remain constantly at work will cause you to lose power of judgement.

Leonardo da Vinci

As previously seen, most people link business activities with struggle and hardship. These people cannot relate business endeavours with being spontaneous, playful and adventurous. Playfulness can be defined as the attitude of letting go of the seriousness, rigidity, and formality which characterises work and business activities.

Playful people tend to adopt a more light-hearted attitude toward business activities and avoid being overeager or pushy. Maslow (1968) defines playfulness as a good-humoured and amusing trait, which naturally goes beyond any state of hostility. These playful individuals tend to be continually engaged with the present moment, even when they pursue their main goals. These people let go of any regret from the past or concern about the future because they know the only moment of power is now. This attitude makes their actions more vital and daring.

In other words, playful individuals are willing to fully harness the present moment with no fear. These people know that "now" is the most valuable stepping stone of what is about to come. Playful people are more open-minded and curious, but also more flexible and experimental. Even though goals are relevant for a playful attitude, these goals are not pursued in an anxious way, but in a more relaxed and detached manner. Murray (1964) observed that all people have the social need of play, which implies:

- To act in a fun, purposeless manner
- To make jokes, laugh, and smile
- To perform activities which release stress
- To partake in games, parties, dancing, etc.

Brown and Vaughan (2010) stated that play is a specific type of mindset, rather than a series of activities. When people adopt a playful attitude, they can interpret situations affecting them in a less dramatic and more resilient manner. People who stand for playfulness do not really believe in working hard, but instead they aim to work smart. These people tend to behave in a spontaneous and thoughtful manner, instead of acting mechanically and automatically. In the business environment, people with a playful attitude never forsake their lives, but positively contribute to all stakeholders while enjoying what they do fully.

When people adopt a playful attitude, they become more receptive and open to new ideas. These people tend to avoid paths well-trodden by others and develop their own ones. Playful people tend to let loose, which prompts them to harness their creative skills and devise new ways to do things.

There is a well-known psychological school of thought called "transactional analysis" (Berne, 1964; Harris, 1969). From this perspective, a person's ego is composed of three parts, which are the parent, the adult, and the child. In different interactions with others, people use different parts (parent, adult, child) and communicate and behave in specific ways which are related to the very parts used. From this perspective, when playful people relate to others, they tend to use their child part. This part is related to relevant traits such as adventurousness, openness, and expansiveness.

Their childlike and light-hearted perspective helps playful people release their imagination freely, which prompts them to envision scenarios beyond current limitations. Nobel (2012) observed that playful people tend to learn more effectively, because they use their whole brains. Playful people are also more prone to experience a state of flow; they can be laser-focused on the task at hand and improve their performance without strenuous effort, but with grace. People who adopt a playful attitude enjoy engaging in challenges and let things unfold smoothly and without pressure.

People with a playful attitude do not follow the rules in force in the work and business environments (such as policies, procedures), which often makes them look anarchic. In other words, these individuals are experimental and improvisational, which might also make them look aimless. They enjoy the process of exploring non-traditional ways of doing things, and avoid getting upset whenever they face setbacks or predicaments. Moreover, these people tend to garner important lessons from their failures and put themselves back in the game.

7.5.3 *Playfulness and Stakeholders*

> If you have fun at what you do, you'll never work in your life. Make work like play and play like hell.

> **Norman Brinker**

> The world of work we are entering in demands that we are more creative, playful and available to have fun. If your work isn't fun, then consider changing something – either the way you work or the work itself.

> **Steve Nobel**

Brown and Vaughan (2010) observed that play activities are performed voluntarily (not driven by a "serious" purpose) and people feel the desire to continue playing because they experience good feelings. These authors also stated these activities prompt people to improvise and experiment creatively, which makes these individuals less focused on themselves and more concentrated on the activities. These specialists concluded playful activities also help people develop new cognitive connections which are valuable for dealing effectively with challenging circumstances; they wisely observed that play acts like a fertiliser for brain growth.

When people relate to stakeholders in a more playful manner, they avoid being overly formal with them, when not needed. Playful people tend to connect to others in a more personal and genuine manner, beyond any social masks or work roles. Besides, playful people aim to develop more constructive and co-operative relationships with other stakeholders, where each part can contribute with their unique talents and skills. These playful individuals are more willing to engage in exploratory and unstructured conversations with others, in order to debate relevant topics from fresher and more creative perspectives.

Nobel (2012) observed that when people relate to others in a playful manner, work and business activities tend to become more productive and creative. Dodgson and Gann (2018) observed that the adoption of an explorative attitude tends to be relevant for business activities, especially when a company faces uncertain or complex circumstances. These authors also stated that "play at work brings progress, enhances our humanity and adds to the distinctiveness of what we can contribute as humans compared to machines."

Bolton and Houlihan (2009) stated that playful activities can increase a person's morale and prompt this individual to act in a more joyous and energetic way. People who adopt a playful attitude to others are less prone to respond in a defensive way. It is important to remember that when in a defensive mode called the fight-freeze-flight response, people cannot fully harness their innermost discerning and creative skills.

As a consequence of the aforementioned benefits, it is important that companies aim to develop more playful interactions with their main stakeholders. Some examples of questions a company's employees should frequently ask themselves to relate to other stakeholders more playfully are:

- How can we perform this specific activity in a more fun manner?
- How can we engage with this stakeholder in a more playful manner?
- What type of non-business activities can be performed with this stakeholder?
- What are different ways to add value to others while being playful?
- What business accomplishments can be celebrated in a fun manner?

Some examples of playful activities can be informal conversations and non-business meals, among others. Sometimes, companies organise relaxing retreats for employees, as an example of a fun activity. These organisations seriously consider these playful activities because they know they prompt people to replenish their vital energy and help them become more efficient in their business activities. Oftentimes, these playful activities also foster a spirit of connection, belonging, and togetherness, especially when they involve the participation of others.

Playfulness can help a company's people adopt a more detached view of business activities. A story shared by Brown and Vaughan (2010) will illustrate this point clearly. According to this story, a CEO met employees at an all-staff meeting to talk about the company's negative outcomes. At the beginning, the CEO blamed himself for these negative performance; afterwards, this man asked attendees to look for foam darts placed under their seats.

Then this individual asked the attendees to shoot those darts at him. As soon as employees started shooting darts, the energy of the room lifted from gloom to glee. After this, the CEO proceeded to explain how future outcomes could be improved, and employees were more open to take these recommendations on board. In this example, the playful interaction enabled attendees to perceive negative outcomes less dramatically.

7.5.4 Playfulness and Laughing

Martin (2006) has observed that humour is a type of mental play, where unrelated thoughts and ideas are mixed up in non-traditional ways. The use of light-hearted and non-offensive humour is a good way to lighten interactions with others. Witty humour makes people feel more comfortable and at ease, especially during stressful circumstances. Good jokes have some incoherence in their scripts, oftentimes crowned by an unexpected punchline, which creates a powerful binding effect among people.

De Bono (1977) observed that humour is a valuable tool which is life-enhancing and accessible to anyone. This author also observed that humour is against any form of solemnity and arrogance, which are so common in business and work environments. Besides, the use of humour contributes to an overall state of well-being and helps develop smoother interactions with others. Ehrenreich (2006) concluded that some people feel naturally compelled to share their joy with others, which strengthens their relationships among them.

Psychologically speaking, humour can be considered as a mental defence mechanism, which people use to convey unpleasant ideas or emotions to others in an ingenious and pleasurable manner. These defence mechanisms are mental subconscious responses usually activated when a person has unpleasant thoughts or feelings (for instance, unacceptable, threatening, or antisocial) that the individual refuses to acknowledge in a proper manner.

Zander and Zander (2002) observed that "humour and laughter can bring us together around our inescapable foibles, confusions and miscommunications, and especially over the ways in which we find ourselves acting entitled and demanding, or putting other people down, or flying at each other's throats." Humour can also be considered an astute way to cope with the tediousness and routine sometimes related to work and business activities; it can also help people put challenging situations into perspective.

On a similar tone, Ramanchadran and Blakeslee (1999) observed that jokes have the function of trivialising troublesome situations, by pretending they do not have any real impact. These authors also concluded that humour helps distract people from anxious states, prompting them to turn off their defensive responses. According to Brown and Vaughan (2010), jokes "are the minimally invasive surgery of a relationship" and they added that jokes "penetrate to a deep entry level without leaving an entry wound." The reader can find below some of the positive effects of laughter on individuals:

- Some studies have concluded that laughter not only creates the opportunity to share glee with others, but also to strengthen bonds with them. Laughter can also help people de-dramatise challenging situations and make them less frightening; complex circumstances seem more approachable and solvable.
- Laughter warms people's hearts because of its noticeable relaxing effect; people become less stressed and more revitalised. The appeasing effect of laughter helps people become more at ease with others and develop a deeper rapport with them.
- Gamon and Bragdon (2002) observed that laughter brings about benefits to the immune system and lowers stress levels. Goleman (1996) observed that laughter prompts people to fully harness their reflective, creative, and critical skills.
- Claflin (1998) observed that laughter increases the heart rate and blood pressure, dissipates any tension, and improves the working of the immune system. This author stated that when people laugh they get a "mini-workout" for their body and brain.
- When people are engaged in laughter and are in a good mood, they are more likely to widen their view and consider a broader range of alternatives to approach current situations.
- Laughter has a therapeutic and cathartic effect on human interactions, which is very relevant during times of conflict. In other words, laughing is prone to brush away nervousness in people, making them less prone to adopt an adversarial attitude toward one another.

The use of humour makes the business environment less formal and more humane. People working for a company should use humour with their main stakeholders in a respectful way, which means avoiding deprecating jokes. Koestler (1964) observed that good humour is generally based on the unexpected, the original, the exaggerated, or the implicit. In a similar vein, De Bono (2004) stated that "humour permits exaggeration and absurdity to make a serious point."

Plester (2009) observed that the use of humour in the workplace can contribute to the development of affinity, cohesiveness, and camaraderie among work colleagues. Price and Price (2013) observed that people who experience positive emotions – for example, the ones stemming from laughter – tend to become more productive and resilient, especially when they face setbacks. According to Martin (2006), "research has also confirmed that humour in the workplace is correlated to better working relationships, greater job satisfaction and increased productivity."

Positive emotional states – for example, the ones stemming from laughter – tend to be contagious. Goleman (2006) observed that people have mirror neurons that replicate the emotional states of others; this phenomenon is called "emotional contagion." When a person experiences a positive emotion, other people around them are more likely to act like that person. On a similar tone, Hatfield et al. (2011) observed that the contagion originates in the mimicry of the others' body language (e.g., facial expression, gestures, etc.) which prompts their emotions to converge.

The appropriate use of humour can warm the work and business environments. The use of occasional jocular anecdotes and light-hearted comments are very effective tools to disrupt any atmosphere of tension in these commonly formal environments. Moreover, Harrold (2007) observed that humour is a good tool to develop rapport with people. Oftentimes, small humorous comments can be used to "break the ice" between stakeholders who have not met previously.

7.5.5 Smiling

Let us always meet each other with a smile, for the smile is the beginning of love.

Mother Teresa

In the business environment, smiling is a universal and inexpensive way of communicating with others. Every time a person smiles at another, a stronger sense of connection between them is developed. When people smile to others, they naturally tend to smile back. McLellan (1996) observed that a "smile is the lighting system of the face and the heating system of the heart." As in the case of laughter, smiling is contagious.

From the emotional perspective, smiling is an unmistakeable display of one's good mood. Smiling and laughing have a very powerful alchemic effect on interactions with others. When people smile (or laugh) with others, any negative emotional state is temporarily cast aside. In other words, people cannot experience a negative emotion (e.g., anger, fear, etc.) and smile (or laugh) at the same time. Some psychological schools of thought assert that when people put a smile on their faces willingly, this gesture releases hormones that prompts their mood to improve.

From the sociological perspective, smiling is a sign of friendliness or non-aggression. When a person genuinely smiles at strangers, their natural defensive responses tend to be turned off. From the communicational standpoint, smiling is a fundamental key to open up a more natural and meaningful conversation. When people smile during a conversation, the rapport between them is improved. Consequently, in the business environment, people should smile more frequently and authentically to develop a livelier connection with others.

Experts in body language agree that honest smiles always involve all the face muscles, while an artificial smile only includes the lower part of the face. This type of smile tends to be shorter. In the case of inauthentic smiles, the lips tend to be stretched sideways, as compared with honest smiles where lips are naturally pulled upwards. An inauthentic smile seems calculating and dishonest and makes people look less trustworthy. Most people recognise a fake type of smile when being approached by those who intend to try to force them to buy a product or service.

Questions for Self-Reflection

- How can I adopt a more generous and grateful attitude toward our company' stakeholders?
- How can I collaborate with our stakeholders on a regular basis?
- How can forgiveness improve the work and business environments?
- How can I introduce more humour and playfulness in the workplace?

Chapter 8

Natural Conversations with Stakeholders

Sometimes the greatest adventure is simply a conversation.

Amadeus Wolfe

8.1 The Need for More Natural Conversations

The first principle in good communication is to treat the other person as a neighbour. Look them in the eye ... and make real contact with them as sharing our human situation.

Godfrey Howard

Clear, complete, truthful, and meaningful communication represents a very important resource in the business and work environments. This type of communication has a positive impact on companies' economic results. The opposite is true; communication problems can affect companies' performance negatively. Communication capabilities are part of what is known as soft skills and help people relate to one another in a more effective manner.

There is an increasing use of technology for communication, for example, emailing, social media, text messaging, and video conferencing, among others. In most cases, technology makes contact with other people easier, which lures most companies to these technological advancements. Honoré (2004) also observed that "technology made it possible to do everything more quickly" and, as a consequence, people are "expected to think faster, work faster, talk faster, read faster, write faster, eat faster, move faster," which is counterproductive for meaningful and authentic communication.

The use of technology often makes the communication process colder and more depersonalised, as compared, for example, with face-to-face interactions. According to Hallowell (1999), when people use technological devices, they tend to feel more disconnected from one another, because there is no "human moment" of real contact between them.

123

Hogg and Vaughan (2002) observed the use of technological devices for communication purposes presents other disadvantages, such as lack of body language and suppression of the amount of information exchanged by the participants. In a similar vein, Locke (1998) observed that computer-mediated communications flatten participants' self-expression. Oftentimes, this communicational technology is purposefully used by companies to make the interaction more formal and less impersonal.

Schrage (1990) stated that the use of technological devices for communication purposes focuses more on the transmission of the message than on facilitating the understanding between the sender and the receiver. This author also observed that the use of these technological instruments for communication purposes does not encourage collaboration between people, because they passively share an experience, instead of actively creating one.

According to Ong (1982), most companies prevalently use the pipeline model for their internal and external communication. This is a one-way communication model in which one participant (for example, a manager) sends chunks of information (e.g., directives, orders, deadlines, etc.) to another participant (for example, employees). Oftentimes, these messages are insufficiently contextualised to be understood in an accurate way. This widespread and practical model leaves aside valuable real interactions between the participants. The use of technological devices is very suitable for the application of the pipeline model.

Keegan (2015) observed that "when communication is important, delicate and potentially ambiguous, you cannot beat face-to-face communication." Personal interactions are superior to other forms of communication because they allow people to obtain instantaneous feedback from others and express their emotions overtly. Lobel (2014) observed that face-to-face conversations make people feel close, not only physically, but also emotionally, creating a more empathetic connection between them.

Personal communication is more expressive, because it includes verbal language (words) and also body language (tone of voice, gestures, posture, etc.), which makes it less prone to misunderstandings. Instead, technology can never reproduce this level of human expressiveness. Therefore, a company's people should always attempt to establish contact with its stakeholders in the most direct manner, whenever possible. For instance, personal meetings and conversations on the phone should be preferred over emails or letters.

8.2 Business Formalities and Natural Conversations

Life is a conversation with the world around us and within us.

Simon Parke

Humans have already changed the world several times by changing the way they had conversations.

Theodore Zeldin

Ong (1982) observed that natural conversations allow people to have more close-knit communion, as compared with written communication, which is more distancing and disengaged. It is important to pinpoint that in the business environment, a great part of the communication is written. According to the aforementioned author, written communication is sequential, with closure but no clear context, where the recipient is often absent and fictionalised.

This specialist concluded that, in contrast, natural conversations are "empathetic and partici-patory rather than objectively distanced," and that there is "real speech and thought" that "exist essentially in a context of give-and-take between real persons." Carlson (1999) observed that in natural conversations, people tend to become more positive, generous, trusting, nurturing, and honest. People who engage in natural conversations are more open and spontaneous, because they feel comfortable with being themselves, as they truly are.

According to Zeldin (2000), a conversation is a joint enterprise and a humbling experience where minds meet, and facts are exchanged and reshaped, bringing about new trains of thoughts. Angell and Rizkallah (2004) observed that interactions aim to co-ordinate and maintain relation-ships with others. These authors also stated that business conversations create structure "because of the way a company organises," which includes "dividing up work tasks, creating business goals, and establishing levels of authority." All these tasks are co-ordinated through human interactions.

In the business environment, there is a myriad of formalities which oftentimes hinder the com-munication process, making conversations structured, distant, and cold. These business conversa-tions do not play out flowingly; they are rigid and unnatural. Consequently, these interactions only help people connect on a superficial level.

For example, in traditional conversations between a company and its suppliers, the most sig-nificant topics tend to be the commercial conditions (price, quality, specifications, etc.) of the transactions between both companies. Any personal aspects related to the individuals engaged in these conversations (e.g., their personal preferences, values, etc.) are purposefully left aside. These non-business topics are considered "irrelevant" for companies' transactions.

Another example can illustrate the previous point more clearly. In the workplace, employees mostly talk to others about topics related to their organisation, such as work tasks to undertake, relevant deadlines to meet, main goals to achieve, projects in progress, and others. Informal topics unrelated to the company's activities are not discussed, because employees are only acknowledged from the perspective of their work roles. Other relevant topics related to employees beyond their work positions (other roles of employees, for instance, as friends, parents, siblings, etc.) are left aside in most companies' conversations.

In traditional conversations, blue collar employees are prone to be acknowledged regarding their manual skills. White collar personnel are more prone to be acknowledged for their rational aspects. None of these business conversations recognise employees as whole human beings with several dimensions, such as emotional, spiritual, physical, and mental aspects.

Work and business roles are predetermined, fixed, and encapsulated categories, which never fully represent the wholeness of the valuable human beings behind them. In the same vein, Rogers (1961) stated that people are always more than their roles because they are intrinsically fluid and living. This prestigious author observed that a person is a "changing constellation of potentialities, not a fixed quantity of traits."

In work and business environments, people continually enact their roles, which makes them feel separate from others. According to Goffman (1969), people play their work roles in a coherent and homogeneous manner, showing the unequivocal signs of these roles, which are intended to be believed by others. These roles have specific ways of expressing and behaving, which are intrin-sically limiting. Consequently, this author observed that, when people play their roles, they are prone to suppress heartfelt feelings and impulses to avoid showing their "all-too-human selves," so they can be accepted by other people. Argyle (1994) observed that people comply with their roles because these roles are interlocked with those performed by the other individuals who they interact with.

However, natural conversations empower people to go beyond these social masks, in order to show themselves as they truly are. Johnstone (1987) observed that "masks are surrounded by rituals that reinforce their power." In other words, every time people "wear" these social masks, they act and speak in an unnatural manner and their conversations become ritualised and structured. This is a very common trait of most traditional business conversations.

These masks often result in people communicating with others in a manufactured, rigid, and unfeeling manner. People's true expressiveness lies concealed behind these social façades. However, when people hold natural conversations, they drop these masks and become more aware of their shared humanness, which prompts them to interrelate in a more expansive and meaningful manner. In simple words, natural conversations bring people much closer.

A person can never be entirely defined by their business role (employee, buyer, supplier, etc.). Natural conversations prompt people to show themselves beyond their roles and functions. Carlson (1999) stated that natural conversations always put the human side of people first, and the role second, which makes people feel they are treated like human beings. Natural conversations leave aside unnecessary formalities to make interactions more real. This type of interaction has a more horizontal approach, which means participants are perceived at the same level, rather than within a hierarchical (vertical) structure.

From the linguistic perspective, the specific traits of the relationship between people engaged in a conversation are implied in the specific words and body language (gestures, tone of voice, etc.) used by them during that interaction. For example, when a boss and an employee hold conversations, the former is more prone to use a more directive tone of voice and more commanding words over the latter than the other way around. In natural conversations, participants tend to use non-directive words and body language, which implies the connection between two human beings in equal conditions, beyond roles, functions, or aspects of status.

As previously seen, traditional business conversations fail to embrace the participants' human side and their complex and unique experiences, because these interactions only cover narrow business topics related to their roles. Natural conversations instead include both business and informal topics. Sometimes, natural conversations can be solely based on personal topics, such as interests, preferences, hobbies, pastimes, family topics, and others, without including any business topic.

Natural conversations acknowledge the fact that each individual has a unique set of values, dreams, preferences, emotions, and expectations. In other words, natural conversations do not have a one-dimensional perspective, as in the case of most traditional business conversations, because participants are considered in a more complete and integral manner, beyond their specific functional role (employee, supplier, customer, etc.).

People who engage in natural conversations can overtly express their needs, values, and dreams. People can be authentic and show their human side, without any fear of being judged by others. These individuals do not feel obligated to "edit" their messages, as commonly happens in most traditional business conversations.

People working for a company should have frequent natural conversations with internal stakeholders (other employees) and external ones (suppliers, customers, etc.). These conversations should include, when possible, both business topics and non-business ones. Natural conversations create a deeper connection between all the people involved, and also strengthen their relationships. These conversations also tend to have a positive impact on a company's performance indicators, such as productivity, quality levels, customer satisfaction, etc.

8.3 Assumptions in Business Conversations

> When you're authentic, you create aliveness and excitement. People instantly tune into you and find you interesting. Sanitised and predictable speaking on the other hand, whether unconscious or deliberate, cuts off connection and creates boredom, disappointment and even mistrust.
>
> **Judy Apps**

All relationships, including business ones, are the result of a series of conversations. Therefore, the destiny of these relationships is mostly affected by the quality of these interactions. In natural conversations, people put aside their own assumptions about others. Assumptions about other people include an overarching set of aspects, such as status, level of intelligence, character, etc. Oftentimes, assumptions about other people mislead the communication process with them.

These assumptions are like screens which cloud people's perception regarding others; therefore, these assumptions have a powerful impact on the communication process. Oftentimes, these assumptions are fragmentary, and also false or unfounded. When people can purposely leave their own assumptions aside, their connection with others becomes more humane and genuine.

Some great philosophers like Descartes observed that people should cast aside preconceptions to gather a true knowledge of reality (Buckingham et al., 2011). Outstanding psychologists like Rogers (1961) stated that flexibility and openness to the communicational experience and unconditional acceptance of one another allows participants to enjoy their interactions more fully. In other words, people are more open and flexible when they drop their assumptions about others.

When engaging in conversations, people can discover their own assumptions regarding others by asking themselves a simple question like "What am I assuming about this person?" This type of question creates more awareness regarding assumptions about others. At the same time, this question facilitates the process of leaving these assumptions aside.

Another relevant question people can ask themselves is: "How can I perceive this person from an innocent and childlike perspective?" The insights via this question can help a person forsake his own assumptions about others in order to perceive them in a more unpolluted manner. This question also helps people connect with the essence of others, their human side.

When a person can perceive others free from these rigid mental labels, the communication process becomes more natural and spontaneous. In those cases, the person can discuss with others relevant topics in a flowing and engaged manner. People who drop their assumptions develop a deeper level of rapport with others, because they can go beyond what is apparent.

8.4 Connecting to Employees in a Natural Way

> Words are windows, or they're walls.
>
> **Ruth Bebermeyer**

In the work environment, typical conversations have covert aspects of power (for instance, company's hierarchical levels) embedded in them. These aspects make conversations in the workplace intrinsically hierarchical and imbalanced (for example, superior–subordinate). In the workplace, people tend to enact their specific work roles in a full and automatic manner.

As seen previously, employees' continuous role-playing hinders the development of a deeper connection between them. In many conversations, roles stand up as borders between people, which hampers their real connection. For example, when a manager talks to a subordinate, the distance and respect for each other's role makes the conversation excessively formal, cold, and impersonal. In most cases, if an employee dares to engage with a manager in a more casual and unstructured way, these attempts are often deemed to indicate a lack of respect toward the hierarchical organisational structure.

As a consequence, most conversations in the workplace are far from being natural. Countless formalities (policies, procedures, etc.) pervading these conversations override any chance of people being spontaneous and connecting with each other in an authentic fashion. In the workplace, but also in business environments, conversations are affected by these hindrances. In extreme cases, conversations become mechanical and dehumanised conversations, resembling interactions between blind automatons.

As seen previously, typical work conversations tend to avoid acknowledging participants' human side. Employees focus on important work tasks during their work time, but they also have other relevant aspects affecting their lives (family, relationships, health, etc.) which are never considered as relevant topics in work conversations. Nonetheless, these personal aspects always play out silently but relentlessly in the background of employees' minds. Moreover, these personal affairs usually affect employees' performance, in most cases, unknowingly.

"Does this mean that employees should only talk about non-business topics?" Not necessarily. There should be a fair balance between organisational topics (deadlines, company objectives, projects, etc.) and non-business ones (emotions, values, preferences, beliefs, habits, etc.).

A simple way to hold more natural conversations in the workplace is to ask others their opinion about any non-business topics, such as sports, well-being, and others. When these non-business topics are included in chats, employees tend to become more engaged and connected to others. Most employees are very opinionated regarding these topics; these themes make these employees reflect on aspects of their humanity.

Therefore, these topics should never be restricted in the work or business environments. These topics are common in all natural conversations; they facilitate valuable interactions between real human beings who connect with one another in a borderless fashion.

8.5 Emotions in Business Conversations

From a psychological perspective, emotional states which are not expressed keep on running on a subconscious level, colouring people's perceptions, thoughts, and actions. Several experts advise people to express their emotional states, not to repress or suppress them. It is also recommended to observe one's emotional states without judging them as negative (sadness, anger) or positive (happiness, etc.). People who openly communicate their emotions to others are prone to experience a cathartic relief.

A natural conversation represents a safe context where people can share their authentic emotions, as a valuable part of their humanness. When people share their emotional states with others, a deeper rapport is developed between them; the latter will also feel compelled to open themselves up emotionally as well. This reciprocal opening of the participants contributes to the development of more meaningful and honest communicational experiences.

Most traditional business conversations are excessively rational and analytical, without including any emotional aspects. Some might argue that in most business conversations individuals often ask others questions like "How are you?", which implies an indirect reference to the emotional aspects experienced by others.

Nonetheless, this type of question is often posed in a merely formal, ritualistic, and mechanical manner, not in an honest way. In other words, the person asking this question does not really intend to connect to another in deep and wholehearted manner. This question's objective is generally to look more sociable in the eyes of others, not connecting to their innermost human aspects.

Instead, a person who engages in natural conversations with others asks them how they feel, and really means it. In a natural conversation, emotions, and other relevant human aspects, are an essential part of the chat. When emotional aspects are integrated to conversations, these interactions become more personal and enriched.

In natural conversations, each participant is encouraged to openly express their thoughts, but also the emotions underpinning them. Instead, in most traditional business conversations, people are prone to repress or suppress most of their own emotional states. People use these self-censoring mechanisms to avoid looking vulnerable before other people, and also as a way to avoid being taken advantage of by them.

In natural conversations, participants' emotions provide the interaction with more substantial texture, meaning, and depth. In these conversations, people show themselves as real emotional beings, which makes them appear more human. These informal encounters gather two human beings in presence, who are authentically interested in knowing more about each other's internal worlds.

Zak (2013) observed that when people share their vulnerable side with others, more trust between them is generated. In a similar vein, Hallowell (1999) stated that, as a result of the emotions conveyed by the participants, these natural encounters have more lasting positive effects for them, such as increased trust, respect, and rapport.

8.6 Goal-Setting and Natural Conversations

Human life has its own laws, one of which is: we must use things and love people.

John Powell

In the business environment, most conversations are unnatural; they tend to be utterly goal-oriented. When talking to others, people have clear and rigid agendas on their minds to follow. These agendas can include, for instance, tasks to perform, projects to implement, deadlines to meet, and other business-related topics.

Agendas set for conversations are generally topic-oriented, not person-focussed. Consequently, when a business conversation is based on specific agendas, this interaction tends to unfold in a colder and more formal manner. Traditional business conversations tend to be rigid and controlling, and the topics discussed by the participants do not come up spontaneously.

Oftentimes, an agenda makes people objectify others, which means considering them as specific means to achieve specific goals related to their own agenda. Instead, natural conversations flow, because the topics analysed are not scripted; people do not aim to tick off predetermined topics from their personal lists.

Sometimes, people participating in a traditional business conversation show their agendas by proposing the topics of interest for the conversation. Other times, people have ulterior hidden motives, which make them subtly sway the conversation toward their own topics of interest.

Besides, many typical business conversations are held in a very limited time. This time limitation prompts people to focus exclusively on the topics related to their own agendas, which makes small-talk irrelevant. Some business conversations do not look like real dialogues, but complex entanglements of each participant's agendas.

As an example, the representatives of two different companies A and B are holding a business conversation. In a typical interaction, the representative of company A will consider the representative of the company B as a "means" to fulfil company A's objectives, and vice versa. The parties do not aim to know each other on a personal level, but to achieve their own goals. Instead, in natural conversations, the other person is never perceived as a means to an end, but as an end itself. Natural conversations aim to explore the human side of others and strengthen relationships with them.

Traditional business conversations have a utilitarian approach; people interact to see what they can get from one another. Instead, in natural conversations, people are not determined to obtain anything from others, but to know others better. In these conversations, the topics to discuss often roll off in a spontaneous and unrehearsed manner, as the result of a dynamic interaction between the participants. People are fully immersed in meaningful dialogues, where personal ideas and stories are articulated and amalgamated in an unstructured manner.

In natural conversations, each person is genuinely curious about one another. When people hold these type of chats, people discuss topics in an experimental and open-minded manner, and not in a definite, directive, or absolute way. Grice (1989) observed that in these interactions, people can make relevant contributions to one another, when required, according to the orientation of the conversation.

8.7 Natural Conversations and Mutual Exploration

Natural conversations are dynamic and generative; the main purpose of these encounters is to explore each other's views in a non-adversarial manner. This type of interaction is always open-ended, which means that there is uncertainty about how it will unfold. During these conversations, a person can propose a topic considered of great value and interest and the other person can engage with it or not, or even change it.

Natural conversations are co-constructed by participants, with no-one controlling the interaction. Senge (1990) observed that, in these conversations, people are willing to drop their own assumptions to observe their own thoughts and others', and also grasp a deeper understanding of the topics discussed. Participants drop assumptions about one another and also assumptions about how the conversation should develop. People also avoid drawing preliminary conclusions regarding topics in progress, which makes the conversation more insightful and meaningful and less constraining.

Research has observed that when people engage in conversation and find commonalities between them, these interactions tend to have a higher engagement and a deeper rapport. In other words, when people find common factors between them (e.g., preferences, values, hobbies, places visited, things learnt, etc.), they feel more connected to one another.

Johnson (1997) observed that, in authentic conversations, each participant willingly comments about their ideas, emotional states, and experiences, which is called reciprocal self-disclosure. In other words, natural conversations are made up of personal and revealing comments, including negative experiences, which create an enhanced sense of intimacy and trust between the participants.

Locke (1998) observed that self-disclosure is more prone to happen upwardly in a hierarchical structure. This author explained that "in a corporate life an employee is far more likely to divulge personal facts about himself to an immediate superior than the superior is to reveal intimacies to his subordinates." Nonetheless, in natural conversations, all participants feel spontaneously encouraged to use self-disclosure with others, regardless of business or work roles.

From the psychological perspective, when people disclose their personal experiences to others, the latter tend to like the former more. Lieberman (2001) observed that people who share their feelings about their negative experiences to others prompts the latter to act in a reciprocal manner, which creates a more trusting bond between them.

Schafer (2015) has observed that self-disclosure generates more attraction in others if the comments have an emotional base, rather than factual, and are specific rather than general. However, this author stated that if a person makes comments which are too intimate, especially when they are early in a relationship, this individual is perceived as less likeable in the eyes of others.

8.8 Natural Conversations and Comfort

Most work and business environments have an accelerated pace and tend to be time-is-money orientated. In these environments, there are some common practices, such as overworking, continuous busyness, multiple deadlines, multitasking and time-management practices, which make people behave in a hurried and unreflective manner and pursue tasks as something to be ticked off from a list.

Consequently, most traditional business conversations are rushed, especially when organisations have plenty of things on their plates. In most companies, time is considered a precious resource, which should never be wasted on non-priority topics or trivial activities. Most companies are continually constrained by various tight deadlines, which in turn limits interactions with others in the work and business environments. In these cases, personal conversations are only held when absolutely necessary.

This time limitation also constrains the length of personal encounters, which prevents people from expressing their ideas fully. These rushed conversations make people feel pressurised and uncomfortable; their need for expression is severely curtailed. In hectic environments, casual or informal conversations are considered a waste of time, and sometimes, plain diversions from the process of achieving a company's objectives. Consequently, these "idle" conversations are strongly discouraged, sometimes in a very subtle manner.

Most dictionaries define the term "slow" with negative connotations such as "sluggish," "dull," "laggard," and others. Honoré (2004) stated that "fast is busy, controlling, aggressive, hurried, analytical, superficial, impatient, active, quantity-over-quantity." This author also observed that natural conversations have a slower pace; slow is "calm, careful, receptive, still, intuitive, unhurried, patient, reflective, quality-over-quality." From this author's perspective, a slower pace allows people to make "real and meaningful connections." In these conversations, people place no restraints on their interaction, because they are willing to experience these conversations fully, without rushing them.

Natural conversations can be mindfully savoured and reflected on, because people are not pushed by any time pressure. Arnold and Plas (1993) observed that "when people take the time to share a joke or a cup of coffee, to pause, think, share and truly listen, trust starts to build." These authors wisely concluded that any time people invest in being more human with others is always well invested.

In natural conversations, the participants can have different opinions on a topic. In those cases, they are inclined to use sentences like "It is interesting to know your specific view on this topic … I feel that this can also be perceived in this way … (exposing the speaker's own view)" or "I understand your perspective on this and I have an alternative viewpoint on this topic, which is …." These sentences are delivered in a calm and friendly tone of voice.

In these conversations, the participants never express their own positions on a topic in an aggressive manner but treat each other with kindness. These individuals adopt a loving attitude with one another, because they each want the other to feel comfortably acknowledged. Therefore, any comments are warmly welcome, never judged.

Some adversarial sentences like "Your view is wrong because …" or "I know what you said is not right …" tend to disconnect people and prompt them to adopt a defensive mode (fight-freeze-flight). In natural conversations, this type of sentence is avoided, because subtle or overt confrontation creates friction and disrupts the flow of the interaction.

In natural conversations, people do not seek approval or acceptance from others – they feel comfortable showing themselves as they truly are. In these conversations, people also feel comfortable with the analysis of an overarching range of topics, which go from external aspects (facts, news, trends, etc.) to internal ones (their own experiences, challenges, desires, etc.).

Consequently, in natural conversations, people tend to adopt a more open-minded attitude, which make them more likely to find commonalities with others as human beings (e.g., moments of tribulation, hard challenges, hopes and dreams, etc.), instead of things separating them. These conversations are more alive because people can express themselves fully. Participants are empowered to break free from any rigid structures which hamper traditional conversations.

8.9 Natural Conversations and Active Listening

Seek first to understand; then to be understood.

Stephen Covey

The majority of people tends to be self-centred most of the time; their main focus is on themselves, not others. Instead, in natural conversations each person is also focused on the other; when a participant talks, the other listens mindfully. People who listen to each other actively tend to fully enjoy the encounter.

Warren (2002) observed that giving undivided attention to others is always an act of love. This author also stated that active listeners concentrate so intently on the speaker that they totally forget themselves. In other words, active listening makes people less self-conscious and more connected to others.

An active listener shows natural interest in what others say, to understand their states of mind and feelings. This individual considers others' ideas enriching because valuable things can be learnt from them. When this person shows interest in others, this individual connects to them on a deeper level. These listeners adopt a generous attitude toward others; they do not try to get anything from others but give them their attention.

An active listener acts like a sounding board which helps speakers articulate and elaborate their message with more clarity and depth. Some authors like Ray and Myers (1989) observed that a person should always listen to others as if this individual was a therapist, willing to discover what is relevant to them, without judging them. Besides, speakers who are given undivided attention tend to feel as if they were the most relevant voice to be heard, which positively contributes to their self-esteem and confidence. Metaphorically speaking, this listener acts like a movie maker who purposely directs the filming lights and cameras on the other person. From this perspective, the speaker is considered as the main "protagonist" on the communicational stage set.

An active listener is fully present, which means this person is centred on the now, avoiding any distracting thoughts about the past or future. The listener is not trying to guess what the speaker is about to say next. Instead, the listener is totally absorbed and engrossed in the speaker's message, which is the most important thing at that moment. This also means the listener avoids multitasking (e.g., reading, taking calls, etc.) during the interaction. Some authors like Tuckle (2015) have observed that, even when a mobile phone is nearby, people tend to engage in a more superficial conversation and their attention becomes less engaged.

In most traditional business conversations, active listening is not possible because people are continually pressurised by multiple deadlines, policies, procedures, and processes. These people have an impending sense of urgency to achieve organisational goals, which prevents them from listening to others in a mindful manner.

Instead, in natural conversations, even though people have priorities to focus on and objectives to meet, they allow themselves to be more patient and listen to others actively in order to connect to them more deeply. Moreover, these individuals enthusiastically encourage others to express their ideas fully and openly.

Besides, an active listener is never anxious about providing the speaker with responses, advice, or suggestions. This type of listener is patient, relaxed, and calm when others are speaking and avoids interrupting their train of thought. The active listener is never interested in blaming, criticising, or arguing with the speaker. This listener acknowledges the message conveyed in a kind, warm, and respectful manner.

8.10 Other Aspects of Active Listening

> It is the province of knowledge to speak, and it is the privilege of wisdom to listen.
>
> **Oliver Wendell Holmes Sr.**

Most people have overanalytical minds, crowded with agendas, expectations, and concerns, which prevent them from listening to others more actively. Carlson and Bailey (1998) observed that during a conversation, a person should slow down, in order to fully experience others without being polluted by restless thoughts. Listeners who slow down become more attentive to what is being said by others and increase their understanding of it. To put it simply, active listeners tend to quieten their mental dialogue to focus only on the ideas expressed by others.

An active listener is always willing to know more about others and understand distinct specific views on different topics. This type of listener fully absorbs the messages conveyed by others and reflects on their ideas. This listener acts like a curious child who silently observes the world around and pays close attention to each of its details. Not only is an active listener attentive to the words expressed by others, but also their body language (e.g., tone of voice, gesture, movements, etc.).

An active listener tends to make frequent nods to non-verbally encourage speakers to deliver their ideas in a complete manner. These listeners also use regular eye-contact and certain words (e.g., "aha," "hmm," etc.) to show their engrossment in the speaker's message. With these signals, the listener aims to satisfy the speaker's need to be fully heard.

When a person listens actively to another, the latter is more likely to listen to the former, because of the principle of reciprocity. Cuddy (2016) observed that when a person listens actively to another, they can develop a more trusting bond. This author also concluded that an active listener is more inclined to provide others with useful suggestions based on what they previously said. Based on ideas previously delivered by others, this person can also ask them insightful questions about their interests, desires, and needs.

8.11 Active Listening, Paraphrasing, Analogies, and Recaps

An authentic active listener also lets others finish their ideas and uses paraphrasing on a regular basis. People who paraphrase repeat the message conveyed by an individual in their own words, to verify that the message was understood accurately. In natural conversations, a person can paraphrase what the speaker said (textual paraphrasing) and also how this person felt (emotional paraphrasing).

Paraphrasing is a valuable skill used to learn more about the other person. The use of this tool can be improved with continuous practice. Rosenberg (2005) observed that paraphrasing should be used when it contributes to a better understanding of others and to adopt a more compassionate attitude toward them, especially when their messages are emotionally charged. A person who paraphrases another uses sentences like "Let me see if understood well what you said … You told me that …," and similar phrases. With this type of sentence, people show that they paid close attention to the messages conveyed by others, which also implies that their opinions are relevant.

An active listener can also use analogies to clarify what was previously said by another. An analogy is a sentence which relates two things which look similar in some way (for instance, "This lake is like a clean mirror"). To that effect, this individual can use sentences, such as "What you said is like ...? Isn't it?" Lastly, an active listener can also recap what the other person said, by observing "I would like to summarise what you told me …." The use of the aforementioned tools prevents people from misinterpreting the message conveyed by the others.

8.12 Natural Conversations and Co-Operation

> Love is at the same time the foundation of dialogue and dialogue itself.
>
> **Paulo Freire**

Plowman (1998) observed that there are several types of interactions involving communication, such as contending, collaborative, compromising, avoiding, accommodating, and reconciling. Natural conversations are always collaborative and constructive; participants always aim to co-operate and support each other during these interactions.

According to Rogers (1961), in natural conversations, people are genuine and show others warm regard, considering them as individuals with unconditional self-worth, regardless of their personal conditions. In these conversations, people contribute to developing a loving environment for others to express their ideas and emotions in a transparent and unrestrained manner. People also show others that they are not being taken for granted, but valued greatly. Moreover, in these conversations, participants relish the togetherness created by these interactions.

Lowndes (2003) said that, in order to have more natural conversations with others, people can imagine they are talking to old friends. These individuals can ask themselves: "How can I connect with this person if he/she was a close friend?" This simple mental "trick" generally makes conversations more flowing, warm, and amicable.

When a person treats others in a friendly and kind manner, they feel compelled to adopt a reciprocal attitude. Besides, a person who considers others as companions avoids detrimental behaviour toward them, such as

- Keeping people waiting before a meeting
- Not returning their phone calls
- Not answering their emails
- Ignoring their comments
- Talking only about business topics

- Centring the conversation on themselves
- Being disrespectful or rude with others
- Not showing appreciation to them

A person who treats others as friends is more inclined to help them explore their ideas and emotional states openly and confidently. According to Rogers (1961), when a person treats others in a conversation like close companions, this individual avoids trampling on their valuable worlds of meaning and feelings, but instead accepts these worlds with no reservation.

8.13 Natural Conversations and Learning

In natural conversations, people share valuable parts of their personal universe with one another. In these encounters, people truly want to learn more from others about their specific views and perspectives on various topics. Each person is willing to submerge themselves in the strangeness of the other. In these natural conversations, participants never adopt an omniscient attitude toward one another; omniscience implies behaving as a know-it-all person. In a similar tone, Freire (2005) observed that "dialogue cannot exist without humility" and "cannot be an act of arrogance."

These conversations can also help people learn more about themselves. For example, people who talk to others about their own emotions relating to a specific situation can gain more clarity about these emotional states. However, some people tend to naturally adopt a defensive attitude toward others and, therefore, are less likely to fully convey their emotional states to them.

In these conversations, any topic can be discussed from a wide range of perspectives. In other words, people are always open to discovering valuable insights from others, regardless of their specific knowledge, background, or business role. Figuratively speaking, in this type of conversation, participants act like inquisitive explorers navigating uncharted territories teeming with hidden treasures to be unearthed. People who engage in a natural conversation always assume that others have valuable things to share with them. Consequently, participants are empowered to talk about any topic, including personal ones.

Luft and Ingham (1955) developed a very useful model which includes four types of topics to be potentially included in a natural conversation. The first type is called the "façade," because it is a topic about one of the participants which is known by this person, but unknown by the other. The second type is called the "blind spot," which is a topic related to one of the participants, unknown by this individual, but known by the other. There is a third type of topic called "arena," which is related to one of the participants and known by both of them, and the last type is named "the unknown" which is a topic about one participant, but none of them know about this topic (Scoular, 2011). Natural conversations can include any of these four types of topics.

Natural conversations are replete with interesting stories about participants' past experiences, challenges, motivations, dreams, and aspirations. It was previously explained that, in natural conversations, people are focused on the present moment, the topics that unfold during the interaction. Nonetheless, participants can comment about their past experiences and future expectations, but perceived and analysed from the present perspective, which means rooted in the now.

Lastly, in natural conversations, each participant adopts a receptive and validating attitude toward each other's comments. In this type of interaction, a person can even show their appreciation to others by saying "Thanks for sharing this, I appreciate your comments." This appreciative attitude represents a powerful way to validate others as unique and valuable human beings.

8.14 Natural Conversations and Meaning

In traditional conversations, the level of communication is commonly kept on a surface level. These conversations are business-related and formal, which does not connect people in a deep manner. Instead, natural conversations are intrinsically deep and meaningful because participants connect with one another beyond their business objectives, roles, formal hierarchies, or power games.

In general, people tend to consider that a conversation is meaningful when they feel acknowledged, cared for, and respected during the interaction. In meaningful conversations, participants adopt a curious attitude toward each other, which makes their bond stronger. In these meaningful interactions, people ask others interesting questions, for example:

- Could you please tell me more about this?
- How did you deal with that situation?
- What are your hopes and expectations about this topic?
- What are your unique strengths and capabilities regarding this?
- What are the challenges you faced regarding this?
- Why is this situation relevant to you?
- What did you learn about this situation?
- How do you feel about this situation?

These questions are generally posed in a friendly tone of voice and adopting an inquisitive attitude toward others. The purpose of these questions is to know more about others, without making them feel pressurised. These questions empower others to contribute to the dialogue with their particular views. When a person asks these questions to another, the latter tends to feel acknowledged, understood and respected.

Natural conversations are meaningful because they truly transform participants in a positive manner for two main reasons. Firstly, these individuals are transformed because they end up knowing more about one another (e.g., their preferences, challenges, values, fears, insecurities, etc.). Secondly, participants also feel transformed because they are able to express themselves in an overt and authentic manner.

8.15 Natural Conversations, Inclusiveness, and Empathy

> Love is our shared identity. The differences we experience in our gender, nationality, politics and religion do not exist in love.
>
> **Robert Holden**

Natural conversations are more casual and personal than traditional business conversations. In these interactions, people avoid using impersonal phrases, such as "It is said …," "It's been completed …," etc. Instead, participants tend to use personal sentences, which involve others more directly. Some examples of these sentences are: "You said …" or "I said …," and similar ones.

In this type of conversation, people frequently use inclusive words (such as "we," "our," etc.), which denote a strong affective connection between the participants. Natural conversations are also inclusive because, as mentioned previously, participants perceive one another as equals, so they experience a deep sense of togetherness.

In natural conversations, participants are empowered to show all their aliveness to the other. In the work and business environments, and oftentimes outside it, most people are afraid to show themselves in an overt manner, because they fear being misinterpreted, rejected or harshly criticised.

During natural conversations, people tend to adopt an empathetic attitude toward one another. Participants put themselves in the positions of one another in order to perceive things from the viewpoint of the other. A compassionate person feels a natural identification with the predicaments and tribulations of others, acknowledges their emotional states, and provides them with loving support.

Besides, a compassionate person has the ability to "read" others' emotional states, through changes in their body language (posture, tone of voice, etc.). The ability to be sensitive to emotions experienced by other people is part of what Goleman (1996) calls "emotional intelligence skills." When a person adopts a compassionate attitude toward others, this individual tends to use phrases such as:

- I understand your viewpoint …
- What you said is very important …
- If I were you, I would feel the same
- In your position, I …
- I really got what you meant …
- I know that this is challenging for you, …
- I comprehend how you truly feel …

In natural conversations, people also engage with others in a more compassionate manner, when they use some sentences in an active voice, for example: "I understand you." Sentences in a passive voice (for instance, "You are understood by me") should be avoided, not only because they sound unnatural, but also because they do not create a real connection with others.

People who adopt a compassionate attitude toward others bring more love into their relationships with them. When an individual is treated in a compassionate manner by others, this person tends to act in a similar way toward them. Consequently, adopting a compassionate attitude is valuable in any type of relationship, including business ones.

Lastly, it is more difficult for people to adopt a compassionate attitude toward others when they use written communication (emails, letters, etc.) because some aspects of humanity (such as body language and tone of voice) are lost in the interaction. Therefore, when the emotions of the participants are involved, it is preferable that people use one-to-one conversations over alternative forms of communication.

8.16 Natural Conversations and Free Expression

In natural conversations, people can express their opinions in a free and overt manner. In this type of conversation, nobody imposes their views on others. Participants share their ideas eloquently and without editing them. In these interactions, participants do not pretend to show a perfect image of themselves to be accepted by others, but honestly share what is inside themselves. According to Apps (2014), natural conversations also include heart talk, which encompasses comments about feelings, values, meanings, and topics of great value to the speaker.

In natural conversations, people say what they mean, but also mean what they say. These dialogues are so honest and revealing that people feel safe, even when they talk about their own negative experiences, mistakes, flaws, and problems. In these conversations, participants fully own their comments using personal sentences, like "I think ...", "I feel ...", "I know ...", and similar ones. In natural conversations, participants avoid misleading or manipulating one another, and speak their words with integrity and transparency.

In these conversations people welcome the discussion of any topic. However, the discussion of potentially contentious topics (such as politics, religion, etc.) is always friendly and respectful. Each participant is curious to know each other's opinions; they are sensitive to the views of others. Participants express their ideas using words that are right for them.

In natural conversations, people tend to avoid convoluted or complex vocabulary to impress others. They also avoid the use of euphemisms and intricate jargon. Instead, participants tend to choose casual and amenable words. The use of clear, spontaneous, and straightforward conversational style helps people create a deeper connection with others.

The well-known quote "condemnation is the root of all evil" is commonly applied to natural conversations. In these interactions, people are prone to adopt a non-judgemental attitude toward others, which means avoiding criticising them, mentally or aloud. When a person avoids condemning others, this individual is addressing their need to be respected and treated with care. Rogers (1961) called this attitude "unconditional positive regard."

In natural conversations people never behave in an aggressive or defensive manner with others; nor do they attempt to exert their power over them. If participants have divergent views on a topic during the conversation, these perspectives are always expressed in a gentle and caring way. In natural conversations, participants are also inclined to adopt an attitude of curiosity toward others. The use of sentences like "This sounds quite relevant/interesting/attractive/important ..." and "Can you please tell me more about this?" is suitable for this type of conversation.

Natural conversations are warm and friendly, which makes people feel safe, at ease, and physically relaxed. From the scientific perspective, there is a continuous connection between a person's physical and mental aspects. Consequently, when people do not feel tense, they are inclined to express their ideas in a more open, spontaneous, and flowing manner. Comfortable people tend to adopt an exploring and inquisitive attitude toward opinions expressed by others. Tense or uncomfortable individuals are prone to adopt a more cautious attitude (connected to the fight-freeze-flight mode).

8.17 Clarity in Natural Conversations

From the perspective of neuro-linguistic programming (NLP), whenever people engage in conversations, they tend to omit, generalise, and distort their messages. People are also prone to simplify their messages for practical conversational purposes, leaving relevant aspects out of the conversation. Their messages also include various assumptions, which oftentimes are not necessarily connected with reality.

NLP provides a series of questions to help people clarify messages received from others. These questions form part of a tool called the Meta Model of Language. People who apply this tool to their conversations obtain more details about unclear and unspecific messages conveyed by others.

For example, if people use vague sentences like "I am stressed." These individuals can be asked a question like "Stressed specifically about what?" in order to know more about the causes of their stress. People who use generalisations like "I am always stressed" can be asked questions such as "Always?" or "Are there any exceptions to this?" Similar questions can be asked to clarify statements including terms like "everyone" and "everywhere," and similar ones.

Most people use nominalisations or terms linked to intangible or abstract things, which cannot be perceived by the senses. Examples of nominalisations are "fairness," "satisfaction," "rest," etc. If a person says "I need motivation," the word "motivation" represents various things to different people (for example: specific training, recognition, more economic rewards, etc.). In this example, the other person could ask a question like "What do you specifically mean by motivation?" to understand the thinking of the other individual.

Sometimes, people use sentences which imply apparent limitations, for example: "I cannot attain a balanced life." In this case, the other person can ask: "What are the obstacles preventing you from having balance?" to probe the apparent limitations. Sometimes, people use statements which entail mind-reading skills, for instance: "I know that this person will not like my work." A person listening to this statement can challenge this idea by asking: "How do you know that this person will not like your work?"

In some conversations, people use statements which include a cause and its related effect. For example, a person says, "I feel demotivated because I have a lot of work." The listener can ask: "How is it that having a lot of work makes you feel demotivated?" to understand details regarding the link between the cause (having a lot of work) and the effect (feeling demotivated).

Oftentimes, people use sentences which include vague verbs, for example: "I rest too much." In this example, this person can be asked the following question: "In which way are you resting too much?" to garner more details about this. People often use other unclear words like "it," "that," or "this," and similar ones. For example, a person who says "It's stressful" can be asked questions like "What is stressful?" to obtain more detailed information.

In the previous examples, people express their ideas unclearly, and the listener adopts an inquisitive and loving attitude and asks them for more details about the ideas expressed. The frequent use of the aforementioned questions helps the listener clarify messages expressed by others, but also shows them this individual has authentic interest in their ideas, which contributes to the development of more clear and meaningful conversations.

8.18 Body Language and Natural Conversations

Body language (gestures, movements, eye-contact, etc.) is the natural complement of verbal aspects (words) in any conversation. Research shows that body language contributes to the communication process more significantly than verbal language. Mehrabian (mentioned in Pease and Pease, 2004) observed that communication is composed of 55 per cent non-verbal, 38 per cent vocal (which includes the inflection and tone of voice), and only 7 per cent verbal (words). This non-verbal language is used to stress certain points of the message or illustrate them more eloquently. These non-verbal cues also help people express their emotions more overtly.

In natural conversations, people use warmer and more relaxed body language, as compared with traditional business interactions. People who engage in natural conversations use their non-verbal language for positive purposes, for example, to show respect to others, pay attention to them, or express appreciation. Some examples of positive uses of body language are mentioned below.

- ▪ When a person listens to others, this individual should face them either from an angle or communicate side-by-side, to make them feel more at ease. This person should never point at others directly because this type of body language can be perceived as confrontational or intimidating by others.

- A listener should use regular eye-contact with others, without staring at them in a fixed manner. This person should remain relaxed and lean toward others while they express their ideas. This non-defensive body language conveys comfort and engagement with whatever others comment about.
- During a chat, nodding is frequently perceived as a valuable non-verbal signal to acknowledge messages being conveyed by others. People who nod to speakers are encouraging these individuals to continue expressing their ideas. Borg (2011) observed that nodding can also be used to acknowledge others or show understanding or agreement.
- A positive body language cue commonly used in natural conversations is smiling frankly and openly at the other person, which increases the rapport between them. Lastly, tilting the head to one side when the other person is speaking demonstrates interest in what is being said.

Some scholars like Pease (2014) observed that, in typical business conversations, people tend to look at the point between the other's eyebrows. This point is commonly used for formal interactions. Instead, in more casual and natural conversations, people are prone to focus on the whole face of their participants. This second point of attention (the whole person's face) is used for so-called "social eye-contact."

Another important body language cue which most experts highlight is showing the palms up when conversing with other; this signal conveys transparency and honesty. All these micro-gestures make other people feel comfortable and valued. In natural conversations, negative body language (e.g., visual avoidance, crossing arms tightly, eye-darting, and staring continually) should be avoided because it does not contribute to the development of a loving connection between the participants.

A very relevant part of body language is the tone of voice. In traditional business meetings, people tend to use a monotonous and formal tone of voice, to appear more serious and professional in the eyes of others. Oftentimes, people can also use this type of tone of voice to hide their own negative emotional states, like fear, and appear confident and calm.

Instead, in natural conversations, people use a warmer and more friendly tone of voice to express their ideas. In these interactions, people naturally use their tone of voice to express various nuances of their feelings in a more expressive manner. The use of a natural tone of voice helps people express ideas to others in a more transparent and trustworthy manner.

8.19 Body Language, Emotions, and Synchronicity

In natural conversations, people avoid repressing their body language, but let it unfold in a spontaneous and lively manner. Instead, in typical business conversations, people tend to display body language which is rigid and ungraceful, for instance, arms crossed, clenched fists, tight and raised shoulders, etc.

This stiff non-verbal language conveys tension, lack of confidence, and a state of defensiveness. These non-verbal signals do not inspire trust, but create distance with others. Goffman (1969) observed that people tend to hide traits (verbal and non-verbal ones) incompatible with their roles, in order to be accepted by others.

In most traditional business conversations, people display solemn and uptight body language, which creates distance with others. According to Giddens (2009), these people are concerned about how they are seen by others, and consequently use different ways of impression management, for example, controlling their body language consciously or unwittingly.

Oftentimes, these signals look inauthentic and make others feel uncomfortable. In these inter-actions, many people try to hide their undesirable emotional states (sadness, fear, anger, etc.) by controlling their body language, which makes them look untrustworthy. According to Goffman (1969), these defensive practices are used by people to preserve a positive impression when they interact with others.

Tense people tend to show a body language which is incongruent with their verbal language, and this can be detected by others very easily. Their non-verbal "armours" prevent these individu-als from expressing their ideas more openly and creatively. Besides, fretful people have more dif-ficulties conveying messages that come from their hearts.

According to Apps (2012), individuals are more prone to hold authentic conversations when they reconnect the energy of their thoughts and emotions with their voice. This author observed that honest conversationalists are emotionally truthful; their tone of voice, gestures, and corporal movements naturally tell others a congruent story, which makes them credible.

Consequently, people who hold conversations with stakeholders should be aware of not con-trolling their own body language. If their non-verbal expression is restrained, they should slightly tense their muscles and then relax them. A second way to become more relaxed is to breathe deeply a few times and relax, causing gestures and posture to become more at ease physically. When people show more relaxed body language, their conversations tend to become natural and flowing.

From the perspective of NLP (neuro-linguistic programming), natural conversations com-monly show spontaneous synchronicity between the body language of participants. Participants seem to mirror one another with their movements, posture, gestures, tone of voice, and other non-verbal signals. Their body language seems to flow, like dancers in a graceful choreography, which increases their connection and rapport during a conversation. Pease and Pease (2004) observed that mirroring is generally perceived as a co-operative behaviour, which makes others feel more comfortable.

Some NLP specialists recommend that people should purposely aim to "match" other's body language to increase the rapport with them. However, other scholars observed that is not advisable because this might look inauthentic and unnatural. In natural conversations, the alignment of participants' body language occurs unforcefully and spontaneously.

8.20 Natural Business Conversations

Entrepreneurs should remember the quotation which goes "thriving business activities are always based on thriving relationships." Natural conversations allow people to bring to the table their authentic human side which benefits the "business" aspects of their relationships. These conversa-tions also help people connect more deeply in their interactions with others. Natural conversations should never be considered as one-off interactions; they should be used on a regular basis.

Business conversations with stakeholders can adopt the perspective of natural conversations in three distinct ways. The first way is to convert the entire interaction into a natural conversation and combine business topics and personal topics in a balanced manner. These interactions con-sider both the business roles of the participants (manager, subordinate, supplier, customers, etc.) and their valuable human side. These conversations are more relaxed and insightful because people are recognised as worthy human beings, not as cogs in the business machinery.

The second way is to use this sequence: natural conversation – formal conversation – nat-ural conversation. These encounters start as a natural conversation (where personal aspects are expressed), then continue with a more traditional conversation (where business topics – deadlines, projects, requirements, etc. – are discussed), and end up with another natural conversation (where personal aspects wrap up the encounter). Even though this second way looks less spontaneous than the previous option, it can create good engagement and support between participants.

The third way is to have a brief natural conversation only at the beginning of the interaction. This preliminary conversation, known as "small-talk," has the objective of "breaking the ice" before entering a formal discussion on business topics for the rest of the interaction. These natural preludes aim to put people in a more positive mood, which often lowers their default mental defences toward one another. This third way does not consider the human dimension of individuals extensively, so this conversation can still sometimes be an unnatural interaction.

In some cultural environments, known as "high context countries," local companies consider the human side of interactions with others as important as their business side. A companies' members must personally know their counterparts in other companies, before doing any business together. In these cultures, companies understand that transactions are based on relationships, which must be developed and nourished over time.

Lastly, it is important that companies encourage the development of natural conversations among their employees. According to Cohen and Prusak (2001), an organisation can do this in several ways: developing comfortable spaces (e.g., communal rooms, lounges, etc.) where people can hold informal frequent conversations, allowing employees to take regular breaks to talk to one another in an informal manner, and privileging whenever possible personal interactions over other ways of communication (email, etc.).

Questions for Self-Reflection

- What formalities can be eliminated to make communication with our stakeholders more natural?
- How can I listen to our company's stakeholders in a more active manner?
- How can I express myself to our stakeholders in a more spontaneous manner?
- How can I encourage our stakeholders to express their ideas and emotions more openly?

Chapter 9

Chapter 9

The Use of Positive Language with Stakeholders

9.1 The Importance of Words for Communication Purposes

Words are the materialisation or overt expression of people's thoughts and emotions. Words are important in business conversations (and also in non-business ones) because they help people analyse, describe, and justify circumstances in specific ways. Words are like building blocks which sustain and strengthen relationships with others. Besides, words act like maps helping people navigate the circumstances affecting them.

- Words are powerful attention-grabbing resources; they can emphasise or direct the attention to different aspects of specific situations. Words can be used to ask questions, to create possible scenarios and to draw definite or provisional conclusions.
- Some words can describe positive sides of a situation, and others can describe its negative ones. Words are powerful tools to frame, shape and interpret reality in different ways.
- Words can be used to express one's values, preferences, desires, objectives and feelings. Words can also people help describe their beliefs and behaviours, as well as justify them. Words are specific ways people enumerate their own qualities and the ones related to others.
- Words can be used to analyse situations and ideas. Words can be used to compare, synthesise, and create alternatives. Words can also be used to persuade others, instruct them and remind them of relevant things.

The human brain uses words when it processes information; consequently the use of words not only affects the thoughts a person has, but also the emotions and physical sensations related to them. In the business and work environments, words can be used in a loving manner: for instance, to acknowledge and praise stakeholders, empower them, support them, and express gratitude to them. Positive words can be used to provide people with feedback about their performance. People who use positive words with others tend to elicit positive emotions and thoughts in themselves and the other people.

The use of positive words shortens the distance between people. Most people have the need to hear positive words about them from others; praises or compliments are like a soothing balm to these individuals.

9.2 Detrimental Impact of Negative Words

In the business environment, people can use negative words with others to condemn them, threaten them, and complain about their unproductive behaviour. People can use negative words to express their anger, regret, or worry about others' behaviour or ideas. In the work environment, words can also be used to backstab others, discriminate against them, and bully them. Every time people use negative words with others, their relationships are affected in a detrimental manner.

It is important to remember that when people receive negative comments from others, they tend to shut down, adopting a fight-freeze-flight mode. This mode has been thoroughly explained in Chapter 3. These individuals often behave in a resentful or uncooperative manner. Sometimes they feel angry, sad, or ashamed in relation to the people who offended them.

There is a very interesting scientific experiment conducted by the prestigious Dr Emoto (2004). In this experiment, this renowned scholar put water into two glasses. Then a group of people said positive words to the water, for instance, "I love you" or "Thank you." Another group of people said negative words to the second glass of water, such as "I'll kill you" or "Fool." The purpose of this experiment was to test the impact of different words on the structure of water.

Afterwards, the water in each glass was frozen and its structure was examined with technical instruments, such as a microscope. In this experiment, Dr Emoto realised that the structure of the water which received positive words had beautiful and harmonious shapes. Instead, the structure of the water which received negative comments showed inharmonious and ugly figures.

The reader might ask this question "What is the lesson here?" It is important to remember that human beings are made up of water, ranging from 50–75 per cent on average (Helmenstine, 2018). Therefore, what people say to others – and to themselves – always has an impact, either positive or negative, depending on the quality of the words used. Therefore, people working for a company should frequently ask themselves the following questions:

- Are we using positive words to convey our messages to others?
- Can we word our messages in a more positive manner?
- Are our words nourishing our relationships with others?
- How can we make our words more loving toward others?
- Are we using the same type of words we want to hear from others?
- How can our words be more grateful, supportive, or full of praise?
- Are we communicating at all with the company's stakeholders?

These questions will help people to reflect on the words they use on a regular basis. Frequent self-reflection on this topic will help these individuals use more positive vocabulary when interacting with others.

9.3 The Power of Using Positive Language

Some social psychology experiments have concluded that people tend to react more productively to positive words, as compared with negative ones. Positive words have a powerful priming effect on people, prompting them to experience positive emotions and dwell on positive circumstances. In a company's environment, the frequent use of positive words could contribute to an improvement in that organisation's performance and productivity levels.

A very large amount of words commonly used in the business environment have a negative connotation. Some examples of these words are "attack," "competition," "strategy," "tactics," "defence," and others. These words have a warmongering connotation, which prompts people to adopt an adversarial perspective toward others. Underneath these words there is an impending sense of fear; people tend to use these terms to protect themselves from external threats. Some examples of these threatening factors are current competitors, potential entrants to the market, etc.

Cialdini (2016) suggested that people in a company should frequently use terms with positive connotations when performing their business activities. From this perspective, companies should use words related to accomplishment, such as "vision," "mission," "goals," "objectives," and similar ones. This specialist observed that, when people use positive words, their attention is engrossed in these very terms, instead of concentrating on competing words (negative terms). Some ways to use more positive terms in the business environment are:

- People should regularly use words related to thankfulness. For example, the use of sentences with stakeholders like "Thank you very much for your comments" have a very positive effect on people receiving this message. Individuals should also offer honest compliments to internal and external stakeholders. For example, managers can say to their subordinates "I like the way you contributed to this project because …", which will impact on these employees in a positive manner. Positive words can affect the receiver's self-image positively.

- People who tell others that they share some positive traits, interests, or preferences with them create a more positive connection, affinity, and sense of togetherness with these individuals. For instance, a person can say to another "I enjoy working on this project, knowing that you are committed in the same way I am."

- People can also comment about their own ideas or experiences, stressing only their positive aspects. For example, these individuals can say to others "The best part of this …" or "The most positive aspect of …," and contribute to a more constructive dialogue with others. This tool can also be used when a person listens to others. In this case, this person can ask others "What are the most positive aspects of what you said?" to redirect their focus toward the positive.

- In a conversation, a listener can also select the most positive comments the speaker has made and ask questions such as "Could you tell me more about …?" to obtain more detailed information about the positive aspects of the message conveyed. In this way, people are also prompted to concentrate on their own previous positive comments.

- An individual who receives a negative comment from another can reword this message in a positive manner. For example, if a person says, "Our levels of sales are very low," the other individual can reframe this comment by saying "I can see that you aim for higher levels of sales; which are the levels you look forward to obtaining?" In this example, the reframing of the message prompts people to feel more positive, because it does not focus on what people do not want, but on their goals and desires.

Robbins (2001) advised to use words which magnify the intensity of positive emotions. For example, people should say "I feel exhilarated," instead of saying "I am having fun," to bring about more positive feelings and thoughts. This author also observed that people should use softening words in relation to negative emotional states. For instance, the person can use words like "I feel slightly concerned," instead of saying "I feel desperate."

A person can also use this tool to comment to others about their emotional states, for example, by saying to them "You look very exhilarated," instead of "You seem to be in a good mood."

A person can also say "You look slightly concerned," instead of "You look desperate." In short, these "intensifiers" and "softeners" relabel people's emotional states and improve interactions with others.

According to Howard (1989), some examples of positive words which can affect the business communication in a beneficial manner are "agree," "care," "fair," "good," "heart," "hope," "love," "sincere," "special," and "new," among others. This author also provides examples of negative words to avoid in business conversations: "afraid," "but," "cannot," "disappoint," "disagree," "dislike," "doubt," "risk," and "unfortunately," among others. For example, instead of saying "Unfortunately, we cannot send the merchandise until you make the payment," a person can say "We would love to send the merchandise once you make the payment."

Lastly, the use of positive language in the business environment is not limited to spoken words. Some researchers analysed the impact of placing banners with inspirational messages on the walls of the workplace. According to the research findings, the use of these positive notes (for example, "You can achieve your goals") affected employees' performance positively. Therefore, it is advisable that companies use this type of positive visual cues in the workplace to boost employees' productivity (Cialdini, 2016).

9.4 Positive Vocabulary and Criticism

As seen previously, a company's employees should frequently use positive language with other stakeholders and avoid delivering negative criticism to them. The well-known saying which goes "Condemnation is the root of all evil regarding relationships" is very applicable to the business and work environments.

When harsh criticism is used in organisations, people affected by these remarks are prone to respond in a reactive mode (fight-freeze-flight). A person can express negative criticism to others in several ways. For instance, threats, ultimatums, sarcasm, humiliating comments, guilt-tripping, and personal accusations are negative forms of criticism.

In the business environment, a person who delivers derisory criticism to others generally does so because of mistakes they made – for instance, missed deadlines, important documentation lost, low quality supplies, delays in the delivery, wrong products offered, etc. For example, managers who say to their subordinates "You cannot do this job well!" do more harm than good to their relationships with these employees.

In this example, managers communicate with employees in an aggressive manner, personalising the conflict, instead of focusing on the problem itself. Managers' snide remarks prompt subordinates to adopt a defensive attitude, which in turn prevent them from improving their work performance. These employees do not feel acknowledged as valuable human beings, and might even feel rejected and unappreciated.

These employees are prone to feel attacked by their managers' negative remarks, which makes these subordinates feel more vulnerable and unsafe. Their natural fear-based response is related to the fight-freeze-flight mode, which prevents them from harnessing their unique analytical and creative skills. In this example, these employees might even become less receptive due to the comments received.

9.5 A Positive Way to Deliver Criticism

Any criticism expressed to a company's stakeholders should be delivered in a non-harmful manner. A person who delivers critiques to others should adopt a compassionate, understanding, and caring attitude toward them. It is important to pinpoint a generally neglected fact: all human beings, with no exceptions, make mistakes.

When mistakes made by others are highlighted in a non-judgmental manner, people are more prone to learn from these mistakes and to act more effectively next time. When stakeholders are given critiques in a respectful way, they are more likely to treat others in a reciprocal manner. Some important characteristics of constructive criticism delivered to a company's stakeholders are discussed in the remainder of this chapter.

9.5.1 Positive Wording

Criticism provided to others must always be formulated in a constructive manner. When possible, the critique should not refer to things that are wrong or mistaken ("This task was done in the wrong way because ..."), but instead focus on things that can be improved ("Next time, this task should be improved in this way ..."). Consequently, a person who delivers criticism to others should avoid guilt-tripping others ("This is your fault"), because it makes them feel as if they acted wrongly on purpose.

Critical comments should never be delivered in a pushy manner ("You must do it this way next time!") because people are likely to feel controlled and pressurised. As seen previously, accusations should also be avoided when delivering criticism to others. Whenever a person adopts an authoritative or accusatory attitude toward others, they are prone to adopt a defensive attitude (fight-freeze-flight) toward this individual.

A person who delivers critical feedback to others should start with some positive comments on what they have done correctly in the past (for example, "I want to highlight your performance last year because ...") After this, the person can continue with the specific critique "Your performance during the last few months can be improved significantly because ...." When criticism is accompanied by an initial positive comment, receivers tend to feel cared for, which makes them feel more at ease and receptive.

Criticism should always be delivered in a respectful manner; harsh words and tone of voice must be avoided. The use of a conversational and warm tone of voice is preferred over a "formal" or "solemn" one. People delivering a critique to others should demonstrate they want the best for them.

Criticism is also prone to be well-received by others, when it includes previous empathic comments about them, for instance "I know that you have been dealing with a massive workload during the last few weeks." This introductory comment makes people receiving the criticism feel acknowledged as valuable human beings, which makes them more open to remarks received.

After people deliver their critiques to others, they can also offer their assistance for the implementation of the suggestions proposed. For example, these individuals can say "I know that the change I am proposing may be challenging for you, but I want you to know I am willing to support you during the process in this way ...." These people adopt a loving attitude to the receivers, which makes the latter feel cared for by the former. As a consequence, this critique is more likely to be taken on board. Whenever possible, the person offering support to another should act as if the latter was a close friend.

When people deliver critical remarks to others, the latter are more likely to act on these comments when they feel appreciated. For example, the person who delivered a critique can say to the other "Thanks in advance for considering these comments" or "Your co-operation on this topic is greatly valued." This type of sentences assumes the other person will take the comments on board, which makes this individual more prone to act congruently with this positive assumption.

9.5.2 Behaviour-Oriented

Criticism must always be expressed with the core objective of preserving the relationship with others. In a similar vein, Fisher et al. (1999) observed that people should always be soft with others, but hard with problems involving them. Unproductive criticism is generally centred on the characteristics of the person criticised (e.g., personality, mental capabilities, manual abilities, etc.). When a person delivers criticism to others based on their qualities ("You are not good for anything"), they are prone to feel negatively labelled and adopt a defensive response.

Instead, constructive critiques delivered to others are focussed on their behaviour (e.g., writing a report, delivering information, etc.), which can be improved in the future. This type of criticism makes people less defensive toward the critiques. Rosenberg (2005) observed that critiques about others' behaviour should always include observations about this behaviour, but not evaluation.

Criticism based on observations describes the current state of reality related to the receiver, in the most objective way possible. An example of this type of criticism is "You have arrived one hour late for the last three weeks" (observation). By contrast, an example of unproductive critique can be "You are incapable of arriving on time." This second example includes the personal evaluative word "incapable," which makes this feedback detrimental.

A person who delivers the critique to a stakeholder should be as clear and specific as possible. General or vague remarks are never of value. For example, instead of saying "I feel that performance can be improved," people should be informed of the specific actionable steps to take in practice to improve their performance. A better way to word this remark is: "Next time I would like things to be done this way ...."

Lastly, unclear generalisations like "always," "never," "all," "none," and others should be avoided. Critiques given to others should always be centred on specific issues. In the business and work environments, situations are unlikely to be "black or white." As a consequence, it is not advisable to use rigid generalisations, because they do not allow any nuances or exceptions to them. Criticism must refer to a particular situation, for instance: "On this occasion ..." or "In this circumstance ...."

9.5.3 Change-Oriented

Sometimes, the receivers of criticism can be offered an incentive for them to change their behaviour in the future. For example, if an employee has a very low performance, the manager can say to this person "If your performance for the next term is improved by 20%, you will be paid a bonus ...." Oftentimes, the offer of a stimulus makes the critique more actionable. Nonetheless, some scholars are of the opinion that offering this type of incentive to others can paradoxically discourage individuals to take action.

As seen previously, when a person delivers constructive feedback on a specific unsolved problem, the receiver should also be given the proposed solution to be implemented, when possible. An example of this could be "I noticed that your performance can be increased by 20% as compared with the previous year. There are some actions such as ... for you to consider that will help you improve your performance."

Sometimes, the person delivering the criticism and its receiver can work out potential solutions to a problem together. An example of this critique could be "I noticed that your performance can be increased by 20% as compared with the previous year. Let's talk about possible ways that will help you improve your performance. Please let me know your opinion about this and I will tell you mine." This approach tends to be more effective because the individual who should make changes is involved in the design of the action to be taken. From this perspective, criticism also represents an opportunity to enhance the receiver's creative capabilities.

As explained previously, criticism should include specific advice on how the receiver should act, which is considered practical support. Besides, the person delivering criticism to others should provide emotional assistance, for example, encouraging them to act, thanking them for their previous contribution to the company, etc. In this way, the person delivering the critique adopts a compassionate and understanding attitude toward the receiver of the remark.

When people want to prompt others to make some changes in their behaviour, they should accompany their criticism with the potential positive impact that this change will generate. An example of this is "There are some actions such as ... for you to consider that will help you improve your performance for next year. If you could perform these actions next time, this will benefit our department in this way ...." From the psychological perspective, when the person who delivers the critique explains to the other the specific benefits of introducing some changes in the future, the latter is more likely to become emotionally invested in the change process.

Sometimes, the critique that a person provides to another can be linked to a goal shared by them. For example, a shared objective can be highlighted in sentences like "If next time you can ..., our relationship will be greatly benefitted in this way ...." The enunciation of a shared goal ("improvement of the relationship") makes the criticism more actionable to the receiver.

As mentioned previously, unproductive criticism makes people feel they are being commanded or told what to do, which makes them less prone to generate any positive change. For example, critiques like "You have to do ... this way ..." generally creates a lot of resistance in the recipient of this order. Instead, when a person uses more indirect phrases, for instance, recommendations, advice, or suggestions to give feedback to others, they are more inclined to accept the remarks.

Sentences like "You could get better results if ..." and "It would be advisable that ..." are more likely to be taken on board. The use of phrases such as "You could ..." or "You can ..." also helps deliver more constructive critiques to others because they introduce an element of choice or possibility. Whenever possible, criticism should be accompanied by the reasons why it is relevant for the recipient to take action on it ("It is a good idea that you ... because of ..."). Research has shown that people are more likely to comply with a suggestion when it is accompanied by the reason supporting this advice, even in cases when the reason is obvious.

Criticism can also be delivered as a question, for example, "What about changing ...?" Once people have delivered their critique to others, they can also say to them "Thanks for considering this suggestion" or "Thanks for your co-operation regarding this." This type of sentences makes the recipient more likely to take on board the remarks received.

Lastly, Rosenberg (2005) stated that when people makes a request to others, they should ask them if their message was correctly understood, for example, with some questions like "Is this clear?" This type of question allows the receiver to avoid mistakes regarding the request made.

9.5.4 Other Aspects Related to Feedback

People who provide others with criticism should clearly explain to them the objective reasons for their comments. For example, a person can provide another with the following "The procedure you have used is not correct because ..." In this case, the person delivering the critique will explain the most appropriate procedures that the receiver should have used, according to regulations, conditions, or any other valid criteria. Critiques supported by objective evidence regarding why things must be done in a certain way are perceived as fairer by the receiver, because they are less prone to subjective interpretation.

When a person delivers criticism to others that might make them feel ashamed, these remarks must be delivered in private. In those cases, the delivery of a private critique is a sign of caring for others' public image. When a person is not sure if the remarks could be perceived as shameful, this individual should deliver these critiques privately.

From the perspective of social psychology, there is a phenomenon known as "fundamental attribution error" which means that oftentimes a person tends to link other people's behaviour to their personal traits (character, personality, intention, etc.) instead of relating that behaviour to external circumstances. For instance, if a person arrives late to a meeting, another person is prone to explain this late arrival by mostly emphasising the characteristics of the former (for example, "This individual arrived late because he is irresponsible and lazy"), instead of considering possible external reasons affecting that individual (for example, "This person arrived late because of a public transport strike").

Therefore, the person who delivers the criticism should always probe for any external reason which might have affected the other person's behaviour to avoid assuming that this behaviour is related to this individual's characteristics. For example, the person who delivers the critique can ask the other questions like "Were you affected by any external factor which prevented you from arriving on time?" In this way, the person delivering the feedback can be more compassionate with the other.

When criticism is of great relevance, the person delivering the remark should hold a personal meeting with the receiver, whenever possible. In the delivery of critiques face-to-face, the person delivering the critical remarks shows the receiver respect and care which strengthens the relationship between them. People who deliver their criticism in person also take personal ownership of the critique delivered.

Sometimes, a person can double-check the main aspects of an issue with the people involved in it, before delivering any critique to them. Sentences like "I would like you to confirm if ..." can be used to avoid mistakes or misunderstandings when delivering remarks to others. The use of these phrases helps confirm that the issue the critique is being delivered on is based on correct information.

Sometimes, critiques can be formulated in a personal way, for instance: "From my perspective ..." or "I think that ...." In other cases, criticism can be expressed in a more impersonal manner, for example: "It will be interesting ..." or "It is necessary ...." From the perspective of this book, oftentimes the personal approach is more authentic and natural than the impersonal one, making the person receiving the critique feel more at ease and receptive.

On some occasions, criticism can be delivered to others in a less forward manner. These remarks are delivered in a less straightforward way, which makes them more likely to be accepted by others. Some softeners, such as "I am a bit curious about one thing ..." can be used to deliver more indirect criticism.

Questions for Self-Reflection

- Why is the use of positive words important for business activities?
- What are the main traits of constructive feedback?
- How can I make other stakeholders feel comfortable when I give them feedback?
- What is the best way to deliver feedback which can potentially affect others negatively?

Chapter 10

Adopting a Loving Attitude toward Employees

10.1 Main Aspects of a Company's Work Environment

Man becomes a "nine to fiver," he is part of the labour force, or the bureaucratic force of clerks and managers ... They all performed tasks as prescribed by the whole structure of the organisation, at a prescribed speed, in a prescribed manner. Even the feelings are prescribed: cheerfulness, tolerance, reliability, ambition, and an ability to get along with everyone without friction.

Erich Fromm

Some organisations treat employees as interchangeable parts of the organisational machinery. Oftentimes, these employees are treated in a dehumanised way, like cogs that can be easily replaced when they do not contribute to a company's objectives. These employees resemble automatons, whose only objective is to be productive. Cohen and Prusak (2001) wisely expressed that the word "employee" has an implicit negative connotation, which means to be utilised or employed. The word "employee" has its origins in the era of the industrial revolution.

Some companies use the term "human resources" instead of "employees." However, the word "resources" can also have a negative connotation because resources are something to be used and oftentimes abused by organisations. Lastly, from a financial perspective, most companies treat employees as "costs," which also has a negative meaning. This type of organisation tends to reduce these costs in different ways (for instance, through work overload, downsizing, etc.) in order to increase its profits, or reduce its losses.

An organisation generally hires people so that they can contribute to achieving the company's business objectives effectively. From this perspective, employees are considered as a means to achieve an end or goal (the company's goals). Companies usually set various goals, such as a bigger market share, more productivity, higher levels of profitability, more efficiency, and higher levels of quality, among others.

Many organisations set their goals without considering the potential impact of the achievement of these objectives on employees and other relevant stakeholders. For example, a company can set an objective of increasing its market share, which might imply that employees have to work overtime for many hours every day. This overtime might create an imbalance between their worktime and their personal activities (family, leisure, etc.), which in turn might bring about employees' dissatisfaction.

Oftentimes, employees are pushed to achieve the company's goals by any means necessary. In those cases, these objectives tend to have a higher priority than employees' well-being. In these situations, the work environment becomes utterly stressful, which prompts employees to adopt a negative attitude toward others. These employees are prone to shut down and act in a passive-aggressive manner; they often become burnt out or overworked. Consequently, the pressure exerted on staff generally does not help them achieve a company's objectives.

Work has a very important impact on the majority of people's lives. Many employees devote a great part of their energy and time to their work activities. Oftentimes, it is difficult for employees to perceive their work as a fulfilling project. Nonetheless, work can be perceived as a gratifying and meaningful activity, especially when it helps employees develop their unique capabilities and harness their full potential.

Work can also be perceived as a valuable endeavour when it makes employees feel acknowledged and accepted as unique human beings. In short, work can significantly contribute to employees' overall well-being and can represent one of the worthiest sources of employees' personal development, growth, and inspiration.

From the perspective of human resources, employees can be considered the most important "asset" of a company, the visible face of an organisation, and the main connection with its customers and other external stakeholders. Employees are also the main creative forces of any organisation and a *meta-resource*, which means a resource with the ability to generate other resources (such as information, products, services, technology, contacts, funds, etc.).

Each employee should be considered as a unique human being with distinct valuable characteristics. As seen previously, none of an employee's traits (such as role, background, qualifications, etc.) defines this individual in a complete manner; employees are intrinsically complex and multidimensional, because of their physical, emotional, rational, and spiritual facets.

Consequently, when managers relate to their subordinates only considering their roles in the company, other relevant aspects of these employees are unfairly left aside. Most employees cannot be as authentic as they would like to in their workplace, if they are not considered from a holistic perspective.

10.2 Limiting Factors in the Work Environment

> The basic philosophy is that if management wants its employees to do a great job with customers, then it must be prepared to do a great job with its employees. Unhappy employees will make for unhappy customers, so unless employees can be successfully taken care of, the success of the organisation on its ultimate, external markets will jeopardised.

> **Helen Peck, Adrian Payne, Martin Christopher, and Moira Clark**

In the following points, several aspects that prevent employees from being treated in a more integrative manner will be thoroughly analysed. These aspects also prevent employees from showing their authentic selves fully.

10.2.1 Organisational Structure

An organisational structure presents different levels of complexity which vary from company to company. This internal structure includes different layers, such as departments, divisions, roles, etc. Some theories of social psychology state that when a person is assigned a specific role (for example, a role within an organisation), this individual is inclined to act congruently with functions and responsibilities related to this role. In an organisation, these roles have specific levels of authority and responsibility, and are located on different levels in a hierarchy within a chain of command.

In the work environment, each role has thorough specifications which the respective employee is expected to fulfil. The specific characteristics and functions of each employee's role tend to be continually reinforced by the interaction with other employees. In the workplace, most employees reinforce their own roles by their natural tendency to comply with the role's specifications and meet related expectations.

Whenever employees enact their role in a company, their other human aspects (spiritual side, emotional states, values, preferences, etc.) cannot be shown overtly, because these aspects are overridden by their work roles. In the workplace, employees' roles are considered more significant and valuable than their other human aspects. Therefore, the latter aspects are put aside, preventing employees from fully showing their unique essence.

10.2.2 Company's Planning Processes

Every company, regardless of its size, develops strategies or plans, which include objectives, tactics, and deadlines. Every plan includes goals, which are the future desired states which a company intends to achieve in a very specific and realistic manner. Some examples of goals are reducing costs, improving profit margins, increasing productivity levels, entering new markets, developing new products, and raising quality standards, among others. These objectives (and the majority of other work topics) tend to be quantitative (based on figures), which makes them easy to measure.

Patel (2005) stated that most companies tend to adopt an attitude which is over-reliant on numbers. Companies are very keen on quantifiable parameters because their achievement is verifiable and easy to document. The use of quantitative indicators can also be used to compare a company's performance levels in different periods. Besides, sometimes employees receive part of their compensation based on these quantitative parameters (for instance, commission based on sales levels) (Klein, 2003).

Cameron (1963) observed that "not everything that can be counted counts, and not everything that counts can be counted." This quote is often wrongly attributed to Einstein. By over-emphasising quantitative aspects, many companies dismiss qualitative aspects (e.g., kindness, rapport, fulfilment, supportiveness, empathy, etc.) which are equally important, but cannot be easily measured.

There is another relevant point related to a company's objectives. A company sets these quantitative goals, as part of their plans, to improve its performance in the marketplace. However, these goals tend to be set in an impersonal manner, which means without considering the specific and unique characteristics and capabilities of people in charge of achieving them.

Companies' plans also include specific actions to be taken to attain these objectives, as well as clear ways to measure their achievement. As a consequence, whenever employees participate in the implementation of these plans, the possibility of being totally spontaneous is limited by the actions predetermined by the plan.

Companies' plans are like structures which determine what to achieve, how to act, and the specific amount of resources to be used for that purpose. All these aspects limit employees' discretion, as they are oftentimes required to abide by them. Therefore, the full use of employees' creative skills is generally constrained by the structural aspects of these plans. In some companies, plans are more flexible, which provide employees with more leeway to act spontaneously and innovatively.

Some companies are relentlessly goal-orientated; their employees are continually pushed to achieve a company's objectives, which generally brings about potential negative effects for employees, such as burnout, employees' alienation and irritability, lack of balance between employees' work and personal activities, and other work-based issues.

10.2.3 *Company's Rules and Procedures*

> Rules tend to show up when people are not clear or trusted. When you know that people have bought into standards, you can give them freedom for decisions and behaviours. If this alignment does not exist, you must micromanage with regulation, expending much more energy in the long run.
>
> **David Allen**

Many workplaces have excessive formal and rigid procedures which regulate employees' activities. These internal regulations can cover a wide variety of topics: procedures regarding data protection, work dress code, ways of addressing a company's communications, format of documents and meetings, etc. This intricate tapestry of rules aims to standardise employees' behaviour and make it predictable and easier to monitor.

In many cases, organisations assume that workers tend to behave unproductively, make wrong choices regarding their work tasks, or even remain inactive, if internal rules are not in force. Companies set these regulations for their employees to act with efficiency and professionalism. These rules also aim for certainty, regularity, consistency, and clarity, which also contributes to increased efficiency and productivity.

These rules are related to the concept of organisational culture, which means how things are commonly done in an organisation. Most rules are explicit (written), but some are implicit, for example, topics that can be conversed about during worktime. Even though these rules aim to provide certainty and order within the organisation, sometimes they become constraining or even stifling for employees.

These rules are intrinsically controlling and directing, because they tell employees what to do and how to perform their work activities. Some regulations can also affect the way employees show themselves to others at the workplace. Oftentimes, these formalities do not allow people to express themselves in a genuine and authentic manner, but only in accordance with the company's rules. When these formal constraints are too limiting, they can also become demotivating.

As a consequence of these rules, in most work environments, the overt expression of employees' feelings is discouraged. The expression of this rich fabric of human aspects is often considered inappropriate because it is not congruent with the company's rules. Therefore, employees are prompted to show a sterilised and bland version of themselves, leaving aside valuable aspects of their human side.

Oftentimes, employees are also discouraged from new ideas and innovative alternative ways to do things, especially when these ideas contradict or confront well-ingrained rules in the organisation. Therefore, the rules that provide the organisation with stability and protect the status quo also prevent the organisation from treading non-traditional paths. However, these rules can prove to be inefficient when the organisation navigates turbulent environments, where a more flexible and adaptive approach is required.

In many workplaces, employees' aspirations, dreams, and other personal affairs do not count as relevant to the company's aims either. Some work environments have an aseptic attitude toward employees' personal aspects, which are considered to be "domestic issues" that could potentially disrupt the natural dynamics of work activities.

Some companies enforce harsh monitoring and disciplinary rules in the workplace which are not aimed at enhancing employees' future performance, but punishing them because of their past mistakes. Oftentimes, these rules are applied in a mechanical manner, without considering specific circumstances affecting each employee.

The relentless application of these regulations makes many employees feel scared and they tend to adopt a defensive attitude (fight-freeze-flight mode), which affects their performance negatively. These employees feel threatened by these rules; consequently, their need for safety and security is not duly satisfied. Employees who adopt this fearful attitude cannot harness their utmost capabilities fully.

Oftentimes, an organisation is more worried about enforcing varying rules and monitoring their compliance in order to control employees' behaviour, than widely clarifying its most relevant values. As seen previously, a company's values imply what the company stands for and what is relevant to the organisation, for example, honesty, care for the environment, integrity, etc. As compared with rules, values tend to be willingly adhered to, not compulsorily complied with, as in the case of rules.

With the development of technological advancements (such as electronic employees' cards to open gates and doors, websites with restricted access, emailing, intranet, CCTV cameras at the workplace, etc.) employees' performance can be monitored to an unimaginable extent. Employees' work "footsteps" become easily "trackable" by the company. However, employees who are controlled on a strict and continual basis by the company feel they are not trusted, and tend to act in a reciprocal manner toward this organisation.

10.2.4 The Organisation's Politics

All companies are affected by their own political aspects. In general, a company's politics includes behaviour from employees at work, which is intentional and covert, in order to attain their personal goals. From the political perspective, employees try to persuade others to increase the influence of the former in an organisation so that these employees' individual goals are attained. Therefore, politics always implies the practical application of different aspects of power by people working in an organisation. Morgan (1986) observed people's power within a company can be based, for instance, on the control of scarce resources, formal authority, and information management, among others.

When people use politics in a positive manner, they try to relate to others in a constructive manner, for example, looking for mutually beneficial agreements with others, being generous and kind with them, and use of objective criteria for decision-making which affect others. These people also tend to recognise others' valuable contributions and unique capabilities, by praising their efforts and commitment. These positive factors imply the existence of a co-operative and supportive work environment.

However, most people tend to assign a negative connotation to the words "organisational politics;" this type of behaviour tends to be perceived as self-serving. From this perspective, a company's politics can include various aspects, such as gatekeeping, gossiping, one-upmanship, turf wars, favouritism, an unfair system of rewards and promotions, backbiting, taking others' praise, and lobbying at top management, among others.

Negative aspects of politics tend to be based on zero-sum game, where some employees win at the expense of others. These factors imply the existence of a competitive work environment where there are scarce resources to fight for. Besides, these negative aspects of politics prevent employees from harnessing their full potential at the workplace; when affected by these factors, employees cannot act in a totally spontaneous and honest manner. Most of these unconstructive practices are based on fear and keep employees from having honest and meaningful communication with others. These practices generate distrust among employees, which is detrimental to the undertaking of co-operative work projects.

These negative aspects of organisational politics prompt employees to act in a defensive manner, taking care of what they do and say to others. In order to navigate all these negative factors, employees tend to develop façades to interact with others in a politically correct, but inauthentic manner. These protective social masks allow employees to perform their work tasks in a less conflictive manner.

Cohen and Prusak (2001) observed that behaviour, either good or bad, spreads by example. These authors stated that workers regularly look for cues in the work environment about how to behave, and what behaviour is banned and which is rewarded. Therefore, negative political behaviour from a group represents a detrimental cue, which prompts other people to act in the same way. In a similar vein, Cialdini (2009) observed that when people have uncertainty regarding how to act, they look at others' actions, which is called "social proof."

10.2.5 Division of Labour

In many organisations, work projects are broken down into tasks. Each task is generally undertaken by specialised employees, who perform it in a routine manner. In those cases, employees are prompted to act in an interdependent and co-operative manner with others who perform other complementary tasks for the same projects. The objective of this division of labour between members of staff is that each employee gets very knowledgeable and efficient in the performance of one or few tasks, which will contribute to increase the company's productivity.

Consequently, most employees do not have access to the overall work project, but only part of it. In these environments, employees are prone to perform the same type of specialised tasks in a continuous manner, which prompts these employees to feel bored and de-skilled. These employees are also demotivated because they cannot harness their innermost skills fully, but only in a limited manner, in relation to their specialised routine tasks.

In some companies, the division of labour is more accentuated, through the development of departments (e.g., finance, marketing, administrative, etc.) with very specialised functions. These internal areas tend to act like "silos" which hold significant shares of power. Oftentimes, these silos act in an uncoordinated way with others, and even create feuds with them over perceived scarce resources.

As a consequence, these employees only enhance skills related to the functions of their positions, leaving aside their other valuable capabilities. Nonetheless, some companies allow employees to work in other posts or departments, or to be trained at skills unrelated to the ones necessary for their position or department.

10.2.6 Fast-Paced Environment

The continual upsurge of changing factors (e.g., new technological gadgets, changing legislation, and the entry of new competitors in the marketplace, etc.) prompts companies to catch up with these changes. Most organisations are teeming with various impending deadlines, multiple schedules, and a multiplicity of business challenges. All these factors tirelessly pressurise organisations, prompting them to develop hectic agendas and rushed activities. Oftentimes, employees are so pressurised by time limitations that they cannot even hold casual conversations with colleagues to strengthen their bonds with them.

In these organisations, employees are trapped in busy schedules, with their time compartmentalised in carefully designed slots filled with countless pending activities to tick off. These employees do not have much leeway to develop meaningful connections with others. These employees tend to have limited vision, mostly oriented to short-term issues.

These organisations tend to prioritise the urgent over the significant. For example, a company might give priority to paying suppliers' invoices over the development of mutually beneficial relationships with its main stakeholders. Most companies have difficulties setting a balance between urgent affairs and paramount ones.

Oftentimes, driven by this continuous change, many companies rush to implement new structures, systems and processes which are not "staff-friendly." These changes create additional friction and busyness in the workplace.

10.3 Other Aspects Preventing Employees' Full Expression

10.3.1 Widespread Collective Activities

In most organisations, various work activities exist which require team-playing among different employees. Working in teams can be very productive because employees can fully express their unique views to others in an open manner. Oftentimes, groupthink is prevalent in teamwork. In those cases, teams have a set of ingrained tenets and ways of performing work activities which cannot be fully challenged by employees. Groupthink has negative effects on employees because they cannot confront the dominant team's viewpoint in order to offer alternative ideas.

10.3.2 Prevalence of Company's Values

A company's values include the different aspects of importance for an organisation. Values are widespread beliefs considered relevant in an organisational environment. These values affect how employees think, feel, act, and interact with others. A company's values are like lenses through which employees perceive reality within the work environment.

When a company recruits new employees, not only does it verify that candidates have the required skills for the job specifications, but it also checks that these individuals have values which are aligned with the company's prevalent values. Besides, when performing work tasks, employees tend to abide by the company's values, to avoid conflicts with other members of staff.

Nonetheless, some of the company's prevailing values are often at odds with those of employees. In those cases, employees tend to show others they are aligned with all the company's values.

This pretence prevents employees from acting in an honest and authentic way, which is according to their own personal values.

10.3.3 Resistance to Change

Many companies are very conservative and tend to avoid significant changes in the way they do business. These organisations prompt employees to perform their activities in a traditional manner. In these organisations, non-traditional business perspectives proposed by employees are not truly welcome. Therefore, employees' creative expression is constrained by the traditional ways of doing things. Sometimes innovative proposals made by employees are considered, but only after going through a lengthy and thorough scrutiny process.

10.3.4 Perceived Limited Resources

Most companies perceive that their own resources (e.g., technology, funds, personnel, etc.) are scarce. This perceived limited availability of resources within an organisation tends to be a source of intra-organisational conflict. Employees working in different areas and departments (e.g., marketing, administration, finance) are prone to fight over these resources. This perceived scarcity of resources prompts employees to act in a competitive manner with other members of staff. In this type of scenario, every employee aims to get the best share of the limited resources, at the expense of the rest of the employees.

This perceived limitation of resources, so common in most companies, also reduces the chances of employees expressing themselves in an authentic manner. As seen in Chapter 3, the assumption that company resources are limited is related to a scarcity mindset.

10.3.5 Over-Reliance on External Factors

Most companies are overly dependent on factors related to their external environment when they perform their activities. These external factors include, for example, competitors' activities, changes in legislation, shifts in fashion trends, upswings and downswings of economic factors, and changes in customer behaviour, among others.

Even though these external factors are relevant to the company, they are generally beyond its control. Many companies perform activities solely driven by these external factors, not focussing on the development of internal factors. Some examples of internal factors are a company's quality levels, productivity, development of new products and services, etc. Among these factors, the development of strong relationships between the members of staff can also be included.

These internal factors are within the company's control, but they are often dismissed for being focused exclusively on external factors. In other words, when a company is mostly focussed on factors relating to its external environment, employees are prevented from improving the company's internal factors (for example, developing new products).

10.3.6 Over-Emphasis on Rational Aspects

Most companies' activities are rationally based. The application of this rational approach can be observed in some examples, such as efficient use of resources, meeting deadlines, efficacious cost-cutting, and thorough analysis of problems, among other aspects. These rational aspects are also shown in the development of meticulous bureaucratic procedures, processes, and systems aimed at making a company more effective and competitive in the marketplace.

This over-emphasis on rational aspects limits the enhancement of other relevant aspects of employees, for example, their spontaneity and creative expressiveness. Overly rational work environments leave no leeway for employees to express emotional or spiritual aspects either, because these aspects are not relevant to the organisational activities. In extreme cases, employees are perceived as mechanical parts contributing to the organisation's machinery.

10.3.7 Other Aspects

The aforementioned factors characterise the majority of work environments. It is possible to add to those factors others, such as the progressive use of telecommuting (also called remote working), the growing use of outsourcing, the increased use of digital resources and automation, the ongoing need for employees' continuous training, the widespread use of flexible work contracts, and the upsurge of new economic sectors which bring about fresh job opportunities, among others.

This book does not suggest the elimination of these factors, which are intrinsic parts of many companies' internal environments. Instead, companies should take into account these factors, but also set conditions which empower employees to harness their unique skills in a more complete manner and express themselves more authentically.

10.4 Nurturing Relationships with Employees

Overworking happens when people make the mistake of taking care of business instead of taking care of relationships.

Robert Holden

The following points will provide practical advice on how to adopt a more loving attitude toward a company's employees. When these recommendations are applied, the work environment become kinder and friendlier, which in turn prompts employees to fully harness their unique skills and talents. Four relevant factors which makes a workplace more loving are:

- Warm work environment
- Diversity and inclusion at the workplace
- Social events
- Time off

10.4.1 Warm Work Environment

Companies and management teams vibrating at a low level can be arrogant, forceful, self-serving, non-caring, and even deceitful. On the other hand, organisations with a higher vibration are much more likely to be socially and environmentally responsible, and committed to higher standards of business ethics and customers service.

Jason Chan and Jane Rogers

10.4.1.1 *Main Characteristics of a Positive Work Environment*

A company's work environment can either facilitate or hinder employees' performance. The work environment is composed of the physical aspects of the workplace, and also the verbal and non-verbal interactions between employees. Knight (1999) observed that a work environment sends a "metamessage" to others, a story of what is going on inside it. When people visit a workplace for the first time, they can infer some of the main traits regarding that company. In a workplace, individuals can pick up specific clues about the company, such as:

- The attitudes adopted by people when interacting with others
- Main characteristics of employees' conversations (body and non-verbal language)
- Emotional ambience of the workplace (e.g., enthusiasm, pessimism, anxiety, etc.)
- Level of comfort and friendliness between employees
- Specific uses of technology by the members of the staff
- Proneness to individualistic activities or collective ones
- Levels of formality and respect for authority
- Levels of comfort and stress experienced by employees
- Employees' pace when performing work tasks
- Level of tidiness and orderliness
- Existence of formal or informal dress code
- Aspects related to planning and strategies (charts, graphs, etc.)
- Use of signage and livery at the workplace
- Architectural aspects of the place (spaciousness, luminosity, etc.)
- Specific location and use of furniture
- Use of shared spaces for socialisation purposes

Without the intention to make any generalisations, the reader can find below a list of factors which contribute to the development of an unloving work environment. This list is not exhaustive.

- These environments are overly formal and oftentimes extremely goal-oriented and competitive. Staff are only committed to the tasks at hand and avoid talking about non-business topics. Employees' personal topics (e.g., dreams, aspirations, emotional issues, health problems, hobbies etc.) are discouraged.
- Employees adopt an unloving attitude toward others and oftentimes act without integrity. Their actions are based on detrimental values, such as selfishness, impoliteness, untruthfulness, dishonesty, and carelessness, among others. Some examples of this behaviour are lying, censoring, condemning, threatening, bluffing, ultimatums, and gossiping, among others.
- In these environments, there are several negative aspects of political behaviour (such as favouritism, backbiting, etc.) which stem from the adoption of an unloving attitude toward others. Employees are treated in an unloving manner and tend to reciprocate, which makes the whole workplace more hostile and demotivating. In this type of environment, the well-known saying which goes "negativity begets more negativity" is applicable.
- Employees are prompted to be over-committed to achieving goals set by the company. For example, they are pushed to overwork, they are given unreasonable deadlines, etc. These employees are prevented from having work–life equilibrium. Oftentimes, these employees become workaholics and isolated individuals, with a proneness to stress and burnout.

■ Employees manipulate others to achieve the objectives of the former. These employees consider others as a simple means to achieve their own ends, instead of treating them as valuable human beings. In these work environments, employees have a short-sighted perspective on relationships; they aim to attain swift gains from others, instead of cultivating mutually beneficial relationships with them.

All these practices create an ambience of distrust between employees. Oftentimes, these staff members also have low morale, which prompts them to adopt an uncommitted and detached attitude toward work activities. These employees frequently experience negative emotional states (e.g., frustration, worry, depression, anger, etc.), which affects their performance in a detrimental manner.

Oftentimes, these employees' negative emotions are based on fear, which impacts negatively on their work relationships. According to Keegan (2015), in unloving environments, employees are more prone to experience different types of fear (e.g., losing jobs, bullying, harsh criticism, intimidation, arbitrary decisions made by others, losing discretion, not fitting in, etc.), which becomes widespread and normalised. This author also observed that in this type of environment, the best employees tend to leave their jobs, because they cannot express their views openly.

Unloving work environments prompt employees to continually adopt a defensive attitude to others, which is related to the fight-freeze-flight mode. This protective mode is closely linked to the reptilian brain, which is the most primitive part of the human brain. In this mode, people tend to protect themselves against perceived threatening factors (for instance, unloving practices from others).

As seen previously, when in this mode, people tend to act in a hyper-vigilant manner and their focus is narrowed down to the threats affecting them, which prompts them to dismiss other aspects. Consequently, their innermost analytical and creative capabilities are temporarily lowered, which creates a negative impact on their productivity and performance.

10.4.1.2 Main Characteristics of a Positive Work Environment

Companies should aim to develop heart-warming work environments. Figuratively speaking, their work environments should be like vessels through which kindness, co-operation, and supportiveness can be continually channelled and spread between staff members. Loving workplaces are intrinsically inspiring and motivating. Every member of staff feels valuable and valued. This type of environment is not arid, stagnant, or inert, but welcoming, dynamic, and warming. These environments celebrate the interdependence of employees, and welcome and appreciate their unique contribution.

In this type of environment, every person is willing to assist others and care for them. This attitude of collaboration and solidarity generates a positive impact on the employees, but also on other stakeholders interacting with these employees directly or indirectly. Employees are the human interface between the company and its external stakeholders; therefore, anything that affects staff members (either positive or negative) also impacts other stakeholders in the same way. Other relevant characteristics of a warm work environment are:

■ Staff members can perform their work activities at a reasonable pace, without feeling pressurised or stressed. Work activities allow employees to have a good work–life balance, including activities from non-work areas (friends, family, recreation, etc.).

- Members of staff feel acknowledged, appreciated, and valued. If employees have work challenges or personal issues (health, family, etc.), they know they will be supported.
- Employees are encouraged to act in a creative manner. Their insightful ideas and innovative behaviour are considered valuable for the company's productivity and competitiveness.
- Personnel have all necessary available resources (stationery, technology, etc.) for them to perform tasks effectively. These employees are provided continuous support and training to enhance their skills and talents.
- The emotional atmosphere of the workplace is positive. People are enthusiastic, kind, and supportive. People show a spontaneous vitality, grit, and willingness for social connection. In this type of environment, creative ideas tend to flourish on a regular basis.
- Employees adopt a continuous attitude of care, trust, and understanding, which improves connection and rapport with others. This type of environment is suitable for the development of collective projects where employees are interrelated in a synergetic manner.
- Staff members are encouraged to regularly hold formal conversations, as well as informal ones. The topics of these conversations are not limited to work matters, but include personal issues. These meaningful dialogues strengthen the relationships between employees.
- Employees attend non-work activities (dinners, informal meetings, etc.) with colleagues, which helps them revitalise their energy and develop stronger bonds.
- Staff members feel fulfilled with the performance of their work tasks, because they know that they are contributing to the company's purpose, which is meaningful and impactful for the marketplace and the community.

In warm environments, employees are more prone to experience positive emotional states (joy, optimism, peace, etc.) on a continuous basis. These positive emotional states tend to affect a company's economic parameters (sales, profits, quality, etc.) in a constructive manner.

In this type of environment, employees are more prone to act with integrity when they relate to others. Their actions tend to be aligned with positive values, such as care, respectfulness, selflessness, transparency, honesty, trustworthiness, fairness, and others. These individuals are more inclined to adopt a loving attitude toward others, which is generally expressed through praise, encouragement, thankfulness, and recognition of others.

In a warm work environment, positive social capital is more likely to develop. This valuable social capital represents the net of relationships at work which stems from mutual respect, engagement, support, co-operation, and affinity. When this capital is developed in the workplace, people experience a sense of community which implies familiarity, belongingness, membership, and trust. This valuable social tapestry facilitates the learning process in an organisation and helps people stick together during dire circumstances. People perceive interdependence with others in a positive way which allows them to develop close-knit work relationships.

Cohen and Prusak (2001) observed that this capital prompts the development of a deep understanding, sharing, and rapport between people, bridging the distance between them; this capital builds up and accrues over time. This capital is what makes people more loyal and committed to the company and less prone to leave it in search for other opportunities.

In most companies, when dire challenges arise, most employees tend to respond negatively (e.g., feeling overwhelmed, becoming anxious, etc.), which prevents them from surmounting issues effectively. These stressful situations make people feel tense and irritable, and oftentimes prompts them to treat others unlovingly.

However, in warm work environments, employees feel supported on a continuous basis, even if the company faces hardship and struggle. In these circumstances, staff members are less inclined to feel stressed, but more empowered to tackle challenges constructively and encourage others to do so. A warm work environment holds people together, especially during rough times. To put it more simply, in difficult times, employees adopt a co-operative and supportive attitude toward others.

In these work environments, people's loving attitude toward others is contagious. As previously seen, the human brain has mirror neurons which tend to replicate the emotional states of others around. When people act in a loving manner toward others, the latter tends to experience similar emotional states to the former. This phenomenon is called emotional contagion (Goleman, 2006).

Likewise, Cialdini (2009) observed that when a person treats others lovingly, they feel compelled to reciprocate to the former. Hawkins (2012, 2013) stated that a person who adopts a loving attitude toward others positively transform their attitude in a positive manner. As explained in Chapters 2, 3, 6, and 7, this scientist stated that love is a high consciousness state which transmutes the lower consciousness states (e.g., guilt, fear, shame, etc.) of people around it. In short, when people treat others lovingly, the whole work environment tends to become more loving.

10.4.1.3 Positive Layout of the Workplace

The work environment also includes its physical aspects: its architectural design. Warm workplaces are designed in a worker-friendly manner; they allow employees to perform their activities in a focused manner and harness skills effectively. These workplaces are spacious and people can walk around them in an unencumbered manner. These places are well-lit and ventilated and they abide by hygiene and safety legislation.

These spaces have comfortable areas for people to socialise, where employees can take some time off and have informal chats with other colleagues. These places are equipped with dispensers for employees to have beverages and some snacks. These leisure spaces should include comfortable furniture for employees to relax and replenish their energy. Some companies include magazines, books, arcade games, or board games for employees to be entertained and to clear their minds.

Wiseman (2013) stated that positive bodily sensations bring about positive emotions. This specialist observed that, when a workplace is set in a way that prompts people to experience *physical sensations* of comfort and warmth, these individuals tend to *feel* (from the *emotional* standpoint) that this place is friendly and warm. Some examples of "warm" conditions that companies can consider for their workplaces are: placing hot water dispensers for beverages (such as tea or coffee), using comfortable chairs with soft cushions, keeping the place well-heated in winter, etc.

Warm workplaces are also orderly and clean. Lobel (2014) observed that spotless places are associated with morality and ethical behaviour, which means that people working there look more trustworthy. This author stated that people tend to link a sensory experience (for example, seeing a clean workplace) with a related state of mind called "embodied cognition" (e.g., thinking that people working there have "pure" intentions).

The workplace is also perceived as warmer when it is kept decluttered. In order to avoid clutter, old documents and paperwork (not necessary to be kept by law) should be regularly binned. The same applies to useless and broken items. Sometimes, certain documents and other items used occasionally can be stored in a room separate from the main work area.

Wiseman (2009) observed that the use of green in the workplace has a positive effect on employees because this colour is linked with relaxation and positivity. This author advised locating some plants and greenery in the workplace because they symbolise creativity and generativity. Hale and Evans (2007) observed that "green symbolises growth, fertility and harmony; it is restful and refreshing."

Lobel (2014) observed that red is associated with danger, which prompts people to feel anxious. Therefore, red should be avoided in the workplace, when possible. Some recommend that workplaces should be scented to make the place more pleasant and uplifting for employees. Lobel (2014) observed that the smell of cinnamon and peppermint can enhance employees' cognitive skills.

Positive visual cues can enhance employees' performance when they are included in the workplace. Research concluded that the existence of banners with positive images in the workplace prompted employees to be more productive. These positive messages continually imprint on the minds of employees prompting them to adopt a more optimistic attitude.

The workplace should include natural light, when possible. Fluorescent lighting should be avoided. In relation to this topic, Brown (1997) observed that this type of lighting "emits a different colour of light and also gives off more radiation" which tends to lead to poor concentration or mental tiredness. This author also stated that the same applies to bulbs that save energy.

Lastly, workplaces should convey when possible principles of equality. This means that all employees should have the same allocation of space, including superiors. Managers should avoid having carefully guarded and luxury offices in order not to create a sense of separation from the rest of the staff. Workplaces with open spaces, for example without cubicles, tend to encourage employees to act in a more trusting and supportive manner with one another. However, Bernstein and Turban (2018) observed in a research study that open spaces actually decrease direct interaction and co-operation between employees who become more likely to use different ways to communicate with colleagues, such as email. This can be due to overstimulation or a lack of privacy which characterises open spaces.

10.4.2 Diverse, Inclusive, and Participative Workplace

Work is love made visible.

Kahlil Gibran

10.4.2.1 The Importance of a Diverse and Inclusive Environment

Most people tend to categorise others in clear-cut groups, for instance, leaders and followers, proactive and reactive, etc. Oftentimes, people who use these classifications tend to stereotype others, for instance: "All these people are …." Stereotyping is about categorising the members of a group in a stringent and simplistic manner, assigning them homogeneous traits without taking into account their distinctive individual qualities.

Social psychologists have observed that people naturally tend to stereotype because of their subconscious biases. However, human beings are far more complex than simple categories. Each person is unique and can never be pigeonholed in rigid compartments. Moreover, all people need to be recognised by their distinct and unique qualities.

As mentioned in Chapter 6, people generally get on better with others with similar characteristics. Nonetheless, a person with a loving attitude toward others intends to relate to them, beyond apparent differences or dissimilarities. A loving person recognises that other people are valuable human beings. Not only should these valuable beings be respected, but their views and values should also be duly acknowledged.

A company which adopts a favourable attitude toward diversity does not focus on any limiting social categories, but on the individual as a human being. This type of company aims to develop a pluralistic work environment that supports the harmonious coexistence and interrelation of people with different qualities.

In inclusive work environments, the unique attributes of each employee (for example, experience, training, qualification, age, cultural background, etc.) are continually acknowledged, celebrated, and enhanced, when possible. A company's employees feel comfortable showing their unique qualities and they are also open to learning from other members of staff. In relation to this, research has observed that when a person feels excluded by others, the same areas of this individual's brain are activated as if this person was experiencing physical pain. Discrimination and exclusion tend to become a very important stress factor.

Therefore, diverse companies are inclined to count on more perspectives to deal with specific business challenges. This provides companies with more flexibility which is very suitable for fast-changing business environments. Kandola and Fullerton (1994) stated that a diverse work environment has several benefits, such as easier recruitment of talented people, reduction in costs of training and turnover, increased employee commitment and satisfaction, improved customer service, higher quality and productivity levels, and more enhanced company's image, among others.

Nonetheless, these authors also observed that some of these benefits are debatable because of a lack of concrete evidence backing them. Richard (2000) has observed that diverse workplaces are positively correlated with a higher performance level, as compared with less diverse ones. Some characteristics of diversity-centred companies are:

- According to Maslow (1968), this type of work environment is growth-fostering, because it is promoting the satisfaction of all the relevant needs of employees. The different types of needs have already been analysed in Chapter 6.
- Every employee is given fair chances to access different work opportunities regardless of their personal qualities and unique background. There are widespread and transparent procedures regarding employees' promotion; new employees are recruited from a perspective of equal opportunity. Employees' appraisal and promotion are based on specific set objectives and merit, instead of being centred on employees' personal qualities.
- Activities related to favouritism are strictly avoided. Favouritism means unfairly preferring some employees over others. This is a common negative practice part of organisational politics.
- All employees are genuinely encouraged to express their distinct views on relevant topics. As a consequence, the analysis of relevant issues becomes wider and enriched. Any discrimination based on specific ages, genders, physical abilities, races, religions, or type of personality (extroverts, introverts, etc.) is unwelcome and penalised.
- The company is committed to the continuous development of a diverse work environment. For instance, employees can be encouraged to informally express their objections and suggestions regarding the work environment. More formal ways of gathering information can also be used, for instance, surveys where staff members are asked about their satisfaction regarding the work environment.
- Sometimes changes in the physical aspects of the workplace are introduced in order to develop a more diverse environment. An example is fitting special lifts for people with mobility difficulties (e.g., people using crutches/walkers, individuals in wheelchairs, etc.).
- Employees are trained through workshops and seminars to make them aware of the importance of a diverse environment. Sometimes, the training can also include the development of specific capabilities necessary to support a diverse work environment.

Some companies take the initiative and spontaneously foster diverse work environment because they want all employees to be treated in a fair and respectful manner; these companies realise that having a diverse workplace is the best thing to do. However, other companies often become more diverse as a result of the pressure of legal rules (for instance, equal opportunities legislation) or pressure from different groups (such as employees, unions, community, etc.).

Many countries have specific legislation which encourages and protects diversity in the workplace. Some regulations aim to prevent discrimination and prejudice against employees in the work environment. For many organisations, respect for diversity represents an important value; these companies have their own organisational policies to guarantee and care for a diverse work environment.

10.4.2.2 Employees' Participation and Acknowledgement

Fromm (1956) observed that all human beings need to overcome their state of separateness from others. In other words, people are intrinsically gregarious, which means social beings who feel compelled to relate to others and be accepted by them. In a work environment, employees need to be regularly validated as relevant parts of the company.

Consequently, a company should make its employees feel they are a special part of the organisation. A company can clearly highlight the reasons why employees are valuable and acknowledge them in different ways:

- Employees can be regularly informed of the company's most relevant achievements. The organisation can pinpoint how employees contributed to these successful outcomes. When employees' contributions are recognised, their engagement tends to increase significantly.
- Employees can also be told about the new endeavours the company will undertake. In these cases, the organisation can highlight the specific contribution expected from employees.
- Employees can also be invited to give their views on projects in progress, or even past endeavours. In these cases, the employees' voice is acknowledged and considered.

Sometimes employees can be given unexpected gifts for their contribution, for example, sending them thank you letters, inviting them to non-business events, and others. Oftentimes, companies use story-telling techniques to make their employees feel more acknowledged and proud of their contribution. These tales show how employees impacted on the company's endeavours in a positive manner.

These stories include employees' feelings, opinions, and actions regarding the company's projects. Impactful stories show the human side of the company: the flesh-and-blood human beings who contribute to its projects. These stories also include the business aspects of the company's achievements (such as profits, revenues, costs, etc.).

Some companies tend to wrongly include in their stories more faceless facts and quantitative parameters than aspects related to their most precious resources, their employees. This makes their stories cold and impersonal, which prompts employees to feel not fully acknowledged by them.

Poignant human stories create a stronger sense of belonging and identification between employees and the company. People easily identify with stories because they convey relevant ideas, values, and experiences in a memorable manner. These stories make employees feel they are a relevant part of a community of contribution to the company's objectives. These stories can be told in different ways, for example, via the company's workshops, emailing, newsletters, internal magazines, press releases, news boards, blogs, and websites, etc.

For example, a company can use a story related to its new business branch. This story could include several elements, such as the challenges faced by employees before opening the branch and activities performed by employees to overcome these challenges, among others.

10.4.3 Social Activities

10.4.3.1 Importance of Social Activities

> Far from standing in opposition to each other, play and work are mutually supportive. They are not poles at opposite ends of our world. Work and play are like timbers that keep our house from collapsing down on top of us ... Work does not work without play.
>
> **Stuart Brown and Christopher Vaughan**

Most people have a need for novelty and fun; they want to explore new experiences and diverse sensations. Nonetheless, most work environments make people feel bored and burdened and oftentimes trapped and overwhelmed. Most work activities are structured, goal-oriented, and logic-based which render them dull and barren.

Consequently, most employees crave social activities, which are intrinsically more interesting and engaging than work. In these events, people can be fully present and let their hair down, away from work pressures. However, most companies perceive these light-hearted activities to be of low value for business purposes. These recreational activities are usually considered irrelevant; therefore, most companies discourage them.

From this book's perspective, these social activities are not frivolous, slacking, or superficial, but of high value. These activities represent the perfect complement to work activities. These activities encourage improvisation and team-playing, and spice up social interactions, which creates more affinity and rapport between people. During these social activities, most people tend to have fun and experience positive emotions, which in turn is very positive for their work tasks. Copious research concludes that people in a positive mood are prone to act more productively and creatively at work.

In a similar vein, Achor (2011) observed that positive emotional states are very important indicators of high success in the work environment. An example of activities which boosts employees' moods is observed in companies like Yahoo! which, for instance, has a massage therapist inside company premises for employees.

10.4.3.2 Importance of Social Activities and Events

> The brightest and most lucrative futures are going to belong to organisations whose people have the courage to risk being human in the workplace.
>
> **William Arnold and Jeanne Plas**

Some of the world's biggest industries are related to entertainment and leisure, for example, tourism, movies, music, etc. These activities are ludic, which means related to play. These playful activities connect people to their early childhood, when their only concerns were to be fed and to play with toys.

A company that regularly organises social events and activities for their employees adopts a loving attitude toward them. Most people working for a company, even boring ones, want to have fun, once in a while. The majority of employees, including those in the highest positions, feel attracted to social activities and events. Some examples of these activities are cocktails, celebrations, award ceremonies, etc.

These activities have a common trait: most formalities and bureaucratic procedures can be temporarily left aside. In this type of event, people can interact with others more spontaneously. People working in different areas (e.g., finance, marketing, etc.) are brought together which increases the affinity between them.

Dr Zak (2013) observed that these social activities foster the natural release of a powerful hormone called oxytocin, which makes people experience an enhanced sense of well-being. As seen previously in Chapters 5, 6, and 7, oxytocin is produced by the human brain and prompts people to feel good and fosters prosocial behaviour like bonding, co-operating, trusting others, etc.

In these social events, there are no work objectives to achieve or pressing deadlines. People can relax and recharge their batteries to resume their work activities more energised. In addition to this, at these events, most people let their guard down and have no hidden agenda, which makes their communications more spontaneous and rooted in the moment. Therefore, conversations include non-business topics (e.g., personal preferences, past experiences, etc.) which make these interactions more real and meaningful. These events constitute a valuable parenthesis over a tedious work schedule.

At these events, the negative aspects of an organisation's politics (e.g., one-upmanship, gatekeeping, favouritism, etc.) are of little value. These social activities prompt participants to feel more at ease and calm. These people are less prone to adopt a defensive mode toward others, as is oftentimes common in the working hours.

Some companies organise social activities in a very limited manner, for instance: Christmas dinner, year-end celebration, etc. When social events are infrequent, employees are left with a glimpse of them. Some organisations argue that these social activities are not a priority due to busy company's schedules. Other companies believe these activities are a waste of time, because they do not generate any profits. Nonetheless, when these events are frequent, employees' performance is affected positively.

10.4.3.3 A Different Standpoint in Social Events

All companies should organise social events on a regular basis to bring their employees closer to one another. As seen previously, these events should be fostered in every company because they strengthen relationships between staff members. Some examples of social activities a company can organise are:

- Regular meetings for socialisation purposes
- Retreats to practice yoga, chi gung, and meditation
- Sports and board games tournaments
- Picnics and other outdoor gatherings
- Cultural visits to museums, galleries, etc.

When a company informs its employees of upcoming social activities, these staff members should be told of the positive effects of these events for them (for instance, better connection, improved rapport, etc.). Sometimes these events can be linked to specific employees' accomplishments. In these cases, these social activities represent a great way of celebrating these attainments and appreciating employees' contribution.

There are companies that consider these social activities irrelevant. Companies which are reluctant to organise social events can gradually add them in an experimental manner to test their outcomes. Here are some of the additional positive effects of these social activities:

- **Positive energy:** All these activities have a celebratory energy, which prompts people to feel positive, which tends to be contagious. As explained previously, people attending these feel-good events tend to adopt a non-defensive mode; at these events, people also tend to be more spontaneous than usual, showing themselves as they truly are.
- **Improvement in productivity:** At these events, people tend to feel less constrained by work obligations, but more energised. As previously seen, these activities are valuable time off which disrupts the monotony and dullness of worktime. These fun activities always have a positive impact on employee productivity due to their revitalising effect.
- **High quality communication:** At these events, people can interact with others in a more personal, open, and lively manner. Participants tend to access human aspects of others beyond their social masks (job or business roles). This type of events is suitable for natural conversations, explained in Chapter 8. These social activities enrich people's communicational interactions and have a positive impact on their relationships.
- **Enhancing of mental capabilities:** Research corroborates that playful social activities contribute to the development of neuropaths in the brains of the attendees, which in turn enhances their creative skills. Researchers also observed that, at these events, people enhance their improvisational aspects, which can be applied to other real-life social situations, especially challenging ones.
- **Relaxing effect:** Many employees regularly suffer from different degrees of stress during working time. When intertwined with worktime, social activities have a refreshing effect on these employees. This type of activity helps stressed employees "unplug" from the fight-freeze-flight mode adopted at work. When employees release stress, their utmost mental capabilities are naturally enhanced.

10.4.4 Time Off

In many organisations, an employee's working time as well as rest time is meticulously regulated and monitored. Oftentimes, organisations believe that time off impacts negatively on their productivity and efficiency levels. Consequently, employees' working time is squeezed in the most fruitful way possible to contribute to the company's objectives.

Some employees are prompted to work on a non-stop mode or for long hours. Some companies wrongly believe that employees become more effective when they overwork or perform without being interrupted. However, research has showed that extended and uninterrupted work decreases employees' productivity because these individuals become mentally and physically tired.

Employees who overwork also create an imbalance between work activities and non-work ones (family, entertainment, etc.), which makes them feel demotivated. As a consequence, these employees become less engaged with the company, which impacts negatively on its main economic indicators (productivity, quality, etc.).

Research also shows that employees who have regular breaks during worktime and work only a reasonable number of hours are more motivated and productive. In other words, employees need this downtime to replenish their energy levels. Consequently, companies should realise that employees are not machines but human beings, which implies the need to recharge their energy regularly.

Schwartz et al. (2010) observed that employees should break every 90 or 120 minutes of working time to avoid becoming restless, irritable, and unfocused. This downtime should never be considered as slackening time, but revitalising one. These authors concluded that people become more productive at work when they move between periods of concentrated focus and intermittent rest time. During these breaks, employees can replete their energy levels, for example, taking a short walk, stretching their muscles, or breathing deeply.

Companies should discourage employees from overworking. Employees' overtime can be simply avoided through reasonable allocation of tasks and by avoiding tight deadlines. With these simple practices, employees are prone to achieve a better balance between their work activities and personal ones.

Employees who do not overwork have more spare time for other activities. In their spare time, people have more choice and control, as compared with the commonly regulated and predetermined activities at work. Russell (1994) observed that workers should have more spare time, not to recover from work toil, but to express themselves through their non-working skills (artistic, sporty, etc.).

Some employees use their spare time to offset needs unmet in the work environment. This spare time also helps employees take their lives less seriously and more light-heartedly, which in turn has a positive impact on their work productivity. Research showed that leisure contributes to people's well-being and gives their lives more meaning, especially when people perform high-quality activities, such as mingling with others, reading, practising sports, hobbies, artistic endeavours, being in contact with nature, volunteering for social causes, etc.

Lastly, employees should be encouraged to have a minimum of daily sleep. Medina (2014) observed that insufficient sleep time drains the brain and hurts attention, memorisation, and reasoning skills. In other words, when employees do not sleep enough, they are less sharp, focussed, and engaged, which diminishes their productivity levels and the quality of their work. Lack of adequate sleep makes people more irritable, less communicative, and more prone to become stressed.

Blackburn and Epel (2017) observed that a minimum of a regular seven hours of quality sleep has several restorative benefits, such as appetite control, consolidation and healing of memories, refreshment of mood, contribution to learning process and reduction of stress-proneness. These authors suggested some tips for better quality sleep, like going to bed at a regular time, doing relaxation exercises, and drinking warm herbal infusions just before going to bed. Lastly, scientists have discovered that all body functions have their own built-in daily rhythmical patterns, called *circadian rhythms*, which can be negatively affected by scarce sleeping time.

Questions for Self-Reflection

- What are the limiting factors in a work environment?
- How can I make the work environment warmer?
- How can I encourage employees' inclusion and participation?
- What fun and social activities can be introduced in our company?

Chapter 11

Additional Aspects of a Loving Attitude to Employees

11.1 Relationships between Superiors and Subordinates

Work brings far more than just money. A satisfying job can also bring structure and meaning to one's life, mental and emotional stimulation, personal relationships, regular opportunity to develop to use and develop skills, social status, self-esteem and a sense of identity.

Paul Martin

Most organisations have an internal structure, which generally consists of different areas (departments, divisions, etc.). This hierarchical structure commonly has people at the higher level (known as management or superiors) who provide people in lower levels (also called subordinates) with commands and directions. The former are also in charge of monitoring the performance of the latter, according to specific procedures. Besides this, managers are often in charge of the planning process, and the co-ordination and allocation of resources to be used by subordinates. In small companies, this structure tends to be simpler than in bigger organisations.

Some people might argue that the terms "superiors," "subordinates," and others have an unloving connotation. However, in this chapter and the rest of the book, terms such as "superiors" and "subordinates," "managers," "employees," and others will be used for practical purposes and simplicity.

Oftentimes, employees feel their managers are rudely commanding them. In other words, managers adopt an unloving attitude toward employees. In these cases, not only do superiors' unkind directions make subordinates feel unsupported, but these commands also prompt these employees to adopt a defensive mode (fight-freeze-flight).

As seen previously, when employees have a defensive attitude, their mental capabilities are temporarily impaired, rendering them more ineffective at performing their work tasks. Superiors' rude orders can make employees feel unacknowledged as valuable human beings. These careless directions prevent employees from giving their best at work.

Employees are linked to the company through work contracts, which meticulously stipulate their rights and obligations at work. However, from the psychological perspective, the employer and employees are also linked by so-called "psychological contracts," which include the expectations that each party (employer and employee) have about one another. Some common expectations that employees have when they work for a company are:

- To be treated with respect
- To be appreciated for their contribution
- To have stability regarding their post
- To use their skills and talents at the workplace
- To work with supportive and friendly people
- To have the necessary resources to work
- To have time for a work–life balance
- To have a reasonable workload
- To have access to rest time and leisure time
- To express ideas and opinions freely
- To receive fair compensation for their work
- To contribute to a meaningful business purpose
- To have a comfortable and safe space to work
- To access opportunities for promotion
- To be taken into account in relevant decisions
- To acquire new valuable skills
- To be supported when personal issues arise

On the other side, employers have expectations as well. Some common examples of employers' expectations about employees are:

- To contribute to the company's objectives on a continuous basis
- To go the "extra mile" when possible
- To respect hierarchy and authority
- To abide by the company's regulations
- To perform tasks efficiently and diligently
- To use their creative and analytical skills to solve the company's problems
- To keep the company's information confidential
- To contribute to a positive work environment
- To be supportive and co-operative with colleagues
- To relate to external stakeholders in a friendly manner

It is important to pinpoint that these psychological contracts are never carved in stone, but evolve over time. These psychological contracts are unwritten, but their effects are very noticeable.

Some companies tend to focus too much on the work contracts (explicit agreements) and dismiss the psychological contracts (implicit agreements). In the workplace, relationships with employees are more prone to thrive when their expectations, embedded in these psychological contracts, are met. Therefore, a good question to ask to employees on a regular basis is "What are your expectations at this company?" and "Are your expectations being met?" This type of question can provide the company with valuable insights in order to strengthen its relationships with employees.

11.2 Guidelines for More Balanced Relationships with Employees

Bautan (2017) observed that employees have two opposite desires: the desire for stability, certainty, and safety on one side, and the desire for freedom and self-expression on the other side. The first need is satisfied through a stable job, steady paycheque, and clear rules to abide by. The second need is satisfied when employees can freely express their voice and show themselves as they truly are, with their distinct attributes, views, and talents. These personal qualities should be duly acknowledged and welcomed by the company. In the work environment, these two opposite needs should be satisfied in a balanced manner.

According to this standpoint, if employees only satisfy their need for stability without any freedom, they are prone to feel coerced and censored by the company. Instead, if employees are given absolute freedom (for instance, no rules to abide by) without taking into consideration employees' need for stability, the workplace can become haphazard and chaotic.

Most companies tend to be biased toward satisfying employees' need for stability, but dismiss employees' need for freedom and expressiveness. Some guidelines regarding a more effective satisfaction of both employees' need for stability, and their need for freedom and self-expression are explained in the following points.

11.2.1 Treat Employees Kindly

Relationships between superiors and subordinates must be nourished on a continuous basis. Superiors must always instruct employees in a warm manner in order to strengthen their relationships. Moreover, employees must feel recognised and valued on a regular basis. Superiors should aim to lovingly engage with subordinates and guide and empower them on a continuous basis. However, it is also important that superiors deliver instructions to employees, so that the company objectives can be achieved in an effective manner. The reader can find below some guidelines to delivering directions in a more loving manner. These guidelines apply to relationships between superiors and employees, and also between colleagues.

- **Soft requests:** Sometimes, superiors believe that if they are warm with subordinates, they will lose authority over them. Nonetheless, superiors can be authoritative and also loving with employees under their control. In the discipline of negotiation, there is a well-known saying which goes "You have to be hard with problems, but kind with people," which implies focussing on solving relevant problems, but also being considerate and caring with relationships (Fisher et al., 1999).
- **Non-intrusive requests**: Sometimes, superiors can make their requests to employees in non-intrusive ways. For instance, a boss asks employees for some relevant personal information of theirs for work purposes; in this example, the superior should kindly request employees for their permission, so they do not feel their privacy is being invaded. This loving attitude toward employees makes them feel more respected, which prompts them to act more collaboratively.
- **Requests as suggestions:** When possible, superiors should frame requests as kind and caring suggestions. For example, instead of saying "You must do this ...!," the superior could use sentences like "It is advisable for you to ...." Sometimes, the superior can adopt an empathic attitude toward an employee using sentences like "If I were you, I would think about ...," and similar ones.
- **Caring requests:** The comments mentioned in the previous point can be accompanied by caring sentences such as "I sympathise with you ...." Sometimes, requests can be made in

an impersonal manner, such as "It is important that …" or "It is necessary that …." In most cases, the use of personal sentences should always be preferred above impersonal ones.

■ **Indirect requests:** A superior can give directions to subordinates framed as questions, for instance "What do you think of doing …?" These requests tend to be perceived as friendlier and warmer than direct statements (e.g., "You must do …"). Some requests can be accompanied by some introductory sentences, such as "I know it might be a tall order, but I would like to know if …," and similar ones. These "softeners" makes the conversation smoother and more flowing.

■ **Plural requests:** Some directions can be formulated using plural sentences, like "We should do …" and "What do you think of us changing …?", among others. The superior can use the plural ("us," "we") even when messages are entirely related to the subordinate. These messages are more comforting because the employees feel as if they were accompanied by their superiors. This approach can also be used to highlight improvements to be made by the employee, for instance "We should be more careful with … next time."

■ **Justified requests:** A superior should make requests accompanied by the specific reasons underpinning them. Research indicates that when people explain the reasoning underlying their requests, recipients are more inclined to act on these requests. Superiors can justify their requests, by using words like "because," or "due to," and others.

Most work conversations tend to be structured and formal. However, conversations between employees should not only be about requests and related business information. Employees should also be encouraged to have frequent casual chats, even with people higher in the hierarchical structure. In these conversations, employees can discover each other's qualities (preferences, values, etc.) and needs (for example, expression, security, etc.).

When possible, managers should take the time to talk to subordinates in personal meetings in order to cultivate these relationships. Cohen and Prusak (2001) observed that many managers wrongly believe that taking time for meetings outside business activities are generally perceived as a luxury, when in fact it is a necessity.

These conversations allow people to develop a deeper heart-to-heart connection with others and show that they truly care for them, on a human level. When superiors hold this type of conversation with subordinates, they can know the staff that work for them better and will be more capable of assigning these employees tasks more aligned with their innermost needs. The topic of natural conversations was analysed in Chapter 8.

11.2.2 Provide Employees with Care

Many companies must contend with red tape and regulations which are more likely to hamper employees' tasks, rather than make them easier. When managers adopt a caring attitude toward their subordinates, they wholeheartedly aim to strengthen their relationship. These managers genuinely want to help their employees, instead of hindering their performance. Consequently, when employees feel supported, their work performance tend to improve. As seen previously, when a person adopts a loving attitude toward others, their intellectual skills are also enhanced significantly.

Managers should always adopt an encouraging and enabling attitude toward their subordinates. Besides, this type of attitude will strengthen the relationships of the former with the latter. In relation to this, Lieberman (2001) stated that people tend to like those they help. In other words, when a person helps another, a stronger connection and rapport between them is developed.

Conversely, Schwartz et al. (2010) observed that "leaders who operate from anger and negativity literally have the power to make their employees sick." These authors also stated that managers should act like "Chief Energy Officers" who are in charge of inspiring, refuelling, and mobilising employees' energy. Moreover, managers should contribute to the development of an empowering work environment, where employees can enhance their unique skills and capabilities.

Everyone deserves to be supported in the workplace, regardless of their current or past level of achievement in the company. Research concluded that employees who are continually supported identify more with the organisation and develop a deeper sense of closeness and belonging to the company.

In some workplaces, people are less prone to support others. In these places, staff members are not used to being grateful to others for their achievements and are less inclined to engage in co-operative projects. In this type of environment, there are no supportive activities, such as mentoring, coaching, and others. Consequently, managers should regularly scan the work environment to detect non-supportive practices and gradually introduce activities which foster support toward employees.

Arnold and Plas (1993) observed that management should always support employees' personal and family lives. From this perspective, a company should adopt an understanding and flexible attitude with its employees, especially when they undergo challenging personal issues, such as new parenthood, death of relatives, illnesses, divorce, etc. Managers should be available for employees to talk to about the main issues affecting them and give their staff members kind and warm assistance.

A company should adopt a caring approach toward employees affected by these challenges, which can include flexible worktime, the possibility of working from home, and leave time, among others. In these situations, a company has a golden opportunity to show it cares for its employees as human beings, beyond their specific work positions.

11.2.3 Support during a Company's Challenging Times

In relation to change affecting a company, most employees are comfortable with the status quo, and therefore they have a natural resistance to change. In the business environment, most of the time, changes are inevitable. These changes can affect different aspects of the organisation, for example, the way it is organised internally, its policies and procedures, the products they sell, the type of customers it serves, and the employees' functions, among others.

When a company supports its employees on a continuous basis, they tend to feel more at ease when they perform their work tasks. Nonetheless, most employees tend to feel anxious when their company goes through challenging times (for example, downsizing, potential bankruptcy, mergers, etc.). Employees might also feel restless when the company is affected by relevant changes in the business environment, for example, new competitors, new technology, or changes in legislation.

In some of these situations, employees tend to feel threatened, which prompts them respond to these factors in a defensive manner. Schein (2009) observed that employees' fear can have different origins, for example, fear of losing their share of power, fear of being incompetent in the new scenario, etc. In these situations, employees are likely to become overwhelmed, which prevents them from tapping into their skills and talents.

Oftentimes, these anxious employees become incapable of tackling challenging circumstances effectively. Goleman (1996) stated that anxious individuals' cognitive functions become severely impaired, which affects their capacity to generate creative solutions to troublesome issues. Sometimes, employees feel powerless and left to their own devices, as if they had to face these challenging situations on their own. Some tips for managers to take into account during challenging circumstances are:

- Some employees are very fearful of the negative effects of change affecting the company they work for. These employees must be thoroughly told the main aspects of change and the main reasons that justify it. In this way, employees' uncertainty and apprehension regarding changing circumstances can be lowered.
- Angell and Rizkallah (2004) observed that during periods of change, managers should always avoid any communication vacuum, where employees do not know or understand what is going on in the organisation. Managers should provide subordinates with loving support and reassurance during turbulent times. Managers should show employees the potential implications of the changing circumstances, especially highlighting benefits that change will bring about for employees. Managers should be a sounding board for subordinates to navigate these changes confidently.
- Hardingham (1992) suggests that managers should help employees to perceive challenging situations in a less threatening manner. This author observed that management should be more encouraging and patient with employees than usual, so that they can feel safe and assisted.
- Sometimes, employees are thoroughly trained regarding the actions to be compliant with the upcoming change. Employees can also be directly involved in the discussion of potential actions to implement in relation to the change.
- When changes affect the organisation, managers can set a transition period for employees to adapt to the new circumstances. In this period, the change can be introduced gradually and smoothly to allow employees to become comfortable and familiar with the new situation.

Sometimes employees can be valid participants of changes to be introduced. In those cases, employees are consulted and their opinion is duly taken on board before any change is implemented. In these cases, employees are also thanked for their contribution of ideas. When a company uses this participative attitude toward change, employees tend to feel more valued, which prompts them to be engaged with the implementation of the change.

Oftentimes, changes affecting an organisation implies a learning process, which includes unlearning old ways of doing things to learn new ones. In some companies, there are people assigned to explain to employees the specific aspects of change affecting them. In this way, employees can feel more supported and can engage with the overall process of change in a more committed manner.

Sometimes, management can even offer valuable incentives to employees who have adopted change, or to encourage people to adopt it. These incentives are very valuable, especially when some employees feel that their situation worsens after the implementation of change.

In a warm work environment, there is a continuous atmosphere of togetherness, which allows employees to handle changing situations in a more effective way. In those cases, employees do not feel on their own, but are accompanied by their colleagues to face the effects of change. This supportive environment acts as a safety net for employees; in this type of environment, the most important values are empathy and solidarity.

11.2.4 Allow Employees to Express Their Views

Oftentimes, companies have topics which are banned from an open discussion with some staff members. Employees should be continually encouraged to give their opinions regarding any topic relevant to the company. Employees' distinct voices must be acknowledged, heard, and respected. When employees' opinions are duly heard, the company's relationship with them is strengthened.

A company should personally thank its employees for their unique valuable suggestions, whenever possible. When employees' contributions are not properly appreciated, they are less likely to express their perspectives in the future.

Employees should be encouraged to fearlessly express their objections, frustrations, and complaints, and management should make employees feel their opinions actually count. As seen previously, employees should also be empowered to express their opinions about changes to be implemented by the company (e.g., new processes, policies, innovative systems and structures, non-traditional activities, etc.) because their view can provide valuable insights into the potential impact of these changes.

At work, employees should be able to express their needs and views assertively, which means being upfront but polite about their own requests and opinions. Assertive employees tend to express their ideas in a firm, but non-aggressive, manner. These employees do not want to beat others with their arguments, but instead consider the needs of all parties involved.

Assertive employees do not want their needs and wants to be dismissed. Instead, they want to feel empowered to make requests or express their opinions with confidence and respect. These employees avoid being hesitant, tentative, pushy or abrasive, and tend to use sentences which start with "I know …", "I feel …", "I would like …", and similar ones.

Many employees are very opinionated regarding different topics and feel the need to express their views when working for a company. These employees are willing to make proposals to improve the workplace and specific tasks related to it. Nonetheless, in many cases, these employees do not express their opinions in the workplace, because they do not want to "rock the boat" or intrude into company affairs. In other cases, employees do not express their views because they are fearful of being penalised for giving their opinions.

Asking employees for their opinions is always very valuable, especially in relation to topics which affect them directly at work. Most employees are generally open to suggesting alternatives which could improve the company's future performance. In order to elicit opinions from employees, managers can ask them questions like "What is your opinion on changing …?" or "Is there anything regarding … that you think could be improved?" This type of question always makes employees feel acknowledged and valued; they realise that their opinion really counts.

Some companies are open to hearing employees' views through formal channels, for example, surveys to find out different aspects of employees' satisfaction regarding different topics (e.g., training, characteristics of the work environment, economic compensation, etc.). This type of survey empowers employees to make contributions to improve work conditions. In those cases, employees' opinions are analysed and oftentimes specific actions are taken to address employees' objections. If these actions are taken, employees should duly be informed of them. According to Blundel (2004), the company can also garner feedback from employees through gatherings known as consultative meetings, where employees can voice their opinions openly.

Cornelissen (2017) observed that some managers are not open to receiving any feedback or suggestions from subordinates for several reasons: fear of receiving negative feedback from employees, the assumption that managers possess better knowledge than subordinates, and intolerance to any dissent stemming from employees, among others. When employees are not actively encouraged to provide suggestions, they are more likely to feel dismissed and unappreciated by the company. In these cases, employees are less prone to be engaged with the company's activities. As a consequence, superiors should always be open to receiving unsolicited suggestions from employees, which must be seriously valued and taken into consideration.

Employees who do not express their views spontaneously should be regularly asked for advice on potential improvements that could be introduced by the company (e.g., new products, services, markets, etc.). Sometimes employees can be encouraged to use creative techniques (brainstorming, mind-mapping, etc.) with other staff members to generate innovative proposals for the company. These creative techniques will be analysed in Chapters 14 and 15.

In most companies, big decisions are made by the members of the staff working at higher hierarchical levels. However, employees on the lower levels can always contribute valuable ideas to the company. Employees can provide their unique perspective on topics relevant to the company. Once suggestions are made by employees, these members of the staff must be updated on the progress of their ideas. As mentioned previously, when ideas suggested by employees are taken on board by the organisation, these employees should also be informed when respective changes will be implemented.

Lastly, Collins (2001) observed that companies should encourage employees to regularly provide "brute facts" affecting the company in a negative manner. Some examples of these facts can be a drop in the company's sales, shrinking of its market share, massive increase in costs, etc. In some work environments, employees are fearful of conveying bad news to others, so these staff members tend to be silent about these negative facts.

Employees should continually be empowered to discuss these facts with management in an open and authentic manner, instead of eschewing them, so that remedial actions can promptly be taken. Collins (2001) also observed that, paradoxically, successful companies are those that are willing to know and face hard facts, but maintain faith in themselves to overcome these challenging issues and eventually thrive.

11.2.5 Delegation of Tasks

In the work environment, all types of control over employees imply that the company does not trust them fully. When a company does not trust its employees, it is adopting an unloving attitude toward them. Most control procedures in a company are based on fear, for example:

■ Fear of employees not knowing how to act in certain situations
■ Fear of employees not working effectively
■ Fear of employees doing things differently
■ Fear of employees not achieving company objectives
■ Fear of employees wasting company resources
■ Fear of employees acting in a deceptive manner (embezzlement, etc.)

In many companies, employees feel they cannot act freely to pursue the organisation's goals in the most effective manner. In these cases, companies do not have full confidence in employees' discernment regarding how to act in the best way. Consequently, these organisations are prone to put in force a myriad of control procedures to guide, discipline, and monitor their staff members. Consequently, employees' actions are not spontaneous, but thoroughly prescribed. Sometimes, employees are not even able to make the most minimal decisions at work without asking their superiors for authorisation. This type of work environment is disempowering for employees because they cannot feel in control of their work activities.

Delegation of relevant tasks to employees is a key factor for a company's success. Delegation allows employees to make relevant decisions without others' approval. The existence of delegation practices within a company is a signal of trust toward employees. From this perspective, employees are not considered to be naughty children requiring control, but instead adult people who can take full responsibility. When employees feel in control of their tasks, they tend to adopt a more collaborative attitude. Instead, when a company adopts a parental (controlling) approach toward employees they tend to feel resentful and behave in a non-cooperative manner.

Delegation, especially in the case of complex tasks, might need to be implemented in a gradual way, in stages. Oftentimes, when a task is delegated, some achievement benchmarks, principles, and standards are set in advance so that the employee takes them into consideration when performing that task. Sometimes the delegation of a task needs additional training to perform it more effectively.

When employees are given relevant discretion at work, they are more motivated and engaged. Not only do these employees feel autonomous, but they also feel more creative, skilful, and capable. In these cases, employees can take ownership of the delegated tasks and enhance their performance in a genuine and unhindered manner. Emerson (1981) wisely said, "Trust people and they will be true to you; treat them greatly and they will show themselves great."

Some superiors adopt a cautious attitude, which implies not delegating anything to their subordinates, until the latter fully gain their trust. Nonetheless, a different perspective is needed; managers should assume employees' capability beforehand, in order to delegate tasks to them. When superiors trust subordinates, the latter are more likely to act in a trustworthy manner.

As seen previously in this book, delegation of tasks satisfies employees' relevant social need of autonomy. D'Souza and Renner (2014) observed that "feelings of mastery, agency, autonomy and control are important and are connected with our sense of wellbeing." When employees are granted freedom to act more spontaneously at work, they feel less pressurised and coerced, which prompts them to contribute to business endeavours in a more willing and meaningful manner. Amabile and Kramer (2011, 2012) observed that autonomy must be accompanied by the supply of enough resources and time to execute the tasks, continuous support from management, and setting of clear goals in order to foster and stimulate employees' work life.

A person who delegates tasks to others lovingly trusts their capabilities. Moreover, by delegating tasks to others, this person implicitly trusts that others will do their best to complete tasks, using their capacities in the most competent manner. A company that trusts employees makes them feel more competent and resourceful; they realise that their contribution is valuable and meaningful. When people are encouraged to act in an autonomous manner, their self-efficacy skills can be enhanced. Research has shown that autonomous employees are more likely to continue working for their company, and even invest in it.

Delegation implies switching from micro-managing subordinates to allowing them to be self-managed. With delegation, employees are encouraged to take the initiative, without being told how to act in each situation. Superiors who delegate implicitly convey to others this idea: "You are a responsible individual and know how to care for yourself and handle things effectively." As seen previously, when delegating tasks, managers should be available to offer their assistance when requested by employees.

As mentioned previously, employees should be given access to relevant resources (technology, information, etc.) to perform their task autonomously and effectively. Pink (2011) suggests that, when possible, workers should be given autonomy over what to do (choosing the task), when to do it (time for performing the task chosen), the team (who to work with to perform a task), and the technique (how to perform a task). As previously explained, employees who are given more autonomy are prone to feel more empowered, capable, and committed.

Delegation can also be related to collective projects. In such cases, the projects can be self-managed by a team, or led by a member of management. In the former case, employees tend to feel more empowered and willing to contribute with their unique skills and talents, as compared with the latter.

Lastly, Hackman and Oldham (1976) observed that, besides autonomy, there are other relevant motivators for employees at work, such as variety of work tasks to perform, meaningful work activities which enhance their skills, the possibility to create valuable outcomes and take ownership of them, and access to feedback about their performance from others. All these factors contribute to employees' satisfaction in a significant manner.

11.2.6 Harnessing Employees' Skills

Every organisation is as healthy as its workforce.

Bill and Cher Nolton

Rogers (1961) observed that all individuals have an "actualising tendency," which means a relevant need to grow and achieve their full potential. Sometimes companies prompt employees to perform activities totally unrelated to their distinct capabilities, and employees find these activities demotivating. When performing these tasks, employees do not feel empowered to give their best; instead they are more likely to feel deskilled.

In those cases, employees are also prone to feel unappreciated regarding their distinct qualities. On the contrary, employees tend to love what they do when they can harness their skills and capabilities. These employees are more engaged at work because they perceive they are distinctively contributing to the company's projects.

Therefore, one of the most relevant company goals should be to harness the unique capabilities of each employee. There are many tests in the market which help companies discover the core strengths of each employee. Managers who adopt a loving attitude trust employees' resourcefulness and encourage them to harness their full potential. These managers avoid allocating tasks to employees which might constrain the unique skills of the latter. These managers instead encourage employees to participate in projects and activities where the employees can contribute with their distinct capabilities.

When employees are given the opportunity to perform some tasks in sync with their unique capacities, they feel more involved and committed to the company. According to Fritz (1991), involvement means that people are genuinely interested and connected to a project because they feel they can contribute to it with value.

Employees who perform tasks not fully aligned with their talents should be encouraged to use their distinct skills to handle these tasks in the most effective manner. Employees need to feel they are using their unique talents, even in tasks that are not completely suitable for them. Employees must also be given tasks where they can unleash their creativity. Most employees feel more fulfilled when they perform tasks where they can be playful and creative.

Superiors should enrol subordinates into projects that help them connect with their innermost capabilities. Zander and Zander (2002) stated that "enrolling is not about forcing, cajoling, tricking, bargaining, pressuring, or guilt-tripping someone into doing something your way." These authors observed that "enrolment is the art and practice of generating a spark of possibility for others to share." In other words, managers should always adopt an affirmative and encouraging attitude toward their employees, so that they can share their talents and apply them to the company's activities.

Besides, by highlighting employees' unnoticed talents, managers can also help employees to learn from their own mistakes, so they can improve their actions in the future. Moreover, managers can help these employees go beyond their self-imposed limitations. When managers adopt this employee-centred attitude, employees are more prone to hone their unique skills so that they can handle work challenges more effectively.

11.2.7 Developing New Skills

In a very positive way, top businesspeople look upon their staff as if they were their children, constantly seeking ways to encourage them and help them develop their full potential both as employees and individuals.

Brian Tracy

Most employees abhor routine and mechanised activities. However, in many companies, employees have to perform the same tasks at work, day in, day out; these monotonous activities leave no leeway for employees' creative expression. Employees have the need to express themselves in a creative manner, and repetitive work activities prevent them satisfying this relevant need.

Sadly, many companies de-skill employees by forcing them to perform hyper-specialised activities over and over. This type of routine also makes employees feel demoralised, because they cannot utilise their creative skills. Some companies have job rotation which allows employees to vary the tasks they perform or work in different areas or departments, which oftentimes make employees more motivated and engaged.

Some companies adopt a perspective of corporate social responsibility (CSR) which implies contributing to social causes (caring for the environment, donating money to charity, etc.). In these companies, employees should regularly be allocated specific tasks which are aligned with their skills and talents, but also have a positive social impact. The performance of these meaningful social activities tends to make employees feel more fulfilled and self-actualised in the work environment.

Not only should managers harness employees' unique skills, but they should also support employees regarding the development of new skills. Superiors should never adopt a complacent attitude toward employees' natural talents, but instead encourage staff members to go beyond their current capacities. This is beneficial for employees' professional development, but also for the company's performance levels.

The work environment should be a place where the employees' learning is fostered on a continuous basis. As employees are regularly trained and their skills heightened, their awareness is progressively raised and their perspective of reality is widened as well. Employees who incorporate new skills also have more tools to analyse and interpret work circumstances; these individuals tend to deal with these situations more effectively. When employees are given the chance to enhance their skills, they can stand out in the work environment.

There are several well-proven ways to help employees learn new skills. These tools give employees the chance to "fail" in a safe environment. Some examples of these instruments are on-the-job training, online and offline workshops, coaching, shadowing others, mentoring, and participation in pilot projects, among others. These tools help employees safely develop capabilities beyond their comfort zone.

Managers should adopt a positive attitude toward the development of subordinates' new skills. When companies have positive assumptions about their employees' ability to develop new capabilities, these expectations become self-fulfilling prophesies. When managers adopt this attitude, employees feel empowered to widen their set of skills, in order to go beyond their current performance levels.

A manager can motivate employees to develop new skills with sentences like "You are the class of employee capable of ...." This positive assumption frequently prompts employees to behave consistently with the capability stated. Employees can also be rewarded for the acquisition of new skills. This reward could be symbolic, for example, providing employees with a training certificate as evidence of the new skills gained. In other cases, employees can receive more tangible rewards, for example, an economic compensation paid to employees for having developed new skills.

11.2.8 Friendly Assessment Process

Many companies have a penchant for assessing employees in a continuous and rigid manner. In these cases, sophisticated systems and processes are set in place to assess personnel's performance. Oftentimes, the intention behind the control instruments is positive, for example, encouraging employees to improve their performance. However, when the assessment is too strict, most employees tend to feel they are not being trusted regarding their work activities.

Some employees feel fearful of this assessment process, especially when it is undertaken on a continuous basis. These employees are prone to feel judged or negatively criticised regarding their effectiveness at work, which prompts them to adopt a defensive attitude (fight-freeze-flight) toward the assessment. As seen previously, this reactive response keeps employees from harnessing their most relevant mental capabilities, which lowers their overall productivity levels. Employees who adopt a defensive mode narrowly focus on the perceived threat (the assessment process), which hinders their learning process at work.

Many employees might even perceive the assessment process as inadequate and intrusive; sometimes employees see themselves as objects whose qualities need to be assessed by the company. These employees feel hindered and continually subject to the company's control, which makes them perform work tasks in a fearful manner. Besides, these employees are also prone to be resentful, because oftentimes superiors are not assessed by anyone. This perceived "unfairness" of the assessment process could also prompt employees to act in a less co-operative manner.

As seen previously, strict and continuous control over employees tends to stifle employees' natural freedom at work. In those cases, employees are prevented from acting in a more spontaneous and creative manner, because of their fear of being detrimentally assessed. This does not mean that employees should never receive any feedback from superiors. On the contrary, assessment can positively contribute to an employee's learning process at work.

According to Egan (2011), for employees' assessments to be constructive, feedback should always be delivered with a caring spirit, which means in an affectionate and genuine manner. This author observes that good feedback is usually confirmatory and corrective. Confirmatory feedback includes actions that the employee performed well, and corrective feedback includes employees' activities that can be improved. Hounsell (2007) states that constructive feedback represents valuable feed-forward, because it helps employees improve their tasks in the future.

Feedback is more constructive when it is delivered within a two-way communicative interaction between the manager and the subordinate. In these cases, employees actively participate in the assessment process. For example, the superior and a subordinate can review performance together. In this case, the manager provides the employee with feedback, and the former is open to receiving comments and requests for clarification from the latter.

This type of assessment puts the employees in a less defensive mode and generates more engagement. In some cases, employees' performance can also be appraised in a more complete manner, for example, by receiving feedback from different stakeholders, such as other employees, customers, suppliers, etc. This is known as 360-degree feedback.

Managers should avoid providing employees with vague or general feedback from the assessment process. The information provided by managers should be specific and actionable. In that sense, constructive feedback should include:

- Aspects that employees perform well, and tips to perform even better in the future
- Different aspects that employees can improve at work (with a focus on employees' behaviour, not on their personal qualities) and practical ways for employees to improve, including desired clear actionable strategies
- Specific reasons why things should be done differently (according to specific criteria such as regulations, company's strategy, etc.) and their potential positive impact on company activities
- Clear examples of how employees can harness their talents more effectively, which can also be accompanied by messages of gratefulness for employees' positive contributions

A caring manager not only provides subordinates with useful feedback, but also follows up with praise when they implement these suggestions. This manager also directly assists them, when necessary.

In psychology, there is the concept of negativity bias, which means that people tend to react more intensely and continually to negative situations than to positive ones. Consequently, when the main focus of feedback given to employees is negative, they tend to become more negatively self-aware of their performance, which prompts their performance levels to plummet. For this reason, superiors should provide feedback which mostly focuses on specific ways for employees to improve their performance in the future, instead of concentrating on their mistakes. From this perspective, the feedback is reaffirming and reassuring, as a relevant part of the employee's process of learning and development.

Constructive feedback always has an empowering and reinforcing effect, which makes employees feel valuable and recognised. This type of feedback represents a valuable source of information which employees can use to improve their performance at work. In other words, this feedback contributes to enhancing employees' self-efficacy skills. This means that employees are prompted to understand, reflect on, and develop strategies to accomplish work objectives more successfully. The enhancement of these self-efficacy skills also entails employees developing positive beliefs about their capability to perform at work in a more productive manner.

When feedback is delivered in a constructive manner, employees are likely to feel more in control, which helps them improve their work tasks in a progressive manner. This type of feedback can represent a very significant tool for employees' encouragement, motivation, and empowerment. Additional aspects on how to deliver constructive feedback were explained in Chapter 9.

11.2.9 Supportive Feedback

> Love is the basis, the foundation of everything, for it is a virtue that is blind to human mistakes, and is never offended. Even in the worst mistakes, it only sees something positive.
>
> **Peter Deunov**

There are other aspects regarding feedback which must be highlighted. As seen previously, superiors should start focussing firstly on what employees are doing well, and secondly, discuss aspects to be improved. In these cases, employees are less likely to adopt a defensive mode. Besides, feedback should always be provided in a kind and gentle manner, with a focus on preserving and strengthening relationships with employees.

When providing feedback, superiors should show an authentic interest in employees' professional development. In addition to this, feedback stemming from assessment should always be delivered in a personalised manner, considering employees' unique strengths and capabilities. Therefore, feedback should avoid comparing an employee with others.

When employees have made mistakes at work, superiors must be compassionate with them. Superiors who adopt a compassionate attitude toward employees are fully aware of challenges affecting them, and they are willing to understand and support these employees in the best way possible. Compassion implies positive qualities (e.g., tenderness, care, thoughtfulness, and loving kindness) regarding others, which strengthens the connection with them.

Superiors must be patient and loving with their employees. From this perspective, employees' setbacks represent stepping stones for them to learn new capabilities and do things better in the future. Most employees obtain valuable insights into their mistakes. Superiors must always believe in their subordinates and their natural capability to overcome challenges successfully. Fritz (1991) observed that "if something is worth doing, it's worth doing poorly until you can do it well."

However, many managers act in a punitive way regarding subordinates' mistakes. This ruthless approach does not help employees overcome work challenges, but instead damages the relationship with them. As a consequence, superiors should always adopt a supportive attitude toward employees, especially when they make mistakes; managers should consider that every employee is a human being, in the process of improving and developing, not a finished work. This positive attitude contributes to strengthen employees' capabilities at work.

Some business coaches observe that the learning process at work always includes making some mistakes; this is inevitable. When subordinates make mistakes at work, managers should ask themselves some interesting questions:

■ How would I like to be treated by others if I am the one making this mistake?
■ How can I be of help and support to this employee?
■ What is the most loving way to provide this employee with feedback?
■ What actionable tips can make this employee feel more confident and capable?
■ How can I help this employee while I care for my relationship with this individual?

This type of question provides managers with interesting insights. When a superior adopts a compassionate attitude toward employees, these staff members are more likely to co-operate and improve their future performance. Conversely, when a superior is harshly judgemental of employees, they are more prone to adopt a defensive mode, which lowers their productivity levels. Besides, a compassionate attitude always creates a warmer work environment, a place where all employees are comfortable working.

If an employee makes a mistake, a compassionate manager tends to show this employee some examples of how things should be done in the future. The manager's explanation is generally delivered in a warm and kind manner. Due to the superior acting in a non-judgemental manner, the employee is prone to feel more confident, self-assured, and assertive.

11.2.10 Appreciation of Employees' Contribution

The topic of gratitude has been explained in Chapter 7. Many companies tend to take employees work for granted, and avoid being thankful to them for their contribution. Some companies adopt an ungrateful attitude toward their employees, dismissing their human side, and ignoring the fact that employees always need to be valued and recognised.

Managers that acknowledge employees' contribution do not look weak, but more humane. When a manager is grateful with subordinates, they tend to behave more co-operatively, which affects their productivity in a positive manner. When employees are overtly appreciated for their positive contribution to the company, they feel encouraged to keep on contributing. A manager who is grateful with employees can also explain to them how their work specifically contributes to the company's overall progress.

Sometimes companies use personal letters to thank employees for their contribution to company objectives. It is possible to highlight employees' contributions by posting thank you messages or articles in different publications (e.g., the company's magazine, official website, newsletters, blogs, etc.). A company that wants to be grateful with employees publicly should primarily pinpoint the aspects of real people (their character, their commitment and grit, etc.) who contributed to the company's positive outcomes, instead of focussing on impersonal raw data (figures, statistics, percentages, etc.).

When a company adopts a grateful attitude toward employees, they tend to feel proud of their contribution to the organisation. Sometimes recognising employees is symbolic; for instance, by acknowledging the most productive employee of the year.

Some companies with a grateful attitude promise a reward to employees who contribute more to the company's objectives. Wiseman (2013) expressed that when a company offers an employee an economic incentive to perform a task, this activity tends be perceived as less valuable and, in turn, becomes less likely to be performed. On a similar tone, Sutherland (2007) observed that "material rewards reduce the attractiveness of pleasurable activities and have little effect on less pleasurable activities once they have been withdrawn."

If a company want to be grateful, it should instead give its employees sincere praise for their valuable contribution to company's purpose. In a similar vein, Pink (2011) suggested that companies should give employees relevant feedback regarding their performance, instead of giving them material rewards (e.g., bonuses), to boost employees' motivation. This author also observed that these material rewards often decrease motivation, lower performance levels, foster dishonest tackling of tasks, and reduce creativity.

Questions for Self-Reflection

- How can I adopt a kinder and more grateful attitude to our company's employees?
- How can I support our company's employees during dire circumstances?
- How can I give our employees more constructive feedback?
- How can our company's employees' skills be harnessed more effectively?

Chapter 12

Adopting a Loving Attitude toward Customers

There is only one boss. The customer. And he can fire everybody in the company from the chairman on down, simply by spending his money somewhere else.

Sam Walton. Founder of Wal-Mart Stores, Inc.

12.1 Love and Customers

Put service first, and money takes care of itself – always.

David Schwartz

Many decades ago, in a business meeting, a famous businessman, who preferred to remain anonymous, emphatically asserted "Customers will wish you well as a company if you truly wish them well." This simple but insightful idea is not commonly applied by many companies, not even those with extensive experience in the business arena. This valuable idea can be applied to any business activity, with no exception whatsoever.

Companies have to care for their customers if they want to succeed in business; to love customers is to appreciate them in an unconditional manner. Many companies focus on the improvement of economic parameters (more sales, increased profits, bigger market share, etc.) without realising that all these indicators are directly related to the degree to which customers are satisfied with the company's products and services. In simple words, when customers are duly satisfied by a company's products and services, these parameters tend to improve accordingly.

There are many good books on marketing which address the topic of customer satisfaction from a strategic perspective. Most of these books do not take into account the human aspects of customers. Every time a company relates to customers, it should acknowledge them as valuable and unique individuals. Customers deserve to be respected and loved; their needs must be duly recognised by companies on a regular basis. Each customer has dreams and preferences which are legitimate, significant, and distinct, and which companies must take into consideration.

As mentioned in Chapters 5 and 6, all individuals long for love from different sources; love is one of their most important needs. It is possible to say that customers look for love each time they buy products and services from companies. This idea might seem strange to many people, but it happens to be true. Customers primarily buy goods and services because of the positive emotional states they seek to experience when using or consuming them.

These sought-after positive emotions can comprise happiness, peace, security, and other positive states. Some schools of thought have observed that all these positive emotional states are directly and indirectly related to love. From this standpoint, there are only two qualities of emotion: the ones related to love (glee, solace, safety, excitement, etc.) and the ones related to fear (sadness, anger, angst, grief, shame, etc.). The emotions related to love are always positive (as compared with the ones related to fear), and these are the ones sought by customers every time they make a purchase.

Oftentimes, customers buy products and services to be accepted by others (e.g., peers, family friends, colleagues, etc.). In these cases, customers make these purchases because of their urge to fit in with others and be complimented by them. In this case, the customer's need for acceptance implies the need to be loved by other people.

In the business environment, many companies tend to take customers for granted; these organisations adopt an unloving attitude to customers. When a company adopts an authentic loving attitude toward customers, it tries to improve the way they are served on a continuous basis. Below there are some questions companies should ask themselves on a regular basis in order to serve customers in a warmer and kinder manner:

- How can we discover more about our customers' distinct needs?
- How can we acknowledge these unique needs more effectively?
- How can we give customers valuable advice regarding their decisions on our products and services?
- How can we enhance their experience and make them feel more fulfilled?
- How can we solve their problems more effectively?
- How can we offer them more valuable products and services?
- How can we be more appreciative and generous to them?
- How can we be more available to sort out their doubts and objections?
- How can we connect to them in a more natural and spontaneous way?
- How can we acknowledge them as valuable human beings?
- How can we be warmer, kinder, and friendlier to them?
- How can we adopt an authentic and wholehearted attitude of service?

Companies can also ask themselves: "How can we be more loving with our customers in a practical and specific manner?" It is important to pinpoint that when customers buy products or services, they generally look for self-fulfilment. Therefore, companies can use these questions to brainstorm and discover more effective ways to make customers feel fulfilled.

12.2 Importance of Customers' Wellbeing

Friendliness is to human understanding what freedom is to men in society – the very atmosphere of growth and development.

Elmer Letterman

Many companies use a vast arsenal of techniques to persuade customers to buy products and services; in most cases, these stratagems tend to be counterproductive. In relation to this, research in social psychology concludes that people are more likely to do something when the message they receive is *not* intently seeking to persuade them.

Instead of purposely trying to persuade customers, a company should treat them as valuable individuals. Therefore, a company's employees should always try to connect to customers more from the heart, instead of the head. From this perspective, each customer is a unique human being, who deserves kindness, love, and respect from the company. It is interesting to notice that many companies treat customers in the opposite manner; these organisations consider customers as faceless figures or statistics who contribute to the organisation's economic results.

Whenever a company interacts with its customers, it should contribute to their well-being on a continuous basis. Companies and customers are deeply interrelated; when customers are fully satisfied, their well-being also impacts on the company's economic results. In other words, customers who are served well by a company tend to come back to buy more products and services, which generates more revenue and profits for this organisation.

Besides, when a company adopts a loving attitude toward customers, this brings about additional benefits for the company, such as more loyal customers, and abundant positive reviews from customers on the company's products and services, among others. A company treats customers in a loving manner when:

- The company makes customers aware of the best products for them
- The company adopts a kind, patient, and friendly attitude toward them
- The company educates customers to help them learn things that are useful for them
- The company aims to develop a mutually beneficial relationship with them
- The company satisfies their needs more effectively over time
- The company acts with integrity on a continuous basis
- The company provides them with truthful and meaningful information
- The company assists them whenever they need help
- The company suggests insightful ideas to meet their preferences
- The company helps them discover their innermost needs
- The company make them feel good whenever they interact with the company
- The company gives them some free goods and services

Most customers truly value these aspects; companies should pay close attention to them every time they deal with customers. These aspects truly strengthen the relationship between a company and its customers, which makes them more inclined to become loyal to the organisation.

12.3 Main Qualities of a Loving Attitude toward Customers

A customer chooses a product based not only on objective appraisal of its use but also on how he or she feels about it. The fact is that the subtle, working as it does on the level of emotions, hunches and intuition, influences the gross; there is no way around it. And business always has to be tuned in to this fact.

Amit Goswami

Dr Hawkins (2012) recommends that employees in direct contact with customers adopt a loving attitude toward them. This prestigious scientist also observed that employees with a loving attitude tend to become more creative, which helps them recommend to customers products and services which are more suitable for them. Besides, this author concluded that an employee with a loving attitude "often converts customers to friends, and customers tend to become loyal." Consequently, when employees treat customers in a loving manner, they tend to develop mutually beneficial relationships with the company.

Customers who feel they are being treated in a loving manner by a company tend to treat the organisation in a reciprocal manner. These customers tend to write positive reviews online on company's products and services or recommend the organisation to other people (relatives, friends, colleagues, etc.). These positive comments from customers are commonly called positive "word of mouth."

These positive comments are spontaneous unbiased expressions of customers' love toward a company which has previously served them lovingly. According to Cialdini (2009), these recommendations provided by satisfied customers also represent prized "social proofs" which validate products and services offered by the company. These comments also help to reduce other customers' uncertainty regarding the reliability of the products and services recommended. When customers spread positive word of mouth regarding certain products and services, they act like unpaid ambassadors who wholeheartedly endorse these goods and services, and want other people to try them.

Besides, customers who are treated in a loving manner by a company's employees are also prone to defend this organisation and its products when other people attack them. These customers tend to be more understanding with the blunders made by an organisation, and also provide this company with kind insights on how to improve their products and services.

In the following points, no specific selling techniques will be explained. Instead, some relevant principles which can help a company adopt a more loving attitude with its customers will be analysed.

12.3.1 Over-Performing

In marketing, the main objective is to satisfy customers' needs appropriately. In other words, companies should offer products and services which meet customers' expectations. However, a company which loves its customers tries to exceed their needs, which implies *over-performing*. This means that a company offers customers more than what is expected by them. Chaston (2004) called it "positive disconfirmation" when the performance of an organisation exceeds customers' expectations. It is interesting to pinpoint that most customers can distinguish between a company with purely economic objectives (more sales, more profits, etc.) and one whose main priority is to satisfy and even exceed their expectations.

According to Wattles (2013), a company should always give customers more than it takes from them. To put it simply, a company should add more value to customers than the value it receives from them. By creating a deliberate imbalance in the value exchanged with customers, not only does the company serve them better, but these customers are also more likely to develop a strong relationship with this organisation.

Moreover, a company which is generous with customers, which means providing them with higher value, makes these customers feel "indebted" with this organisation. As a consequence, because of the principle of reciprocity, these customers tend to act in generous manner with this company. For example, these customers might come back to the organisation to buy new products and services, or they might recommend this company to other customers. This principle can be applied not only to customers, but also other stakeholders of the company, such as employees, suppliers, intermediaries, etc.

Besides, when a company delights its customers, which is giving more than they expect, this organisation creates a long-lasting impression on them. This type of organisation aims to develop a long-term relationship with customers, instead of focusing only on a one-off transaction.

An alternative perspective states that customers have problems which should be solved by companies in the most effective manner. For example, when customers are looking for a package holiday, they have a problem (e.g., they experience boredom, stress, etc.) and want specific companies (for example, tourism agencies) to solve it in the best way (for instance, package holidays). The companies prone to become wealthier are the ones which solve customers' problems most effectively, which also implies adopting a loving attitude toward customers.

A company with a loving attitude toward customers also provides them with valuable presents. Customers are likely to feel more connected to the company because of having received these gifts. These presents must always be given by the company with no strings attached, which means unconditionally. To put it more simply, if a company only provides customers with gifts if they meet specific conditions (for instance, they get free gifts only if they buy the company's other products), these customers are prone to feel bribed. Some examples of items a company can give customers free of charge are:

- Product samples
- Free e-books, reports, newsletters
- Free services (delivery, repair, training, installing, etc.)
- Free advice and consultation
- Vouchers
- Free trial period

This generous approach implies a demonstration of love from the company to its customers. However, the majority of companies adopt the opposite approach; they are primarily focused on *getting* from customers, which implies obtaining more sales, increasing the level of profits, gaining more loyalty from customers, etc.

Instead, when a company gives its best to customers first, revenue and profits will later ensue in a spontaneous and effortless manner. If a company adopts a generous perspective, the company will not have to pursue and retain customers, because they will be naturally attracted and pledge allegiance to it.

12.3.2 Trustworthiness

When a company is offering products and services with a superior performance, it is generating trust with customers. Trust is a very important factor when a customer and a company depend on each other. Morrison and Firmstone (2015) list some factors which create trust, such as reputation, accountability, and familiarity, among others. From the psychological perspective, familiarity between customers and a company not only increases trust, but also brings about liking between them. According to Pearce (mentioned in Baumeister and Leary, 1995) familiarity between people also brings about mutual assistance, as it also does in the case of dependency between them.

When trust between a company and its customers is increased, their relationship is strengthened, and potential disagreements and misunderstandings are prone to be reduced. High levels of trust also increase rapport, connection, and commitment in the interactions between a company and its customers. When people trust each other, over time, this trusting bond tends to get stronger, but it can also disappear in the blink of an eye.

According to Mitchell et al. (1998), some factors which allow companies to develop trust bonds with their customers are: reliability, benevolence, probity, and satisfaction. Other relevant aspects are fairness in the deals and fulfilment of what was agreed by the company and the customer. It is interesting to pinpoint that these trust bonds tend to develop over time, as a result of a positive assessment of each other's actions.

Rosseau et al. (1998) observed that trust implies the acceptance of a situation of vulnerability, where a person has positive expectations regarding the intentions and actions of another. As seen previously, trust is generally built over time and assessed in a continuous manner. When a person trusts another, the former believes that the latter will not take advantage of the former. In other words, when customers trust a company, they believe it will behave in a predictably benevolent manner toward them. Consequently, these customers are less prone to adopt defensive or aggressive behaviour toward this organisation. To put it simply, when customers trust a company, they are less prone to adopt a fight-freeze-flight mode toward this organisation.

Trust represents a compass that guides customers through their relationships with a company. When trust toward an organisation is broken, customers realise this in a retrospective manner, by analysing the company's past actions. Even when countless rules and conditions can be set to protect customers, these regulations are generally a poor substitute for authentic trust. Moreover, sometimes a truly trusting relationship makes these rules unnecessary.

Many companies resort to a wide range of cajoling stratagems in order to "force" customers into buying products and services. From this book's perspective, customers' needs must always be satisfied in a loving manner, which implies avoiding manipulative techniques and gimmicks. These cajoling techniques tend to create distrust between customers and the company using these tools.

Some examples of these ploys are: to exaggerate products' benefits to mislead customers into buying them; to increase the customers' "pain" in order to offer a way to assuage it; to deride products and services offered by other organisations in order to differentiate a company's own offerings; to hide the fine print on contracts so that customers make uninformed decisions, etc.

Sisodia et al. (2015) observed that some companies tend to adopt a perspective of hucksterism – which implies the use of aggressive selling techniques that have no regard for customer needs. These authors stated that this type of selling behaviour is more noticeable in companies whose employees' main compensation is tied to sales quotas. Some additional aspects regarding manipulative marketing techniques will be discussed in Appendix C.

12.3.3 *Attitude of Service*

> Render more service than that for which you are paid and you will soon be paid for more than you render.
>
> **Napoleon Hill**

Most companies focus on selling their products and services to customers; however, the traditional sales approach tends to create different levels of friction between the company and its customers. Instead, companies that adopt a loving attitude toward customers focus on serving them, not on selling them products and services. This type of company realises that their business activities are more about serving customers (which means being customer-oriented) than focusing on the company itself.

Some employees tend to feel inferior when serving customers. It is important to clarify that serving never means servitude; instead, serving always implies adding value for customers and improving their lives to a small or large extent. An authentic attitude of service toward customers also entails treating them in a loving manner. Employees who serve customers lovingly feel it is an honour to assist them.

From this perspective, companies encourage customers to make the best decisions regarding their purchases of goods and services. These companies understand that customers' needs are relevant, and for this reason they try to satisfy them effectively. This type of company is determined to support customers before, during, and after the selling process. From this standpoint, a company wants its customers to make the best decisions for them, even when this implies not buying anything at all, or buying products and services from other organisations.

When a company changes its intent by adopting an attitude of service, customers can feel this in a subtle but powerful manner. As seen previously, when a company serves customers, they do not feel coerced into a commercial transaction, but instead truly acknowledged, supported, and respected. Customers do not want to feel bullied into purchasing a product or a service.

When an employee has a serving attitude, this person relates to customers in a more open manner, wholeheartedly wanting the best for them. As seen previously, when adopting a loving attitude, the employee will aim to inform customers of their best options, indicating the most suitable one for them.

Besides, when a company serves customers, it wants them to only buy products or services which they have full confidence in. In other words, the company wants customers to make fully informed purchase decisions, without any hesitation. When customers make their purchasing decisions based on the best information to hand, they are less prone to feel regretful afterward. This type of company does not want customers to feel they have bought a product which does not actually meet their innermost needs.

If the company instead "pushes" customers to buy its products and services, they are more likely to become resentful with this organisation, and their relationship will be harmed. As seen previously, many companies regularly use stratagems to cajole customers and prompt them to buy products and services they do not really need. These ploys generally work once, because when customers discover they have been deceived, they tend to cease the relationship with that company. These commercial ruses never contribute to development of a long-term relationship between the company and customers.

With a loving attitude, a company's employees act as supportive coaches with customers. As mentioned previously, this type of employee provides customers with the most valuable information and advice for them to make the most informed decision. In other words, the attitude of service implies guiding customers to make their best choice, which implies total respect for their sovereignty when they make purchasing decisions.

Customers always want to know what is in it for them regarding a product or a service. A company with a serving attitude toward customers always considers their well-being and avoids keeping these customers by any means. As a consequence, when a customer is effectively served by a company instead of being manipulated, a bond of trust is created and strengthened between them. In order to serve customers in the best way, employees should always ask customers questions like:

■ What is the most relevant attribute of this type of product/service?
■ What benefits do you want to obtain from this type of product/service?
■ What are your real motivations when buying this type of product/service?
■ What type of experience do you want to have regarding this type of product/service?

- How can this product/service make your life better?
- What are the ideal characteristics of this type of product/service?

When customers provide the company with specific answers to these questions, the organisation can get to know customers better in order to offer them products and services matching their criteria and preferences. Sometimes, customers might not have accurate or definite answers to the aforementioned questions. In those cases, it is the function of sellers, based on their expertise and experience, to educate and provide specific information about the alternatives that are potentially suitable for these customers.

It is important to highlight a very obvious point, which is generally dismissed by many companies. Some products and services which could be beneficial for certain customers could be totally detrimental for others. Therefore, company employees should treat each customer as a distinct human being with specific needs and preferences. This point will be thoroughly discussed later in this chapter. Wolhorn (1977) observed that a company's employees should treat customers in the same way these employees would like to be treated if they were customers. In relation to this, Greenleaf (1991, 1996) observed that leading companies are the ones that make customers happier and fulfilled while being served.

Many salespeople become too eager to obtain a purchase from customers, and customers frequently feel the salespersons' anxiousness. When salespeople act in an anxious manner, customers are likely to be put off. In those cases, customers feel that the salesperson does not want the best purchase for them, but for the company.

Many employees want to close the sale at all costs and forget to thoroughly explore the distinctive customer's needs. In those cases, it is advisable that salespeople change their focus from "selling mode" to "serving mode," which implies knowing more about customer's unique preferences. In relation to this, customers have different criteria when buying a product or service, such as trustworthiness, quality, branding, packaging, delivery services, financing, etc.

Sometimes a company can also help its customers discover their latent or unobvious needs; in other words, customers might not be clear about their preferences. In these cases, company employees can kindly interact with customers to discover and explore their hidden preferences and needs, as well as potential products and services which are suitable to them.

The company's employees should position themselves as experts about the product and services being offered to the customers. By standing out as knowledgeable about a company's products and services, salespeople can provide the best advice to customers. The main purpose of the salesforce is to guide customers throughout the buying process in a friendly manner.

However, the expert knowledge possessed by salespeople should always be balanced with the knowledge that customers have about themselves, which includes their own needs, desires, and values. The harmonious combination of these two types of knowledge places the seller in a better position to offer customers loving support so that they can make good purchasing decisions.

As explained previously, a company which adopts a loving attitude toward its customers is aimed at offering them the best value possible regarding its products and services. When a company focuses on offering outstanding value to customers, their needs are more likely to be met. Moreover, when customers have good experiences stemming from a company's products and services, they tend to feel cared for and loved by this company. These positive emotions experienced by customers make them more likely to be loyal to that company, and their relationship tends to become stronger over time.

Some companies use processes and systems that help customers analyse, select, and buy products without any assistance from a seller. This is part of the self-service trend, where customers can become self-reliant. Some examples of this are websites where customers can buy or book online, and supermarkets where customers select and buy products on their own and pay for them through an electronic cashier.

In all these cases, there is no interaction between customers and a company's employees, which can make the company's service to customers look impersonal. In these cases, the company should provide customers with assistance from its employees in different ways (on the phone, in person, virtual chat, etc.) in order to make their customers' experience warmer and less impersonal.

12.3.4 A Sharing Attitude

Research corroborates that when a person shares anything personal with another, the latter tends to be more open with the former. Moreover, Cialdini (2009) observed that every time a person gives something to another this person feels naturally compelled to naturally reciprocate, which means acting in a similar manner. This principle is known as reciprocity and affects all social interactions.

A company's employees can apply this principle to all interactions with customers. When talking to a customer, sellers can make a casual comment about their own needs. For example, when showing a specific product to a customer, a seller can say "In relation to this type of product, I generally like ...." When sellers are open to confessing their own personal needs and preferences to customers, the latter are more inclined to talk about their own needs.

In order to improve their communication with customers, salespeople can make comments not only about their own personal preferences, but also about their own values, hobbies, interests, and any other personal aspects. By doing so, salespeople present themselves as more authentic individuals, which prompts customers to open up reciprocally. When customers hear these comments from a salesperson, they tend to lower their defensive barriers during the sales process.

Bryant (2009) observed that when people show themselves vulnerable before others, which implies being transparent, honest, open, and accepting of their own shortcomings and mistakes, this creates a stronger connection with them. Consequently, when sellers show themselves to be vulnerable and human, they are more prone to build deeper rapport with customers. In other words, when sales people trust customers with aspects of their own personal stories, customers are more likely to trust these sellers with their own.

Besides, when salespeople share their own personal information with customers and they reciprocate, some common aspects between the speakers are likely to be found; for example, similar tastes, identical preferences, etc. As seen previously, research has demonstrated that when a person finds commonalities with another, more affinity is created between them. In relation to this, Wiseman (2009) have observed that, according to research, people tend to like each other more when they agree on things they dislike, rather than on things they like.

The principle of reciprocity and sharing can be applied in other ways. As mentioned previously, companies, for example, can give away different things to customers: free samples, truthful and relevant information, useful advice, technical support, etc. According to the principle of reciprocity, customers that received these gifts from a company are prone to give something back to this organisation. For example, customers can give positive recommendations about the company to their friends, and customers can also give their loyalty to the company.

12.3.5 Spontaneous Approach

Many employees engage in conversations with customers in a scripted and unnatural manner. Some companies make salespeople memorise scripts to use with customers. When talking to customers, these sellers appear artificial, like robots, and no authentic rapport is developed between them. This structured way of communicating is ineffective in developing relationships with potential or current customers. Customers are very intelligent and easily perceive when a company uses canned stories to meet its own interests.

A company can adopt an alternative perspective by leaving its own hidden agenda aside and approaching customers in a natural and spontaneous manner. Natural communication is a key factor for companies to engage with customers from a long-term perspective. From this standpoint, the company's priority is to serve its customers in the best manner, not to entice them with verbal gimmicks. When customers are really deemed important, employees let the conversation unfold spontaneously and effortlessly. In this communicational approach, sales people do not try to veer the conversation in any specific predetermined direction.

Not only does this conversational approach improve the connection with customers, but it will also make them feel more comfortable, which contributes to building mutually beneficial relationships. The topic of natural conversations has been thoroughly explained in Chapter 8.

12.3.6 Full Connection

Most companies get in contact with their customers on several occasions: before, during, and after the purchasing process. According to McGrath and MacMillan (2005), the consumption chain is the sequence of interactions between a company and its customers. Some examples of these interactions are: customers' request for information about products or services, arrangement of the main purchasing conditions, delivery of products, sorting out complaints, etc. It is important to highlight that a company's employees should always add value to customers in each of these interactions.

The aforementioned authors advise companies to identify their main employees that get in contact with customers in each of these interactions and encourage these staff members to fully acknowledge customers' needs in a responsive, diligent, and friendly manner. In other words, in each interaction, employees should make things easier, faster, and simpler for customers. However, some companies tend to relate to customers in a halfway fashion. In relation to this, there are several obstacles which affect the quality of the connection between a company and its customers. Some examples of these hindrances are:

- **Lack of full information:** Sometimes companies withhold information that is relevant to customers. These companies act in a very calculated or dishonest manner, which prevents the chance of a real and deep connection with customers. Customers should always be provided with the most significant information for them to make the best purchasing decision.
- **Lack of personalised approach:** According to Brandenburger and Nalebuff (1996), when a company does not take the time to develop its relationships with customers, it is as if this company was selling standardised and undifferentiated products and services, similar to the ones offered by any other organisation. The development of strong relationships with customers adds value to customers, in the same way products and services offered by a company do. Therefore, it is important to care for the relationships with customers and nurture them on a regular basis, avoiding treating customers as "numbers" or "undifferentiated" individuals.
- **Lack of undivided attention:** Some companies do not develop a deep connection with customers because they do not provide them with full attention. Company employees must have a laser-focus on customers when engaging with them. All distractions (e.g., picking up a phone call, etc.) must be avoided in order to acknowledge customers in a respectful

manner. A company's employees can use active listening skills when the customer is talking. These employees can also paraphrase what customers say and clarify relevant points to avoid misunderstandings.

- **Lack of presence:** Some employees are not fully present when interacting with customers. Presence implies being focused on the now. Many employees tend to be distracted by thoughts about the past (e.g., memories) or future (e.g., worries, expectations). For example, when talking to customers, some employees think about the best way to close the deal with them; other employees are concerned about potential customer objections. The previous examples are focused on the future, which prevents employees from being fully engaged with the customers in the now. When employees focus on the present moment, their main priority is to understand customer's needs in order to meet them effectively.

- **Lack of kindness and warmth:** A full connection with customers also implies treating them in a polite and amicable manner. For instance, a company can kindly request customers' permission to ask for some aspects about personal information in order to show them more details about the company's products. Employees can also show their kindness toward customers in other ways. For example, some power gestures of warmth are grinning or smiling to customers in a friendly manner. Some other positive body language signals are nodding and making continuous eye contact when the customers is speaking. All these actions improve the rapport between a company and its customers.

- **Lack of continuous support:** Some companies are limited to offering assistance to customers during the buying process. In order to develop more affinity with customers, a company should also offer them kind support after they have bought the product. This includes, for example, listening to customer complaints, providing customers with clarification about the use of a product, etc. A company can also offer customers valuable support before the buying process, for instance, by providing them with the most complete online information regarding the organisation's products and services, so that these customers can check it before interacting with this company.

- **Lack of comfort:** Some employees do not make customers feel at ease. When an employee engages with customers, this person should prompt them to feel comfortable. When customers are treated in a friendly manner, they are more prone to experience positive emotions and link these emotional states to the company. Most purchasing decisions have an emotional component. Therefore, when customers feel good during their interactions with a company, they are more likely to develop a deeper connection with this organisation.

- **Lack of high value:** Some companies provide customers with little or no value. In order to develop long-lasting relationships with customers, companies must offer high value, but also add more value to them on a continuous basis. For example, a company should improve their products and services on a regular basis, because customers are very demanding and their expectations tend to become gradually higher over time. If a company does not innovate on a regular basis, other companies in the market will.

As seen previously, no customer wants to feel pulled or rushed into purchasing a company's products and services as a result of frightening, manipulating, or misleading strategies. These ploys create no connection with customers, but push them away. Not only do customers want to feel in total control of their actions when buying a product or a service, they also want to be acknowledged as valuable and unique human beings, who deserve to have their need for full connection duly satisfied.

12.3.7 Soft-Touch Approach

The majority of sales workshops teach selling techniques (e.g., different alternatives to close deals, ways to answer customers' objections, scripts to identify customers' needs, etc.) which are unnatural, and sometimes blatantly manipulative. As seen previously, the right approach of a company's employee when approaching customers is not to try to sell something to them, but instead to show genuine interest in their needs. When a salesperson is truly interested in a customer, the latter is more prone to show interest in the former.

Salespeople commonly use traditional selling techniques which includes elements of control and manipulation. When sellers use these techniques, customers often feel "forced" to make decisions in a certain way, as a result of the pressure exerted on them. Most customers perceive these sellers as untrustworthy and unreliable. Salespeople who are pushy typically take actions like:

- Trying to focus on their company, instead of customers
- Treating customers in an inauthentically kind manner
- Hiding or distorting information which is relevant to customers
- Talking only about commercial topics and avoiding talking about personal ones
- Talking negatively about competitors
- Enunciating needs which customers do not actually have
- Trying to offer products and services convenient for the company, not customers

Customers can usually "smell" when a seller is pushy, sleazy, and inauthentic; they can easily perceive when the selling process does not feel "correct" or "real." Customers can also perceive the feeling of desperation from a forceful seller, which pushes them away. When customers perceive a lack of integrity in the salesperson, they automatically adopt a defensive attitude (fight-freeze-flight). In those cases, customers are prone to shut down their interactions with the seller.

No company can gain customers by pushing them into buying its products and services. Instead, when a company's employee acts in an unworried manner, which means not being continually centred on getting sales, customers tend to feel more comfortable. Moreover, when a company focuses on serving customers, they naturally respond in a more positive manner to its products and services.

As seen previously, hard-selling and pushiness is never related to a loving attitude toward customers. To that effect, when a salesperson adopts a loving attitude toward customers, this seller avoids trying to persuade them by using cajoling or misleading ploys. Social psychologists have observed that when a person is overly and purposely trying to persuade others, they are less likely to be effectively persuaded, because the former tends to be distrusted by the latter.

It is interesting to pinpoint that customers can feel when they are being treated in a fair and supportive manner. Customers can easily distinguish a company that wants to thrust its products onto them from a business which wants to serve them in the best way. This second type of company is primarily aimed at providing customers with the best advice, so that they can make the best decision to satisfy their needs. Consequently, when approaching customers, sellers should ask themselves "Am I being pushy with customers or am I trying to help them in the most honest manner?"

There is another relevant point to highlight. Companies that sell products or services with several technical characteristics (sizes, materials, functions, etc.) often have to educate customers. These technical aspects should always be explained to customers in the clearest and most simple way, avoiding any technical jargon when possible. A seller who provides customers with information about these technical aspects should avoid bragging about this knowledge, so that customers do not feel ashamed of not having this knowledge (Allen and Wotten, 1998).

In those cases, a seller can say to a customer "You might have realised that there are different models of ... I would like to explain this further ..." or "It is relevant for you to know a bit more about ...," so that customers can feel acknowledged and respected. In order to clarify these technical traits, sellers can use visual props (such as photos, samples, drawings, etc.) to make their explanations clearer (Allen and Wotten, 1998).

12.3.8 Transparency

Lack of transparency is related to the previous points regarding a seller's manipulative attitude. When sellers are transparent, they avoid providing customers with misleading or untruthful information. Instead, sellers' lack of transparency tends to generate distrust, which in turn harms the relationship with customers. Some examples of stratagems purposed to misguide customers are:

- Provision of incomplete information
- Disclosure of false information
- Incremental requirements to buy the product
- Unreal scarcity of products and services

In relation to the last example, a company pretends that the supply of their products (or services) is limited, when this is not true. In those cases, most customers tend to covet these items more intensely, because they are perceived as scarce.

None of the aforementioned stratagems create a trusting and loving bond with customers. In all these cases, customers perceive that the company is lying to them. In other words, a company promises something to customers which is not the real deal. The use of this type of ploy backfires, making a company appear untrustworthy in the eyes of customers.

Consequently, a company should always aim to supply its customers with truthful and complete information so that they can make well-informed buying decisions. A company with integrity always provides customers with honest information and lovingly guides them before, during, and after the buying process. These companies actually want the best for their customers; their helpful attitude makes customers feel more supported, as well as comfortable. Figuratively speaking, these companies behave as a loving parent who continually gives their best advice to their children, but also encourages them to make the best decision.

Transparent companies always communicate the full range of aspects regarding their products and services. These companies are always willing to educate customers in a caring manner, so that they can make their most well-informed buying decisions. When a company acts with integrity, it is more likely to capture customers' minds (making them aware of the company's products and services), but also their hearts (which implies building a long-lasting trusting bond with them).

12.3.9 Openness

Many companies try to sell their products and services to customers without knowing their distinct needs in detail. Customers are wise and insightful; they can thoroughly teach any company about their unique needs. Therefore, companies should always be open to being introduced to the customers' unique world, which includes their needs, values, and expectations.

It is important that companies be empathetic, which means seeing reality through customers' eyes. A very effective way to know what customers want is to listen to them actively on a continuous basis. The main aspects of active listening have been explained in Chapter 8, which included natural conversation.

Another powerful way is to ask customers various open questions, such as "What …?", "Why …?", "Who …?", "When …?", and similar ones. These questions prompt customers to share more insightful information about themselves. When interacting with customers, companies should avoid asking them closed questions, which generally have short answers, for instance "yes" or "no." This type of question does not provide as much relevant information about customers' preferences.

12.3.10 Specific Approach

Many companies say that they want to serve customers in the best way. Nonetheless, it is important to highlight that the word "customers" is just a general and abstract concept which never defines clearly the specific, particular, and concrete human beings who look for products and services according to their distinct preferences. Not all customers are alike, even when they share some characteristics with others.

When the company focuses excessively on the concept "customers," it runs the risk of missing the unique human aspects of the individuals to be served. According to De Mello (1990), the concept of "customers" is not fixed and unchanged; instead, each customer is a living being and therefore dynamic. He added "words are pointers, they're not descriptions." Oftentimes, words hinder the real connection with reality. In relation to this, Watts (1955) observed that "in practice we are all bewitched by words," and "we confuse them with the real world, as if it were a world of words …," and "we are dismayed and dumbfounded when they do not fit."

Companies must realise that each customer has unique tastes and preferences. Consequently, companies should discover and acknowledge these distinct customers' needs in order to offer them products and services that are actually suitable for them. A company which adopts a loving attitude toward its customers tends to do its best to meet their distinct expectations.

Some questions a company's employees should ask themselves are: "What are the specific needs and motivations of this customer?" or "What unmet needs do I perceive in this customer?" These questions create more awareness and understanding of what specific customers are looking for, which in turn helps a company serve them in a more loving manner.

According to Wellemin (1998), customers have needs related to the tangible aspects of the products or services (such as quality, design, reliability, etc.) and other needs which are more related to intangible aspects of the purchasing process. This second group of needs (intangible) are as important as the first group (tangible). Some examples of needs of customers related to intangible aspects of the purchasing process are:

■ To be acknowledged regarding their unique needs and preferences
■ To be treated with care and respect all through the purchasing process and also after it
■ To be actively listened to regarding comments and objections about products and services
■ To be provided with accurate information about the product or service in order to make their best decision
■ To feel comfortable (physically, emotionally, and mentally) during the buying process
■ To be offered a relevant set of alternatives in order to choose the most appropriate one
■ To receive continuous support from the company in case of clarifications or claims
■ To be delivered what was promised by the company

- To be offered the possibility of changing, replacing, or returning products or services
- To have the terms and conditions of the purchase respected by the company

It is important to understand that customers do not only buy specific products and services from a company. At the same time, customers are "buying" how the company behaves with them and how they treat them over time, and this counts as much as the products and services themselves.

12.3.11 Segmentation and Uniqueness

In marketing, there is a well-known concept called "segmentation" which means dividing the market (total group of customers) into segments (parts of market). Each segment is composed of customers with the same characteristics (for example, age, occupation, gender, lifestyle, etc.). Even though customers are commonly gathered in homogeneous subgroups (called segments), each single customer must also be considered as a distinctive individual.

Above all, each buyer is a unique human being, who cannot be replicated. Consequently, each time a company interacts with a customer, the organisation should focus on discovering that customer's distinctive needs in a thorough manner.

Many companies tend to treat customers in a quantitative manner, which means that each customer is a number to the company. This approach toward customers is unloving because it aims to depersonalise them. Instead, when a company adopts a loving attitude toward customers, they feel they are not a figure or a component of an impersonal group to that organisation; each customer is considered as a valuable and distinct individual.

A loving company also prompts customers to express and articulate their own needs in a clear and overt manner. When interacting with customers, this type of organisation makes customers feel a deep sense of conviction that they are making the right choice regarding the products and services offered by this company. This organisation adopts a humanised approach toward customers, which contributes to the development of stronger relationships with them.

A loving organisation shows continuous genuine curiosity regarding customer preferences. This type of company adopts a learning attitude; it honestly wants to know more about customers in order to serve them better. In other words, when a company is fully aware of each customer's unique needs, the organisation is more capable of offering products and services which resonate with them. When a company is fully aware of the singular needs of each customer and understands them in a thorough fashion, customers are more inclined to feel connected to this organisation.

It is important to remember that all customers want to be cared for by a company. Consequently, whenever customers complain against a company, this organisation should always take their objections as signals of customers' unsatisfied needs. This company should exhaustively analyse this valuable feedback to adopt a more loving attitude toward these customers and address these objections in a more effective manner. Moreover, negative feedback received from customers often helps to develop better products and services in order to satisfy customers' needs more effectively.

12.3.12 Emotional Enhancement

The main purpose of the marketing discipline is to satisfy customers' needs. The concept of satisfaction implies that customers experience pleasant emotional states in relation to the products and services they buy. These positive emotional states could be of a different kind, for example, peacefulness, happiness, excitement, etc. In all these cases, products and services are connected to specific emotional experiences triggered by them.

From the psychological perspective, all human actions, including buying behaviours, are motivated by two main drivers: experiencing pleasure or avoiding pain. For example, a person goes to the cinema because he wants to have fun (pleasurable experience). A person, for example, who contracts insurance policy does so because he wants to be covered in case of an accident (avoidance of pain). In these cases, customers want to experience positive emotions or, at least, shun negative ones.

Nonetheless, if we look more closely into these examples, it is possible to say that customers always want to experience positive emotional states. When the person buys the insurance, for example, this individual does not only want to avoid the pain of not having insurance coverage (avoidance of pain), but he also wants to be at peace (pleasure-seeking).

The main responsibility of companies is to enable customers to have a positive emotional experience. Oftentimes, this experience can be composed of an array of various encounters or episodes, which should make a positive impression on customers. For example, customers can have a good emotional experience when consuming the products and services bought, but also during the buying process itself. Consequently, if a company adopts a loving attitude toward its customers, every time it interacts with them, they are more likely to experience positive feelings. When a customer is prompted to experience positive emotional states, this individual becomes more co-operative with the company and open to receiving support from it.

Many companies only focus on offering the best products and services and managing specific aspects of the sales process. However, these companies forget to enhance the customers' overall experience. A company should always do its best to make customers feel positive emotions each time they interact with the organisation. These interactions do not include only the buying process, but are also related to activities after sales, such as delivery of products, returns, and repair or replacement of products, among others.

The company should purposely enhance different points of contact with customers to prompt them to experience positive emotional states. For example, the company should have an attractive and interesting website, develop enticing packaging for its products and have visually appealing layout for its stores, etc.

Sometimes, customers feel restless or uncomfortable during the buying process because of different reasons (e.g., confusing information, limitation of time, etc.). In most cases, the company can do something to make customers feel more at ease, so that they can experience positive emotional states during the buying process. For example, if customers experience negative emotions because they are confused about the information regarding a product, the company should provide comprehensive clarification so that they can experience a more positive emotional state.

It is important to pinpoint that when buying products or services, customers commonly face different types of risks, which vary depending on the type of product or service. Solomon et al. (2006) observed that customers face:

■ Monetary risk (customers want to spend money wisely and not waste it on products or services which do not satisfy their needs)
■ Functional risk (customers want the product and service to be effective, which means that it provides the benefits promised)
■ Physical risk (customers want the product or service to be safe, secure, or healthy, without affecting their health or physical integrity)
■ Social risk (customers want the product or service to be accepted by their close circle, for instance, relatives and friends)
■ Psychological risk (customers want the product or service to contribute positively to their self-esteem and status)

In relation to this, a loving seller when interacting with customers can make them feel more at ease and confident regarding these risks. In other words, when purchasing a product or a service, customers should feel the aforementioned risks are eliminated. For example, in relation to monetary risk, the seller can explain why a product or service is good value for money; in relation to the functional risk, the sales individual can explain to the customers how a product or service satisfies their needs. In relation to the physical risks the seller can explain, for example, how to use the product in a safe way.

In some cases, a customer can experience negative emotions after buying the product or service (for instance, regret, guilt, etc.). From the marketing perspective, this is called cognitive dissonance, which is the result of incongruence between a customer's beliefs and behaviours. Customers tend to experience negative emotional states because they believe the product or service they purchased was not the right choice. When buyers experience this dissonance, they feel the product or service purchased really does not satisfy their needs, or might not be fully convinced about it.

In this case, the company can interact with customers to clarify doubts they could have about the products bought. The company can also provide buyers with reassuring comments that they made the right buying choice. However, in the case that the customer really believes the product does not meet their needs, the company should be willing to provide customers with a refund. All these actions generally make customers feel better; these actions can transmute customers' post-purchase regrets into positive emotional states.

When customers regularly experience positive emotions in relation to a company and its products, they are more likely to be loyal to this organisation and develop a long-term relationship with it. In those cases, customers are also more prone to recommend the company's products or services to relatives, friends, and acquaintances.

As previously explained, this positive customer experience does not have to be limited to the sales process. The relationship between the company and its customers can be reinforced over time. A company can strengthen its relationships with its customers in different ways; for example, by sending customers emails with the latest news about product launches or valuable articles, or sending customers free gifts or coupons. Companies can also use this nurturing approach even with customers that got in contact with the company but did not buy any products from them.

From a wider perspective, all departments which make up an organisation (manufacturing, administrative, financing, etc.) should be customer-oriented. All these departments should contribute, directly or indirectly, to a more positive customer experience. For example, the manufacturing department should aim to produce goods which cater to the customer's needs, not the company's needs. Likewise, the administrative department should send documents (for instance, invoices, receipts, etc.) in a way that makes the customer's purchasing process easier.

All the company's employees should be reminded and even trained so that they adopt a customer focus on a regular basis. These employees should be devoted to the satisfaction of customer needs, which means making these customers feel positive emotions. All the company's departments (manufacturing, administrative, etc.) should work in a co-operative and integrative way in order to serve customers in the best fashion.

12.3.13 Warm Appreciation

Your customers don't just want the product or service. They want what your heart has to give them.

Mark Silver

Appreciation has several meanings; one of them is being thankful. A company can develop a strong link with its customers when it is grateful to them. For example, some companies show their appreciation to customers by sending them letters or emails and thanking them for their custom. When a customer buys a product from a company, this organisation should express its gratitude in a personalised manner whenever possible. For example, the message of thankfulness sent to the customer should include a personal touch, including specific aspects of this particular custom. This personalised approach makes the expression of gratitude look warmer.

In other words, companies should avoid using the same standardised templates to express their gratitude to all customers when possible. An example will clarify the aforementioned point. If a letter is sent to customers, their names and specific characteristics of the products bought should be included. Some other particular aspects of that purchase should be highlighted, for example, why the customer made a good choice buying the products.

That gratitude note can also include the honest desire that the customer fully enjoys the products purchased. This letter can also comment on the continuing willingness of the company to provide this customer with additional information of value, whenever needed. Lastly, the desire to strengthen the relationship with this customer beyond this purchase can also be expressed in that letter.

There is another relevant point to highlight. From the psychological perspective, when an employee is grateful with customers, they are more prone to have positive thoughts, which create and reinforce their neural networks, which in turn contributes to these customers having a more positive attitude toward this organisation.

As recently explained, customers must always be thanked for their custom. Besides, customers must also be genuinely appreciated when they do not make any purchase from the organisation. In those cases, the company can be grateful to customers for having spent their time looking at its products, or for having shown an interest in them.

Lastly, there is another meaning of appreciation, which is to realise the intrinsic value of something or someone. There is a saying which goes: "what you appreciate increases in value." From this perspective, a company which appreciates customers values them greatly and is truly interested in thoroughly knowing their preferences in order to meet their expectations more effectively.

12.3.14 Welcoming Feedback

Many companies really hate when customers complain about their products and services. However, when a company adopts a loving attitude toward its customers, their complaints and objections are instead kindly welcomed and thanked. This type of company also informs customers that their feedback is valuable and therefore it will be thoroughly analysed.

When customers complain, the company should always be inquisitive and sympathetic to them. To that effect, customers should be asked about the specific motivations of their complaints in order to deal with them effectively. In other words, companies should always be open to amicably discuss with customers their complaints, in order to address them accordingly.

When customers have complaints about a specific product or service, a company's employees should always act as supportive advisors. Customers' comments must be acknowledged with no delay. In those cases, the company should show a spirit of service and willingness to introduce necessary changes to satisfy customers' needs in a proper manner. Sometimes the company cannot offer a quick solution to customers' complaints. In those cases, the company should promise customers they will analyse their issues more thoroughly and offer them specific answers as soon as possible.

Oftentimes, customers' complaints or objections are not clear enough. As a consequence, the company should ask for clarification, for example, by paraphrasing or recapping customers' critiques. Sometimes a company can also use a pre-emptive approach in relation to customers' complaints. For example, after having shown a product, a company can ask its customers a question like "Are there any points regarding this product which you are not sure about?" In all the aforementioned cases, any feedback given by customers is worthy information which should be thoroughly analysed to offer a better service to customers.

12.3.15 *Story-Telling*

Some customers love to be engaged in simple stories about the company and its products and services, as well as its experiences and viewpoints. When a company uses the story-telling technique, the stories must be presented in an engaging, simple, and amenable way so that customers can identify and connect to these tales. A good story can create a state of intimate connection between the company and the customer.

When story-telling is used, the stories must be delivered in a natural, articulate, and spontaneous manner. In other words, customers must never perceive the stories as canned or scripted. Besides, the stories used must always be relevant to the situation at hand; for instance, the demonstration of a product. If possible, the story should also include real people who customers can identify with. For example, if a seller is explaining the potential benefits of a specific product to a customer, some examples of other customers who have benefitted from this product in the past are significant. The story can include different elements, such as:

■ Reasons which make the story relevant and suitable for the situation at hand
■ Descriptive analysis of situations of the story context (where and when this story unfolds)
■ Relevant facts or highlights regarding the story
■ Thoughts and emotions experienced by the participants of the story
■ Sensory comments (related to the five senses, sight, hearing, touch, taste, and smell)
■ Specific evidence underpinning different aspects of the story (for instance, objective facts)
■ Metaphors, examples, comparisons, rhetorical questions, and analogies
■ Situations of conflict or predicaments faced by participants, and how these challenges were overcome over time
■ Brief recap or summary of the story and recommendations stemming from the tale

The story-telling should implicitly include clues about values, principles, and the purpose of the organisation the salesperson (story-teller) is working for. As mentioned previously, when a company uses story-telling with customers, it should link facts to identifiable real people. For example, if a seller comments about the company's recent outstanding selling performance, the data of sales can be related to specific salespeople working for this organisation, including their real names when possible. When story-telling is used in a genuine manner, tales told to customers can easily touch their hearts and prompt them to take action.

Cohen and Prusak (2001) stated that stories which start like "This happened to me ..." or "I witnessed ..." are more engaging and authentic than second-hand tales. Guber (2011) observed that people are prewired to engage with good stories that are attention-grabbing, which means providing listeners with an emotional experience in order to spur them into action.

A company can also use stories to make its customers imagine the experience of enjoying a certain product or service if they bought it. In those cases, story-telling techniques prompt customers to have an approximate vision of their future experience with the product or service offered by the company. To that effect, Yeung (2011) suggests that companies use sentences such as "Imagine that you …" as part of their story-telling process. The use of story-telling becomes more relevant in the case of services offered by a company (training, transport, etc.) which are intangible by nature.

Questions for Self-Reflection

- How can I make customers feel more comfortable?
- How can I create more trust in relation to customers?
- How can I adopt a more obliging attitude toward customers?
- How can I use story-telling when I interact with customers?

Chapter 13

Adopting a Loving Attitude toward Other Stakeholders

13.1 Suppliers and Intermediaries

Most companies are fully reliant on suppliers of products and services for their business activities. Sometimes a company does not sell its products and services directly to customers, but through intermediaries such as wholesalers, retailers, and agents. Both suppliers and intermediaries add significant value to the products and services offered by the company in a direct or indirect manner.

Some of the principles regarding other stakeholders (employees and customers) previously explained in this book can also be applied to suppliers and intermediaries, taking into consideration the specific characteristics of these stakeholders. A company should adopt a continuous loving attitude toward its suppliers and intermediaries, by taking specific actions, for instance:

13.1.1 Continuous Communication

Companies should always be open to interacting with their intermediaries and suppliers on a continuous basis. When a company has frequent communication with these organisations, the amount of misunderstandings and conflicts are significantly reduced. Sometimes a company can contact its suppliers and intermediaries for no specific business reason. In those cases, the company approaches these organisations just to have some small-talk with them to nurture the relationships with them. A company can also organise non-business activities to improve its relational aspects regarding these stakeholders. Some examples of these activities are:

- Informal lunches or dinners with suppliers and intermediaries
- Casual visits to their venues
- Sending them presents or letters on special occasions
- Phoning them to talk about trivial topics (politics, sports, etc.)

Besides, a company can congratulate its suppliers and intermediaries on their recent achievements (for example, opening up a new branch, or obtaining a quality certification, etc.), or greet them on their anniversary. All these activities create an atmosphere of comfort and trust between the organisation and these stakeholders. Throughout these activities, the company can develop more humanised contact with its stakeholders.

However, some companies act the opposite way; their interactions with stakeholders only have specific business objectives (for example, placing orders, renegotiating terms and conditions of agreements, etc.). Other companies contact suppliers and intermediaries in such an infrequent manner that their relationships with them are never strengthened significantly.

In some cases, the lack of communication with these companies is related to an attitude of impoliteness; for example, when a company receives a phone call or email from one of its suppliers and it does not to return this call or answer that email promptly. This careless behaviour affects the relationships between the company and these external stakeholders negatively.

Some companies argue that they are "overly" busy (e.g., multiple business projects, several tight deadlines, etc.) to cultivate their relationships with external stakeholders, such as suppliers and intermediaries. However, the core factor of any successful business activities is based on strong relationships with stakeholders. For instance, any relevant business aspects (e.g. launching new products, generating more revenue, increasing the market share, increasing profits, etc.) are built on healthy relationships with a company's stakeholders.

As mentioned previously in this book, a very effective way for a company to strengthen its relationships with suppliers and intermediaries is to be authentic and trustworthy. In other words, a company should always provide reliable and accurate information to these stakeholders. Truthfulness always generates trust between the company and its suppliers and intermediaries. A company which acts in a dependable manner prompts its stakeholders (e.g., suppliers and intermediaries) to act in the same manner. When a company provides credible and complete information to other organisations, its relationships with them are strengthened in a significant manner.

Sometimes, when a company and its intermediaries and suppliers trust one another very well, there may be no need to develop a formal contract; the word given suffices. In those cases, not only do companies save the cost of drafting, enforcing, and monitoring a contract, but their commitment also grows much stronger over time. However, not using contracts will not be a suitable way of working for many companies.

A company should always be confidential with stakeholders. Confidentiality means keeping critical or strategic information about them in a safe manner. A confidential company shows a caring attitude by continually protecting this information and avoiding any data leakage. When a company adopts this attitude toward its stakeholders, they are more prone to disclose sensitive information. The principle of confidentiality applies not only to suppliers and intermediaries, but also to other stakeholders (for instance, employees, customers, etc.).

Besides, when a company is trustworthy with its suppliers and intermediaries, it is willing to admit its own mistakes as quickly as possible. This honest attitude commonly generates even more trust between the company and its stakeholders. However, many companies are reluctant to admit their mistakes, which makes them less credible before other organisations.

13.1.2 Unselfishness

Every time a company negotiates agreements with its suppliers or intermediaries, it should avoid adopting a bargaining attitude toward them. A bargaining company tends to ask itself "What can I get from this organisation?" This unloving attitude is only centred on the company's needs and dismisses completely the needs of the other party. When a company adopts this selfish approach on a continuous basis, its relationships with its stakeholders are prone to become weaker over time.

Instead, when a company adopts a loving attitude, it is more prone to negotiate with stakeholders in a friendly way and ask itself the following questions:

- How can we be more considerate with this organisation's specific needs?
- What can we give to this organisation to satisfy their needs properly?
- How can we strengthen the valuable relationship with this organisation?
- What agreement can be proposed that fairly satisfies the needs of both parties?

A company should always aim to develop tailor-made agreements with its suppliers and intermediaries and avoid the use of standardised contracts. The company should use customised contracts which should fairly take the specific needs of both parties into account. Besides, a company should only look for business agreements with stakeholders which are mutually beneficial, which means that the unique needs of each party are properly met.

These win–win agreements endure the passage of time, as compared with lopsided agreements which tend to be short-lived. This type of agreement is possible when the organisation thoroughly knows the distinctive needs of the other party. When a company does not thoroughly know the main needs of the other organisation, it should ask it about its main interests.

Some useful questions a company can ask its stakeholders for this purpose can be: "What are the main aspects you are looking for in a potential agreement between us?" and "Why do you want …?" A company can also ask itself the following question: "How can we satisfy their needs in a more effective manner?"

Whenever a company does business with its suppliers and intermediaries, all contractual terms and conditions between them should be the result of a fair exchange of proposals from both sides. In other words, both companies should participate in the construction of agreements, which means that none of them should impose terms on the other. Agreements with stakeholders should always be based on consensus and aim to have a long-term perspective, when possible.

In mutually beneficial agreements, the interests of each party are cared for; no participant obtains unfair benefits at the expense of the other. These business contracts always bring about the highest good for all parties involved. In other words, this type of agreement is always transparent, fair, and amicable.

During the process of arriving at these agreements, the parties should avoid performing manipulative actions, such as exaggerated requests, offering false alternatives, bluffing, ultimatums, and unnecessary delays, among others. Some companies tend to use this type of detrimental behaviour in order to obtain more benefits from the agreement than the other party. From the perspective of this book, the relationship of a company with these organisations should always be consensual; no parties must be forced to be with one another.

13.1.3 Respecting Commitments

> The truth of the good old maxim, that 'Honesty is the best policy,' is upheld by the daily experience of life; uprightness and integrity being found as successful in business as in everything else.
>
> **Samuel Smiles**

An organisation that trusts another expects that the latter will abide by contractual obligations agreed by both parties. A trustworthy organisation is expected to act in a benevolent manner with others; this type of company tends not to perform any opportunistic or deceptive action to take advantage of others. It is interesting to highlight that when a company expects another organisation to behave honestly, this often becomes a self-fulfilling prophesy. Oftentimes, companies tend to act in congruence with others' expectations of them.

When a company and its external stakeholders (for instance, suppliers and intermediaries) trust each other, they know that they will naturally keep their commitment to one another over time. However, some companies promise things to their suppliers and intermediaries in the heat of the moment, which later cannot be delivered. These organisations do not keep their word with these stakeholders. A company which fails to respect its commitments with other organisations is prone to be distrusted in future transactions.

Consequently, a company should only assume commitments with these organisations if it can fulfil them in a proper manner. This type of organisation acts with integrity. According to Hendricks and Ludeman (1996), integrity is the foundation of any business relationship; the lack of integrity creates "entanglement" between companies, not real relationships. These authors observed that integrity is about being honest with oneself and others.

Before assuming any commitment, a company should always ask itself "Will we be really capable of delivering what we are about to promise?" and "Will this agreement positively contribute to the business purpose of both companies?" A company which answers these questions honestly is more likely to act with integrity with other organisations.

Lastly, a company which could not deliver its promises should sincerely apologise to the organisation affected. A company in fault should always take full ownership of this situation, making no excuses or untruthful comments. Besides, this company should clearly and swiftly explain the reasons for not keeping its word and offer compensation, when possible, for the inconveniences created. When a company adopts this attitude, its relationships with its external stakeholders are strengthened.

13.1.4 Soft Conflict-Solving

A company should always treat its suppliers and intermediaries in a warm and kind manner, even during arguments or disagreements with them. If external stakeholders behave rudely with the company, this organisation should remain calm and loving all the same. A company should never reciprocate when it is treated disparagingly, condescendingly, or abrasively by others; if it does, the conflictive situation tends to escalate and becomes personal. Companies should also use calming and constructive statements which help each other release any state of tension and overwhelm, and be at ease. Consequently, a company which adopts a loving attitude to its suppliers and intermediaries is more inclined to solve problems with them in an amicable manner.

Nonetheless, many companies use antagonistic methods, such as lawsuits, to resolve controversies with their stakeholders. These "hard" methods should never be a priority for a company; they should be left as the last resource to be used. Oftentimes, not only do these hard methods not mitigate the conflicts, but they exacerbate them.

A company which has conflicts with its stakeholders should be flexible and open to exploring different alternatives with these organisations in a creative manner. Conflictive situations must be resolved in a way that brings about the best outcomes for all parties involved. These agreements should be based on valuable principles, like fairness, mutual care, respect, and co-operation, among others.

The potential solutions to a conflictive situation between two organisations should be the result of the active participation of all parties involved. Therefore, companies should avoid taking unilateral actions (for example, a lawsuit) to solve problems with their external stakeholders, because this is detrimental to their relationship. Butler and Hope (2008) observed that a relationship is like a system, where each party is a component of the system; therefore, when one party tries to introduce changes that could negatively affect the other, these changes tend to be resisted and this affects the whole relationship.

In order to solve an issue sensibly, companies should adopt a co-operative attitude with one another. This attitude implies the use of empowering sentences like "I propose that we work on this together …", and similar ones. A company which faces conflicts with its suppliers and intermediaries can also create more affinity with them by regularly using inclusive vocabulary. A company can use inclusive terms like "we," "our," and "ours" when it interacts with stakeholders. For example, a company can use sentences such as "We can develop a mutually beneficial relationship over time."

A company should always approach any conflictive situation with its suppliers and intermediaries in a upfront, but kind manner. Therefore, companies should avoid unproductive behaviour, like threats, accusations, blaming, offending, and similar ones. In relation to this, Dooley (2010) recommends to "fight fire with kindness." In other words, a conflict between companies can never escalate if these organisations avoid personalising this issue. The main objectives regarding a conflictive issue is not only to try to solve it in the best way possible, but also to preserve the relationship between the organisations involved.

An effective way to handle conflicts with stakeholders is using kind and assertive communication. Davis et al. (2008) observed that being assertive implies recognising any differences of perspective regarding others, but also being willing to express these differences in a calm, clear, and firm manner. Assertive people are not aggressive with others; these people do not feel uncomfortable expressing their distinct views on an issue in a kind manner. Moreover, assertive people are empathetic because they are always open to considering the perspectives of others.

All business transactions include commercial aspects (such as price, volume, quality, etc.) but also relational aspects (such as trust, confidence, comfort, respect, etc.). These two aspects, commercial and relational ones, are inextricably interrelated. As a consequence, a company should never focus exclusively on the commercial aspects of an agreement and dismiss the relational ones. Both aspects are equally important for the development of a long-term relationship with suppliers and intermediaries.

13.1.5 Co-Operative Attitude

A company with a collaborative attitude toward its suppliers and intermediaries tries to support them in the best way possible. This type of company continually collaborates with its stakeholders, especially in circumstances beyond what was contractually agreed with them. This collaborative company usually asks: "How can we be more helpful to these stakeholders?"

For instance, a company signs a contract with a retailer to sell their products. In this contract, there is no condition which obligates the company to provide free samples to this retailer. Nonetheless, a company which adopts a co-operative attitude toward this retailer will tend to provide this intermediary with free samples, even if this has not been stipulated in the contract. In this case, the company gives the retailer the samples because the company knows they are of value to this intermediary. When a company adopts a co-operative attitude toward its external stakeholders, its relationships with them become stronger and more stable over time.

Besides, a company should express its gratitude to its suppliers and intermediaries for adding value to the products bought by customers. For example, a company buys high-quality raw materials from its suppliers; these materials add value to the product manufactured by this organisation. Customers are also prone to appreciate the quality of the materials used in the product they buy from that company. In this case, suppliers indirectly add value to the final customers.

Another example will also clarify this point. For instance, a company sells its products to retailers and these intermediaries show these products in a very well-located and finely decorated place, which grabs customers' attention. In this case, the retailer also adds value to the product to be purchased by final customers. Consequently, a company should frequently express its gratitude to its suppliers and intermediaries for the value they add to final products to be bought by customers.

Lastly, a company which co-operates with its suppliers and intermediaries provides them with valuable information (for example, customers' feedback, latest market trends, etc.) on a regular basis. This valuable information can help these stakeholders enhance their performance and add higher value to their products and services.

13.2 Competitors

13.2.1 Love and Competitors

Companies invest millions to find out inside knowledge about their competition, their products and customers, and even their plans. Most business books include numerous strategic approaches to outpace competitors. Moreover, the concept of "competitors" not only is well-used in the business environment, but also in other areas, like sports.

Competition implies that there is a "race" that companies have to "run," in which there can only be one "winner" and many "losers." As seen previously in this book, the whole concept of "competition" is based on fear. The concept of "competitors" is related to a scarcity mindset, previously seen in Chapters 3 and 4. Some misleading but common assumptions stemming from this concept are:

- There is not enough space for all companies in the market.
- Customers are scarce, so each company has to fight with the competition to win them.
- Competitors are always considered as impending external threats to a company.
- The marketplace is a battlefield where companies only thrive by outpacing one another.
- An important part of a company's resources needs to be allocated to outsmarting competitors.
- Competitors' activities must be monitored on a continuous basis.
- If a company does not beat its competitors, it will be beaten by them.
- All companies must continually offer better products to not be defeated by competitors.
- Almost all types of strategies are justified to outpace competitors.

From this book's perspective, companies should stop using the words "competition" and "competitors." The use of these concepts implies that other organisations are perceived as threats a company should fear, or forces that it should defend itself from. Moreover, a company which uses terms like "competitors" or "rivals" to identify other organisations in the business environment tends to respond to them reactively.

From the psychological perspective, this defensive response is related to fight-freeze-flight mode. As previously explained, in this survival mode, people's analytical and creative capabilities are temporarily impaired. Besides, a company which considers other organisations as "competitors" is prone to be excessively aware of their activities, which prevents this company from adopting a proactive attitude. Sometimes, this type of company can be tempted to outpace its competitors by all means, even immoral or illegal ones, for example:

- Stealing or copying intellectual property owned by other companies
- Slandering other organisations
- Hacking into other organisations' websites
- Entering into price wars with other companies
- Performing activities related to industrial espionage
- Using comparative advertising to debase other companies
- Limiting the access of competitors to markets
- Poaching talent from other companies
- Use of predatory prices to push other companies out of the market

Some countries penalise some of these activities with stringent legislation. In other cases, some of these activities are not regulated legally, but nonetheless, they are considered immoral. A company which performs any of these activities does not act with integrity regarding other organisations in the marketplace.

13.2.2 A More Positive Approach Regarding Other Companies

This book offers an alternative view on organisations traditionally considered as "competitors." These businesses can be perceived as positive forces, instead of threatening factors. To that effect, "competitors" can be a valuable source of feedback for an organisation. From this perspective, a company should avoid adopting an aggressive or defensive attitude toward these so-called "competitors," but instead have an open and curious perspective regarding them.

Oftentimes, a company can be inspired by "rival" organisations in valuable ways that help it improve its business activities. A company can also take these "competing" organisations as powerful motivators, preventing it from dwelling in stagnation and complacency. Besides, a company can consider organisations selling similar products and services as teachers to learn from. Moreover, a company can obtain relevant information about successful approaches used by other organisations regarding:

- Their distinct approaches on customer service
- Their quality standards
- The unique value delivered to customers
- Their relationships with stakeholders
- Their innovative products and services
- Their non-traditional recruitment processes
- Their creative business models
- Their ingenious ways to price products
- Their partnerships with other companies
- Their environmental consciousness
- Their alternative distribution
- The sophistication of their product design
- Their non-traditional use of technology
- Their unique promotional strategies

In other words, these companies can be considered as models to emulate. A business can consider these companies as worthwhile references to orientate its own activities. In the business literature, when a company "borrows" some excellent aspects or processes from other companies, it is called external benchmarking. When a company benchmarks, it adopts certain aspects of excellence used by other organisations, but generally adapts them to its specific and unique needs.

Sometimes other companies represent the living evidence of wrong business behaviour. This is the other side of the topic discussed recently. When other organisations act in unethical and unloving ways, a company can use them as reminders of the business practices *not* to be adopted. Some examples of negative practices are companies which mislead buyers to obtain their business, organisations which are reluctant to take customers' complaints seriously, etc. A company can take these negative models in order to act in the opposite manner, for instance, by treating customers with honesty and integrity.

Competitors can also be considered as potential business partners. In other words, companies who offer products or services of a similar type or category can develop strategic alliances, in which all participants benefit. These alliances represent synergetic platforms where business partners are more prone to share various resources (e.g., technology, information, sources of supply, contacts, distribution channels, customers, funds, etc.) with one another. Oftentimes, these partnerships help members share business risks and reduce costs.

These partnerships imply a certain degree of affinity between the participants, and a sense of camaraderie and companionship with them. However, a company which only perceives other organisations as competitors to be beaten will not be able see them as potential partners for business activities.

Some business coaches observe that a company should never compete with other companies, but with itself. From this perspective, a company should take itself as the main reference to outpace. Over time a company should gradually raise its bar, and commit to improve their products, services, processes, and systems in a proactive and sustained manner. A company should continually better itself, not for the fear of "competitors," but because it wants to serve customers in a superior way.

13.3 Communities

> I am I plus my surroundings and if I do not preserve the latter, I do not preserve myself.
>
> **José Ortega y Gasset**

13.3.1 Relevance of Communities

McIntosh et al. (1998) observed that companies have different types of responsibilities: economic (related to economic viability of the organisation in the marketplace), legal (related to the company's strict abidance with legislation), and social and environmental (considering a society and the environment as relevant factors when performing business activities). Some businesses only aim to respond to economic and legal aspects, dismissing the environmental and social ones. In any case, all business activities have an impact on each of the aforementioned aspects, which companies should be fully aware of.

Businesses are social organisations. Consequently, a community is always a relevant factor for any company's business activities, because without a community, there is no business. In other words, companies are never run in a vacuum; there cannot be companies offering their products and services without people buying them. Without a community, there cannot be people who work for companies either. Besides, without a community, there cannot be intermediaries and suppliers. Companies also benefit from other resources from a community, such as infrastructure (roads, bridges, etc.).

Therefore, all companies should be supportive and committed to their communities. To put it more simply, organisations must always be caring and generous with their communities. Moreover, businesses must act as catalysts for positive social change and add significant value to their communities by improving the lives of their members.

A company which has a loving attitude toward its community abides by some relevant principles such as responsibility, solidarity, benevolence, respectfulness, honesty, and fairness, among others. This type of company will support its community without compromising any of these values, even if doing so could achieve economic benefits for the organisation. Community-oriented organisations have a higher level of awareness than other companies.

A company which adopts a loving attitude toward its community goes beyond the well-known perspective of corporate social responsibility (CSR). In the case of CSR, the company supports certain causes (e.g., donations, social events, foundations, etc.) which can contribute to the community in a positive and specific manner. From the CSR perspective, a company aims to solve some significant problems affecting communities and positively contribute to their development.

Instead, when a company has a loving attitude toward its community, this represents the general perspective the company uses to perform *all* its business activities, not specific ones. In other words, this is an ongoing perspective, which is not limited to specific activities or projects. A company which adopts a loving attitude toward its community aims to support it in a proactive manner. This community-oriented perspective is imbued in everything that the company does. From this standpoint, all business decisions (strategic, tactical, and operational ones) are analysed and implemented considering their social impact on the community.

In economics, the impacts of a company's production of goods and services on the social environment are called "externalities." These externalities can be positive (for example, the use of renewable energy) or negative (for instance, throwing industrial waste in a river). From this perspective, a company with a loving attitude toward its community consistently avoids any business actions which might cause harm to the community; in other words, this organisation will aim to eliminate any negative externalities.

At the same time, this type of company is also committed to continually increasing the amount of activities which have tangible positive effects on the social environment, benefitting it directly or indirectly. In other words, this organisation wants to purposefully bring about positive externalities.

Many companies perform activities related to CSR because they want to improve its image and reputation. In this case, the support to the community is a mere exchange; the organisation offers more assistance to the community in exchange for a better image. Instead, a company with a loving attitude toward its community does not look for anything in return for their good actions. A company who truly cares for its community spontaneously connects with and impacts on it in a meaningful manner. As seen previously, all of the company's activities and practices are driven by their direct or indirect contribution to the community.

13.3.2 Community-Oriented Activities

A company with a loving attitude understands that the community is one of the most important resources to count on. This company understands that it is closely and continually linked to its community; all the benefits the company obtains from its business activities (e.g., revenues, profits, company image, reputation, etc.) come directly or indirectly from its community. Therefore, these companies understand these communities should be continually assisted and cared for.

A company cannot fully thrive if its community does not meet its basic needs. Therefore, a company and its community are inextricably bound; they have a shared destiny. They are interdependent because they need each other to prosper. Companies with a loving attitude to communities can positively contribute to them in different ways, such as:

- Not polluting the environment and having green policies (e.g., use of renewable sources of energy, recycling, use of ecological manufacturing technology and processes, efficient management of waste material, green quality certifications, etc.)
- Treating employees with respect and dignity, paying them fair salaries, and allowing them to enhance their natural skills and develop new ones; not violating employees' rights in the workplace
- Performing business activities in a warm and friendly manner, respecting the cultural traditions, values, and customs of its community
- Leading social projects, such as charities, donations, organisation of community events, free training, internships, sponsoring events, among others
- Treating other companies fairly, considering the possibility of them becoming business partners
- Developing joint projects with non-governmental organisations, governments, and local communities
- Developing fair deals with all company intermediaries (suppliers, intermediaries, etc.) continually supporting them, especially during difficult times
- Hiring people with low resources from the local community
- Abiding by relevant legislation (e.g,. work regulation, quality norms, etc.) regarding business activities
- Avoiding any illegal activities such as smuggling, bribing, forfeiting, hacking, tax evasion, etc.
- Development of partnerships with different representatives of communities such as councils, associations, chambers of commerce, etc.

Among the activities that can also be included is the investment in companies which have a positive impact on the community. For example, a conscious company, when investing, prefers to buy shares in organisations that have a positive social impact. Some examples of this type of company are educational institutions, recycling companies, communication companies, health organisations, etc.

On the contrary, companies that have a negative social and environmental impact are, for instance mining corporations, gambling organisations, weaponry manufacturers, tobacco manufacturers, etc. A conscious company tends to avoid investing in this second type of companies, which means, for example, not buying shares of this company.

Besides this, conscious companies also aim to provide products and services which contribute positively to the community. Oftentimes, when a company acts in a conscious manner, its activities are also related to the concept of sustainability. A sustainable approach implies that the company's activities have a positive impact not only on the social environment, but also on future generations. An example of this sustainable activity is the implementation of green policies, whose main purpose is to care for the environment, which impacts positively not only on current communities, but also future ones.

Mackey and Sisodia (2014) stated that a company should behave as a citizen of the community. Companies should always assist their community, especially when it faces relevant challenges. For instance, there are many examples of companies who helped communities who were affected by natural disasters, like floods, tornados, etc.

Some conscious organisations thoroughly analyse the main problems affecting their community and develop specific action plans to offer the community support regarding these issues. Moreover, some conscious companies monitor the impact of their community-oriented activities and summarise these positive impacts in a report; this report can be presented to the community and other relevant stakeholders.

Lastly, when a conscious company is about to implement a business project with potentially relevant impacts on a community, this organisation tends to consult some representatives of the community before taking any action regarding this project. The purpose of this consultation is to hear these representatives' views and consider their suggestions regarding the business project.

13.3.3 Other Aspects Related to Communities

When a company adopts a loving attitude toward its community, its activities are based on integrity. This type of company becomes a model to emulate for other organisations because of its positive impact on society. The products and services offered by a community-conscious company have a social plus, which makes them preferred by many customers over offerings from non-conscious organisations.

When a company develops strong relationships with its community, multiple benefits are brought about for both parties. The most obvious benefits are the tangible positive effects of the company's activities on its community. Besides this, the company also obtains relevant benefits, such as an improvement in its image and reputation, higher employee motivation and engagement, and wider company visibility, among others.

There is an increasing quantity of customers preferring companies which have a positive impact on communities. These socially conscious customers choose products and services sold by this type of company, because their purchases indirectly benefit the community. Community-oriented companies also act like a magnet for talented human resources; many highly skilful people are very keen to work for this type of organisation.

Therefore, it is important that organisations adopt a community-oriented attitude. In order to adopt a more loving attitude toward its community a company can ask itself these questions on a regular basis:

- Are our activities creating a positive impact on our community?
- What are the actual impacts of our activities on the community?
- How can lives of community members be enhanced by our activities?
- How can we make a more significant positive impact on our community?

Lastly, it is important to pinpoint that there are other stakeholders which will not be analysed in this book, such as financial organisations, government, business partners, potential and current investors, the media sector, unions, pressure groups, regulatory bodies, non-governmental organisations, academia, and trade associations, among others. Nonetheless, most principles explained in this text can be applied to these stakeholders.

Questions for Self-Reflection

- How can our relationships with suppliers and intermediaries be improved?
- How can we adopt a more constructive attitude toward competitors?
- How can our relationships with the community be improved?
- What activities can we perform that will have a positive impact on the community?

Chapter 14

Love and Creativity

14.1 Meaning of Creativity

> Life itself is a creation, a work in progress, unfolding and revealing itself even as it is being created.
>
> **Robert Fritz**

Every good product, service, or organisation started with an idea in the mind of someone. Consequently, creative skills are a meta-resource, which means a valuable resource that helps individuals and organisations generate other resources. People are masterful artisans of each thing they do in their life; each of their actions, thoughts, emotions, and words has the distinctive signature of their creative craftsmanship. When people create, a part of them is splintered into their creations. As seen previously, creativity is a very important human need, which is closely related to the need for self-expression. Even though it is not easy to define creativity some suggested meanings of this term are:

- Creativity is the development of new alternatives beyond traditional ones.
- Creativity is going beyond the status quo, the current state of things.
- Creativity is stretching one's mind toward uncharted territories.
- Creativity is being as endlessly inquisitive as a child.
- Creativity is bringing thoughts into being.
- Creativity is becoming aware of new aspects of reality.
- Creativity is going beyond ingrained assumptions.
- Creativity is a generous act which gives new ideas away.
- Creativity is unfolding one's mental landscape from the inside out.
- Creativity is imagining situations beyond current limitations.
- Creativity is playing with several hypotheses on a topic.
- Creativity is widening one's perception beyond the known.
- Creativity is using one's imaginative skills to produce something original.
- Creativity is dwelling on potential future scenarios.
- Creativity is welcoming fresh perspectives on long-standing issues.
- Creativity is the restructuring of current categories or developing others.

- Creativity is gracefully going beyond any resistance to change.
- Creativity is the eradication of self-censorship.
- Creativity is going beyond hackneyed ways of doing things.
- Creativity is multiplying potential perspectives on a topic.
- Creativity is devising innovative ways of perceiving reality.
- Creativity is being playful and freely engaged with ideas.
- Creativity is being curious and spontaneous, like an explorer.
- Creativity is mentally experimenting with the untested.
- Creativity is developing new ways to solve current problems.
- Creativity is giving birth to uncharted worlds.
- Creativity is adding incremental value to others.
- Creativity is a relevant asset in fast-changing scenarios.

McKenna (2012b) states that "creativity is a neurophysiological state ... where we have seemingly unlimited access to our greatest potential." All human beings are natural creators; they are continually developing new activities, thoughts, and perspectives – they cannot avoid it. People's creative potential is embedded in their DNA; creativity is an innate capability of all human beings. People are more creative and resourceful than they believe they actually are.

Fritz (1984) observed that creating is always an act of love. This author stated that "in the creative process, love is generative rather than simply responsive" (Fritz, 1991). This prestigious scholar concluded that people who create bring about something out of nothing and they love their creation to exist (Fritz, 1984, 1991). In other words, every creation has its creator's love embedded in it. In a similar vein, Montagu (1957) observed that "love enables the person to treat life as an art which the person as an artist is continually seeking to improve on in all its aspects."

14.2 How Creativity Works

To see things in the seed, that is genius.

Lao Tzu

The creative process works through different mental operations: for example, the innovative combination of existing elements of a topic, modification of its current elements, simplification or sophistication of them, and partition of a topic into different subcomponents. The human mind has the capacity to store information (e.g., facts, objects, people, circumstances, etc.) into limiting and rigid mental models (De Bono, 1970). However, the use of creative techniques helps restructure the information enclosed in these models in a different manner.

People who create are willing to explore uncharted territories. Consequently, these people avoid being traditional, or complacent, but instead are inquisitive and open to new perspectives. Klein (2003) observed that creative insights help people change the way they understand, perceive, feel, and desire.

Osborn (1948) observed that our mind is composed of two parts: a judicial part which assesses, analyses, and makes comparisons and choices, and a creative part, which develops ideas and visualises. These two parts are complementary; the creative mind can provide the judicial part with new insights, and the judicial mind can set some limits on the creative part.

From the psychological perspective, the mind can be divided into the conscious and subconscious mind. The conscious mind is related to one's waking state: reasoning, perception, and interpretation of the environment. This part of the mind is continually related to the subconscious one, which acts below the level of people's awareness. The subconscious mind is related to one's beliefs, values, intuition, emotions, creativity, past conditioning, and management of bodily functions. This part of the mind manages a massive amount of information as compared with the data dealt with by the conscious mind.

Scientists have observed that the human brain is composed of the two hemispheres, which have different functions. The left hemisphere is more lineal, logical, verbal, numerical, and analytical. The right hemisphere is more related to creative thoughts, imagery, symbolism, spontaneity, playfulness, intuition, and emotional aspects.

When a person is creative, the two hemispheres interact at all times collaboratively. Some specialists have observed that creative people are more prone to use their right hemisphere, which helps them have a more holistic view of things. Nonetheless, other specialists like Sawyer (2006) concluded that there is no clear evidence of the relationship between creativity and the right brain. From this perspective, creative skills involve the whole brain. Greene (2012) observed that creative activities do not involve only the mental processes, but the whole self, which includes the emotions, character, energy, and also the mind.

Gardner (2006) states that there are seven types of intelligence: body intelligence (related to physical skills), verbal (related to expression), spatial (related to the use of space), logical (related to solving problems), emotional (related to understanding one's own feelings and the feelings of others), spiritual (related to spiritual aspects, like one's role in the world), and creative. From this perspective, creative intelligence implies the capability to create new realities. Even though people are related to all these types of intelligence, each individual will be naturally prone to harness some types of intelligences more than others. Creative intelligence can be enhanced by using the techniques suggested later in this book.

Wallas (1926) observed that the creative process has four stages: preparation (when people garner and organise sufficient information about a topic), incubation (when the topic is left aside, people focus on unrelated or trivial tasks and leave their subconscious minds to work on the issue), illumination (when insights about the topic spontaneously arise, oftentimes in an unfinished manner), and verification (the final idea is tested and conveyed to others). The aforementioned four stages tend to overlap in practice.

From this perspective, creativity implies the use of both the subconscious mind (for the incubation and development of ideas) and the conscious mind (to gather initial information, and to assess and select the most appropriate ideas). Creative skills are generally used in combination with logical skills: people can use a creative approach to generate multiple options to tackle issues, and then use their logical capabilities to select the most suitable one. As explained previously, creativity often implies breaking down an issue into its sub-elements, to use as they are, or to modify them or even recombine them with others.

14.3 Characteristics of People Who Create

New ideas start with some recognition of an incomplete pattern. This is about noticing that there is something missing or that something could be improved.

Max McKeown

People are always creating either purposefully or unintentionally. It does not really matter if their creations are small (e.g., preparing an attractive dinner for friends, engaging in an interesting conversation with a relative, etc.) or big (e.g., discovering a new medicine, developing new technology). Oftentimes, people are not even aware they are thinking and acting in a creative manner. Some characteristics of people who use their creative skills are:

- **Endlessly curious:** Creative people are inquisitive and non-complacent regarding current facts and circumstances. These people are very flexible and believe that products, services, processes, and individuals can always improve. Ray and Myers (1989) call the process of discovering new symbols and forms regarding a topic "creative courage." Rogers (1961) stated that creative people are prone to "toy with elements and concepts" in an exploratory manner. These ruthlessly curious individuals tend to ask countless questions, such as "What are other ways to …?" and similar ones. Creatives are playful; they approach issues in a childlike and light-hearted manner, continually looking for new approaches and perspectives. These individuals explore things playfully, which makes them more resilient and enduring when their attempts fail. Sawyer (2006) observed that creative people are internally motivated; they find exploration of new alternatives so enjoyable that they often find themselves losing the notion of time. Creative individuals have a knack of exploring new ideas, while they enjoy the process. These unremitting people have a high tolerance to uncertainty and ambiguity.

- **Open-minded:** As seen previously, the human brain stores information in very rigid structures or mental models, which makes it difficult to devise new alternatives and options. To that effect, creative people go beyond their mental structures, and temporarily put them aside, or completely dismiss them. Oftentimes, creative people are capable of observing a well-known situation from different fresh perspectives. These people are prone to delay their judgement on a specific topic for a while in order to explore a myriad of different approaches related to that topic. These individuals are also prone to develop new ideas, considering elements from completely unrelated fields. For example, fast food chains have taken the concept of the assembly line, which comes from an unrelated sector like the automobile industry, in order to serve customers more quickly.

- **Visionary:** Creative people are prone to stretch themselves beyond the ideas commonly held by average people. Creative individuals' revolutionary spirit does not conform to what is currently done, used, or established for a long time. They can shape the future by developing innovative products, services and ways of solving problems, which most people do not even dare to imagine. Creators are willing to take risks in order to explore untraditional perspectives, risks which are considered unacceptable by other people. Creative people have forward vision which helps them to develop potential scenarios to deal with challenging circumstances more effectively. Oftentimes, creative individuals are perceived by other people as daydreamers or naïve thinkers. These people hold on to their innovative vision tightly and aim to put it into action. Marden (1917) observed that "men succeed in proportion to the fixity of their vision and invincibility of their purpose."

- **Prolific:** Creative people generate multiple ways to approach challenging topics. Firstly, creative people are prone to develop a myriad of options to approach an issue. In other words, creative individuals firstly focus on the quantity of alternatives over their quality; all possible approaches are welcome without being judged prematurely. In a second stage, these people concentrate on quality over quantity. In other words, from the pool of ideas generated previously, creative individuals select the most feasible to be later analysed more thoroughly.

- **Questioning:** Creative people have the tenacious commitment to tread unknown and untested paths, and go beyond prejudices, assumptions, and widespread beliefs. They never believe that things should be a certain way. Stengberg (mentioned in Garnham and Oakhill,

1994) observed that these people are mentally self-governed; they prefer to set their own rules rather than follow or assess the rules of others. By being self-governed, they are more prone to generate original and valuable ideas.

- **Receptive:** Creative individuals are more open to receiving new insights in a non-judgemental manner. Creative people know that illumination, or the generation of new ideas, cannot be forced; it happens spontaneously. Oftentimes, creative insights come unexpectedly, as a result of a combination of specific activities (e.g., thinking about an issue, researching on a topic, etc.) and taking a rest (not doing anything). Moments of solace and silent contemplation are ideal to receive creative insights, because one's mental chattering is temporarily paused. Besides, a creative person knows that insights can be whispered to them in different ways (e.g., words, images, symbols, emotional states, physical sensations, conversations with people, books, etc.).

- **Determined:** Creative people are proactive; they continually aim to reach out for new ideas. Creative people are also patient because they know that good ideas often take time to incubate and develop. Sometimes, new ideas come up half-boiled and need more time to develop. Hall (1995) says that ideas are like babies who should be cared for and nourished during their growth. Creative individuals try out new ideas on a continuous basis, knowing that sometimes their ideas will work well in practice, and some will not. These individuals consider these "failures" as learning experiences, which can be used to do things differently in the future. Creative people never give up, especially when their ideas don't take off.

Creative people tend to experience positive emotions on a regular basis. Profuse research observes that people who experience positive emotions are more prone to engage in creative thinking, because they tend to analyse varying data in a broad manner (instead of narrowly focusing on specific information) and develop various high-level mental connections with that information. In other words, when people experience positive emotional states, they are more inclined to explore information in non-traditional ways.

Lastly, creative individuals relish a myriad of valuable discoveries developed by many people who painstakingly devote their time to innovation. Moreover, creative people also feel compelled to move in that direction, providing mankind with their own valuable contribution, in order to make the world a better place.

14.4 Business Objectives and Creativity

If we listened to our intellect … we'd never go into business because we'd be cynical … You've got to jump off cliffs all the time and build your own wings on the way down.

Ray Bradbury

Many of the ideas you have, if not immediately and obviously valuable in the moment, contain the germ of something that may be useful.

David Allen

Many people strongly believe that creative techniques are more related to artistic disciplines (such as painting, sculpture, etc.), not to business activities. Nonetheless, creativity is suitable for business activities, but also fundamental to any company's success. Oftentimes, business activities are performed in scenarios characterised by ambiguity, constant change, uncertainty and unpredictability. Consequently, creativity represents a paramount tool for companies to thrive in, in these scenarios.

From the business perspective, the fundamental role of creativity is to add more value for customers and other stakeholders (employees, intermediaries, community, suppliers, etc.). Consequently, creativity can be applied to any business situation and activity. Moreover, some companies adopt the creative approach as part of their business philosophy. The use of creative tools has different objectives. The list below includes some examples of potential uses of creative tools; this list is only indicative, not exhaustive.

- To develop new products and services
- To improve characteristics of current products and services (performance, speed, etc.)
- To define new uses for current products and services
- To create intellectual property assets (trademarks, patents, etc.)
- To increase customers' satisfaction and loyalty
- To generate alternative business models
- To analyse business problems in several ways
- To harness a company's main capabilities differently
- To simplify products, services, procedures, and processes
- To develop a better work environment
- To manage data more efficiently
- To add new services (delivery, prepayment, etc.) to current products
- To strengthen relationships with the company's stakeholders
- To improve the company's productivity and competitiveness
- To obtain information in non-traditional ways
- To prepare a different assortment of products and services
- To re-position products and services in customers' minds
- To implement new management methods
- To design new packaging and packaging for current products
- To improve the company's image and reputation
- To develop new ways of buying products and services
- To develop innovative solutions to conflicts with stakeholders
- To improve the company's internal communication
- To manage business information in a more innovative manner
- To generate word of mouth in a non-traditional manner
- To re-locate company activities in an innovative manner
- To train and motivate employees in different ways
- To dispose of goods in an alternative manner
- To reduce company costs (R+D, manufacturing, marketing, etc.)
- To outsource activities to external organisations
- To develop new categories of customers
- To use different materials or manufacturing processes
- To implement non-traditional ways of transporting and storing goods
- To develop different ways to contribute to the community
- To use innovative distribution channels
- To recruit personnel and professionals in a non-traditional way
- To implement different environmentally friendly actions
- To design more attractive promotional activities and events

- To develop new ways to price the offerings
- To offer innovative financial conditions for buyers
- To enter unexplored markets
- To develop beneficial partnerships with other companies
- To create attractive offers in a negotiation process
- To develop other ways to increase an online presence
- To develop new ways to improve quality levels
- To develop new company strategies
- To develop more socially responsible activities
- To reformulate the company's mission and vision
- To restructure the organisational chart (departments, areas, etc.)
- To implement non-traditional ways of using technology
- To develop different ways of managing time
- To design new customer service activities

The current global era makes creativity even more necessary than before. The globalisation process includes several factors, such as continuous launches of new products and services, countless technological breakthroughs, interconnectedness of countries' economies, and development of new disciplines (robotics, nanotechnology, etc.), among others.

In this global scenario, many companies realise that the enhancement of their staff's creative skills can help them thrive in this fast-changing and tumultuous scenario. Kao (1996) observed that in the past, organisations pursued technology, capital, and raw material as their differential advantage in the market, but nowadays companies are looking for the creative advantage, which includes "imagination, inspiration, ingenuity, and initiative."

It is important to pinpoint that organisations themselves are creations as well; their projects constantly unfold and readjust with the aim to fulfil their business purpose. Kim and Mauborgne (2015) observed that some creative companies develop new marketplaces (named blue oceans), instead of focusing on the well-known marketplaces (called red oceans). These authors stated that these companies create value and innovate on a continuous basis, providing customers with offerings they are not accustomed to or ready for.

14.5 Main Hindrances to Creativity

Every new idea is a mashup or remix of one or more previous ideas.

Austin Kleon

Just as weeds choke out flowers in a garden, too much judgement tends to choke out the imaginative talent with which we were born.

Alex Osborn

Even though creativity seems to serve uncountable business objectives in the business environment, many companies do not take the chance to develop creative activities. For example, when things are going well, most companies are not compelled to innovate. Good ideas often come out of dissatisfaction, when things are not working in the way they expected. For instance, when a company is pleased with their customer service processes, this organisation will be less incentivised to innovate these processes.

In contrast, a company which is frustrated regarding its business activities tends not to act in a complacent manner, and instead looks for alternative ways to improve these very areas. Another incentive to developing non-traditional ideas is when customers provide the company with negative reviews and complaints. This negative criticism can represent a valuable trigger for a company to find new ways to improve their products, services, and processes.

Some traditional companies are prone to become threatened when change needs to be implemented. These organisations resist change, and fear the unknown. They prefer to do things "as usual." Oftentimes, these organisations become quickly outdated and their products and services become obsolete. In those cases, these organisations keep on using outdated methods, even when they do not work any longer. These companies have a functional fixation on how they perceive circumstances. Narang and Devaiah (2014) call this resistance to change "gravity mindset."

Some common expressions of these companies are: "We have tried similar ideas previously," "There is no need to change what works …," "It is not possible to change this …," or "This will take a lot of time or effort …," among others. Hamel and Prahalad (1996) observed that "what prevents companies from creating the future is an installed system of thinking," which includes unchallenged assumptions and narrow views of threats and opportunities.

Complacent companies tend to act in a non-creative manner. These short-sighted organisations consider that their products, services, and processes, and even their business models cannot be improved. Morgan (1997) observed that "many products and services become 'prisoners' of their underlying concept," and even though they stem from good ideas, these ideas become unchallenged and prevent companies from innovating. Creative processes imply different degrees of change that companies should be willing to take. Some other hindrances preventing companies from adopting a creative attitude are:

- **Short-term orientation:** Many companies have a hectic schedule, which includes countless meetings, tight deadlines, overworking, etc. Oftentimes, these companies tend to focus mostly on the short-run, for example, activities like paying the bills, and serving current customers, among others. In these organisations, creative activities are not prioritised because employees have to deal with urgent tasks. In contrast, creative companies are strategic; they tend to adopt a long-term perspective. These organisations understand that some innovative insights take time to develop, therefore, these organisations avoid rushing creative ideas. These organisations also realise that some creative ideas need to go through a process of experimentation, adjustment, and testing to see if they are feasible or not.

- **Rigid mental categorisation:** As seen, previously, the human mind has a natural tendency to categorise and store information in rigid mental classifications. Consequently, any new information is kept in one of the pre-existing categories. Oftentimes, these categories do not have any practical application, when facing new circumstances. Most people tend to stick to their limiting mental categories without challenging them. Creative people are instead prone to question their mental categories, modifying or recombining them, or even creating new classifications.

- **Copying others:** Some companies adopt the same perspectives and methods used by other organisations, regardless of their suitability for the specific dynamics of the former. Many companies are prone to thoughtlessly emulate what is in fashion or currently trending in the marketplace. Companies which adopt this passive attitude are unwilling to undertake creative projects, which harness their unique resources. Nonetheless, some companies analyse what works for other organisations, but also creatively adapt these aspects to apply them to their own specific reality. This approach is called benchmarking and is considered a creative tool, which will be analysed later.

■ **Fear of uncertainty:** Most business people have a fear of uncertainty. These people perceive unpredictable situations as threatening, which makes them feel anxious and powerless. Therefore, these individuals tend to develop patterns, routines, and regularities to avoid uncertainty. As seen in Chapter 4, companies aim to counteract uncertain scenarios in different ways: researching, planning, budgeting, agreeing on contractual terms, etc. People who fear uncertainty are less prone to develop creative ideas, which always implies taking risks. Creativity is naturally related to possible courses of actions, which involve ambiguity and uncertainty. In the creative process, no positive results can be guaranteed; at first, people who develop new ideas cannot know if their ideas will work on a practical level.

■ **Strict planning:** In most companies, work tasks need to be purposeful; these organisations are aimed to achieve specific company objectives, such as increasing productivity, improving customer service, etc. These companies develop plans which include realistic goals to help them prioritise their tasks, use their resources effectively, and reduce uncertainty about future scenarios. As seen previously, goals are future desired states or educated guesses, which are based on the analysis of relevant internal factors (company's talents, capabilities, etc.) and external ones (customers, suppliers, etc.). Unfortunately, these goals are often set in an inflexible manner, which renders them useless when the situation motivating them has changed significantly. Companies with rigid goals act in predictable ways to achieve them, which makes these organisations incapable of taking non-traditional actions. These companies are keen on "predicting" their future outcomes. In relation to this, Klein (2003) observed that creative insights are never predictable, but disruptive: "they come without warning, take forms that are unexpected, and open up to unimagined opportunities."

■ **Lack of confidence:** Some people do not consider themselves creative, because they have self-limiting beliefs regarding creativity. As seen in Chapter 3, beliefs always dictate how a person thinks, feels, and acts. Therefore, people who have detrimental beliefs about creativity will not make any attempt to use creative techniques. Some examples of these negative self-dialogues are: "Artists are the only creative people," "I was not born creative," "I am not a genius," "I do not have a creative mindset," and "I cannot see creative ways to do this." These people are unwilling to explore new perspectives, because they believe that they are not capable. In other words, they do not trust their innermost creative skills.

■ **Stress:** In stressful situations, people tend to adopt a defensive attitude, which is related to fight-freeze-flight mode. In this mode, their analytical and creative capabilities are temporarily diminished. Their minds are focused on the threatening factors affecting them. In stressful circumstances, there is no need for the exploration of new ideas, which is the basis of the creative process. Stressed people tend to be tense, fretful, and agitated. Creative insights are more likely to emerge when people are calmed and relaxed. Tomasino (2007) observed that when people experience negative emotions, their discerning skills and intuitive assessments are impaired, leading them to have more inflexible thoughts and actions. In a similar vein, Wiseman (2009) observed that stressed people are less creative and more risk-averse; they tend to use routine methods to analyse circumstances and have more rigid behaviour.

■ **Mental biases:** As explained previously in Chapter 4, people have mental biases, also called cognitive distortions. These subconscious patterns of thought prevent people from apprehending circumstances clearly and directly. Oftentimes, these mental biases stop people from accessing their inner wisdom and prevent them from tackling life circumstances effectively.

Some examples of these mental distortive patterns are: exaggerating or minimising things, neglecting relevant factors in a situation, relating uncorrelated matters, "predicting" future scenarios, jumping to conclusions swiftly, among others. Not only do these biases prevent people from harnessing their discerning capabilities, but also their creative ones.

■ **Thoughtless abidance by the rules:** Many companies are beset by countless rules (e.g., formal procedures, policies, etc.) which are not critically questioned over time. In general, these purposeful restraints are mechanisms for control and order within a company; they are generally based on fear of uncertainty and chaos. However, creativity always implies freedom, improvisation, and experimentation. Companies which are burdened by rules tend to act in a mechanistic manner; this is opposite to a creative approach, which implies flexibility and open-mindedness. Most employees abide by these norms thoughtlessly and automatically. In these work environments, people are criticised and even punished when they use experimental approaches and do not do things "by the book." When criticised, these staff members tend to adopt a fight-freeze-flight mode, which prevents them from harnessing their creative capabilities. People who abide by the company's regulations are prone to behave in a serious and structured manner. Creative people instead tend to adopt a playful and even chaotic attitude, which defies rigid formalities. Creativity implies going beyond the rules, and oftentimes breaking them and making new ones.

■ **Groupthink:** Many organisations show a phenomenon called groupthink. In these companies, people want consensus and avoid considering other alternatives besides the ones already accepted by the majority. Dissent is overtly or subtly dismissed by group pressure. Consequently, people tend to provide the same opinions as the rest in order to avoid being disapproved by them. McKenna (2012a) observed that groupthink "amounts to an intentional erosion of one's critical faculties as a result of adopting group norms." Research shows that the internal dynamics of these organisations is based on unanimity and homogeneity of views. The open discussion of topics is discouraged and nobody wants to stand out. According to Wiseman (2009), decisions made in these organisations can be riskier and more daring or more conservative than the ones made individually by each member, because their opinions tend to reinforce one another.

■ **Lack of awareness:** Profuse research has observed that many of the actions that people take daily are on autopilot. Oftentimes, people are unaware of their routine ways of doing things. Scientists have observed that repeated actions strengthen specific neuro pathways in the brain, and make them more active, which reinforces the routine behaviour. These habits become more ingrained over time, which prevents people from developing alternative behaviours. Sometimes, habitual behaviour is useful to save time and be more effective, but this behaviour becomes unsuitable in novel or ever-changing situations, which generally require a more proactive and creative approach.

■ **Silo structure:** Most companies have a compartmentalised internal structure where each department acts as a "silo," which often has scarce interaction with others. This silo structure is based on the effective division of labour; each internal area is specialised in specific tasks. The incomplete data possessed by each silo prevents it from developing an integrative and holistic analysis of a company's issues. This rigid organisational structure hinders the development of innovative and synergetic solutions, because inputs from different silos or departments cannot be duly considered and integrated. This bureaucratic structure kills the possibility of collective creativity.

■ **Perfectionism:** As mentioned previously, most people working for organisations are goal-oriented; they want to do things in the right way to attain these goals. However, when people generate creative ideas, a few of them might be successful, but most will not be. Besides, creative ideas are developed gradually, and are often tested and modified several times. The "errors" found during the creative process represent necessary stepping stones to develop future fruitful ideas. Successful creators are not ashamed of making mistakes because they know those errors provide them with insightful clues on their path to outstanding creations. Errors show people what does not work and prompts them to act in alternative ways.

There are a few other relevant topics to analyse. Most companies tend to use black or white patterns of thinking. In these organisations, employees tend to classify facts and situations in a binary manner, such as profit – loss, co-operation – competition, traditional – modern, winner – loser, growth – decline, etc. From this limited perspective, a company is less likely to develop alternative views, which generally includes nuances, new combinations, reformulation of traditional classifications, use of analogies, and development of innovative categories.

It is important to acknowledge that creativity is related to imagination and the development of new ideas. Because of this intangible element, many companies consider that creative activities do not contribute to the company's economic results in a tangible and substantial manner. Therefore, the actual usefulness of a creative approach is harshly criticised by many organisations. These companies tend to use a quantitative approach which gives priority to what is precisely measurable (e.g., sales, profits, number of customers, etc.) and dismiss what is not quantifiable (e.g., intuitive insights).

It is important to analyse the relationship between knowledge and creativity. In general, knowledge constitutes a relevant springboard on which creative techniques can be applied. People must be educated to interpret circumstances affecting them in a more complete manner. Moreover, most psychologists agree that creativity is centred on a specific domain or discipline, and previous preparation (which implies training and collecting related information) on that discipline is needed to develop creative ideas.

This knowledge represents the "raw" input that the creative person will work on to develop non-traditional insights. It is a myth that people create *ex nihilo* (out of nothing); they always create based on combining and transforming their current knowledge. However, when people have solemn respect for the knowledge they possess, without challenging it, these individuals are less prone to develop new ideas.

Many knowledgeable people think in a structured and rigid way, which prevents them from developing non-traditional approaches. Moreover, Sawyer (2006) observed, that beyond a certain point, education becomes a *hindrance* for the enhancement of creative skills. Some experts also state that specialised knowledge can prevent a person from developing fresh ideas to deal with complex and dynamic circumstances. Creative people continuously challenge established and well-accepted knowledge and are open to and flexible about exploring innovative ideas.

14.6 Traditional Creative Tools

Ideas no longer belong to business … Business belongs to ideas.

Will Murray

Genius is no more than childhood recaptured at will.

Charles Baudelaire

A very simple creative tool anyone can use is note-taking. Businesspeople should form the positive habit of taking note of any relevant topics related to business activities; valuable ideas come up and disappear fleetingly. Rando (2014) observed that "language is the oxygen of thinking; it allows thoughts to breathe and live, to become full-blooded."

People who put their ideas on paper do not have to depend on their memory skills. Besides, taking notes give people a clearer and more articulate description of a topic. When taking notes, people can retrieve information, assess it later, modify it, and even combine it with other data.

For instance, people can write down twenty potential solutions to a problem per day. By making the list, people can "unload" or "map" the ideas they have in their minds. Whenever people enumerate these ideas, they should not restrain or censor themselves; any idea should be included, even those considered "unreasonable" or "far-fetched." Some ideas on that list can be modifications of previous ones. At the end of the week, this list should be rationally analysed to select the most promising ideas.

Another way to do this exercise is to write any idea about a topic down in a non-stop way and without editing. Later, these notes can be thoroughly analysed to find relevant patterns and insights into them. Afterwards, these notes can be refined and edited if necessary. Geniuses like Leonardo da Vinci kept countless notebooks with handwritten and graphical ideas.

Written ideas are longer lasting as compared with spoken ones; therefore, these notes can be reviewed more thoroughly later. Afterwards, these notes can also be elaborated, illustrated, edited, reformulated, or combined with other notes. In other words, written notes represent a valuable source of additional ideas to be utilised in the future.

However, some authors like Buzan and Buzan (2003) observed that note-taking tends to obscure significant words among all the notes taken and represent time wasted because it tends to include unnecessary notes. These authors are of the opinion that note-taking does not necessarily stimulate creativity. In conclusion, there are different views on the effectiveness of this tool. Therefore, everyone should try note-taking and see if it works for them because each individual is different.

Below there are some examples of other valuable creative techniques. This list of tools is indicative, not complete. Companies can use these tools to achieve any of the objectives mentioned in Section 14.4 of this chapter. The use of creative techniques should be a positive habit that everybody takes up. The use of these tools helps people unearth their unique creative skills.

14.6.1 Mind-Mapping

This well-known technique was popularised by Buzan (2002). In order to use this tool, people must consider a relevant idea (e.g., a problem to be solved) and put it in a circled box in the middle of a blank page. This main topic should be broken down into subcomponents which branch out and are shown as little boxes around the main topic, connected to it with lines.

This technique helps people see relevant topics visually. These topics can be analysed in a holistic manner, including their main components. Buzan (2002) observed that this tool stimulates "whole-brain" thinking (the use of both left and right hemispheres) and gathers a large amount of information in one place, which helps people make more creative choices.

Some organisations use these mind-maps to develop their strategies, to deliver business presentations, to organise meetings, and to manage product innovation projects, among others. These maps can be prepared individually or collectively and they can be reformulated several times.

14.6.2 Drawing

The use of words limits the possible mental associations between valuable ideas. Instead, drawings allow people to develop more links between ideas, without being hampered by the intrinsic limitations of words. Edwards (1993) observed that "drawing is a global (whole) skill" which represents "a particular way of seeing" that allows people to tap into their "inventive, imaginative, intuitive powers."

Koestler (1964) stated that visual images are powerful "vehicles of thought" and non-verbal or pictorial representations, which are beneficial for creative purposes. This author observed that oftentimes "language can become a screen which stands between the thinker and reality." The use of images is related to the right-brain hemisphere which is linked to a non-linear, intuitive, and holistic perspective. Instead, the left brain is more related to rational, critical, and structured thinking.

For instance, people working for an organisation can draw a business problem affecting them. This visual representation of the issue can prompt these people to draw potential approaches to solve it. These potential solutions can be drawn in a clear, vivid, and detailed manner. The use of graphs and drawings help people hone their creative skills, because these drawings are not constrained by the specific meaning of words or the structure of sentences. The pictures originally drawn can be modified and fine-tuned as more ideas come up.

14.6.3 New Viewpoints

This is a well-used creative tool which involves the analysis of a topic from different viewpoints. An organisation regularly analyses its problems from its own perspective. Nonetheless these problems can be analysed from the perspective of different stakeholders: for instance, employees, customers, suppliers, competitors, community, the media, etc. Each of these stakeholders has a unique way of perceiving and interpreting circumstances.

For instance, when a problem affects one department (e.g., the marketing department), the problem can be analysed from the perspective of other departments (e.g., administrative, finance, etc.). The problem can also be analysed, imagining it from the perspective of other companies in the sector or different industries.

A topic can be analysed, imagining how it would be approached by different professionals or experts (e.g., doctors, lawyers, musicians, etc.). A topic can also be analysed from the perspective of several personalities (e.g., Richard Branson, Will Smith, etc.). Some useful questions for imagining these alternative perspectives "How would ... analyse this situation?", "What specific solutions would ... provide?", and "What would ... do?"

Some other ways to use this tool are to imagine how other unrelated people would analyse a topic. For example, a person can ask questions like "How would a person from Mars analyse this topic?", "How would a beggar analyse this topic?", or "How would a toddler perceive this subject?", among others.

This tool helps analyse issues with fresh eyes and in a multidimensional way, including a wide range of distinct viewpoints. People who use this technique can generate new perspectives on a topic, without being "polluted" by previous knowledge about it. These individuals can temporarily leave aside any of their rigid categories, assumptions, values, or beliefs.

14.6.4 What If Method

This creative method is simple and straightforward. When people use this tool, they should imagine possible scenarios, in which there are no limitations of resources (e.g., funds, technology, time, etc.). A person who uses this technique is thinking in a hypothetical manner.

When a person does not set any limitation to the analysis of an issue, this individual is more capable of generating potentially fruitful alternatives to tackle it. The use of this method is speculative and based on potential options regarding an issue, which do not include any hindrance. The use of this tool also helps people shift from a negative mood (based on the problem) to a positive emotional state (based on possible solutions).

In order to use this technique, a person can ask questions like "What if …?", "What will happen if …?", or "How would things be if …?", and similar ones. When these probable scenarios are imagined, it is easier for a company to work out specific ways to achieve them from a backward perspective.

14.6.5 *Benchmarking and Analogies*

This technique is commonly used by companies and it involves taking into account traits, processes, or procedures used by other companies and applying them to their own organisations, with the adaptations needed. Oftentimes, a company can consider outstanding aspects of other organisations as starting points and improve these aspects in order to apply them internally. A company can take as a reference organisations with practices of excellence from the same industrial sector or different industries.

These benchmarks can also be internal, for instance, when a company sees excellent aspects in one of its own departments (e.g., marketing, finance, etc.). In these cases, the organisation aims to apply these outstanding aspects to other departments whose performance needs to be improved. The application of these aspects tends to require adaptation to the distinct characteristics of the receiving department.

This technique is related to the use of analogies. An analogy implies the use of certain similarities between the topic being analysed and aspects taken from unrelated topics (e.g., components of nature, functions of the body, dynamics of societies, etc.). When ideas are taken from different fields, the creative tool is also called cross-fertilisation.

Some people confuse analogies with metaphors. To put it simply, a metaphor is an implicit comparison (e.g., "Our company is a rocket"). Instead, analogies are explicit comparisons (e.g., "Our company is like a rocket"). The connection between the two elements (in this example "our company" and "a rocket") in metaphors and analogies can be direct or indirect. According to Bragg and Bragg (2005), the use of these tools often helps transfer the underlying principles of a situation (in the example, how a rocket works, why it works, etc.) to another situation ("our company").

14.6.6 *Brainstorming*

This is a meeting where participants take turns to express their views on a common topic. These opinions are expressed freely, without any fear of being censored. In other words, all ideas are welcome and nobody criticises others' ideas. The use of this tool entails the temporary abandonment of criticism in order to allow non-traditional ideas to pop out.

The ideas expressed by each participant can be noted on a blackboard or flipchart for everyone to see. In these meetings, there could be a person who is responsible for taking note of all the ideas exposed during the encounter. All types of ideas are taken on board, even the seemingly outlandish. Sometimes, these meetings are attended by employees working for different departments (marketing, manufacturing, etc.) which makes the interaction richer and more diverse.

The use of this tool helps a company generate a large amount of non-traditional ideas about a specific topic. The ideas expressed in the meeting are later analysed by attendees from a rational perspective. Companies can also break a problem into parts with each part being analysed by specific brainstorming groups.

On one side, Wiseman (2009) observed that, according to research, the use of brainstorming proved to be less effective than the individual development of creative ideas. This is due to a phenomenon called "social loafing" or "diffusion of responsibility," which implies that in a group each member is less inclined to make their best effort, because they become over-reliant on other people's contribution. On the other side, Johnson (2010) observed that brainstorming always represents a valuable tool to develop serendipitous connections.

There is another version of this tool called *brainwriting*. When participants use this technique, they individually write their ideas on small pieces of paper, and then they are shown on a board. Another version of brainwriting is when there is only one piece of paper which is passed around, and everyone takes turns to add their own ideas to it.

14.6.7 Disney Strategy

This strategy was explained by Robert Dilts (1994) and it is said to have been used by Walt Disney. This strategy includes three sequential stages: the dreamer, the realist, and the critic. In the first stage (the dreamer), people envision what can be done creatively regarding a specific topic. In the second stage (the realist), people aim to analyse how creative ideas stemming from the previous stage (the dreamer) can be implemented in practice, considering their feasibility.

In the last stage (the critic), people focus on any criticism of these ideas: for example, why these ideas can fail in practice. In this last stage, people will also consider information from their previous unsuccessful experiences, as well as projected potential setbacks related to the ideas.

14.6.8 SCAMPER

This technique was originally developed by Osborn (1948). This acronym is S for substituting elements, C for combining with other factors, A for adapting, M for magnifying or modifying, P for putting or using for other purposes, E for eliminating or reducing, and R for reordering (or inverting). This technique can be used to solve problems related to products, services, processes, and business models.

For instance, a food company analyses one of its products (cereal). In this case, the company can modify part of that product (for example, its packaging) or combine this product with others in an assortment (for example, launching a package which includes boxes of cereal with different flavours). This organisation can also adapt the product for specific users (for example, cereal for children) or magnify the product by offering a family pack instead of an individual one.

This company can also promote the product for other uses, for example, if the cereal is promoted as nourishing, it can be promoted as energy-boosting. This organisation can also eliminate aspects of the product, for instance, taking out some ingredients (e.g., sugar, preservatives, etc.), or reordering the product: for instance, offering individual cups with cereal for daily use.

A product can be broken down into its parts, and different aspects of SCAMPER can be applied to each of them. Bragg and Bragg (2005) suggest a very interesting question when using this model which is: "What factors can be reduced/eliminated/created for this product or service regarding the sector standards?"

14.6.9 Use of External Words

These are considered as trigger words, which are randomly related to the topic subject to analysis. Any words can work as a trigger and these words can be taken from a dictionary, any other book, TV programmes, etc.

For example, if the company is looking for a new "customer service approach," this topic can be related to any random word such as "tree," "cup," "running," and any other ones. The use of random words prompts the creation of new mental connections which can contribute to the development of new ideas.

14.6.10 Framing

A topic can be reformulated in many ways by changing its focus. Framing is a very useful tool to generate fresh ideas stemming from different perspectives. Some examples of framing can be found below:

- A topic can be defined in a more general manner, or in a more detailed way.
- A topic can be examined from a long, medium, or short-term perspective.
- A topic can be analysed considering its impact on a department, the whole organisation, or the business environment.
- A topic can also be analysed taking into account its rational aspects or emotional aspects.
- A topic can also be evaluated from the viewpoint of its positive aspects, or from the perspective of its negative aspects.
- A topic can be considered from the perspective of its past aspects, or considering its future implications.
- A topic can be analysed from the perspective of possibility, or from the viewpoint of certainty.
- A topic can be analysed taking into account all its aspects or structure (holistic view), or its components (partial view).
- A topic can be examined considering its main aspects, or taking into account secondary traits.

The aforementioned examples are not exhaustive. Organisations can use framing considering other perspectives besides the ones mentioned previously.

14.7 Additional Comments on Creativity

The aforementioned set of techniques should be used even in cases where things are working well. Everything is perfectible, which means things can always be improved; it is important not to rest on one's laurels and to avoid being complacent. People are naturally resistant to change, so creativity stretches their views beyond their comfort zone and beyond their natural ways of perceiving things. Companies can use a combination of these creative techniques in different orders: for example, first using brainstorming, and then mind-mapping.

Lastly, some people are resistant to change and prefer the status quo, which is related to the "endowment effect." This means that these people are comfortable with what they already have, even when it is negative. These people are less likely to use creative tools. Other people are affected by the *Eistellung effect*. This means that when people find a specific solution to a given problem, they are less likely to come up with new ideas. These people are also less prone to use creative techniques.

Questions for Self-Reflection

- What does creativity mean to me?
- What are the attributes of creative people?
- What are the main obstacles in our company regarding creativity?
- Which techniques can be used to perform more creative business activities?

Chapter 15

Additional Aspects of Love and Creativity

15.1 Creating is Also Asking New Questions

Look and you will find it – what is unsought will go undetected.

Sophocles

15.1.1 Importance of Questions

We hear only those questions for which we are in a position to find answers.

Friedrich Nietzsche

Solving the problem is the exciting part, not knowing the answer. Once the conjuring trick is explained, it loses its magic.

Paul Arden

Most people have a few default responses when they face a problem: for instance, they gather additional information, listen to experts, and analyse the issue thoroughly. Oftentimes, people avoid tackling the problem or decide to postpone its analysis. A good way to solve a problem is to ask several questions related to it. Toddlers learn through asking continuous questions to explore the world around them; their relentless curiosity prompts them to ask countless questions in a repetitive and varying manner. Adults are also prone to ask questions about different topics (such as relationships, health, career, etc.).

Companies also tend to pose questions such as "Will this product work?", "Which is the best way to obtain new customers?", or "Where are the most interesting markets to sell our products", among others. Many companies enrol their staff on seminars, workshops, and other training events with the purpose of answering those relevant questions.

Consequently, a very straightforward creative technique is to ask varying questions, especially non-traditional ones. These questions could be asked in relation to any aspect of a company's activities, for instance: business challenges, issues relating to a product or service, relationships with specific stakeholders, strategy aspects, etc. Every time a question is posed, new alternatives regarding a target topic are more likely to come up. To that effect, questions represent wonderful creative tools to solve seemingly unsolvable problems.

Questions are empowering and expansive starting points; they develop a field of valuable possibilities. People who ask frequent questions tend to loosen their mental processes and leave any ingrained assumptions aside. Besides, questions help people challenge statements which include the words "must" and "should." The most creative questions are not comforting, but instead challenging and daring.

According to Robbins (2001), questions shape thoughts and responses to experiences, and create a more fulfilling life. Moreover, questions act like lenses which allow people to see reality in different ways. When people are stuck in a rut, they can use questions to find and develop new paths. Oftentimes, the answers to questions do not come straightforwardly, they are gradually processed before one can see the answers clearly.

Some people refrain from asking questions because they are shy or because they do not want to look silly or ignorant. However, asking questions is always a wise approach which implies inquisitiveness and exploration. Questions are expansive, because they help clarify topics in order to explore uncharted avenues related to them. Different questions focus on distinct aspects of a topic, which helps analyse it in a multifaceted way.

From the creative perspective, there is no such a thing as a silly question; therefore, any question is welcome. Some other functions of asking question as a creative tool are:

- Questions can help people reflect on relevant topics.
- Questions can challenge perceived limitations.
- Questions can help individuals formulate problems more clearly.
- Questions can open new lines of research on a topic.
- Questions can identify priorities regarding a topic.
- Questions can prevent people from swiftly jumping to conclusions.
- Questions can help define a problem in a wider or narrower manner.
- Questions can help connect different problems.
- Questions can help prioritise different aspects of an issue.
- Questions can disrupt automatic patterns of thinking and ingrained perceptions.
- Questions can be the starting point for asking additional questions.
- Questions can help restructure information in a non-traditional manner.
- Questions can help find meaning to unclear situations.
- Question can identify the key elements of a topic.
- Questions can probe hypothetical scenarios.
- Questions can develop new alternatives and widen choice.
- Questions can help summarise or recap relevant ideas.

From the creative perspective, the objective of asking questions is to generate the largest amount of answers possible, even those that are seemingly unfeasible or far-fetched. At a later stage, these answers will be screened out from a perspective of feasibility and practicality.

15.1.2 Examples of Useful Questions

A prudent question is one-half of wisdom.

Francis Bacon

Questions stimulate creative thinking, which help companies navigate the business journey in a meaningful and insightful manner. Sometimes, it is necessary to ask different questions to probe a specific topic. Some examples of questions to be asked are:

- What are other less known characteristics/uses/objectives/dimensions/perspectives of …?
- What are unwanted consequences of …?
- What can be added up to/taken off from …?
- What is possible in relation to …?
- What other factors are related to …?
- What are the underlying assumptions regarding …?
- What is the opposite of …?
- How would … be approached if we started afresh?
- What are the proactive/reactive aspects of …?
- How can … be examined more thoroughly?
- Why is … relevant to our company?
- What are the main obstacles preventing …?
- What are the main principles underpinning …?
- What was learnt from …?
- How can … be simplified?
- What is the exception to …?
- How can I satisfy customers' needs more effectively with …?
- How might … be worsened/solved?
- What are other ways to reduce costs/increase performance/improve the design …?
- What are the traditional and non-traditional activities related to …?
- Who are the main people affected by …?
- How can … be seen differently?
- How can this be improved regarding …?
- Does … feel right?
- How can I differentiate … from …?
- Where can information about … be obtained?
- What are the main time aspects related to …?
- How can I surmount the obstacles related to …?
- What do I already know about …?
- What resources can be leveraged to improve …?
- How can … be more useful in other contexts?
- How can … be reframed?
- What is the best/worst scenario regarding …?
- What are metaphors or analogies related to …?
- What are the unique or distinct aspects of …?
- What are the reasons for …?
- What are the different ways that … can fail/succeed?
- What are the missing aspects/repetitive aspects of …?
- What are the ambiguous/uncertain/uncontrollable aspects of …?
- What are the rational/emotional aspects related to …?
- Which are the internal/external factors affecting …?
- How do other companies deal with …?
- Why is … urgent for our company?

- What should have happened when ... was solved?
- What are the precedents for ...?
- What are the priorities regarding ...?
- What is the most radical idea regarding ...?
- What are the advantages/disadvantages/strengths/weaknesses of ...?
- If we had unbounded resources, what could be done with ...?
- What aspects of ... can be emulated?
- Who will benefit from ...?
- How will they benefit from ...?
- What are the other meanings of ...?
- What actions should be taken regarding ...?
- How would an outsider perceive ...?
- How would an expert deal with ...?
- How can conflicting goals regarding ... be resolved?
- What are the main and secondary factors related to ...?
- What other aspects of value are related to ...?
- What are other ways that ... can work?
- What are the ideal circumstances for ... to succeed?
- What are the limits of ...?
- How can I articulate the idea of ... more clearly?
- Does ... provide customers/employees/community with great value?
- What were the previous solutions to ...?
- What are the main drivers fostering ...?
- What are the main trends affecting ...?
- What are the causes/consequences of ...?
- What are the main parts/structure related to ...?
- What are the commonalities/differences ...?
- What metaphors/analogies can be applied to ...?
- What is the main pattern in relation to ...?
- Which are the temporary/permanent aspects of ...?
- How can the parts of ... be organised in a different manner?
- How is the top organisation in the market dealing with ...?
- What partnerships can be developed to deal with ...?
- What are the simple traits/complex traits of ...?
- What disciplines/fields can I learn more about ...?
- What are the qualitative/quantitative traits of ...?
- What are the compulsory/voluntary features of ...?
- What are the strategic/tactical aspects of ...?
- What would an improved version of ... be?
- What are other examples of ...?
- What are central/peripheral characteristics of ...?
- What are the general/particular aspects of ...?
- How can ... be modified/reduced/augmented/combined with other factors?

It is also useful to ask questions from the opposite perspective of a topic to generate new ideas. For example, if the topic is "good customer service," a creative question regarding this topic is "What is bad customer service?" In this example, the question can provide insights into how *not* to act in relation to customers. O'Connor (2001) observed that people can also ask questions about questions: for example, "What is the most valuable question we need to ask about …?"

When posing these questions, people should adopt an attitude of curiosity, flexibility, and open-mindedness. Not all questions enumerated previously will be applicable to every topic. Companies should choose the most suitable questions for each situation under analysis, leaving irrelevant questions aside.

There is another important point to highlight, which is the topic of concepts. Concepts are general classes of categories. Atkinson et al. (1981) observed that "concepts foster cognitive economy by dividing the world into manageable units" because "the world is full of so many different objects that if we treated each one as distinct, we would soon become overwhelmed."

In relation to this topic, De Bono (1998, 2013) suggests a very interesting question, which is "What is the operation concept of this?" This specialist observed that concepts are general and abstract "junctions in the mind" which help people develop different alternatives to put these concepts into action. Consequently, concepts cannot be implemented directly, but through specific ideas. This author also mentioned that in the case of fast food restaurants, the main underlying concepts for their business activities can be "good location," "savoury food," "fast customer service," and others. By analysing and clarifying these concepts, a company can devise different creative alternatives to put these very concepts into practice.

15.2 Non-Traditional Tools for Creativity

> Unless man can make new and original adaptations to his environment as his science can change the environment, our culture will perish. Not only individual maladjustment and group tensions, but international annihilation will be the price we pay for a lack of creativity.
>
> **Carl Rogers**

15.2.1 Meditation

Even though some consider meditation a non-business practice, it has been used by global companies such as Google, Apple, and others to develop creative ideas and concepts. Some studies have demonstrated that regular meditation enhances mental capabilities and reduces levels of structural stress, rendering the body more relaxed. People's inner wisdom is generally clouded by their continual mental ruminations. However, when people meditate, their minds become more tranquil, which allows these individuals access to their valuable inner knowledge.

Research has found other benefits of meditation, such as revitalisation of the body and decluttering of the mind. Meditation also helps people cast a fresh and light gaze into their inner world. People who meditate are more prone to achieve a state of balance, peacefulness, and overall well-being. All these benefits contribute to the generation of more creative ideas.

There are different ways to practice meditation. One well-known way to meditate is to sit in or lie down in a comfortable and quiet place. Then close the eyes, relax the body and focus on the breathing, feeling the air on the upper lip when inhaling and exhaling. People can mentally scan their bodies to detect any tension and imagine it flying away, like a passing cloud. The meditative process can be performed by repeating a mantra such as "Om," "love," or any other, but meditation can also be done silently.

As mentioned, when people meditate, they should continually focus on their breathing, by following each inhalation and exhalation. Whenever the meditator's mind goes astray or is distracted, this individual should gently bring it back to the original point of concentration (the mantra or the breathing, whichever is used). If thoughts or emotions come up during this process, people should observe them in a non-judgemental way and let them go. Some practical uses of meditation for business activities are:

■ During meditation, a person can pose questions like "What are alternative ways to improve our customer service activities?" to look for creative insights. Answers to these questions might come during the meditation process or afterwards. During meditation, a person is more prone to incubate innovative alternatives to solve an issue.

■ Meditation brings serenity which allows the analysis of challenging situations in a more focused manner; people who regularly meditate are less prone to worry and complain. Consequently, meditation is useful for business people who are continually challenged by troublesome issues.

■ A meditative state is optimal for the generation of creative thoughts, because it naturally squashes any defensive state (fight-freeze-flight) which usually pervades a great part of work environments. As seen in this book, this reactive state is detrimental to the generation of creative insights.

15.2.2 Development of Intuition

Neither a lofty degree of intelligence nor imagination nor both together go to the making of genius. Love, love, love, that is the soul of genius.

Wolfgang Amadeus Mozart

Intuition is information obtained from the subconscious mind. This information is received as insights, not stemming from the use of rational capabilities. These insights are obtained in the form of thoughts, images, sounds, or sensations. This information summarises complex ideas simply, and it can often be obtained through specific experiences: for example, meeting a person, engaging in conversation, reading a certain book, etc.

People should avoid reacting negatively to these insights, but welcome them instead. Intuitive insights are creative and beyond the habitual way of thinking. Many people tend to distrust these sudden and often unexpected insights, because they often cannot be rationally explained or justified. Sometimes these insights do not make immediate sense, which prompts people to discard them without giving them a second thought.

In business activities, intuitive insights can be very valuable, especially when there is limited time to make decisions. When people follow their intuition, their actions tend to be more graceful and effortless. In uncertain business scenarios, intuition can also provide valuable clues on how to proceed. Many entrepreneurs built their business empires based on their hunches. There are different ways to be more receptive to these insights:

15.2.2.1 Contact with Nature

People who are in regular contact with nature are more prone to receive creative insights. The passive observation of natural landscapes has a soothing effect, which contributes to the generation of intuitive insights. When people are in contact with graceful, lush, and harmonious natural places, their mental chattering is lessened and their minds are more receptive to insightful ideas.

15.2.2.2 Asking Questions

People can ask themselves relevant questions to solve specific challenging situations. These questions can be asked before going to bed, when meditating, or when in a calm and relaxing state, for example, having a shower or taking a bath. Spontaneous intuitive insights into these questions tend to come up afterwards, in the moment least expected.

15.2.2.3 Delving into the Issue

For instance, a person wants an answer to a question regarding an issue: "What materials can I use for this new product?" Firstly, this person can obtain introductory information about this topic from different sources: books, magazines, websites, etc. This person can also enumerate possible solutions on a piece of paper. After dwelling on this topic for a while, it is best to give this issue a rest, which means not thinking about it. During that time, the answer to the question incubates "behind the scenes" and tends to arise effortlessly.

15.2.2.4 Being Calm

Intuitive insights are more likely to arise when a person is calm, emotionally and mentally, and physically relaxed. Activities like yoga, swimming, or walking in a quiet place are a few examples of activities which make people slow down and become more receptive to intuitive insights.

15.2.2.5 Being in the Present

Insights are more likely to pop out when people are fully focused on the now. When individuals are engrossed in the activity at hand, their minds are less prone to ponder the past (e.g., guilt, criticism, e.g.) or the future (e.g., worry, fear, etc.). People who are centred on the now do not resist what is, but engage with it. These people can be fully aware of the current experience, which opens their minds to insightful information.

People are more prone to receive intuitive or inspirational insights when they adopt a humble and open-minded attitude. Intuitive insights can never be produced at will or forced; they come spontaneously. However, people can be more prone to receive these insights when they adopt a calm, receptive attitude. Other ways to generate intuitive insights are mentioned in Appendix G.

Klein (2003) observed that intuition is the way people translate their own experience into action; consequently, people become more intuitive regarding a field or discipline, as they gain more experience in it. This scholar stated that people with intuitive skills perceive relevant cues from a situation at hand, which leads them to see other cues. From this perspective, intuitive people can imagine future scenarios based on these patterns, which can help them decide how to act in specific circumstances.

In other words, intuitive people have the ability to make diligent and subtle distinctions, in a split second, without going through a lengthy analytical process. Klein (2003) observed that intuitive skills are useful for situations where there is time pressure, expert knowledge is needed, when there are unclear goals, and in dynamic (but not complex) conditions.

15.3 Selection of Creative Ideas

Creativity in business is not different from all other expression of creativity: They begin with questions, not answers.

Amit Goswami

The techniques explained in this chapter and the previous one can be used to generate a myriad of creative ideas regarding a topic. From the creative perspective, being prolific with ideas is always recommended. As seen previously, creative thinking and rational thinking complement each other; the former generates a wide range of options on a topic and the latter narrows down the options within those viable alternatives according to specific criteria.

The objective of this realistic screening of creative ideas is to minimise risks (e.g., financial, commercial, etc.) relating to its implementation. De Bono (2013) explains that companies that are sensitive to value can appreciate the value of an innovative idea. Consequently, ideas stemming from the use of creative techniques can be analysed from a rational perspective, considering different practical aspects, such as:

- Distinct benefits of the idea
- Intelligibility and simplicity of the idea ("Is the idea easy to understand?")
- Main audiences benefiting from the innovative idea (e.g., customers, employees, etc.)
- Main audiences affected negatively by the implementation of the idea.
- Social impact of the implementation of the idea
- Time necessary to implement the idea
- Potential co-operation needed from specific stakeholders (suppliers, intermediaries, etc.)
- Suitability of the idea for customers/employees/suppliers/intermediaries
- Accessibility to technology to develop the idea
- Availability of economic resources to implement the idea
- Estimated risk/return related to the implementation of the idea
- Compliance of the potential implementation of the idea with current legislation
- Feasibility of technical aspects related to the idea (specifications, designs, etc.)
- Possibility of prototyping the idea
- Possibility of enhancing or improving the idea
- Alignment of the idea with well-known ideas or concepts
- Potential replicability of the idea by others in the market
- Possibility of legal protection of the idea (e.g., patents, etc.)
- Possibility of the application of the idea to various products, services, or processes
- Alignment of the idea with the company's mission
- Potential unforeseen consequences of implementing the idea (e.g., delays, staff training, etc.)

When analysing creative ideas, people can also ask if these ideas make others' lives easier, safer, more comfortable, and more pleasurable. Oftentimes, innovative ideas have a relevant positive impact on the world, to a small or big extent. Murray (n.d.) suggest that, when testing an idea, business people can ask questions like "How do we feel about this idea?" to obtain some intuitive insights on the topic.

From the sociological perspective, creative ideas are ultimately validated by the social context (also called the "field"). In the entrepreneurial world, this field is composed of customers, other companies, media, community, government, and experts, among others. Oftentimes, different departments of the company (e.g., finance, marketing, manufacturing, etc.) are consulted regarding ideas; in other cases, ideas are discussed with external specialists on the topic.

Other stakeholders can be consulted by the company in order to test the viability of an idea: for instance customers, business partners, suppliers, intermediaries, etc. The company can even consult the community, if the implementation of an idea has a significant social impact.

15.4 Innovation and Creativity

Before you can think out of the box you have to start with a box.

Twyla Tharp

15.4.1 *Main Aspects of Innovation*

Innovation involves a natural tension between chaos and order. If too many new ideas are followed nothing ever gets finished. If too many old rules are followed nothing ever gets improved.

Max McKeown

Trott (2012) highlights that innovation is "the management of all activities involved in the process of idea generation, technology development, manufacturing and marketing of a new (or improved) product or manufacturing process or equipment." The idea of innovation is not limited to products, but can be extended to services, management activities, administrative processes, and also marketing activities.

Innovation means the practical application of fresh ideas by a company, including their commercial exploitation. Drucker (2007) observed that innovation is motivated by various factors, for example, changes in the industry and market, changes in demographic factors (e.g., employment levels, population growth, literacy levels, etc.), the upsurge of new knowledge, and changes in people's perception regarding a topic, among others. Below there are other interesting ideas about the innovation process:

- All products and services need improvement; if not, over time, they run the risk of becoming useless or obsolete.
- During the development of innovative products and services the company should harness its unique talents and core capabilities.
- Innovation is not related to one specific department (marketing, R+D, etc.); it should always be part of a company's philosophy which pervades all its aims and activities.
- The novel combination of knowledge possessed by an organisation and knowledge from other fields can prompt the generation of outstanding ideas.
- The innovation process should harness a company's main strengths and capabilities and also consider the opportunities and threats in the business environment.
- Innovative companies tend to adopt an outstanding attitude of service toward customers; these organisations want to satisfy customers' needs in the most effective manner.
- Dominant ways of doing things and ingrained conventions must always be challenged, questioned, and rebelled against during the innovation process.
- A company should never start with the innovation process when its products become commoditised or copied by others; the company should start this process much earlier.

- Forsaking old ideas gives place to the unfolding of new ideas; ideas which are not fruitful at present can later become productive, reformulated, or combined with other ideas.
- Potential economic outcomes stemming from the innovation process are often difficult to quantify; this should not prevent a company from adopting a proactive innovative approach.
- No innovation is an island, but directly or indirectly related to a previous series of innovations developed by the organisation, or other companies and individuals.
- Perceiving flaws in things that apparently work well can be a very important source of innovative ideas; therefore, companies should always monitor what works for further improvements.
- The generation of innovative ideas can come from different sources: contact with customers, employees' comments, other companies' activities, trends, publications, highlights in other sectors, etc. Any information can be a valuable input for creative insights.
- Any opportunity to solve a relevant problem in a better way is a starting point for innovation; problems are opportunities (in disguise) for innovation.
- Innovation not only implies the development of non-traditional ideas, but also the testing of these ideas from a commercial, technical, and financial perspective.
- Companies that are extremely risk-averse are prone to prevent themselves from innovating; innovation implies risk and uncertainty and potential rewards are not easily commensurable.
- The first vision of a new product or service is not always crystal-clear; oftentimes, ideas develop gradually over time and consequently, patience and determination are key factors in innovation.
- Any feedback from customers in any of the interactions with a company is valuable input for further innovation; thus, customers can actually be considered co-creators.
- Customers can also be considered in any of the stages of the innovation process (e.g., sharing their needs, launching a new product, etc.); customers can be a relevant factor to test the commercial feasibility of a new product as well.
- Innovative companies tend to face two types of uncertainty: about the final outcome of their innovation process, and about specific ways to achieve a desired result.
- Companies should always allocate sufficient time and resources for innovation; the innovation process tends to take more resources than estimated.
- A company's innovation process should be flexible due to its intrinsic uncertainty, so tight deadlines should be avoided.
- An innovative product does not always have to be disruptive or ground-breaking; any change, whether slight or significant, that adds more value to customers can be considered innovation.
- Assumptions about what is preferred by the market as innovation should be avoided; market preferences must be carefully researched and fully tested.
- Many brilliant ideas are generated in response to employees' or customers' dissatisfaction; all products and services should be improved on a regular basis, even the ones that serve customers effectively.
- Current industrial sectors are never still; they are always dynamic and coexist with emerging and declining sectors. A company should aim to go beyond the limitations of the sector it belongs to, by reshaping that sector, creatively combining elements from different sectors, or even creating a new sector.
- The innovation process should not be handled in an extremely serious and formal manner; a playful and exploratory attitude should preferably be adopted.

- All innovative products and services impact on the organisation and its environment; the development of innovative products and services should always consider the potential ethical implications for the company's stakeholders.
- Some innovative products and services can also benefit other stakeholders besides customers, e.g., communities; these innovations must always be preferred over the rest.
- There is always uncertainty and unpredictability regarding the results of the innovation process. Therefore, adaptiveness and open-mindedness are needed throughout the process.
- Some outcomes from the innovation process can be applied to more than one product and service; an innovative product or service can also stack up the characteristics of various current successful products and services.
- Some innovations are disruptive or radical (they create a new market), some instead are a modification or natural progression of what already exists (they serve current markets).
- All innovative products or services should have some points of contact with the products they replace; customers must identify common traits between old products and new ones, even in the case of radically innovative products.
- There is no limit to the improvement of any product or services; creative development is unbounded. However, excessive formalities or rigid control procedures within an organisation could limit innovation.
- Failed attempts during the innovation process can become stepping stones to successful tries; companies can always learn from unsuccessful products, services, processes, and business models.
- Observing how customers relate to products and services can provide valuable insights for innovation purposes; the most relevant judge of the value of the outcomes of the innovation process is the market.
- The quest for new business opportunities and innovative ideas should never end or become stagnant; innovation routines and habits should be continually fostered all over the company.

According to Lafley and Charan (2008), innovation is the process of converting new ideas into economic results (revenues and profits), which always entails being customer-focused. These authors stated that innovation is also a social process which implies getting on board with staff from different departments and areas, who should share their learning, challenges, and ideas. This perspective implies fostering open communication among the different areas and departments of a company. According to McKeown (2014), all innovative ideas should also take into consideration relevant habits and ingrained traditions, which can represent relevant hindrances to the acceptance of non-traditional ideas.

15.5 Tips for Companies to Enhance Their Creative Resources

> Great minds discuss ideas; average minds discuss events; small minds discuss people.
>
> **Eleanor Roosevelt**

In organisations, creativity and innovation can be fostered not only to resolve problems, but also to exploit untapped opportunities. Managers should continually remind employees that creative thinking and experimentation is not only legitimate, but greatly welcomed. Management should encourage and reinforce creative behaviour in their staff. In order for the company to thrive, all staff members should get involved in creative activities on a regular basis.

When possible, all company departments (marketing, administrative, manufacturing, etc.) should directly or indirectly contribute with their insights to the innovation process. As seen previously, all sources of information, internal or external, are potential drivers to prompt innovation activities. However, chance and serendipity can also become relevant factors in the innovation process.

Sometimes the innovation process can be developed in partnership with other organisations, which provide the valuable input for the innovation process. As explained previously, all non-traditional ideas should be tested regarding their usefulness and their operative and practical aspects. Companies can purposefully take specific actions to increase innovation in their organisations. Some examples of actions to be considered by a company are:

15.5.1 Declaration of Innovation

Sloane (2007) suggested that all companies should write their own declaration of innovation. According to this author, this declaration should include the reasons for innovation (why), the areas to innovate (what), and the request that employees commit to a continuous innovation process. Additionally, this author mentioned that this statement can include specific resources to be allocated for innovation, aspects related to management and monitoring of the innovation process, the commitment to look for ideas from various sources, and declaration of continuous involvement in this process. This statement should be made public to all the company's employees, who should be reminded of it on a continuous basis.

15.5.2 Creative Time and Spaces

All employees should have specific time compulsorily blocked off to generate new ideas for the company, as part of their worktime. This is important because many employees avoid trying to develop creative ideas because of their hectic and busy schedule. Organisations should also have designated rooms, known as "safe environments" for employees to perform creative activities. Thompson (1992) suggested the development of bright workplaces (with incandescent or natural lighting), whose walls shows the company's vision and mission to foster innovation. This author also suggested playing calming baroque or classical songs as background music in the workplace because this type of music stimulates creativity. The workplace can have furniture which encourages open interaction between employees, which can help generate collective ideas. Wiseman (2013) observed that the use of natural plants in the workplace also prompts people to be more creative. Lastly, whiteboards can be stuck on the walls and can be used if intuitive insights arise.

15.5.3 Creative Meetings

The company should organise frequent brainstorming sessions, within each department. These meetings should last around 15 minutes and each participant should be able to freely and openly express their ideas on a common topic. Participants of these meetings should avoid censoring phrases to new ideas, such as "It is not practical," "It seems too difficult," and other similar phrases. There should be a person designated to jot down all the ideas exposed. These meetings could include members from other departments. The ideas obtained in these meeting should be analysed later and test their feasibility (financial, technical, commercial, etc.).

15.5.4 Fun Activities

Research has shown that activities which prompt people to experience positive emotional states help them harness their creative and intuitive capabilities more effectively. For instance, the workplace can be equipped with arcade and board games to be used during break time. Besides this, the company should organise social fun events (such as staff dinners, sports competitions, retreats, etc.). In this type of events, staff members are more prone to "let their hair down" and forsake fight-freeze-flight mode, which is common in most work environments. By being relaxed and at ease, employees' creative skills are naturally enhanced. As seen previously in Chapter 10, these events are revitalising and re-energising and empower employees to later go back to work with a fresher approach on challenging work issues, which also impacts positively on productivity levels.

15.5.5 Avoid Groupthink

In some companies, groups are formed whose members are unwilling to stand out with their own opinions; these individuals tend to conform with their group. Consequently, in any group, dissent should be encouraged and alternative perspectives on topics welcomed. People outside the group should also be able to give their alternative views on specific issues; external consultants or advisors can also provide disruptive opinions on relevant topics. In order to avoid groupthink, McKenna (2012a) suggested dividing a group into different subgroups, which will each analyse different aspects of the same topic. Scoular (2011) suggests that some of the participants in a group can adopt a critical view on a topic, by playing "devil's advocate."

15.5.6 Record of Brilliant Ideas

Companies should keep a collective record of creative ideas, including those whose implementation is not immediate or temporarily not suitable. All employees should contribute to these records. This record can include ideas stemming from the use of creative techniques, including the ones that did not pass the feasibility test. These ideas can also come from other sources, such as suppliers, customers, intermediaries, competitors, organisations from other sectors, the community, etc. These attractive ideas can come from other non-traditional sources, such as movies, magazines, songs, books, cultural environment, etc. The brilliant ideas can also come from different disciplines, such as physics, philosophy, history, etc. This record is useful because the company can recombine, adapt, simplify, or augment these ideas to apply to the company's issues. These records could include different categories of topics, and creative ideas can appear in more than one category. The access to these records should be open to all employees. There is specific software in the marketplace to keep records of creative ideas and projects.

15.5.7 Ideas Incubators

These are projects or areas inside the company whose main objective is the development of new ideas. In these incubators, people can freely and openly work on new perspectives or different issues, and develop innovative ideas in a prolific and unhampered manner. These incubators represent a safe haven where unconventional or non-traditional ideas are developed and welcome. These incubators can even thoroughly explore areas which seemingly work well for the organisation.

15.5.8 Reward Creativity

The company should set organisational policies that stimulate the generation of new ideas by its employees. To that effect, a company should provide employees with specific incentives for the development of creative perspectives. These incentives could be economic (e.g., additional compensation, bonus, etc.) or non-economic (e.g., free transport tickets, additional annual leave, etc.). There could also be regular contests where members of the work team can propose their innovative approaches and be awarded valuable prizes. The generation of creative ideas should not be limited to specific departments (e.g., marketing or research and development), but affect the whole organisation.

15.5.9 A More Loving Environment

Maturana and Bunnel (1998) observed that love enhances people's creative capabilities and also expands their intelligence. When the workplace is warm, and people treat each other in a more caring, kind, and respectful manner, and they feel safe and appreciated, these people are less prone to experience the fight-freeze-flight response which temporarily impairs all thinking skills, including creative ones. The main characteristics of a warm workplace have been explained previously in Chapter 10.

15.5.10 Creative Brief

This tool has been suggested by Udall and Turner (2008). This a one- or two-page report, which includes the following elements: a question prompting insightful analysis regarding a specific topic, the motives as to why this question is strategically relevant, the aim and objectives of the activities to be performed in relation to this question, the desired results and what they should look like, deadlines and timelines for the process, and support and resources available. This brief can prompt the company's employees to generate innovative ideas.

15.5.11 Open Feedback

Companies can adopt an open attitude to criticism from staff. To that effect, companies should welcome any type of comments from its personnel, both positive and negative ones. The company can set a suggestion box in order to encourage employees to provide anonymous suggestions. Cornelissen (2017) observed that this tool opens up the company's internal communication channels. Some know-it-all managers are very reluctant to use this tool, because they are afraid of any criticism from employees. Companies should encourage feedback from both internal and external stakeholders. This feedback provides the company with valuable insights that are stepping stones to develop non-traditional approaches: new processes, new products and services, new business models, new goals, etc.

15.5.12 Embed Creative Techniques during Worktime

It should be a policy to train employees in the use of different creative techniques, which have been described in this book. These training events could be workshops, seminars, or conferences. These events should explain practical tools for employees to apply to real-life scenarios. When employees perform their work activities, they should be granted a minimum "leeway" for them to explore creative perspectives. Medium- or long-term projects should also include a percentage of the worktime to be devoted to the generation and testing of new alternatives.

15.5.13 Opportunities Audit

When a company discovers a valuable opportunity, this could be a relevant starting point to develop creative ideas to harness this opportunity. However, most organisations do not allocate any time to discover and explore opportunities because they are focused on urgent tasks (e.g., paying the bills, chasing suppliers, etc.). De Bono (1978) suggests that companies should formally implement a process to find new opportunities. This author observed that the opportunities detected can be listed in a report (which includes a description of the opportunities, benefits, potential actions to take, resources and assistance needed, sticking points and timing). This author also observed that there could be an Opportunity Manager who facilitates and co-ordinates the tasks of the Opportunity Team. This independent team is in charge of looking for opportunities, using inputs within the company and outside it. This team will be interrelated to other areas of the organisation. From this perspective, there could also be an opportunity Task Force, which will deal practically with the opportunities discovered by the Opportunity Team, using specific resources allocated for that purpose.

15.5.14 Continuous Improvement Quality

Companies should monitor all their activities, products, and services on a continuous basis in order to assess their potential for improvement. All areas of the company should be evaluated, not only those which do not work well. When carrying out this assessment, all assumptions on how things "are" and "must be" have to be left aside temporarily. The company should adopt an approach of possibility, exploration, and openness. This perspective is based on the principle that everything is perfectible and can be improved over time.

15.5.15 Encourage Collective Creative Activities

As seen previously, some important collective activities are brainstorming meetings. Besides these, collective creation can also be attained through the development of partnerships with varying institutions, such as universities, research centres, other companies, associations, and government organisations. This type of alliance with creative aims represents a fertile environment for the generation of insightful and fresh ideas.

15.5.16 Creativity Audit

Kao (1996) observed that companies can audit some indicators regarding their creativity on a regular basis. This author suggest that companies ask questions like "What are the main creative resources possessed by our organisation?", "How many creative projects have come into fruition?", "What were the circumstances that prompted our company to undertake creative projects?", "What are the current hindrances to our creativity," "How can our company emulate outstanding creative organisations?", "Who are the most creative staff members in our organisation?", and "What systems are in place to generate, store, and apply creative ideas?", among others.

15.5.17 Innovation Goals

A company can set specific and realistic objectives regarding its innovation process. For example, an organisation can set a goal of developing three new products or services per year. The progress of attainment of these goals should be monitored on a continuous basis. The topic of goals is explained more thoroughly in Appendix G.

15.5.18 Attributes Assessment

McGrath and MacMillan (2005) recommend a valuable tool to continually improve products and services. These authors suggest that a company should map the main attributes of its products and services using classifications like satisfiers, neutral attributes, and dissatisfiers. From this perspective, satisfiers are positive attributes which prompt customers to experience positive emotions, neutral attributes make customers behave nonchalantly, and dissatisfiers are negative attributes which prompt customers to experience negative emotions. Companies should hold regular meetings to brainstorm ways to increase the satisfiers for their products, and reduce or eliminate their neutral factors and dissatisfiers. In a similar vein, Kim and Mauborgne (2015) observed that a company can analyse a product or service offered by companies in the sector, and identify elements which can be eliminated, those which can be reduced, factors which can be increased, and elements which can be created.

15.5.19 Premortem Assessment

This tool was suggested by Klein (2003). This technique consists of imagining the worst result for a project, product, or activity. From this failure, the company should thoroughly visualise and analyse the sequence of factors and actions bringing about that negative outcome. The purpose of this analysis is to discover what would have been done wrongly if this negative result is obtained, and how actions could have been improved; a list can be made with the potential causes of the failure. This technique to anticipate negative scenarios was originally used by the ancient Stoics (who called it *premeditatio malorum*, or "pre-vision of evils"). Stoics used to mentally rehearse or predict things which could go wrong regarding specific situations by asking specific questions (such as "What if this goes wrong?") and then imagining the actions to take. Research has shown the use of this tool can help companies detect potential challenges affecting their endeavours in order to take effective action, in case they occur. This tool can also help companies take preventive action to avoid the potential causes of failure, when possible.

Questions for Self-Reflection

- Which questions can help me perform more creative business activities?
- Which non-traditional tools can help me become more creative?
- How does our company deal with innovation?
- How can a more creative work environment be developed?

Appendix A: Stress and Business Activities

When we overwork, we under enjoy.

Susan Jeffers

Looker and Gregson (2010) state that stress is a "mismatch between perceived demands and perceived ability to cope," which implies that a person has too many demands or too few resources to deal with those demands. Sometimes stress can also stem from few demands, even though this is less common. In other words, stress is a person's defensive response to a perceived threat from the environment.

Stressed people appraise that they will not be capable of dealing with the stressing factors effectively. Csikszentmihalyi (2002, 2003) states that workers are more prone to become stressed when the level of work required from them is highly challenging as compared with their skills. From the psychological perspective, stressful events tend to be more impactful when they are uncontrollable or unpredictable.

Stress usually brings about physical symptoms (for example, tension, fast heartbeats, etc.), emotional states (anger, fear, etc.), thoughts (worries, ruminations, etc.), and behaviour (avoidance, inaction, self-medication, etc.). These aspects interact with each other in a negative cycle. Stress can also be contributory to the development of different health conditions, such as backache, lowered immunity, depression, headaches, heart attacks, etc.

Some say that a reasonable amount of stress improves achievement, but it is difficult to determine what is "reasonable." At first, when people feel stressed, they might feel more energised, but after a while they become depleted, out-of-control, and fretful. The mind–body system is only built for arousal for a short time.

Perceived stressors trigger people's fight-freeze-flight response, which lowers their discerning and creative skills, bringing about temporary cognitive impairment. In this reactive mode, the person's focus is narrowed down to the threatening factor. If this alarm system is activated for a period of time long enough, the body is not allowed to recover properly.

Most business environments are intrinsically stressful because of multiple factors: multitasking, tight deadlines, scarcity of resources, absence of support, demanding requirements, unrealistic objectives, etc. For example, at work, some common stressors are a lack of autonomy, countless bureaucratic procedures, technological fast-paced change, role ambiguity, shift work, unfair treatment, unfamiliar tasks, lack of feedback and support, insufficient skills, authoritarian commands, confusing goals, boredom, bullying, overworking, unhealthy work–life balance, lack of planning, low-quality communication, lack of recognition, etc. Some relevant changes (change of job, promotion and demotion, downsizing, mergers and acquisitions, etc.) can also represent stressing factors.

In the business environment, stress brings about negative outcomes such as lack of motivation, avoidance of challenging tasks, harsh arguments, workaholic attitude, accidents, foggy thoughts, irrational decisions, low creativity and productivity, lack of co-operation, slow judgement, etc. Bevelin (2017) observed that stressed people tend to be more suggestible than unstressed ones. Stress also has a significant impact on other areas, such as family, health, etc. In all cases, stress always indicates that some necessary changes must be made. Below there are some simple actionable tips to relieve the symptoms of stress in the business and work environments.

a) Self-Awareness

A stressed person should purposely take some time off, when possible, to be more self-aware; these individuals should observe early signs of stress in their body (like muscular tension and accelerated breathing). The body of a stressed individual tends to become blocked and its vital energy does not flow well. When practising self-awareness, Bacci (2002) suggested that individuals should focus on their breathing and internal states (e.g., emotions and physical sensations), instead of concentrating on what they want to achieve (e.g., aims and objectives). In other words, people should dwell on their internal states and observe them quietly. Besides, when individuals become aware of tension in different areas of their bodies, they can intently tense their muscles and then relax. Individuals can also imagine that the tension is being released from their body like a flying cloud. People can also stretch their whole body like a slothful cat in order to relax their muscles.

Individuals can also use diaphragmatic or abdominal respiration to become more aware of their breathing and calm it down naturally. People can even be aware of their breathing while they go through their daily activities, especially when they face dire challenges. A person can also use introspective questions to prompt emotions and thoughts to pop up, such as "What is going on in me at this moment?" or "What am I feeling now?" The objective of these questions is to enhance people's internal awareness and help them articulate their own emotional states in words.

b) Exercise and Other Activities

Exercise is a powerful self-care tool, which helps release stress naturally. Exercise also revitalises muscles, bones, and tissues, improves blood circulation, and helps detox the body. Besides, exercise helps release endorphins, which contributes to an overall sense of well-being. Frequent exercise contributes positively to one's self-esteem. Research concludes that exercise reduces proneness to stress and increases life expectancy.

Some physical activities like jogging and gym exercises are excellent to release tension. Stretching exercises and aerobic exercises (such as dancing, cycling, and running) and exercise routines to tone muscles (e.g., lifting weights) are also advisable. Some disciplines are naturally de-stressing for example, yoga, chi-kung, tai chi, meditation, etc.

Meditation improves the overall working of the body, quietens the thoughts, and relaxes the body. Frequent practice of meditation makes people feel more vital and energetic. Meditation enhances concentration and problem-solving processes. The meditative state is also suitable for receiving intuitive insights and creative ideas.

c) Healthy Habits

In order to avoid worsening stress symptoms, a person should have a healthy diet. A balanced ingestion of fats, carbs, and proteins should be considered. A good nutrition programme generally includes a multivitamin and mineral complex, taken on a daily basis. Some specialists like Abrams (2017) suggest the intake of magnesium, calcium, vitamin C, vitamin B5, and vitamin B6, as well as Biotin. Advice from a doctor or nutritionist should always be sought by individuals on what constitutes a balanced diet for them.

Some food recommendations are well-known and common sense. For example, some products to avoid are junk food, products with preservatives, canned food, overtly salty or sugary items, foods with high-fructose corn syrup, fried products, caffeine, and alcohol. People should eat more leafy green vegetables, fruit, beans, whole grains, seeds, legumes, and nuts. Natural, organic, fermented, and vegetable-based food should be chosen over highly processed items. Some specialists also recommend eating lean protein, and cold-water fish in moderation. Sufficient water should be drunk to remain hydrated all over the day.

Some healthy fats, such as olive oil, oily fish, and avocado should be preferred over fats in processed food. Food ingestion should be unhurried, and over-eating should be avoided; small and regular portions should be ingested and chewed slowly. When eating, the person should mindfully concentrate on their food, avoiding mental wandering over work-related problems. It is important not to skip meals during the day. Emotional eating should be avoided; for example, eating to combat boredom, tension, or anxiety is not beneficial.

d) Alternative Activities

Rosenberg (2005) observed that oftentimes stress is caused by unmet needs, which makes it important for people to ask themselves "What are my unmet needs in this situation?" People who use this question can obtain some insights about their main needs, which will help them meet them in alternative ways. For instance, if people do not feel fulfilled at work, they can look for other activities outside work for their self-realisation.

A person should devote frequent time to activities that this individual yearns to do, not obligations. These activities help people recover their energy levels and become more revitalised. A person should choose activities which prompt them to experience positive moods and laughter when possible. These activities will vary from person to person, but all of them help people slow down and become more at ease.

For instance, some people like reading positive literature (motivational books, spirituality, etc.), which is very inspiring and oftentimes calming. Others like to be in contact with natural places (parks, lakes, etc.) to become more revitalised. Some people are keen on activities like dance, sports, and hobbies and creative activities (music, writing, etc.) which help the person wind down.

Some people like to give themselves treats: for example, bubble baths, sauna, dinners out, or some other activities like cooking, travelling, etc. Other people like to have professional massages, which improve circulation, release tension, and calm pain. Research has also shown that performing activities which prompt people to experience positive emotional states, such as watching comical movies, are of great help to overcome stress.

Some specialists also advise helping others: for example, volunteering or charitable activities. These altruistic activities switch the focus from oneself to others, which makes people feel at ease. People also feel good because they contribute to noble social causes.

e) Better Work Organisation

Stressed people should slow down their work pace, avoiding hectic schedules when possible. Complex business projects should be broken down into more actionable and easier steps. A person should avoid undertaking tasks uninterrupted for lengthy periods of time. Some useful questions stressed people can ask themselves are, "Am I overloaded with activities?" and "How can I manage my activities in a more calm and enjoyable manner?"

Regular short breaks should be taken during work time to avoid exhaustion and overwhelm. These breaks can also be included in the personal diary to be respected, as if they were carved in stone. Multitasking should be avoided because it goes against undivided focus and effectiveness. When people perform many simultaneous activities, they are more prone to make mistakes because their focus is scattered. Employees should be engrossed in one task at a time, and temporarily disengage from other activities.

At night, a person can make a list of things to do during the following day. To do lists can also help people declutter and clear up their minds and give them an instant emotional boost. Relevant activities should always be prioritised over trivial ones; the former should have specific blocked time to tackle them. Sometimes, different ways to approach each of the forthcoming tasks can also be included on the list. Besides, realistic goals should be set and reviewed on a regular basis, avoiding a perfectionist attitude when pursuing them. When possible, some tasks should be delegated to others, or worked on in co-operation with other colleagues.

f) Improved Discernment

When stressed people dwell on irrational ideas or catastrophic thoughts, they can ask themselves specific questions like "Are these threatening factors real or imagined?", "What are the chances of these threats occurring?", "What is the evidence of this?", "What is a more realistic view of this?", and "What is the worst that can happen in relation to this?", among others. These types of questions help people change their perception of external circumstances, and prompt them to feel calmer and more in control.

Stressing circumstances should be promptly recognised and can also be written down and framed more positively in order to avoid reacting to them. A person should identify the actions to be taken in relation to these situations. The person should also use more positive vocabulary; for example, "challenge" instead of "problem," or "I choose to feel more energised," instead of "I feel exhausted."

Blackburn and Epel (2017) observed that people can deal with stressful circumstances by framing them as challenges, instead of threats. These authors stated that people can feel excited and confident before these circumstances, by using phrases such as "I am excited" and "I have what it takes," which in turn will create positive effects in their minds and bodies.

Lastly, a person can reflect on current challenging circumstances in order to look for creative solutions to them. In Chapters 14 and 15, several creative tools (such as analogies, brainstorming, etc.) were thoroughly explained.

g) Social Aspects

People could look for support from others (colleagues, relatives, friends, etc.) when feeling overwhelmed with stress factors. These individuals can talk to others about their own worrying issues to unload their minds and also receive useful tips. In this way, stressed people can feel cared for and assisted by others, which reduces their anxiety and tension. A stressed person should always look for uplifting people and avoid surly ones. Positive social interactions can represent a very restful refuge from hectic business and work schedules.

People tend to feel less stressed when they are more generous, supportive, and grateful with others. When a person adopts a loving attitude toward others, stress is naturally pushed away; love and stress are incompatible. People with a kind attitude take the focus off themselves and place it on others. Research has shown that when people are more grateful, they have lower stress levels, and their negative emotional states (fear, anger, etc.) are replaced with positive ones (peace, contentment, etc.).

Lastly, a person should seek for a balance between work and other life areas (health, family, hobbies, etc.) as a priority. Overworking always brings about several trade-offs and imbalances in the rest of these areas.

h) Other Aspects

When individuals are stressed, they can use self-suggestions to calm themselves down. Some statements like "Relax," "I am capable," "I am tranquil," or "I allow myself to be still" can be effective to become more relaxed. By mentally repeating these sentences, a person can focus on positive things, instead of concentrating on threatening factors.

People can also become more positive by asking themselves questions like "What good things happened today?", "What good things are likely to occur?", and "What am I grateful for?", and similar ones. The objective of these questions is to prompt positive thoughts, in order to replace stressful ones.

Visiting natural places, like parks, lakes, mountains, and other places of natural beauty can also represent relevant stress busters. According to Blackburn and Epel (2017), these natural places allow people to disconnect from the myriad of stimuli bombarding them on a continuous basis, which in turn makes them more tranquil.

Lobel (2014) observed that having a shower after a hectic day not only makes people feel cleaner, but it also helps them eradicate any trace of stressful experiences they have had during the day. When having a shower, the person will feel cleaner, more revitalised, and less prone to be burdened down by stressing circumstances.

Brewer (2010) suggests keeping a stress diary. In this diary, people should frequently jot down the time of the day they felt stressed, the stress intensity, the stressful situation, the feelings, and negative responses related to that situation. In this diary, potential effective courses of actions to respond to the stressing factors can also be included.

Appendix B: Mindfulness and Business

Most of the time, a person's brain is prone to focus on the future (worries, expectations, etc.) or the past (regret, guilt, etc.). The human mind is also naturally inclined to judge everything (for example, good, bad, big, small, etc.). People who practice mindfulness concentrate on themselves (their thoughts, emotions and physical sensations) or focus on different aspects of the environment around them (people, things, places, etc.) with undivided attention and in a non-judgemental manner. Consequently, mindful people tend to be less reactive.

Individuals who intently practice mindfulness are centred on the present moment and use their five senses (touch, sight, smell, hearing, taste) fully. As seen previously, people tend to see reality through the lenses of their mental biases (e.g., exaggerating, mind-reading, drawing quick conclusions, etc.). Salzberg (2014) observed that mindfulness helps people cut through their mental biases to get in direct contact with themselves and their surroundings. Tart (mentioned in Fontana, 1999) observed that mindfulness helps people see things as they are, instead of how they want them to be.

Research notes several benefits of mindful practice, such as less tiredness, better communication skills, higher self-esteem, improved memory skills, fewer distractions, heightened awareness, improved decision-making, more creativity, lower stress levels, enhanced performance, and less emotional reactivity, among others. Collard (2014) observed that mindful individuals tend to be more vital, enthusiastic, grateful, and compassionate. The continuous use of mindful techniques also has a positive impact on relationships and the overall well-being of a person. Below there are some potential uses of mindfulness in the business environment.

- Mindfulness can be used as part of active listening to a company's stakeholders. When a person is actively listening to another, the former can become a silent observer of the latter's movements, gestures, tone of voice, emotions, and words. Mindful listening contributes to a better comprehension of the speaker's message. Mindful listeners temporarily silence their inner dialogue to pay full attention to what is being said. This type of listener adopts a more empathetic attitude toward a speaker.
- With mindfulness, a business person can fully concentrate on projects of great importance (contracts, strategies, product innovation processes, launching of new items, etc.). Mindful practice can help people focus on the priority tasks at hand, without being distracted by trivial ones. Mindful observation can also be used to avoid multitasking, which lowers productivity, according to research. In other words, mindfulness also allows people to manage relevant tasks in a more productive manner.

- Mindful practice can be used by business people who suffer from stress. Stressed people who practice mindfulness can become more aware of their thoughts, emotions, sensations, and the overall environment. When they do so, they can assess threatening factors (e.g., excessive workload, tight deadlines, etc.) in a calmer and more insightful manner. A mindful person will tend to avoid responding to stress factors actively. Verni (2015) observed that mindfulness helps people focus on the "raw data" at present, lessening their ruminations and facing the business challenges in a less stressed manner.

- Mindfulness can help business people become better learners. As seen in Chapter 4, running a business implies continuous self-education and training. When people practise mindfulness on a regular basis, they can fully focus on the knowledge to be learnt and affect the learning process positively. Besides, a mindful learner has a clear understanding of relevant knowledge and reasons underpinning it. Lastly, mindful people tend to apply the new knowledge learnt to specific situations in a more meaningful manner.

- With mindful practice, business individuals can become more aware of their negative emotions, such as anger, sadness, fear, and others. These emotions negatively colour thoughts and activities when unchecked. A person with a mindful attitude does not aim to control these disturbing emotional states. Instead, this person observes their emotions and allows them to be, without judging or criticising them. By doing so, any turbulent emotion tends to naturally subside. Verni (2015) stated that mindful people are more inclined to recognise their negative emotions and disengage from them, if necessary. When people have full emotional awareness, they are less prone to have unproductive behaviour which could bring about negative consequences.

- With the regular practice of mindfulness, a business person can avoid automatic behaviours. Many business people perform their daily activities on autopilot. For most routine activities, a person has no need to be fully conscious of the task at hand. Nonetheless, many business people tend to be less effective when they respond automatically to new challenges (e.g., entering a new market). In those cases, a more thorough and creative analysis is relevant. Mindful business people are fully aware of the task at hand and can develop more innovative ways of approaching it. Besides, many business individuals have negative habits (e.g., answering emails late, etc.) which affect the company's performance in a detrimental manner. People who start to act mindfully can replace negative habitual responses for positive ones. This type of person is also more prone to act authentically and spontaneously, instead of heedlessly and automatically.

- Webb (2016) suggests that when people start feeling the signs of stress (irritability, tension, fatigue, clouded thoughts, reactiveness, etc.), they should take a mindful break. During this break, these individuals should pause any current activity and breathe deeply, focussing on the area of their bellies; this is called abdominal respiration. These people can also sit in an open space or natural landscape, and breathe slowly and calmly, while they are mindfully aware of the surroundings. During that break, people can also scan their body and imagine any tension subsiding. During the day, people should take regular breaks of around 5–10 minutes to start feeling more revitalised.

- Mindful people can be more aware of the interconnectedness of all that exists. For example, when people are working for a company, they can be aware of their interdependence with other members of staff. A mindful person considers the workplace to be a co-operative space where each person supports one another and contributes to the company's purpose. From this perspective, successful work projects are never the result of an individual, but of collective effort. Likewise, a company's success is never considered a result of the organisation itself, but instead the contribution of all valuable stakeholders, such as suppliers, intermediaries, external advisors, etc.

■ Mindful business people can make better decisions. Mindful people are fully focused on the present moment, which prevents them from being dragged down by turbulent thoughts and emotions from the past or the future. Mindful individuals tend to be calmer, which allows them to make unhurried and wiser business decisions. These people are less prone to respond to challenges in a reactive or thoughtless manner. These individuals tend to be more flexible and in control, when they solve business problems. A business person who adopts a mindful attitude is prone to make decisions more clearly and objectively, without being taken by distracting thoughts and emotions.

■ Mindful people tend to pay more attention to the details. People with a mindful attitude are more observant; they can perceive details in any situation that most individuals have taken for granted. A person fully engaged in the present moment can discover different aspects of the environment (people, things, places, experiences, etc.) and also of themselves (thoughts, emotions, physiological states). When people are aware of what is going on around and inside themselves, their analysis of situations is more thorough and meaningful. This increased awareness can also help people detect hidden opportunities in the business and work environments.

■ A mindful person can deal with difficult conversations in a more compassionate manner. Some business people face challenging conversations with stakeholders: for example, talks about the cancellation of a supply contract, or a meeting arranged to fire an employee, and downsizing the company structure, among others. A mindful person is capable of telling others about a conflicting issue in a calm and kind manner. A mindful individual is also more prone to use objective criteria (for example, statistics, market price, etc.) to solve conflictive situations with others in a fair manner. A person with a mindful attitude truly cares for the relationships with others stakeholders, and tends to address conflictive situations more lovingly.

Appendix C: Marketing and Manipulation

Tricks and treachery are the practice of fools that have not wit enough to be honest.

Benjamin Franklin

C.1 Consumption and Consumerism

The majority of customers in the marketplace look for new products, services, and experiences on a regular basis. Most customers are utterly attracted by novelty and innovation. Hyde (2012) observed that, as customers, "sometimes we go to the market to taste estrangement, if only to fantasise what our next attachment might be." Oftentimes, customers obtain a very short-lived sense of satisfaction from their purchases, which prompts them to engage in buying again. Not only do customers create a continuous demand for innovative offerings from companies, but customers are also one of the main drivers of an economy. Moreover, customers represent the main, and oftentimes the only, source of income of most companies.

Honoré (2004) observed that consumerism has contributed to the development of the fast-paced society and "tempted and titillated at every turn, we seek to cram in as much consumption and as many experiences as possible." In relation to this, Martin (2006) observed that "our consumerist culture encourages people to strive after things that they believe, often wrongly, will bring them happiness in the future" and "they find it hard to enjoy the present because their thoughts are focused on a future state they have not yet attained and perhaps never will."

Customers have different motives for buying products and services, like social acceptance, safety, simplicity, status, comfort, novelty, autonomy and independence, time-saving, entertainment, curiosity, and low cost, among others. The different types of needs of a company's stakeholders, including customers, were thoroughly explained in Chapter 6.

C.2 Marketing Strategies and Manipulation

Most companies actively use different marketing stratagems (e.g., events, advertising, free samples, etc.) to persuade customers to buy their products and services. In relation to this, Baker and Martinson (2002) observed that authentic persuasion is based on relevant principles, such as truthfulness, authenticity, respect, fairness, and social responsibility. In a similar vein, Parson (2004) highlighted the importance of veracity, non-malfeasance (not harming others), beneficence (doing good to others), confidentiality (respecting privacy of others), and fairness when interacting with customers.

Nonetheless, it is also very common to see customers disappointed because of having been enticed by deceptive or manipulative stratagems implemented by companies. These manipulative ploys aim to reduce customers' natural freedom of choice, and force them into choosing specific pre-selected alternatives.

Some examples of companies' disrespectful behaviour toward their customers are the use of pushy sales techniques, continuous unsolicited telephone calls, and the delivery of junk mail and intrusive spamming, among others. Some companies through attractive advertising campaigns aim to promote needs which are superfluous and also showcase idealised role models (e.g., the successful entrepreneur, the vital young man, the perfect lady, etc.) which can often confuse customers regarding their innermost fundamental needs. Organisations that use these ruses have no interest in developing sustainable relationships with customers which exceed specific transactions. These companies tend to put any potential mutually beneficial relationships with customers on the back-burner, which makes this approach extremely short-term-oriented.

Many companies are not interested in taking the time to create an emotional connection and rapport with customers in order to discover and acknowledge their unique needs. In many cases, companies completely ignore customers' specific and unique preferences. Some companies do not have the least interest in making customers feel that the product they buy is right for them.

Sometimes, customers are not treated as human beings, but as mere means (impersonal figures in a company's database) to potentially contribute to achieving a company's economic results (profits, sales, etc.). In all these situations, customers tend to feel blatantly utilised, which makes them suspect a company's real intentions when they interact with this organisation. These customers perceive that companies are not being authentic, which prompts these very customers to act in a similar way.

Consequently, companies should adopt a thoughtful and loving attitude when they interact with customers. Each encounter with customers should be considered as an opportunity to develop and strengthen fruitful relationships with them. These golden occasions should empower companies to offer more value than expected by customers in order to delight them.

C.3 Other Aspects of Marketing Strategies

Every time customers get in contact with a company, this organisation should kindly and warmly accompany and guide them over the buying process, which means before, during, and after the purchase. When a company assists customers in an insufficient manner, they can think that this organisation does not care enough for them. A company's employees should continually check if they are adopting a kind and warm attitude toward customers. A good question to be posed is "Are we supporting this customer enough?"

Customers tend to feel very upset when a company does not fulfil its promises (for example, delays in the delivery of products, delivering goods of inferior quality, etc.). Therefore, whenever a company makes the promise, this organisation should meticulously deliver what was agreed. Companies should avoid over-promising and under-delivering, because customers will feel deceived.

There are a few other points companies should take into account when interacting with customers. Interactions with customers should consider human contact, more especially in the case of online purchases. When possible, personal interactions or conversations on the phone should always be preferred over the ones which are only technology-based, like email or online chat.

Lastly, companies should be committed to continually improving the performance and quality levels of their products and services. Organisations should invest enough resources on research and development of new offerings for customers. When a company offers innovative products to customers, they are inclined to be very grateful for this.

Appendix D: System Thinking and Organisations

No mind is an island; each man is part of the main.

John Donne

D.1 The Importance of Companies as Systems

Science suggests the next step of human evolution will be marked by the awareness that we are all interdependent cells within the super-organism called humanity.

Bruce Lipton and Steve Bhaerman

Companies can be considered dynamic and complex living systems with the capability to adapt to changes in the business environment. A system is a synergetic set of interrelated components which link to one another in a direct or indirect manner. Synergy means the company is more than the simple summation of its components. O'Connor and McDermott (1997) observed that "a system is an entity that maintains its existence and functions as a whole through the interaction of its parts." From this perspective, a company behaves as the organising or structuring principle of its components.

Each of the departments, sections, divisions, or teams can be considered as subsystems. Despite being continually managed and monitored; the behaviour of a company's subsystems is often difficult to predict. Moreover, changes in any of these components affects the system as a whole. At the same time, the company belongs to bigger systems: for example, its industrial sector (group of companies offering similar products and services).

The company is also part of a wider system, the business environment, which includes not only competitors, but also suppliers, intermediaries, media, customers, business partners, and the community, among others. Not only does a company continually interact with its external environment, but this organisation also has a shared view of this environment, sets a common purpose and acts toward it as a common front. The business environment is also considered a system affected by a myriad of uncontrollable and often unpredictable factors (e.g., economic, legal, cultural, technological, etc.).

From a global perspective, the world is becoming increasingly interconnected. National economies are increasingly interrelated, as the result of international trade flows (import, export, foreign direct investment, etc.), technological advancements (internet, satellite, etc.), and financial aspects (international loans, etc.), among others. Therefore, it is also possible to consider the world as a complex and dynamic system.

D.2 Main Characteristics of Companies as Systems

As with any system, there are boundaries which separate the company and its internal environment from the external environment. From this perspective, the most important activity in an organisation is to effectively manage the flows (products, services, information, etc.) which go through and within the company's boundaries.

A company's activities should always be analysed from a holistic perspective, considering the contribution of each of its components. In a similar vein, Goleman (2014) observed that, in order to analyse systems, people should use a panoramic span of attention. An analysis considering, for example, the contribution of just one of a company's departments is incomplete. Consequently, when a company develops its strategies, this organisation should allow the participation of these departments in the process of planning, when possible.

It is important to break down the components of the company as a system, and analyse how these components interact with one another. As in any system, all parts of a company contribute to the whole to different extents. This analysis should also consider the impact of the company on its external environment, which is the bigger system the company is inserted in, and vice versa.

Continuous feedback is obtained as the company's components relate with one other, and also when this company as a whole relates to its external environment. This feedback can confirm that the company is going in the right direction, so this organisation will keep on acting in the same way. This feedback can also indicate that the company should correct its course of action, and choose an alternative one. In this case, feedback prompts the company to make some adjustments to achieve a state of balance (also known as homeostasis).

As a system, a company has inputs (e.g., supplies) and outputs (e.g., products to be sold). An organisation also has throughputs, which is the transformation of inputs into outputs by adding significant value to them. Successful companies add value to these exchanges, which means that the outputs will have a superior value to the inputs.

When a company is considered a system, none of its parts should be analysed in isolation, but in relation to the whole. Thus, when a company adds value to customers through its products and services, it should take into account the contribution of different internal departments (manufacturing, administrative, marketing, etc.). This organisation should also consider the value added by components of the bigger system that the company is inserted in (company's suppliers and professional advisors, etc.), as well as the company's intermediaries (e.g., wholesalers and retailers the company sells its products to).

D.3 Systems, Objectives, Decision-Making, and Environments

The majority of companies are goal-oriented. These organisations set objectives and perform activities to achieve these goals in an integrated manner. A company on its way to attain its goals is always subject to changes in its internal or external environment. Therefore, when a company sets its objectives, it should consider both its internal and external environments. Sometimes the objectives must be reformulated according to changes in those environments. Objectives set by a company should consider potential impacts on components of the bigger system the company belongs to (e.g., suppliers, customers, community, etc.).

From a systemic perspective, when a company takes actions to achieve its objectives, these actions are always related to events, which are beyond an organisation's control. Oftentimes, these external events have unpredictable and uncontrollable consequences. Besides, any change in the company system not only modifies the organisation itself, but also impacts on its external environment. Great and small changes (both internal and external) affect the whole company system. This complex interrelation of internal and external factors makes the long-term consequences of these changes difficult to predict.

It is possible to see a simple example of these interrelated factors. For instance, if a company's employees become more engaged and motivated, they are more prone to serve customers more kindly, which in turn could create stronger loyalty ties between them and the company. Consequently, all business decisions should be made considering not only small components within the company system, but also the bigger context the organisation is inserted in. Oftentimes, decisions a company needs to make are affected by undetected factors from its subsystems or from the bigger system the organisation belongs to.

As with any human system, the company has homeostasis, which implies that it will adapt to changes in its internal environment (e.g, employees, etc.) and its external environment (e.g., competitors' activities, changes in customers' trends, etc.), in order to remain stable over time. Both the internal environment of the company and its external environment are impermanent and subject to continuous development.

Not all factors in a company's external environment affect the organisation as a system in the same manner. Some companies as systems are more inclined to collapse when they are affected by impactful factors; for example, a company with low levels of sales is more prone to shut down when the national economy is in an economic depression. Fiebleman and Friend (1945) observed that a company is more likely to survive an ever-changing business environment when it is tenacious, determined, and flexible.

D.4 Other Aspects of the Systemic Perspective

The analysis of company problems (for example, lack of qualified staff) tend to be related to other problems (for example, financial problems, etc.). Therefore, problems should never be considered in isolation, but in relation to other troublesome issues. From this perspective, it is important for companies to step back and reflect on the whole set of problems and their interrelated aspects, considering the whole picture. From the systemic perspective, no problem occurs independently, but in relation to others.

Individuals working for a company, and outside it, can also be considered as systems. People are multidimensional: they are affected by emotional, spiritual, physical, and mental aspects. These individuals also have different roles, such as worker, parent, friend, relative, etc. These people also belong to bigger systems, such as groups of friends, relatives, colleagues, etc.

From the employee's perspective, systems like family, friends, and others are equally as important, if not more so, as the organisation the employee works for. The way these individuals perform their activities in some of these systems (for example, the family circle) tends to impact others in the systems they belong to (e.g., group of work colleagues).

Many companies consider their employees in a fragmented way; for example, taking into account only their job or work role. These companies also tend to consider their external stakeholders purely in relation to their specific business roles (e.g., suppliers, buyers, etc.). Instead, the systemic approach fosters a multifaceted perspective, which goes beyond reductionist working and business roles. From this perspective, work activities allocated by a company to its employees consider other employees' dimensions besides their work roles, so that employees can achieve a balance between their work tasks and other areas of their lives (family, friends, etc.).

In a company, each department or internal division should be aware of their valuable contribution to the whole company system. All parts of the company system should add value in a consistent manner. These subsystems should also be aware of the interaction with one another, considering the possibility of assisting each other and working in a co-operative and co-ordinated manner. Moreover, a company should hold frequent cross-departmental meetings, which implies the participation of different areas of this organisation (marketing, finance, etc.). These meetings can bring a more integrative picture of the company's challenges and opportunities, and can be a viable environment to brainstorm creative courses of action to deal with them.

Consequently, the interplay between different parts of the organisation should always be taken into consideration. The level of conflict among these components can be reduced significantly when each subsystem adopts an integrative and non-fragmentary view of business activities.

Business activities can be analysed in a fragmented manner: for example, from the viewpoint of the company itself. However, this analysis can also be more overarching when it considers the unique perspectives of customers, suppliers, community, government, etc. Most companies are prone to assess business situations by considering only one or few of these possible viewpoints. In those cases, the general picture is not perceived; the valuable interplay between these distinct perspectives is generally dismissed.

It is also important to pinpoint that the company's strengths, capabilities, and talents are inter-related to one another. All these elements add value in an integrative manner. Nonetheless, these positive internal aspects are also related to negative ones (a company's weaknesses). Consequently, these negative factors often counteract positive ones, creating final negative outcomes.

From a systemic perspective, a system tends to be slowed down by its weakest factors. This principle can be applied not only to the level of strengths and weaknesses, but also on the level of departments, divisions, and teams. The weakest department, division, and team tend to slow down the whole company's system. Therefore, some relevant questions a company can ask itself on a frequent basis are:

- What is the contribution of this department, section or team to the bigger company system?
- How does a change in this department, section, or team affect the company as a whole?
- What is the contribution of this company to the business environment system as a whole?

Appendix E: Compassionate Negotiation

E.1 Conflicts and Organisations

All organisations tend to have several conflicts within them and with other companies. These conflicts have various origins, such as different values and beliefs, emotional unrest, perception of limited resources, and diverse goals, among others. Some conflicts are internal, which include the same area or different areas within a company (e.g., marketing, finance, etc.). Other conflicts are external, for example, between an organisation and its external stakeholders (suppliers, intermediaries, etc.). Companies use different techniques (negotiation, lawsuits, mediation, etc.) to solve these conflicts.

Some conflicts escalate because of a participant's personal aspects (e.g., personality) and others because of substantive aspects (e.g., quality, price, etc.). Oftentimes, these conflicts damage relationships, which are the most relevant assets in an organisation. From a traditional perspective, every conflictive situation tends to be perceived as a fixed pie; a participant can only get a bigger slice at the expense of the other. This perspective is based on a scarcity mentality, which is fear-based. This fear can adopt different forms, such as fear of losing resources, fear of not being right, and fear of being controlled, among others.

It is possible to say that most conflicts are based on the lack of a loving attitude towards others. The existence of conflict implies, to a certain extent, participants' perception of separation from each other. Each party gives preference to their "right to be right" over their "duty to care for others." However, if companies adopted an attitude of open-mindedness and show a warmer heart, most conflicts could be amicably resolved, and oftentimes avoided.

E.2 The Importance of a Loving Attitude toward Conflicts

Companies which act based on noble principles (e.g., compassion, care, forgiveness, gratitude, etc.) are less prone to engage in any conflictive situations with their stakeholders. These organisations also give priority to the human aspects of each participant in any negotiation process, in order to preserve and strengthen their relationships with them. There are some recommendations organisations can use when they have disagreements with their stakeholders:

- Express one's needs in clear and simple language. Use positive vocabulary when possible and focus on what you want, avoid centring on what is not wanted.

- Invite others to convey their needs overtly. Acknowledge others' opinions overtly ("I appreciate your comments, thanks for letting me know!").
- Avoid mind-reading or guessing the other's opinions and preferences. Use open questions, paraphrasing, clarifications, and recaps in order to understand other's comments clearly.
- Encourage others to elaborate on their ideas with sentences like "Tell me more about ...." Listen to them in an active manner, by being totally focused and absorbed in their comments and without interrupting them. Keep an inquisitive attitude, even during rough times.
- Look for similarities with the other participants. When people converse about their similarities, they are naturally prone to feel affection for one another.
- Don't ignore or avoid conflictive situations, hoping they will be resolved by themselves over time. Perceive any conflictive situation as an opportunity to learn from one another in order to strengthen the relationship with each other.
- Try to interpret comments from the other participant from the most loving perspective, even seemingly negative ones. When a person makes a detrimental comment, paraphrase it from a positive standpoint. Assume that others have the best intention to reach an agreement.
- Use words which imply a connection between the participants, for example, "let's," "us," "we," and "our," among others. When possible, eliminate words, like "I," "my," or "mine."
- Avoid using manipulative stratagems, such as ultimatums and false deadlines, among others. All these ploys prevent participants from achieving a mutually profitable agreement and damage the relationship.
- Acknowledge others' emotions; allow them to be expressed overtly. Rosenberg (2005) observed that when each person can express their vulnerabilities, conflicts can be solved more easily. Emotional states generally signal the person's most relevant interests.
- Be empathetic with others' emotional states, using sentences like "It looks like you feel ...." Suggest break time when emotions are becoming increasingly heightened to avoid potentially destructive escalation.
- Avoid adopting a defensive attitude toward others which is generally based on fear. Never respond to aggressive comments in a reciprocal manner. Identify one's emotions regularly and express them calmly using sentences like "I feel ..." without blaming others.
- Avoid personalising the conflictive situation (for instance, discussing personal traits). Personal conflicts are more prone to escalate.
- Approach the conflict in a positive mood, whenever possible. When participants experience positive emotions, they tend to develop more creative solutions to it.
- Know that an appreciative and a generous attitude toward others prompts them to feel more positive emotional states. The use of sentences like "Thanks for your contribution" and similar ones is beneficial for the negotiation process.
- Acknowledge the significance of achieving a higher-level goal that should be arrived at by a mutually satisfactory agreement, which not only preserves, but also strengthens the relationship between the participants.
- Realise that partial agreements often create momentum for bigger ones. Sometimes agreements can have a trial period to test their effectiveness in practice. There could be a transition period from the current situation to the implementation of an agreement.
- Ask others to suggest solutions to the conflict; make them feel like valuable participants in the development of the agreement. Ask questions like "What do you suggest we should do?"
- Consider the other participant as a partner, not as an adversary. It is important to recognise and encourage others to continually contribute to the development of an agreement.

- Allow others to express their opinions openly. Focus on active listening to others firstly, in order to be heard by them afterwards, especially when discussing challenging issues.
- Avoid exerting power over the other party. Avoid any imbalance of power as it creates resentment, distrust, and unwillingness. Show care for others to prompt them to open up.
- Try to imagine creative solutions to the conflict alongside the other participant. Look for fair solutions which consider both parties' interest. Pose interesting questions like "What would a solution look like if we meet our interests and yours?"
- Break down the conflictive topic into subparts: for example, a price can be broken down into: money to be paid, currency used, possibility of financing, etc. Look for creative variations to these variables.
- Understand that negotiation processes are generally based on more than one variable (for example, quality, price, transportation, etc.); these variables (and their subvariables) can also be recombined in a creative manner to arrive at an agreement.
- Avoid attacking, judging, criticising, and ignoring others, which displays an unloving attitude toward others. Realise that these strategies don't make people feel acknowledged and recognised as legitimate participants.
- Be flexible in the design of any potential agreement, which must be based on equality, co-operation, inclusiveness, and fairness. Solve obstacles or deadlocks in a co-operative and creative manner, and always avoid making decisions unilaterally. Ask others for their opinion, instead of commanding them.
- Learn more about values of the other participant, which indicate what is important for them. Ask questions like "What is really important for you in this situation?" to discover the other person's values.

Some other points can be highlighted. Participants should find a common ground during the negotiation process. O'Connor (2001) suggested that every participant should frequently use tools like "chunk up" and "chunk down." For example, a company has a disagreement with a supplier about the commercial terms of a transaction between them. In this example, the parties can use "chunk up" to agree on higher order objectives. For instance, these participants might agree that beyond this specific agreement, they want to preserve their business relationship (high-level objective). The parties can also use chunk down; in this case, participants can explore more specific parts of the agreement (e.g., price, quality, etc.), when appropriate.

E.3 Other Relevant Aspects to Be Considered

Each party should aim to discover the other's interests, which are the real needs behind their positions (or requests). Positions are just one of many strategic ways to satisfy one's interests. However, there are often several ways to address each other's interests. Participants who do not know each other's actual interests can ask the other questions like "Why do you want this?" Conversations during the negotiation process should unfold around both participants' interests to find ways to fairly meet them.

According to Kelley (1990), participants in a negotiation process should avoid using *ad hominen* arguments, which dismiss the argument of others by attacking them in a personal way. According to this author, an example of this type of erroneous argument is: "The agreement cannot be reached because you are not capable of understanding the complexity of this transaction."

Caspersen (2015) suggested that one's comments should always be focused on the interaction with the other person ("You left the room suddenly") based on one's observation, instead of making personal judgements on how they are ("Your behaviour is rude"). All observations should be made in a warm and loving manner.

The participants should also aim to always use assertive vocabulary, which implies communicating one's needs in a calm and firm manner, instead of doing so in an aggressive way. Caspersen (2015) suggests the use of sentences like "When (the triggering event) happened, I felt (my feeling) because (my need/interest) is really important to me. Would you be willing to (request a doable action)?" to express one's emotions, needs, and requests.

All agreements should be based on objective principles (e.g., statistics, expert opinion, market average price, etc.), not arbitrary ones. Each participant should ask one another about the objective evidence that justifies their own position. Kelley (1990) observed that participants should avoid providing subjective arguments ("This is the price that I want") or emotional ones ("In your heart, you know that this is the best price…").

Lastly, Leech (1983) suggested a conversational maxim to contribute to an agreement with others. According to this maxim, each party should reduce the amount of statements which imply disagreement, and instead maximise those statements which imply agreement. An example of statements which imply agreement is: "I am sure that we will develop a co-operative agreement working together."

Appendix F: Empathetic Use of Social Media

F.1 Main Characteristic of Social Media

The social media platforms are valuable environments, through which companies can engage with their different stakeholders. These platforms allow companies to develop two-way communication, tantamount to personal conversations. These virtual tools are participative because people can openly and overtly express their opinions, either positive or negative.

Some companies use different social media platforms to enhance their image; these virtual environments provide organisations with priceless visibility and an online presence. All information published on social media is shown in real time and in a direct manner.

Social media is an easy-to-use, integrative, and democratic environment, because it allows individuals and organisations to develop networks, whose members can be accessed directly. On these social platforms, information can be disclosed with immediacy. Belonging to a virtual community contributes to a sense of bonding between the participants. Nonetheless, in this virtual environment, it is often difficult to verify the trustworthiness and credentials of the participants.

These platforms are relevant socialising spaces, where virtual relationships with others can progressively be developed; they are also equalisers because of their free access for everybody. Relationships online tend to be strengthened by sharing common interests and learning from one another on a regular basis. Therefore, the use of specific ways of communicating ideas (like story-telling) is very common and valuable.

Virtual relationships cannot be compared with the realness and authenticity of offline relationships. Online interactions are less complete and deep, and more intermittent and ephemeral than offline ones. Many people argue that on social media, there is no human connection with real people, but with abstract profiles which seem to look good to try to grab others' attention.

Nonetheless, these platforms allow participants to connect with people or organisations which would otherwise not have been possible, if it were not for social media. Lindgren (2017) observed that online platforms represent computer-mediated environments of affinity where participants can experience "*virtual togetherness.*"

Tuten and Solomon (2017) observed that social media has four main purposes: developing communities (which involves online networking sharing, socialising, and chatting), social publishing (which includes editorial activities with content generated by the user), social commerce (which includes retailing and customer service activities), and social entertainment (music, games, art, etc.). These authors also stated that people engage in social media for different reasons: affinity, utility or personal gain, helping others, curiosity, and ego-validation, among others.

Safko and Brake (2009) observed that there are several categories of social media, such as social networking, publishing (blogs, wikis, etc.), photo, audio, video, microblogging, livecasting (online radio and TV), virtual worlds, gaming, productivity applications (Gmail, Yahoo!, etc.), aggregators (gathering and sharing information, for example, Reddit, Yelp), RSS (sending information useful for your organisation), search (Google search, Yahoo! search), mobile applications, and interpersonal tools (Skype).

F.2 Companies and Social Media

Social media, as audience-oriented platforms, allow companies to post messages, upload pictures and videos, or publish articles with no cost. In that sense, the barriers to entry to these platforms are very low; all companies can publish content online, regardless of their size.

Companies who utilise social media should always adopt a generous attitude; they should provide their audience with valuable free content on a regular basis. The content published should be changed frequently, avoiding rehashing previous information. New content should be distinct and attractive, and aim to cater to the audience's needs.

Companies should never use these platforms to hard-sell their products or services. Any reference to company products or services should be subtly included, preferably after having provided substantial free high-quality content. McKenna (2012a) expressed the view that social media platforms can be used for story-telling: for instance, by telling tales about successful customer experiences. Safko and Brake (2009) state that the main objectives of the content published on social media should always be communication, collaboration, education, and entertainment. This content could include both opinion and factual information.

Messages posted by a company should be congruent across all social media platforms, which means they should not have any contradictions. All these messages published by an organisation should support one another, as part of the company's overall digital communication strategy. These messages should also be coherent with the rest of the messages conveyed by the organisation in other ways: for example, events, mail, adverts, company's website, etc.

Most companies need to become more active on social media and regularly publish attractive content. The content published defines the organisation and distinguishes it from other organisations. A company should choose content which piques the audience's curiosity and prompts them to participate willingly. There is a positive correlation between high-quality content posted by an organisation and the endorsement it receives from audiences.

Authentic and worthy content generates the spontaneous engagement of community members. A company which posts high-quality information on a frequent basis tends to be perceived by visitors as a caring organisation. Oftentimes, companies replicate their content in several platforms, using different formats. In those cases, several platforms can also be linked to one another.

When possible, after new content is posted the company should invite their audience to participate and also express their views and opinions on the information published. Companies can also pose open-ended questions to prompt the audiences to participate. Most community members are very opinionated; they have the urge to express their views overtly and freely. Every time members of an audience give their opinions, a company can obtain valuable insights. On social media platforms, individuals are empowered to comment about topics in an open and fluid manner, through digital, sociable, and non-face-to-face interactions.

F.3 Other Aspects of Companies and Social Media

These content-oriented platforms are popular because they foster the equal participation of individuals and organisations. Consequently, companies should never censor any opinion, even negative ones. This attitude positions a company as transparent in the eyes of the audience. However, companies should never allow community members to be offensive or aggressive with their comments. Clear participation rules based on respect and inclusiveness should be clearly set and disclosed by the company.

These virtual spaces are useful to debate relevant topics, oftentimes in a heated manner, and are paramount sources of relevant feedback about a company's activities, products, and services. Oftentimes, companies consider audience members' comments as starting points for making adjustments in their offerings.

A company should regularly express its views regarding different topics on these platforms. Companies representatives can directly connect to audience members in order to clarify doubts or offer them valuable advice. Companies can also use social media as an online research tool to scan trends, consumption patterns, and technological advancements.

Customers always leave valuable "footprints" on social media platforms to be used by a company as data to improve its products and services. Companies can assemble a myriad of traces left by customers on social media platforms for research purposes. The use of this online research tool is low-cost because all the information is available online, free for the taking. Organisations can complement this data with information from other sources, such as interviews, focus groups, etc.

Social media always empowers individuals to express their views openly, without being subject to any gatekeeping or editing forces. This trait makes social media more credible than traditional media, because customers can share their reviews and recommendations of products and services unrestrainedly.

Customers' comments cannot be controlled by companies, which makes these comments more trustworthy. These reviews and recommendations are known as word of mouth. Oftentimes, specific pieces of content become viral, which means they are cascaded swiftly and profusely over a virtual community.

Appendix G: Additional Ways to Generate Intuitive Insights

When people regularly focus on their desired states (the goals they want to achieve) they are activating their reticular activating systems (R.A.S.). As seen in Chapter 1, the R.A.S. is the part of the brain which screens out irrelevant information in the environment and helps a person detect relevant data. The working of this system is congruent with a well-known saying which goes "what you focus your attention on, increases."

In simple words, if a person concentrated on a topic frequently that person will tend to receive valuable insights (e.g., opportunities, people, places, situations, and information) related to this very topic and also automatically discard any information unrelated to it. The activation of the R.A.S. can be obtained in different ways, which are prone to bring about intuitive insights:

G.1 Setting Objectives

Research has shown that people who set clear objectives for different areas of their lives are more prone to succeed than those who don't. Purdie (2010) observed the objectives must be set using the SMARTENUP acronym, which means specific, measurable, attainable, realistic, time-bound, enthusiastic, naturally defined, understood by the individual or the company's people and (well-) prepared.

A company's goals should also be congruent with the mission and corporate aims. From the systemic perspective, a company's objectives should also consider the impact on different stakeholders (employees, customers, suppliers, community, etc.).

Objectives should be measurable in order to know they have been adequately achieved. However, as seen previously, some qualities, such as kindness, generosity, gratitude, and compassion cannot be measured accurately, because they are not quantifiable.

O'Connor (2001) observed that a person or organisation that sets objectives should include other elements such as specific evidence that objectives have been achieved, necessary resources to achieve these outcomes, and potential benefits of achieving these goals. This author also observed that objectives must be congruent with other objectives and with the identity of the objective-setter. This specialist also recommends that companies and individuals set goals that are worthy and ambitious, especially for the medium and long term.

Objectives are cues people use to meet their needs; a person who sets objectives tends to be more motivated to find effective ways to achieve them. Goals should always be worded in a positive way, by focusing on the desired state, not on what should be avoided. When a person words goals, they should avoid words which imply lack (e.g., "I want ..." or "I wish ...") and use positive wording instead (such as "I choose ..." or "I deserve ...").

From a rational perspective, Covey (1992) observed that objectives should always include what the person or organisation wants to achieve, why the person wants to achieve these goals, and how these objectives will be attained. From an intuitive perspective, when people set their goals, they should not be focused so much on "how" these goals will be achieved. Instead, these individuals should be centred on their desired states frequently, and be receptive to any useful intuitive insights into ways to achieve these goals. Some other relevant aspects related to objectives are:

■ Setting goals is a powerful strategic and motivating tool which helps people move forward in a more effective and planned manner. When people are focused on specific goals, they are more likely to gain momentum and less prone to be sidetracked. Nonetheless, if the goals are too rigid, the person can have difficulties adapting to changing circumstances.
■ The objectives to achieve (for example, to find a solution to a specific problem) can be written on a piece of paper in a clear manner. When people read their objectives regularly, their R.A.S. are reactivated, and their brain will tend to laser-focus on information relevant to these objectives.
■ Amabile and Kramer (2011, 2012) observed that setting clear and meaningful objectives is a valuable tool to generate creative insights, especially when a person has time to work on their attainment. These authors also concluded that minimal daily progress regarding these objectives can contribute to the development of creative and outstanding ideas.

Fritz (1984, 2003) observed that not only should people set their goals, but also recognise and accept their current state (status quo) and confront both (goals and current states) to create "structural tension," which tends to be resolved as people take creative action to achieve these goals. This author also stated that the objectives should be set to create end results (e.g., going toward wanted situations) and not to solve problems (e.g., getting rid of unwanted circumstances).

The aforementioned perspective is related to a model used in business coaching activities called GROW, which means G for setting Goals (and envisioning them), R for comparing them with the current Reality (present circumstances), O for assessing the most adequate Options, and W for taking respective actions (Will).

G.2 Use of Envisioning

The human mind cannot differentiate real things from imagined ones. Visualisation is a transformative tool which implies forming mental images, by using the five senses internally. When people visualise a desired state frequently, these images are embedded in their subconscious minds, which with the help of the R.A.S. will find effective ways to achieve these very states. Visualisation has been used by great luminaries such as Einstein, da Vinci, and Tesla, among others.

People should visualise their desired state in a vivid and detailed way. Images must be as compelling and vivid as possible. When people visualise, they can use colourful images and also include other senses (tactile sensations, sounds, etc.). People can also imagine the positive emotions they would experience when the objectives have already been achieved.

During the visualisation process, the images must be in the "first person;" people should imagine themselves as the protagonists, not as mere witnesses. It is not advisable for people to view themselves in a detached way (as a witness of themselves). When people practise visualisation regularly, the gap between their current state and their desired one tends to be bridged gradually. Allen (2003) observed that positive envisioning improves the quality of a person's perception, feelings, thoughts, and decisions; this specialist also observed that "a vision of a desired future allows you to focus on an improved condition."

Envisioning is used by many companies worldwide. In some cases, when the company's people mentally see the future desired state, they can also envision in a backward manner the steps that would have been required to arrive at the achievement of this desired state. The use of visualisation also imprints the subconscious with vivid images, which will help the person incubate innovative approaches to the situation visualised.

Lastly, Wiseman (2009) develops the concept of doublethink. From this perspective, not only should the people visualise their desired goals, but they should also devote some time to imagining potential issues which might affect the achievement of these goals, and imagine how to surmount these difficulties. This specialist stated that the doublethink tool proved to be more effective than only visualising future desired states, because the imagining is accompanied by the realistic assessment of potential difficulties.

G.3 Use of Positive Statements

The use of positive statements also called "affirmations" is also a powerful tool to obtain intuitive insights. These statements are worded in a positive way and can stem from goals previously set. When a person continuously repeats these affirmations, mentally or aloud, they become embedded in their subconscious minds; with the help of their R.A.S., they will be guided to find effective ways to attain the outcomes related to these affirmations.

A person should repeat these positive statements in an assertive manner. If possible, they should also evoke emotions congruent to the ones they expect to experience when these outcomes are attained. These positive commands should be worded in a personal and meaningful manner. Present tense should be used to word these statements ("I choose ...," "I allow ...," "I see myself ...," "I deserve ...," "I feel well doing ...," "I am empowered to ...," or "I enjoy ..."), avoiding words which imply lack (such as "wish," "desire," "want," and any similar ones). When employed on a regular basis, these statements programme the person's mind positively, and helps this individual develop insightful alternatives.

Bibliography

Abrams, R. C. 2017. *Body wise. Discovering Your Body's Intelligence for Lifelong Health and Healing.* London: Blue Bird.

Achor, S. 2011. *The Happiness Advantage. How a Positive Brain Fuels Success in Work and Life.* London: Virgin Books.

Alderfer, C. P. 1972. *Existence, Relatedness and Growth: Human Needs in Organizational Settings.* New York, NY: Free Press.

Alessandra, T. and M. O'Connor. 1998. *The Platinum Rule. Discover the Four Basic Business Personalities and How They Can Lead You to Success.* New York, NY: Warner Book.

Allen, D. 2003. *Ready for Everything. 52 Productivity Principles for Getting Things Done.* New York, NY: Viking.

Allen, P. and G. Wotten. 1998. *Selling.* Harlow, UK: FT Prentice Hall.

Alofs, P. 2013. *Passion Capital. The World's Most Valuable Asset.* Toronto: Signal.

Amabile, T. and S. Kramer. 2011. The Power of Small Wins. *Harvard Business Review.* [Online] Available at: https://hbr.org/2011/05/the-power-of-small-wins (Accessed: September 16, 2018).

Amabile, T. and S. Kramer. 2012. The Progress principle: Optimising Inner Work life to Create Value. *Rotman Magazine.* Winter 2012: 28–33

Angell, P. and T. Rizkallah. 2004. *Business Communication Design: Creativity Strategies and Solutions.* New York, NY: McGraw-Hill.

Apps, J. 2012. *Voice and Speaking Skills for Dummies.* Chichester, UK: Wiley.

Apps, J. 2014. *The Art of Conversation. Change Your Life with Confident Communication.* Chichester, UK: Capstone.

Arden, P. 2006. *Whatever You Think, Think the Opposite.* London: Penguin Books.

Argyle, M. 1994. *The Psychology of Interpersonal Behaviour.* London: Penguin Books.

Arnold, W. W. and J. M. Plas. 1993. *The Human Touch. Today's Most Unusual Program for Productivity and Profit.* New York, NY: Wiley.

Ashkanasy, N. M. and C. E. Ashton-James. 2007. Positive Emotion in Organizations: A Multi-Level Framework. In Nelson, D. and C. L. Cooper (Eds.). *Positive Organizational Behaviour. Accentuating the Positive at Work,* 57–73. London: Sage.

Assagioli, R. 1974. *The Act of Will.* London: Wildwood House.

Atkinson, R., Smith, E., and Bem, E. et al. 1981. *Hilgard's Introduction to Psychology.* New York, NY: Harcourt Brace College Publishers.

Autry, J. A. and S. Mitchell. 1998. *Real Power. Business Lessons from the Tao Te Ching.* London. Nicholas Brealey.

Bacci, I. 2002. *The Art of Effortless Living.* London: Bantam Books.

Baker, S. and D. L. Martinson. 2002. Out of the Red-Light District. Five Principles for Ethically Proactive Public Relations. *Public Relations Quarterly.* 47(3), 12–15.

Bailes, F. 2004. *Basic Principles of the Science of Mind.* Marina del Rey, CA: De Vorss Publications.

Barge, J. K. and C. Oliver. 2003. Working with Appreciation in Managerial Practice. *Academy of Management Review.* 28, 124–142.

Barsade, S. G. and O. A. O'Neill. 2014. What's Love Got to Do With It? A Longitudinal Study of the Culture of Companionate Love and Employee and Client Outcomes in a Long-Term Care Setting. *Administrative Science Quarterly.* 59(4), 551–598.

Baudelaire, C. 2010. *The Painter of Modern Life*. London: Penguin Classics.

Baumeister, R. F. and M. R. Leary. 1995. The Need to Belong: Desire for Interpersonal Attachments as a Fundamental Human Motivation. *Psychological Bulletin*. 117(3), 497–529.

Baumeister, R. F., Bratslavsky, E., Finkenauer, C. et al. 2001. Bad is Stronger than Good. *Review of General Psychology*. 5(4), 323–370.

Bautan, Z. 2017. Being Populist Is Not Always Bad (in Spanish). Ser Populista No Es Siempre Malo. *Perfil Newspaper*. January 9, 2017. [Online] Available at: www.perfil.com/internacional/zygmunt-bauman-s er-populista-no-es-siempre-malo.phtml (Accessed: September 16, 2018).

Bayer, L. 2016. *The 30% Solution. How Civility at Work Increases Retention, Engagement, and Profitability*. Melbourne: Motivational Press.

Beck R. C. 2012. *Motivation. Themes and Principles*. Upper Saddle River, NJ: Pearson Education.

Bell, C. R. and J. R. Patterson. 2007. *Customer loyalty guaranteed: Create, lead, and sustain remarkable customer service*. Avon, MA: Adams Business.

Berne, E. 1964. *Games People Play*. New York, NY: Grove Press.

Bernstein, E. S. and S. Turban. 2018. The Impact of the 'Open' Workspace on Human Collaboration. *Philosophical Transaction of Royal Society B*. 373(1753). [Online] Available at: http://dx.doi.org/10.1098/rstb.2017.0239 (accessed December, 19 2018).

Bevelin, P. 2017. *Seeking Wisdom*. Sweden: Post Scriptum.

Bill, L. 2002. *Power up Your brain*. London: Nicolas Brealey Publishing.

Blackburn, E. and E. Epel. 2017. *The Telomere Effect. A Revolutionary Approach to Living Younger, Healthier, Longer*. London: Orion Spring.

Blundel, R. 2004. *Effective Organisational Communication. Perspectives, Principles and Practices*. Harlow, UK: FT Prentice Hall.

Bridges, C. 2017. *In Your Creative Element. The Formula for Creative Success in Business*. London: Kogan Page.

Briskin, A. 1998. *The Stirring of the Soul in the Workplace*. San Francisco, CA: Berrett Koehler Publishers.

Bodian, S. 2006. *Meditation for Dummies*. Indianapolis, IN: Wiley.

Bolton, S. C. and M. Houlihan. 2009. Are We Having Fun Yet? A Consideration of Workplace Fun and Engagement. *Employee Relations*. 31(6), 556–568.

Borg, J. 2011. *Body Language. How to Know What's Really Been Said*. London: Pearson.

Bragg, A. and M. Bragg. 2005. *Developing New Business Ideas. A Step-by-Step Guide to Creating New Business Ideas Worth Backing*. Harlow, UK: FT Prentice Hall.

Brandenburger, A. M. and B. J. Nalebuff. 1996. *Co-Opetition*. New York, NY: Doubleday.

Brewer, S. 2010. *Cut Your Stress. An Easy-to-Follow Guide for Stress-Free Living*. London: Quercus.

Brooksbank, R. 2002. *Hot Marketing. Cool Profits. 200 Proven Sales and Marketing Ideas to Grow Your Business*. Sydney: McGraw-Hill.

Brown, P. and S. C. Levinson. 1987. *Politeness. Some Universals in Language Usage*. Cambridge: Cambridge University Press.

Brown, S. 1997. *Practical Feng Shui. Arrange, Decorate and Accessorize Your Home to Promote Health, Wealth and Happiness*. London: Ward Lock.

Brown, S. and C. Vaughan. 2010. *Play. How It Shapes the Brain, Opens the Imagination and Invigorates The Soul*. New York, NY: Penguin Group.

Bryant, J. H. 2009. *Love Leadership. The New Way to Lead in a Fear-Based World*. San Francisco, CA: Jossey Bass.

Buckingham, W., Brunham, D., Hill, C. et al. 2011. *The Philosophy Book*. London: DK.

Burg, B. and J. D., Mahn. 2010. *The Go-Giver. A Little Story About a Powerful Business Idea*. Penguin Books: London.

Bushe, G. R. 2011. Appreciative Inquiry: Theory and Critique. In Boje, D., Burnes, B. and J. Hassard (Eds.). *The Routledge Companion to Organizational Change*, 87–103. Oxford: Routledge.

Bushe, G. R. 2013. The Appreciative Inquiry Model. In Kessler, H. (Ed.). *Encyclopedia of Management Theory*. Los Angeles, CA: Sage. [Online] Available at: http://www.gervasebushe.ca/the_AI_model.pdf (accessed December, 19 2018).

Butler, G. and T. Hope. 2008. *Manage Your Mind*. Oxford: Oxford University Press.

Buzan, T. 2000. *Head First. 10 Ways to Tap into Your Natural Genius.* London: Thorsons.

Buzan, T. 2002. *How to Mind Map. The Thinking Tool That Will Change Your life.* London: Thorsons.

Buzan, T. and B. Buzan. 2003. *The Mindmap Book. Unlock Your Creativity, Boost Your Memory, Change Your Life.* London: BBS Books.

Buzan, T. and C. Griffins. 2014. *Mind Maps for Business. Using the Ultimate Thinking Tool to Revolutionise How You Work.* Harlow: Pearson Education.

Cameron, W. B. 1963. *Informal Sociology, a Casual Introduction to Sociological Thinking.* New York, NY. Random House.

Campbell, D., Coldicott, T. and K. Kinsella. 1994. *Systemic Work with Organisations. A New Model for Managers and Change Agents.* London: Karnac Books.

Campbell, E. (Ed.). 1992. *A Lively Flame.* London: The Aquarian Press.

Campbell, E. 1996. *Love and Relationships.* London: Thorsons.

Cannon, W. 1915. *Bodily Changes in Pain, Hunger, Fear and Rage: An Account of Recent Researches into the Function of Emotional Excitement.* New York, NY: D. Appleton.

Cardone, G. 2011. *The 10X rule. The Only Difference Between Success and Failure.* Hoboken, NJ: Wiley.

Carlson, R. 1999. *Don't Sweat the Small Stuff at Work. Simple Ways to Minimize Stress and Conflict While Bringing Out the Best in Yourself and Others.* London: Hodder and Stoughton.

Carlson, R. and J. Bailey. 1998. *Slowing Down to the Speed of Life. How to Create a More Peaceful, Simpler Life from the Inside Out.* London: Hodder and Stoughton.

Cash, A. 2013. *Psychology for Dummies.* Hoboken, NJ: Wiley.

Caspersen, D. 2015. *Changing the Conversations. The 17 Principles of Conflict Resolution.* London: Profile Books.

Castells, M. 1996. *The Rise of the Network Society.* Malden, MA: Blackwell Publishers.

Chan, J. and J. Rogers. 2015. *Infinite Abundance. Becoming a Spiritual Millionaire.* Manchester, UK: Light Foundation.

Chaston, I. 2004. *Knowledge-Based Marketing. The 21st Century Competitive Edge.* London. Sage.

Chersniske, S. A. 1998. *The DHEA Breakthrough.* New York, NY. Ballantine Books.

Childre, D., Martin, H. and D. Beech. 2000. *The HeartMath Solution. The Institute of HeartMath's Revolutionary Program for Engaging the Power of the Heart's Intelligence.* New York, NY: Harper Collins.

Cialdini, R. 2009. *Influence. The Psychology of Persuasion.* Boston, MA: Pearson.

Cialdini, R. 2016. *Pre-suasion. A Revolutionary Way to Influence and Persuade.* London: Random House Books.

Claflin, E. 1998. *Age Protectors. Stop Aging Now!* Emmaus, PA: Rodale.

Clare, J. 2018. *Storytelling. The Presenter's Secret Weapon.* London: Lionsden Publishing.

Cohen, D. and L. Prusak. 2001. *In Good Company. How Social Capital Makes Organizations Work.* Boston, MA: Harvard Business School Press.

Collard, P. 2014. *The Little Book of Mindfulness.* London: Gaia.

Collin, C., Benson, N., Ginsburg, J. et al. 2012. *The Psychology Book.* London: DK.

Collins, J. 2001. *Good to Great.* London: Random House.

Collins, J. and J. Porras. 2005. *Build to Last. Successful Habits of Visionary Companies.* London: Random House.

Collison, C. and G. Parcell. 2004. *Learning to Fly. Practical Knowledge Management from Leading and Learning Organizations.* Chichester, UK: Capstone.

Conner, D. 2010. Spiritual Wholeness. Operationalizing the Intangible. In Shelton, C. and M. Lynn (Ed.). *Good Business. Putting Spiritual Principles into Practice at Work.* Unity Village, MO: Unity House. 28–51

Cooper, R. and A. Sawaf. 1998. *Executive EQ. Emotional Intelligence in Business.* London: Orion Business Books.

Corley, T. 2009. *Rich Habits. The Daily Success Habits of Wealthy Individuals.* Minneapolis, MN: Langdon Street Press.

Cornelissen, J. 2017. *Corporate Communication. A Guide to Theory and Practice.* London: Sage.

Covey, S. 1992. *The 7 Habits of Highly Effective People. Powerful Lessons in Personal Change.* London: Simon & Schuster.

Cranwell-Ward J., Bacon, A. and R. Mackie. 2002. *Inspiring Leadership. Staying Afloat in Turbulent Times.* London: Thomson.

Csikszentmihalyi, M. 2002. *Flow. The Classic Work on How to Achieve Happiness.* London: Rider.

Csikszentmihalyi, M. 2003. *Good Business. Leadership, Flow and the Making of Meaning.* London: Coronet Books.

Cuddy, A. 2016. *Presence. Bringing Your Boldest Self to Your Biggest Challenges.* London: Orion Publishing Group.

Cyrulnik, B. 2009. *Resilience. How Your Inner Strength Can Set You Free from the Past.* London: Penguin Books.

Daft, R. and G. Huber. 1986. *How Organizations Learn a Communication Framework. Organizations as Information Processing Systems.* College Station, TX: Department of Management, Texas A&M University.

Dalai Lama and H. C. Cuttler. 1998. *The Art of Happiness. A Handbook for Living.* London: Hodder and Stoughton.

Dalmasio, A. 2012. *Self Comes to Mind. Constructing the Conscious Brain.* London: Vintage Books.

Davis, M., Eshelman, E. and M. McKay. 2008. *The Relaxation and Stress Reduction Workbook.* Oakland, CA: New Harbinger Publications.

De Barren, S. 1988. *You Are the Key.* London: Wellspring Publications.

De Board, R. 1978. *The Psychoanalysis of Organizations. Psychoanalytic Approach to Behaviour in Groups and Organizations.* London: Tavistock Publications.

De Bono, E. 1970. *Lateral Thinking.* London: Penguin Books.

De Bono, E. 1977. *The Happiness Purpose.* London: Penguin Books.

De Bono, E. 1978. *Opportunities. A Handbook of Business Opportunity Search.* London: Penguin Books.

De Bono, E. 1986. *Tactics. The Art and Science of Success.* Dorset: Fontana.

De Bono, E. 1998. *Simplicity.* London: Penguin House.

De Bono, E. 2004. *How to Have a Beautiful Mind.* London: Vermillion.

De Bono, E. 2013. *Thinking to Create Value.* Malta: Kite.

De Botton, A. 2010. *The Consolations of Philosophy.* London: Penguin Books.

De Botton, A. 2016a. Economic Demand. *School of Life.* January 11, 2016. [Online] Available at: www.youtube.com/watch?v=VvTzaNUDVms (Accessed: September 16, 2018).

De Botton, A. 2016b. How to Remain Calm with People. *School of Life.* July 4, 2016. [Online] Available at: www.youtube.com/watch?v=du035tg-SwY (Accessed: October 5, 2018).

Decety, J. and W. Ickes (Eds.). 2011. *The Social Neuroscience of Empathy.* Boston, MA: MIT Press.

De Mello, A. 1990. *Awareness.* Grand Rapids, MI: Zondervan.

Deunov, P. 2004. *Love Is All-Forgiving. Reflections on Love and Spirituality.* Deerfield Beach, FL: Health Communications Inc.

DeVrye, C. 2000. *Hot Lemon and Honey. Reflections for Success in Times of Change.* Manly, Australia: Everest Press.

Dilts, R. 1994. *Strategies of Genius. Volume 1.* Capitola, CA: Meta Publications.

Dilts, R., Hallbom, T. and S. Smith. 2012. *Beliefs. Pathways to Health and Well-Being.* Carmarthen, UK: Crown House.

Dixon, N. 2000. *The Organization Learning Cycle. How We Can Learn Collectively.* Aldershot, UK: Gowen Publishing Limited.

Dobelli, R. 2014. *The Art of Thinking Clearly.* New York, NY: Harper.

Dodgson, M. and D. M. Gann. 2018. *The Playful Entrepreneur. How to Adapt and Thrive in Uncertain Times.* Padstow, UK: Yale University Press.

Dooley, M. 2010. *Infinite Possibilities. The Art of Living Your Dreams.* Hillsboro, OR: Beyond Words.

Drucker, P. F. 1973. *Management: Tasks, Responsibilities and Practices.* New York, NY: Harper and Row.

Drucker, P. F. 1999. *Managing Challenges for the 21st Century.* New York, NY: HarperBusiness.

Drucker, P. F. 2007. *Innovation and Entrepreneurship. Practice and Principles.* Oxford: Elsevier.

Drummond, N. 2002. *The Spirit of Success. How to Connect Your Heart to Your Head in Work and Life.* London: Hodder and Stoughton.

D'Souza, S. and D. Renner. 2014. *Not Knowing. The Art of Turning Uncertainty into Opportunity.* London: LID.

Duckworth, A. 2017. *Grit. Why Passion and Resilience Are the Secrets to Success.* London: Vermilion.

Duncan, T. 2002. *High Trust Selling. Make More Money in Less Time with Less Stress.* Nashville, TN: Thomas Nelson Publishing.

Dweck, C. 2012. *Mindset. How You Can Fulfil Your Potential.* London: Robinson.

Dyer, W. 1976. *Your Erroneous Zones.* New York, NY: Quill.

Dyer, W. 1989. *You Will See It When You Believe It.* New York, NY: Avon Books.

Edwards, B. 1993. *Drawing on the Right Side of the Brain. How to Unlock Your Hidden Artistic Talent.* London: Harper Collins.

Edelman, M. W. 1993. *The Measure of Our Success: A Letter to My Children and Yours.* New York, NY: Harper Perennial.

Egan, G. 1994. *The Skilled Helper. A Problem-Management Approach to Learning.* Monterey, CA: Brooks Cole Publishing Company.

Egan, J. 2011. *Relationship Marketing. Explore Relational Strategies in Marketing.* London: FT Prentice Hall.

Ehrenreich, B. 2006. *Dancing in the Streets. A History of Collective Joy.* New York, NY: Metropolitan Books.

Ellis, A. and R. Harper. 1997. *A Guide to Rational Living.* Hollywood, CA: Melvin Power Wilshire Book Company.

Emerson, R. W. 1981. *Emerson's Essays.* New York, NY: Harper Perennial.

Emery, F. (Ed.). 1959. *System Thinking.* London: Penguin Books.

Emoto, M. 2004. *The Hidden Messages in Water.* Hillsboro, OR: Beyond Words Publishing.

Engelhart, M. and T. Engelhart. 2008 *Sacred Commerce. Business as a Path of Awakening.* Berkeley, CA: North Atlantic Books.

Enos, R. 2018. 7 Sketches That You Won't Believe Represent a State of Anarchy. *Collective Consciousness.* August 2018. [Online] Available at: www.collective-evolution.com/2018/08/19/7-sketches-that-you-wont-believe-represent-a-state-of-anarchy/ (Accessed: September 16, 2018).

Ericsson, K. A., Krampe, R. T. and C. Tesch-Romer. 1993. The Role of Deliberate Practice in the Acquisition of Expert Performance. *Psychological Review.* 100(3), 363–406.

Ettlie, J. E. 2006. *Managing Innovation. New Technology, New Product and New Services in a Global Economy.* Oxford: Elsevier/Butterworth Heinemann.

Evans, J. 2012. *Philosophy for Life and Other Dangerous Situations.* London: Rider.

Fayol, H. 1949. *General and Industrial Management.* London: Pitman.

Ferriss, T. 2017. Why You Should Define Your Fears Instead of Your Goals. July 14, 2017. [Online] Available at: www.youtube.com/watch?v=5J6jAC6XxAI (Accessed: September 16, 2018).

Fiebleman, J. and F. W. Friend. 1945. The Structure and Function of an Organisation. *Phil. Rev.* 54: 19–44.

Fisher, R., Ury, W. and B. Patton. 1999. *Getting to Yes. Negotiating an Agreement Without Giving In.* London: Random House.

Ford, C. and D. Gioia (Eds.). 1995. *Creative Action in Organizations. Ivory Tower Visions and Real World Voices.* London: Sage.

Fox, E. 2010. *The Mental Equivalent.* Princeton, NJ: Princeton Licensing Group.

Fox, M. 1995. *The Reinvention of Work. A New Vision of Livelihood for Our Time.* San Francisco, CA: Harper.

Fontana, D. 1999. *Learn to Meditate. The Art of Tranquillity, Self-Awareness and Insight.* London: Duncan Baird.

Forgas, J. P., Bower, G. H. and S. Krantz. 1984. The Influence of Mood on Perceptions of Social Interactions. *Journal of Personality and Social Psychology.* 20, 497–513.

Frankl, V. 2006. *Man's Search for Meaning.* Boston, MA: Beacon Press.

Fredrickson, B. 2013. *Love 2.0. How our Supreme Emotions Affect Everything We Think, Do, Feel and Become.* New York, NY: Hudson Street Press.

Freire, P. 2005. *Pedagogy of the Oppressed.* New York, NY: Continuum.

Friedman, A. and S. Miles. 2006. *Stakeholders. Theory and Practice.* Oxford: Oxford University Press.

Fritz, R. 1984. *The Path of Least Resistance. Principles for Creating What You Want to Create.* New York, NY: Fawcett Books.

Fritz, R. 1991. *Creating.* New York, NY: Fawcett Columbine.

Fritz, R. 1999. *The Path of Least Resistance for Managers. Designing Organizations to Succeed.* San Francisco, CA. Berrett Koehler Publishers.

Fritz, R. 2003. *Your Life as Art.* Newfane, VT: Newfane Press.

Fritz, R. 2007. *Elements. The Writing of Robert Fritz.* Newfane, VT: Newfane Press.

Fromm, E. 1956. *The Art of Loving.* New York, NY: Harper & Row.

Fromm, E. 1966. *Fear of Freedom.* London: Routledge & Keegan Paul Ltd.

Fromm, E. 1976. *To Have or to Be?* London: Abacus.

Gallo, C. 2011. *The Innovation Secrets of Steve Jobs. Insanely Different Principles for Breakthrough Success.* New York, NY: McGraw-Hill.

Gamon, A. and D. Bragdon. 2002. *Building Mental Muscle. Conditioning Exercises for the Six Intelligence Zones.* London: Pocket Books.

Gamon, A. and D. Bragdon. 2003. *Building Left-Brain Power: Conditioning Exercises and Tips for Left-Brain Skills.* New York, NY: Walker & Company.

Gamon, A. and D. Bragdon. 2008. *Learn Faster, Remember More.* New Lanark, UK: Geddes and Grosset.

Gardner, H. 2006. *Multiple intelligences. New Horizons in Theory and Practice.* New York, NY: Basic Books.

Garnham, A. and J. Oakhill. 1994. *Thinking and Reasoning.* Oxford: Blackwell.

Gasper, K. and L. A. Spencer. 2018. Affective Ingredients: Recipes for Understanding How Affective States Alter Cognitive Outcomes. In Diener, E., Oishi, S. and L. Tay (Eds.). *Handbook of Well-Being.* Salt Lake City, UT: DEF Publishers. [Online] Available at: www.nobascholar.com/chapters/41/download.pdf (Accessed: December 20, 2018).

Gelb, M. 1998. *How to Think Like Leonardo da Vinci. Seven Steps to Genius Every Day.* London: Thorsons.

Giddens, A. 2009. *Sociology.* Cambridge: Polity Press.

Gilbert, P. 2009. *The Compassionate Mind.* London: Constable.

Gilbert, P. and Choden. 2013. *Mindful Compassion. Using the Power of Mindfulness and Compassion to Transform Our Lives.* London: Robinson.

Goffman, E. 1967. *On Face-Work: Interaction Ritual.* Harmondsworth: Penguin Books.

Goffman, E. 1969. *The Presentation of Self in Everyday Life.* New York, NY: Penguin Books.

Goldsmith, M. and M. Reiter. 2008. *What Got You Here Won't Get You There. How Successful People Become Even More Successful.* London: Profile.

Goleman, D. 1996. *Emotional Intelligence. Why It Can Matter More Than IQ.* London: Bloomsbury.

Goleman, D. 1998. *Working with Emotional Intelligence.* London: Bloomsbury.

Goleman, D. 2006. *Social Intelligence. The New Science of Human Relationships.* New York, NY: Bantam.

Goleman, D. 2014. *Focus. The Hidden Driver of Excellence.* New York, NY: Bloomsbury.

Goleman, D., Kaufman, P. and M. Ray. 1995. *The Creative Spirit.* New York, NY: Plume.

Good, D., Lyddy, C. J., Glomb, T. M. et al. 2016. Contemplating Mindfulness at Work. An Integrative Review. *Journal of Management.* 42(1), 114–142.

Gorman, P. 2004. *The Game of Business and How to Play It.* London: Big Sur Publishing.

Goswami, A. 2014. *Quantum Creativity. Think Quantum, Be Creative.* London: Hay House.

Gottman, J. 1994. *Why Marriages Succeed or Fail.* New York, NY: Simon & Schuster.

Grant, P. (Ed.). 2005. *Business Psychology in Practice.* London: Whurr Publishers.

Gray, A. E. 2015. Speak: Some Thoughts on Somatic Psychotherapies in International Contexts. Somatic Psychotherapy Beyond Borders. *Somatic Psychotherapy Today.* Fall 2015, 5(4), 30–37.

Greene, R. 2012. *Mastery.* London: Profile Books.

Greenleaf, R. 1991. *The Servant as Leader.* Indianapolis, IN: The Robert K. Greenleaf Center.

Greenleaf, R. 1996. *On Becoming a Servant-Leader.* San Francisco, CA: Josey-Bass Publishers.

Grice, H. P. 1989. *Studies in the Way of Words.* Boston, MA: Harvard University Press.

Griffith, J. 2016. *Freedom. The End of Human Condition.* Sydney: WTM Publishing and Communications PTY Ltd.

Guber, P. 2011. *Tell to Win. Connect, Persuade and Triumph with the Hidden Power of Story.* London: Profile Books.

Hackman, J. R. and G. R. Oldham. 1976. Motivation Through the Design of Work: Test of a Theory. *Organizational Behavior and Human Performance*. 16, 250–279.

Haidt, J. 2006. *The Happiness Hypothesis. Putting Ancient Wisdom to the Test of Modern Science*. London: Arrow Books.

Hale, G. and M. Evans. 2007. *The Feng Shui Bible. A Practical Guide for Harmony and well-being*. Wigston, UK: Lorenz Books.

Hall, D. 1995. *Jump Start Your Brain*. New York, NY: Warner Books.

Hall, E. T. 1981. *Beyond Culture*. New York, NY: Anchor Book.

Hallowell, E. 1999. The Human Moment at Work. *Harvard Business Review. Jan–Feb 1999 Issue*. [Online] Available at: https://hbr.org/1999/01/the-human-moment-at-work (Accessed: September 16, 2018).

Hamel, G. and C. K. Prahalad. 1996. *Competing for the Future*. Boston, MA: Harvard Business School Press.

Hamilton, D. 2010. *Why Kindness Is Good for You*. London: Hay House.

Hardingham, A. 1992. *Making Change Work for You*. London: Sheldon Business Books.

Harris, T. A. 1969. *I'm OK – You're OK*. New York, NY: Harper & Row.

Harrold, G. 2007 *De-stress Your Life in 7 Easy Steps*. London: Orion.

Hatfield, E., Rapson, R. L. and Y. L. Le. 2011. Primitive Emotional Contagion: Recent Research. In Decety, J. and W. Ickes (Eds.). *The Social Neuroscience of Empathy*. Boston, MA: MIT Press. [Online] Available at: www.neurohumanitiestudies.eu/archivio/Emotional_Contagion.pdf (Accessed: December 20, 2018).

Hawkins, D. R. 2012. *Letting Go. The Pathway of Surrender*. London, UK: Hay House.

Hawkins, D. R. 2013. *Power vs. Force. The Hidden Determinant of Human Behavior*. Carlsbad, CA: Hay House.

Heineman, B. W. Jr. 2008. *High Performance with High Integrity*. Boston, MA: Harvard Business Review Press.

Hellinger, B., G. Weber and H. Beaumont. 1998. *Love's Hidden Symmetry. What Makes Love Work in Relationships*. Phoenix, AZ: Zeig, Toucker & Co.

Helmenstine, A. M. 2018. How Much of Your Body Is Water? The Percentage of Water in the Human Body Varies by Age and Gender. *ThoughtsCo*. June 01, 2018. [Online] Available at: www.thoughtco.com/how-much-of-your-body-is-water-609406 (Accessed: September 16, 2018).

Hendricks, G. and K. Ludeman. 1996. *The Corporate Mystic. A Guidebook for Visionaries with Their Feet on the Ground*. New York, NY: Bantam Books.

Herzberg, F. 1968. *The Work and the Nature of Man*. London: Staples Press.

Hill, N. 1928. *The Law of Success*. Meriden, CT: Ralston University Press.

Hill, N. 2016. *Think and Grow Rich*. Shippensburg, PA: Sound Wisdom.

Hillman, J. 2006. *The Soul's Code. In Search of Character and Calling*. New York, NY: Warner Books.

Hogg, M. A. and G. M. Vaughan. 2002. *Social Psychology*. Harlow, UK: Pearson.

Holden, R. 1992. *Stress Busters. 101 Ways to Inner calm*. London: Thornson.

Holden, R. 2008. *Success Intelligence. Essential Lessons and Practices from the World's Leading Coaching Programme on Authentic Success*. London: Hay House.

Holiday, R. 2004. *The Obstacle is the Way. The Ancient Art of Turning Adversity to Advantage*. London: Profile Books.

Holton, B. and C. Holton. 2010. Soul Management. In Charlotte, S. and L. Martha (Eds.). *Good Business. Putting Spiritual Principles Into Practice At Work*. Unity Village, MO: Unity House. 61–68.

Honoré, C. 2004. *In Praise of Slow. How a Worldwide Movement is Challenging the Cult of Speed*. London: Orion.

Hounsell, D. 2007. Toward a More Sustainable Feedback to Students. In Boud, D. and N. Falchikov (Eds.). *Rethinking Assessment in Higher Education*. London: Routledge. 101–113.

Howard, G. 1989. *Getting Through. How to Make Words Work for You*. London: David and Charles.

Hyde, L. 2012. *The Gift. How the Creative Spirit Transforms the World*. Edinburgh: Canongate Books.

Ingham, J. 2017. *The Social Organization. Developing Employee Connections and Relationships for Improved Business Performance*. London: Kogan Page.

Isaacson, W. 2012. The Real Leadership Lesson of Steve Jobs. *Harvard Business Review*. April, 2012. [Online] Available at: https://hbr.org/2012/04/the-real-leadership-lessons-of-steve-jobs (Accessed: December 20, 2018).

Jeffers, S. 1991. *Feel the Fear and Do It Anyway*. London: Arrow Books.

Jeffers, S. 2003. *Embracing Uncertainty. Achieving Peace of Mind as We Face the Unknown*. London: Hodder and Stoughton.

Jobs, S. 2008. Steve Jobs' 2005 Stanford Commencement Address. March 7, 2008. [Online] Available at: www.youtube.com/watch?v=UF8uR6Z6KLc (Accessed: September 16, 2018).

Johnson, D. 1997. *Reaching Out. Interpersonal Effectiveness and Self-Actualization*. Boston, MA: Allyn and Bacon.

Johnson, S. 2010. *Where Good Ideas Come From. The Seven Patterns of Innovation*. London: Penguin.

Johnstone, K. 1987. *Impro. Improvisation and the Theatre*. London: Methuen Drama.

Kahneman, D. 2013. *Thinking, Fast and Slow*. New York, NY: Farrar, Straus and Giroux.

Kahneman, D. and A. Tversky 1984. Choices, Values, and Frames. *American Psychologist*. 39(4), 341–350.

Kandola, R. and J. Fullerton. 1994. *Managing the Mosaic. Diversity in Action*. London: Institute of Personnel and Development.

Kao, J. 1996. *Jamming. The Art and Discipline of Business Creativity*. London: HarperCollins Business.

Kassorly, I. 1985. *Go for It*. London: Warner Books.

Kay, J. 2011. *Obliquity. Why Our Goals Are Best Achieved Indirectly*. London: Profile Books.

Keegan, S. 2015. *The Psychology of Fear in Organizations. How to Transform Anxiety into Well-Being, Productivity and Innovation*. London: Kogan Page.

Kelley, D. 1990. *The Art of Reasoning with Symbolic Logic*. New York, NY: W.W. Norton & Company.

Kim, W. C. and R. Mauborgne. 2015. *Blue Ocean Strategy. How to Create Uncontested Market Space and Make the Competition Irrelevant*. Boston, MA: Harvard Business School Press.

Klein, G. 2003. *Intuition at Work. Why Developing Your Gut Instincts Will Make You Better at What You Do*. New York, NY: Currency.

Kleon, A. 2012. *Steal Like an Artist*. New York, NY: Workman Publishing Company.

Knight, S. 1999. *NLP Solutions. How to Model What Works in Business to Make It Work for You*. London: Nicholas Brealey Publishing.

Koestler, A. 1964. *The Act of Creation*. London: Hutchinson & Co.

Kofman, F. 2013. *Conscious Business. How to Build Value Through Values*. Boulder, CO: Sounds True.

Kolb, D. A. 1973. *Organizational Psychology. An Experiential Approach*. Englewood Cliffs, NJ: Prentice Hall.

Kotler, P., Keller, K. L., Brady, M. et al. 2009. *Marketing Management*. London: Pearson Education.

Kukk, C. 2017. *The Compassionate Achiever. How Helping Others Fuels Success*. New York, NY: HarperOne.

Kuykendall, L., Boemerman, L. and Z. Zhu. 2018. The Importance of Leisure for Subjective Well-Being. In Diener, E., Oishi, S. and L. Tay (Eds.). *Handbook of Well-Being*. Salt Lake City, UT: DEF Publishers. [Online] Available at: www.nobascholar.com/chapters/31/download.pdf (Accessed: December 20, 2018).

Lafley, A. G. and R. Charan. 2008. *Game-Changer. How You Can Drive Revenue and Profit Growth with Innovation*. New York, NY: Crown Business.

Laloux, F. 2014. *Reinventing Organizations. A Guide to Creating Organizations Inspired by the Next Stage of Human Consciousness*. Brussels: Nelson Parker.

Leech, G. 1983. *Principles of Pragmatics*. London: Longman Group Ltd.

Leonard, G. 1992. *Mastery: The Key to Success and Long-Term Fulfilment*. New York, NY: Plume.

Lessem, R. 1993. *Business as a Learning Community*. Maidenhead, UK: McGraw-Hill.

Letterman, E. 1962. *Personal Power Through Creative Selling*. New York, NY: First Collier Books.

Lewis T., Amini, F. and R. Lannon. 2001. *A General Theory of Love*. New York, NY: Vintage Books.

Lieberman, D. 1997. *Instant Analysis*. New York, NY: St Martin's Griffins.

Lieberman, D. 2001. *Get Anyone to Do Anything*. New York, NY: St Martin's Griffins.

Linden, C. 2013. *Stress Free in 30 Days*. London: Hay House.

Lindgren, S. 2017. *Digital Media & Society*. London: Sage.

Litvinoff, S. 2005. *The Confidence Plan*. London: BBC Books.

Liu, E. and S. Nope-Brandon. 2009. *Imagination First. Unlocking the Power of Possibility*. San Francisco, CA: Jossey Bass.

Lobel, T. 2014. *Sensation. The New Science of Physical Intelligence*. London: Icon Books.

Locke, J. 1998. *The De-Voicing of Society. Why We Don't Talk to Each Other Anymore*. New York, NY: Simon and Schuster.

Loehr, J. and T. Schwartz. 2003. *The Power of Full Engagement. Managing Energy, Not Time, Is the Key to High Performance and Personal Renewal*. New York, NY: Free Press.

Looker, T. and O. Gregson. 2010. *Manage Your Stress for a Happier Life*. London: McGraw-Hill.

Lorenz, E. 1993. *The Essence of Chaos*. Seattle, WA: Washington Press.

Lowell, B. and C. Joyce. 2007. *Mobilizing Minds. Creating Wealth from Talent in the 21st Century Organization*. New York, NY: McGraw-Hill.

Lowndes, L. 2003. *How to Talk to Anyone. 92 Little Tricks for Big Success in Relationships*. London: Element.

Luft, J. 1970. *Group Processes*. Palo Alto, CA: National Press Books.

Luft, J. and H. Ingham. 1955. *The Johari Window, a Graphic Model of Interpersonal Awareness. Proceedings of the Western Training Laboratory in Group Development*. Los Angeles, CA: University of California.

Lundvall, B. A. (Ed.). 1992. *National System of Innovation: Toward a Theory of Innovation and Interactive Learning*. London: Pinter Publishers.

Lundvall, B. A. and B. Johnson. 1994. National Systems of Innovation and Institutional Learning. (Sistemas Nacionales de Innovación y Aprendizaje Institucional). In *Revista Comercio Exterior*. 44(8). Agosto 1994. México. 695–704.

Mackey, J. and R. Sisodia. 2014. *Conscious Capitalism. Liberating the Heroic Spirit of Business*. Boston, MA: Harvard Business Review Press.

Maclelland, B. 2007. *Prosperity Through Thought Force*. New York, NY: Cosimo.

Maltz, M. 2015. *Psycho-Cybernetics*. New York, NY: Perigree.

Manby, J. 2012. *Love Works. Seven Timeless Principles for Effective Leaders*. Grand Rapids, MI: Zondervan.

Marden, O. S. 1917. *How to Get What You Want*. New York, NY: Thomas & Crowell.

Martin, P. 2006. *Making Happy People. The Nature of Happiness and Its Origins in Childhood*. London: Harper Perennial.

Maslow, A. H. 1943. A Theory of Human Motivation. *Psychological Review*. 50, 370–396.

Maslow, A. H. 1954. *Motivation and Personality*. New York, NY: Harper & Row.

Maslow, A. H. 1968. *Toward a Psychology of Being*. New York, NY: D. Van Nostrand Company.

Massey, H. and D. Hamilton. 2012. *Choice Point. Align Your Purpose*. London: Hay House.

Maturana H. and P. Bunnel. 1998. Biology of Business. Love Expands Intelligence. *Presentation at the Society of Organisational Learning Members' Meeting*. Amherst, MA. [Online] Available at: www.researchgate.net/publication/240275459_The_Biology_of_Business_Love_Expands_Intelligence (Accessed: September 24, 2018).

Maturana Romesin, H. and G. Verden-Zoller. 1996. The Biology of Love. In Opp, G. and F. Peterander (Eds.). *Focus Heilpadagogik*. Munchen/Basel: Ernst Reinhardt. Available at: https://www.terapiacognitiva.eu/cpc/dwl/PerMul/biology-of-love.pdf (Accessed: December 20, 2018).

Maturana Romesin, H. and G. Verden-Zoller. 2008. *Origin of Humanness in the Biology of Love*. Charlottesville, VA: Imprint Academic.

Maxwell, J. 2009. *How Successful People Think. Change Your Thoughts, Change Your Life*. New York, NY: Centre Street.

May, R. 1994. *The Courage to Create*. New York, NY: Norton & Company.

McBride-Walker, S. M. (n.d.). *Toward a Working Definition of the Construct of Fear in the Management Sciences*. Cleveland, OH: Department of Organizational Behavior. Weatherhead School of Management Case, Western Reserve University. [Online] Available at: https://weatherhead.case.edu/departments/organizational-behavior/workingPapers/WP-16-01.pdf (Accessed: September 24, 2018).

McGrath, R. G. and I. C. MacMillan. 2005. *Marketbusters. 40 Strategic Moves That Drive Exceptional Business Growth*. Boston, MA: Harvard Business School Press.

McGuinness, M. 2015. *Motivation for Creative People. How to Stay Creative While Gaining Money, Fame, and Reputation*. Lateral Action Books.

McIntosh, M., Leipziger, D., Jones, K. et al. 1998. *Corporate Citizenship Successful Strategies for Responsible Companies*. London: Financial Times Management.

McKenna, E. 2012a. *Business Psychology and Organizational Behaviour*. Hove: Psychology Press.

McKenna, P. 2012b. *I Can Make You Smarter*. London: Bantam Press.

McKeown, M. 2014. *The Innovation Book*. London: Pearson.

McLellan, V. 1996. *Wise Words and Quotes*. Wheaton, IL: Tyndale House Publishers.

Meares, K. and M. Freeston 2008. *Overcoming Worry. A Self-Help Guide Using Cognitive Behavioral Techniques*. London: Robinson.

Medina, J. 2014. *Brain Rules. 12 Principles for Surviving and Thriving at Work, Home, and School*. Seattle, WA: Pear Press.

Miller, L. 2009. *Mood Mapping. Plot Your Way to Emotional Health and Happiness*. London: Rodale.

Milligan, A. and S. Smith. 2008. *See, Feel, Think, Do*. London: Marshall Cavendish.

Mitchell, P., Reast, J. and J. Linch. 1998. Exploring the Foundation of Trust. *Journal of Marketing Management*. 14, 159–172.

Montagu, A. M. F. 1957. *The Direction of Human Development*. London: Watts.

Morgan, G. 1986. *Images of Organization*. Newbury Park, CA: Sage.

Morgan, G. 1997. *Imaginization. New Mindsets for Seeing, Organizing, and Managing*. San Francisco, CA: Berret Koehler/Sage.

Morrison, D. and J. Firmstone. 2015. The Social Function of Trust and Implications for e-Commerce. *International Journal of Advertising*. 19(5), 599–623.

Mulford, P. 2015. *Your Forces and How to Use Them*. Hollister, CA: Yoge Books.

Murphy, J. 1988. *The Power of the Subconscious Mind*. Excalibur.

Murray, B. (n.d.). *A Career Can Turn on a Big Idea*. Momentum.

Murray, D. 2009. *Borrowing Brilliance. The Six Steps to Business Innovation by Building on the Ideas of Others*. New York, NY: Gotham Books.

Murray, E. J. 1964. *Motivation and Emotion*. Englewood Cliffs, NJ: Prentice-Hall.

Narang, R. and D. Devaiah. 2014. *Orbit-Shifting Innovation. The Dynamics of Ideas That Create History*. London: Kogan Page.

Nardi, B. 2005. Beyond Bandwith. *Computer Supportive Co-Operative Work (CSCW)*. 14(2), 91–130.

Neill, M. 2013. *The Inside-Out Revolution. The Only Thing You Need to Know to Change Your Life Forever*. London: Hay House.

Nelson, B. and P. Economy. 2010. *Managing for Dummies*. Hoboken, NJ: Wiley.

Nelson, D. and C. L. Cooper (Eds.). 2007. *Positive Organizational Behaviour*. London: Sage.

Nobel, S. 2012. *The Enlightenment of Work. Revealing the Path to Happiness, Contentment and Purpose in Your Job*. London: Watkins.

Novak, D. and C. Bourg. 2016. *O Great One: A Little Story About the Awesome Power of Recognition*. New York, NY: Penguin Random House.

Oakley, E. and D. Kroug. 1994. *Enlightened Leadership. Getting to the Heart of Change*. New York, NY: Fireside.

O'Connor, J. 2001. *NLP Workbook. A Practical Guide to Achieving the Results You Want*. London: Thorsons.

O'Connor, J. and I. McDermott. 1997. *The Art of Systems Thinking*. London: Thorsons.

Ogunlaru, R. 2012. *Soul Trader. Putting the Heart Back into Your Business*. London: Kogan Page.

Ong, W. J. 1982. *Orality and Literacy*. London: Matheun.

Ornish, D. 1999. *Love and Survival. 8 Pathways to Intimacy and Health*. New York, NY: William Morrow & Company.

Osborn, A. 1948. *Your Creative Power*. New York, NY: Charles Scribners.

Panza, C. and A. Potthast. 2010. *Ethics for Dummies*. Hoboken, NJ: Wiley.

Parke, S. 2010. *One-Minute Mystic*. London: Hay House.

Parson, P. 2004. *Ethics in Public Relations. A Guide to Best Practice*. London: Kogan Page.

Patel, K. 2005. *The Master Strategists. Power, Purpose and Principle in Action*. London: Hutchinson.

Pease, A. 2014. *Body Language*. India: Manjul Publishing House.

Pease, A. and B. Pease. 2004. *The Definite Book of Body Language. The Hidden Meaning Behind People's Gestures and Expressions*. London. Orion.

Peck, H., Payne, A., Christopher, M. et al. 1999. *Relationship Marketing. Strategy and Implementation.* Oxford: Butterworth Heinemann.

Peters, T. 1994. *The Pursuit of Wow. Every Person's Guide to Topsy-Turvy Times.* London: McMillan.

Pfeiffer, V. 2001. *Positive Thinking.* London: Thorsons.

Pink, D. 2011. *Drive. The Surprising Truth About What Motivates Us.* New York, NY: Riverhead Books.

Plester, B. 2009. Healthy Humour: Using Humour to Cope at Work. *Kōtuitui: New Zealand Journal of Social Sciences Online.* 4(1), 89–102. [Online] Available at: www.tandfonline.com/doi/abs/10.1080/1177083x.2009.9522446 (Accessed: September 24, 2018).

Plowman, K. D. 1998. Power in Conflict for Public Relations. *Journal of Public Relations Research.* 19(4), 237–261.

Polanyi, M. 1967. *The Tacit Dimension.* London: Routledge and Keagan.

Powell, J. 1999. *Why Am I Afraid to Tell You Who I Am?* Grand Rapids, MI: Zonderban.

Price, A. and D. Price. 2013. *Introducing Leadership. A Practical Guide.* London: Icon Books.

Pugh, D. S. and D. J. Hickson. 2007. *Writers on Organizations.* London: Penguin Books.

Purdie, J. 2010. *Life Coaching for Dummies.* Chichester, UK: Wiley.

Race, P. 1995. *Who Learns Wins.* London: Penguin Books.

Ramanchadran, V. S. and S. Blakeslee. 1999. *Phantoms In the Brain. Human Nature and the Architecture of the Mind.* London: Four State.

Rando, C. 2014. *You Can Think Differently. Change Your Thinking, Change Your Life.* London: Watkins.

Ray, M. and R. Myers. 1989. *Creativity in Business.* New York, NY: Broadway Books.

Reivich, K. and A. Shatté. 2002. *The Resilience Factor. 7 Keys to Finding Your Inner Strength and Overcoming Life's Hurdles.* New York, NY: Broadway Books.

Richard, O. C. 2000. Racial Diversity, Business Strategy, and Firm Performance: A Resource-Based View. *Academy of Management Journal.* 43, 164–177.

Ritt, M. 1998. *Napoleon Hill's Keys to Positive Thinking.* London: Piatkus.

Robbins, A. 2001. *Awaken the Giant Within. How to Take Immediate Control of Your Mental, Emotional, Physical & Financial Destiny!* New York, NY: Fireside.

Robbins, A. 2014. Tony Robbins: 6 Basic Needs That Make Us Tick. *Entrepreneur.* December 4, 2014. [Online] Available at: www.entrepreneur.com/article/240441 (Accessed: September 25, 2018).

Robbins, M. 2017. *The 5 Second Rule. Transform Your Life, Work and Confidence with Everyday Courage.* Savio Republic.

Roberts, K. 2004. *Lovemarks: The Future Beyond Brands.* New York, NY: Powerhouse Books.

Robinson, K. and L. Aronica. 2009. *The Element. How Finding Your Passion Changes Everything.* London: Penguin Books.

Robles, M. 2012. Executive Perceptions of the Top 10 Soft Skills Needed in Today's Workplace. *Business Communication Quarterly.* 75(4), 453–465.

Rodenburg, P. 2007. *Presence. How to Use Positive Energy for Success in Every Situation.* London: Michael Joseph.

Rogers, C. 1961. *On Becoming a Person.* London: Houghton Mifflin Company.

Rogers, C. 1969. *Freedom to Learn.* Columbus, OH: Charles and Merrill Publishing Company.

Rogers, C. 1991. *Client Centred Therapy.* London: Constable.

Rosenberg, M. 2005. *Nonviolent Communication.* Encinitas, CA: Puddledancer Press.

Rosenfield, L., Hayes, L. and T. Frentz. 1976. *The Communicative Experience.* Boston, MA: Allyn and Bacon.

Rosseau, D. M., Sitkin, S. B., Burt, R. S. et al. 1998. Not Different After All: a Cross-Discipline View of Trust. *Academy of Management Review.* 23(3), 393–404.

Russell, B. 1994. *In Praise of Idleness.* London: Routledge.

Safko, L. and D. Brake. 2009. *The Social Media Bible. Tactics, Tools, and Strategies for Business Success.* Canada: Wiley.

Salzberg, S. 1995. *Lovingkindness. Revolutionary Art of Happiness.* Boston, MA: Shambala Classics.

Salzberg, S. 2014. *Real Happiness at Work. Meditations for Accomplishment, Achievement and Peace.* New York, NY: Workman.

Sawyer, R. K. 2006. *Explaining Creativity. The Science of Human Innovation*. Oxford: Oxford University Press.

Schafer, J. 2015. Self-Disclosures Increase Attraction. *Psychology Today*. March, 2015. [Online] Available at: www.psychologytoday.com/us/blog/let-their-words-do-the-talking/201503/self-disclosures-increase-attraction (Accessed: September 25, 2018).

Scheffer, M. 1990. *Bach Flower Therapy. Theory and Practice*. London: Thorsons.

Schein, E. 2009. *Corporate Culture Survival Guide*. San Francisco, CA: Jossey Bass.

Schloss, D. P. 2001. *If at First, You Don't Succeed, Buy This Book!* Motivation Plus.

Schrage, M. 1990. *Shared Minds. The New Technologies of Collaboration*. New York, NY: Random House.

Schwartz, D. 1979. *The Magic of Thinking Big*. London: Pocket Books.

Schwartz, D. 1986. *Maximize Your Mental Power*. London: Thorsons.

Schwartz, T., Gomes, J. and C. McCarthy. 2010. *The Way We're Working Isn't Working. The Four Forgotten Needs That Energize Performance*. New York, NY: Free Press.

Scott, D. M. 2017. *The New Rules of Marketing and PR. How to Use Social Media, Online Video, Mobile Applications, Blogs, Newsjacking, and Viral Marketing to Reach Buyers Directly*. Hoboken, NJ: Wiley.

Scoular, A. 2011. *The Financial Times Guide to Business Coaching*. Harlow: Pearson.

Seligman, M. 2006. *Learned Optimism. How to Change Your Mind and Your Life*. New York, NY: Vintage Book.

Senge, P. 1990. *The Fifth Discipline. The Art & Practice of the Learning Organization*. London: Century Business.

Senge, P., Scharmer, C. O., Jaworski, J. et al. 2004. *Presence. Exploring Profound Change in People, Organizations, and Society*. New York, NY: Currency Double Day.

Shapiro, E. and D. Shapiro. 1994. *A Time for Healing. The Journey to Wholeness*. London: Piatkus.

Shelton, C. and M. Lynn (Ed.). 2010. *Good Business. Putting Spiritual Principles into Practice at Work*. Unity Village, MO: Unity House.

Siebold, S. 2010. *How Rich People Think*. London: London House.

Silver, M. 2015. *Getting to the Core of Your Business*. Heart of Business Press.

Silver, Y. 2017. *Evolved Enterprise. An Illustrated Guide to Re-Think, Re-imagine and Re-Invent Your Business to Deliver Meaningful Impact and Even Greater Profits*. Washington, DC: Ideapress Publishing.

Simon, C. 2016. *Impossible to Ignore. Creating Memorable Content to Influence Decisions*. New York, NY: McGraw-Hill.

Sirgy, M. J. and D. J. Lee. 2018. The Psychology of Life Balance. In Diener, E., Oishi, S. and L. Tay (Eds.). *Handbook of Well-Being*. Salt Lake City, UT: DEF Publishers. [Online] Available at: https://www.nobascholar.com/chapters/55/download.pdf (Accessed: December 30, 2018).

Sisodia, R., Wolfe, D. and J. Seth. 2015. *Firms of Endearment. How World-Class Companies Profit from Passion and Purpose*. Upper Saddle River, NJ: Pearson.

Skinner, T. 2003. *Beyond the Summit. Setting and Surpassing Extraordinary Business Goals*. London: Random House.

Sloane, P. 2003. *The Leader's Guide to Lateral Thinking Skills. Powerful Problem-Solving Techniques to Ignite Your Team's Potential*. London: Kogan Page.

Sloane, P. 2007. *The Innovative Leader. How to Inspire Your Team and Drive Creativity*. London: Kogan Page.

Sloman, J. 2008. *Economics and the Business Environment*. Harlow, UK: Prentice Hall.

Smiles, S. 1859. *Self-Help*. London: John Murray.

Smoth, R. 1986. *Personal Growth and Creativity*. Worthing: Insight Edition.

Solomon, M., Bamossy, G., Askegaard, S. et al. 2006. *Consumer Behaviour. A European Perspective*. Harlow, UK: FT Prentice Hall.

Steiner, R. 1986. *The Philosophy of Spiritual Activity*. New York, NY: Anthroposophic Press.

Steiner, R. 2014. *Knowledge of the Higher Worlds. How Is It Achieved?* London: Rudolf Steiner Press.

Stutz, P. and B. Michels. 2012. *The Tools. 5 Life Techniques to Unlock Your Potential*. London: Vermillion.

Sunderland, M. 2007. *What Every Parent Needs to Know. The Incredible Effects of Love, Nurture and Play on Your Child's Development*. London: DK.

Sutherland, S. 2007. *Irrationality*. London: Pinter & Martin.

Tapscott, D. 1996. *The Digital Economy. Promise and Peril In the Age of Networked Intelligence*. New York, NY: McGraw-Hill.

Tharp, T. 2006. *The Creative Habit. Learn It and Use It for Life*. New York, NY: Simon and Schuster.

Theodore, J. 2011. *Lessons from the Life of a Salesman*. London: Books of Africa Ltd.

Thompson, C. 1992. *What a Great Idea. Key Steps Creative People Take*. New York, NY: Harper Perennial.

Thompson, G. 1995. *Fear: The Friend of Exceptional People*. Chichester, UK: Summersdale.

Thurston, J. 2017. *Kindness. The Little Thing That Matters Most*. London: Thorsons.

Todd, S. 1997. *Think Like a Genius*. London: Bantam Press.

Tomasino, D. 2007. The Psychophysiological Basis of Creativity and Intuition: Accessing "the Zone" of Entrepreneurship. *International Journal of Entrepreneurship and Small Business*. 4, 528–542.

Tracy, B. 2010. Service and Satisfaction. In Shelton, C. and M. Lynn (Ed.). *Good Business. Putting Spiritual Principles into Practice at Work*. Unity Village, MO: Unity House. 9–15.

Trott, P. 2012. *Innovation Management and New Product Development*. Harlow: Prentice Hall.

Tuckle, S. 2015. *Reclaiming Conversation. The Power of Talk in Digital Age*. New York, NY: Penguin.

Tuten, T. L. and M. R. Solomon. 2017. *Social Media Marketing*. London: Sage.

Tversky, A. and D. Kahneman. 1974. Judgement Under Uncertainty: Heuristics and Biases. *Science*. 185(4157), 1124–1131.

Udall, N. and N. Turner. 2008. *The Way of Nowhere. Eight Questions to Release Our Creative Potential*. London: Harper Collins.

Valtonen, H. 2016. Risk Management. *Investment Foundations Program*. Chapter 18. CFA Institute. [Online] Available at: www.cfainstitute.org/en/programs/investment-foundations (Accessed: December 19, 2018).

Verni, K. 2015. *Practical Mindfulness. a Step-By-Step Guide*. London: DK.

Von Hildebrand, D. 2009. *The Nature of Love*. South Bend, IN: Saint Augustine's Press.

Wallas, G. 1926. *The Art of Thought*. New York, NY: Harcourt, Brace and Company.

Walter, D. 2005. *De-Junk Your Mind*. London: Penguin Books.

Warren, R. 2002. *The Purpose Driven Life. What on Earth Am I Here For?* Grand Rapids, MI, Zondervan.

Wattles, W. 2013. *The Science of Getting Rich*. Theclassics.Us.

Watts, A. 1955. *Wisdom of Insecurity. A Message for An Age of Anxiety*. New York, NY: Vintage Books.

Webb, C. 2016. *How to Have a Good Day. Harness the Power of Behavioural Science to Transform Your Working Life*. London: Crown Business.

Weick, K. 1995. *Sensemaking in Organizations*. London: Foundation for Organizational Science.

Wellemin, J. 1998. *Successful Customer Care in a Week*. London: Hodder and Stoughton.

West, D. and J. Ford. 2015. *Strategic Marketing: Creating Competitive Advantage*. Oxford: Oxford University Press.

Whitaker, A. 2016. *Art Thinking. How to Carve Out Creative Space in a World of Schedules, Budgets, and Bosses*. New York, NY: HarperBusiness.

Wickham, P. 2004. *Strategic Entrepreneurship*. London: Prentice Hall.

Wiest, B. 2013. *101 Essays That Will Change the Way That You Think*. Williamsburg, VA: Thought Catalog Books.

Wills, F. and D. Sanders. 1997. *Cognitive Therapy. Transforming the Image*. London: Sage.

Wilson, E. 2007. *Stress Proof Your Life. 52 Brilliant Ideas for Taking Control*. Oxford: Infinite Ideas.

Wingfield-Stratford, E. 1969. *Good Talk. A Study of the Art of Conversation*. London: Lovan Dickson.

Wiseman, R. 2009. *59 Seconds. Think a Little, Change a Lot*. London: Macmillan.

Wiseman, R. 2013. *The As If Principle. The Radical New Approach to Changing Your Life*. New York, NY: Free Press.

Witten, D. and A. T. Rinpoche. 1999. *Enlightened Management*. VT: Park Street Press.

Wolhorn, H. 1977. *Emmet Fox Golden Keys to Successful Living and Reminiscences*. New York, NY: Harper & Row Publishers.

Worline, M. C. and J. E. Dutton. 2017. *Awakening Compassion at Work. The Quiet Power That Elevates People and Organizations*. Oakland, CA: Berret Koehler.

Yeung, R. 2008. *Confidence. The Art of Getting Whatever You Want*. Harlow: Pearson.

Yeung, R. 2011. *I Is for Influence. New Science of Persuasion*. London: Macmillan.

Zak, P. 2013. *The Moral Molecule. How Trust Works.* London: Plume.

Zander, R. S. and B. Zander. 2002. *The Art of Possibility. Transforming Professional and Personal Life.* New York, NY: Penguin Books.

Zeldin, T. 2000. *Conversation. How Talk Can Change Our Lives.* London: Hiddenspring.

Ziauddin, S. and I. Abrams. 1999. *Introducing Chaos.* London: Icon Books.

Zohar, D. and I. Marshall. 2004. *Spiritual Capital. Wealth We Can Live By.* London: Bloomsbury.

Index

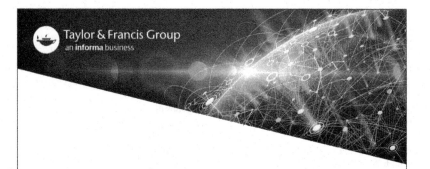